TALKING TO LEARN
Conversation in
Second Language Acquisition

Editor
Richard R. Day

NEWBURY HOUSE PUBLISHERS, Cambridge
A division of Harper & Row, Publishers, Inc.
New York, Philadelphia, San Francisco, Washington
London, Mexico City, São Paulo, Singapore, Sydney
1 9 8 6

Library of Congress Cataloging-in-Publication Data
Main entry under title:

Talking to learn.

1. Language and languages—Study and teaching—Ad-
dresses, essays, lectures. 2. Language acquisition—
Addresses, essays, lectures. 3. Conversation—Study
and teaching—Addresses, essays, lectures. I. Day,
Richard R.
P53.29.T34 1986   418'.007   85–25472
ISBN O–88377–317–1

NEWBURY HOUSE PUBLISHERS
A division of Harper & Row, Publishers, Inc.

Language Science
Language Teaching
Language Learning

CAMBRIDGE, MASSACHUSETTS

First printing: February 1986

Printed in the U.S.A.   2 4 6 8 10 9 7 5 3

Contents

Section Three: Task, Talk, and Learning

Section Four: Outside the Classroom

INTRODUCTION

Richard R. Day
University of Hawaii

The purpose of this anthology is to make available in a single volume reports of second language acquisition research relating to conversation among native speakers and nonnative speakers, and nonnative speakers with other nonnative speakers, both in the classroom and outside the classroom. With one exception these articles have not appeared elsewhere, and they represent the latest advances in the role that conversation plays in the process of second language teaching and learning.

Examination of the relationship between conversation and second language acquisition is relatively new. Its origins can be traced to a ground-breaking article by Hatch (1978), in which she called for a new approach to the study of second language acquisition. Hatch observed that the focus of research in the 1970s on *form* and the limited work on *function* overlooked *how* a second language is learned. She claimed that new insights into the process of second language acquisition could be gained from an analysis of conversation. Hatch wrote:

It is not enough to look at input and to look at frequency; the important thing is to look at the corpus as a whole and examine the interactions that take place within conversations to see how that interaction, itself, determines the frequency of forms and how it shows language functions evolving. (Hatch 1978: 403)

Hatch noted that the basic assumption of researchers in both first and second language acquisition was that the learner, whether a child learning his or her first language or a nonnative speaker learning a second or foreign language, first learns various structures and how to combine them into sentences or utterances and that the learner gradually acquires a repertoire of these structures. It was further assumed that in some as yet unknown fashion the learner then put these structures to use to carry on conversations.

Hatch advanced the possibility that perhaps the reverse of this assumed process was true: "One learns how to do conversation, one learns how to interact verbally, and out of this interaction syntactic structures are developed" (Hatch 1978: 404). Hatch's evidence for her claim was based on studies of children acquiring first and second languages and on reports of adults learning second languages.

Hatch's thinking, which was influenced by earlier work in child first language acquisition (e.g., Scollon 1974), sparked a great deal of interest by researchers in second language acquisition. Larsen-Freeman edited a collection of articles (1980) which focused on the role of discourse analysis in second language acquisition. Among the more influential studies was Long (1981), in which he claimed that the modification of interactional input to the second language learner was the necessary and sufficient condition for second language acquisition (1981: 24).

The chapters in this volume address the issues raised by Hatch, Long, and other researchers from a variety of points of view. Section One presents some theoretical concerns. Section Two contains chapters that focus on the nature of conversational interaction in the classroom, both content and ESL, where students are attempting to learn English as a second language. The focus on language in the classroom is continued in Section Three, but looking more closely at small-group or task activities. The papers in the final section look at the nature of conversations that learners have with both other ESL learners and native speakers outside the classroom.

REFERENCES

Hatch, E. 1978. Discourse analysis and second language acquisition. In E. Hatch (ed.). *Second Second Language Acquisition: A Book of Readings.* Rowley, Mass.: Newbury House. 401–435.

Larsen-Freeman, D. (ed.). 1980. *Discourse Analysis in Second Language Research.* Rowley, Mass.: Newbury House.

Long, M. H. 1981. Input, interaction, and second language acquisition. In H. Winitz (ed.). *Native Language and Foreign Language Acquisition, Annals of the New York Academy of Sciences,* 379: 259–278.

Scollon, R. T. 1974. One child's language from one to two: the origins of construction. Ph.D. dissertation, University of Hawaii, 1974.

TALKING TO LEARN
Conversation in
Second Language Acquisition

Section One

SOME THEORETICAL ISSUES

INTRODUCTION

Richard R. Day

The two chapters in this section help to set the stage for the issues that are treated in the three other sections of the book. The first is by Hatch, Flashner, and Hunt. Hatch, as noted in the introduction to this volume, has been credited with being among the first to call for a different look at the way second languages are acquired. The second chapter is by Sato, who, through a longitudinal, functionalist study of the development of a Vietnamese-English interlanguage, examines the issue of necessity/sufficiency of conversation in second language acquisition.

Hatch et al. propose a framework through which we may understand language, language acquisition, and language use. In keeping with Hatch's earlier work, the experience model is not restricted to one aspect of language (e.g., syntax or phonology) but attempts to account for all of what the authors call the "subsystems" of language. It is their claim that "language clarifies and organizes experience and, conversely, that language grows out of experience." Further, they claim that "the development of language is not completely preordained and internally driven."

Hatch and her colleagues attempt to substantiate their claims by examining data from both first and second language acquisition. They then present the experience model, which, they note, is based on work by other researchers. Crucial to the model is the concept of a "knowledge structure"—previous information about or experiences with the situation in which the learner is involved, including the language associated with the situation. Their presentation of a knowledge structure is similar to what others have referred to as a "schema" or a "formal schema" or a previously acquired knowledge structure (cf. Carrell 1984). Second language acquisition is guided by interaction with others (e.g., an ESL teacher) in an associated set of experiences.

These sets of experiences, which are different for different types of learners (e.g., foreign language learners vs. immersion learners), fulfill many roles, including setting preferred structures for discourse, highlighting important information, and clarifying syntactic organization.

The experience model also involves an abstract production system, which is developed to give "language expression to knowledge structures." It is a three-level model, consisting of a conceptualizer, formulator, and articulator. It is important to stress, as do Hatch, Flashner, and Hunt, that the model does not merely focus on the syntactic system but is flexible enough to deal with the organization of conversation at many levels of speech.

In the second chapter, Sato's research of the development of a Vietnamese-English interlanguage (IL) makes more specific earlier claims by Hatch on the role of conversation in second language acquisition. She follows the development of past time reference (PTR) by two young Vietnamese brothers over a 10-month period, tape-recording their conversations in a wide range of situations.

Sato believes that the conversations her subjects had with NSs facilitated their *performance* in English; however, she is reluctant to conclude that the subjects' *acquisition* of all the linguistic devices that signal PTR was aided by their conversations. She provides evidence to show that the conversations her two subjects had with NSs helped in the acquisition of some linguistic features, but not with others.

Sato's work is particularly important for advancing our knowledge of the role of conversation in second language acquisition. As she notes, this role is a complex one, being influenced by a wide variety of factors, including the languages involved in interlanguage development, the particular features of the target language, and the usefulness of various conversational modifications and adjustments that NSs make in their conversations with NNSs.

When we compare Sato's results with the experience model of Hatch and her colleagues, we find that Sato's work refines the claims of the experience model. The latter attempts to explain second language acquisition in terms of experiences; Sato finds that there are specific factors that can be isolated and identified as being implicated in the process.

REFERENCE

Carrell, P. L. 1984. Evidence of a formal schema in second language comprehension. *Language Learning*, 34 (2): 87–112.

1

THE EXPERIENCE MODEL
AND LANGUAGE TEACHING

Evelyn Hatch, Vanessa Flashner, and Larry Hunt
University of California at Los Angeles

THE FRAMEWORK

The experience model is not technically a model. Rather, it is a framework including a model, which has as its goal an understanding of language, language acquisition, and language use. In this framework, language is a way—perhaps the best way—of making our experiences understandable to ourselves and to other people. The focus of such a framework may seem diffuse since it does not center on just one linguistic level, for example, syntax. If various subsystems at times take prominence, it is in terms of what they can contribute to making experiences comprehensible. The subsystems are differentially involved for various goals. For example, each of the following pairs interact:

How to interact	Conversation structure
How to organize experience	Frames and text types
How to identify concepts	Lexicon + lexical rules
How to highlight/emote	Suprasegmental rules
How to make relations clear	Pragmatic/syntactic organization
How to be explicit/accurate	Morphosyntax, phonology

The continuous interaction of experience with interlinked cognitive, social, and linguistic systems should show how development evolves.

In this framework, we claim that language clarifies and organizes experience and, conversely, that language grows out of experience. That is, the development of language is not completely preordained and internally driven. Thus, language is developed as a way of structuring experience as that experience takes place. In interactions, the discourse frames, the scripts for interactions, develop: the language appropriate to the interaction builds on this development; and the language, in turn, refines the frame.

Without further explication, let us consider examples that illustrate this in first language acquisition. Freedle and Lewis (1977) claim that interactions such as those illustrated below convey meaning, albeit uncertain meaning, and provide a base for a more formal communication system of language and gesture.

> F is sitting in her seat holding a rubber toy which is tied to the side of the chair. Mother has her back to F as she reaches for a dish. F squeaks a rubber toy making noise. As a "consequence," F kicks her feet and squeals with apparent delight. Mother turns toward F smiling and vocalizing. F quiets, eyes fixed on mother. Mother touches F's face. F vocalizes and moves her hands toward mother. Mother sits in front of F and vocalizes to her. F watches mother and listens, Mother pauses, F vocalizes. Mother touches F and vocalizes to her. F vocalizes. (Freedle and Lewis, p. 158)

As Richards and Schmidt (1983) show, more formal instructional sequences in turn taking and conversational openings and closing continue over time. The structures may continue to develop over months, even years of interaction.

> Woman: Hi.
> Boy: Hi.
> Woman: Hi, Annie.
> Mother: Annie, don't you hear someone say hello to you?
> Woman: Oh, that's okay, she smiled hello.
> Mother: You know you're supposed to greet someone, don't you?
> Annie: Hello (hangs head).
> (Richards and Schmidt, p. 128)

Such experiences provide instruction for the development of conversational structure. And the conversations, in turn, provide a source for the development of lexical and syntactic structures.

Early childhood experience often concerns identification and manipulation of objects. This experience is reflected in language. Consider, for example, the voluminous research on interactions of caretaker and child that emphasizes the "here and now" of object identification and description (such as numeracy, color, possession, and location) and of action and causation labels. The early emergence of "this N" (this baby), "this color" (this red), "this my," "WH N" (where dolly?), "N Adj" (car allgone) is a reflection of attempts to make the nature of objects clear to self and others in conversational interactions.

In relating these experiences to language, the rules of conversational cooperation (Grice 1975) are invoked. The caretaker does not nominate topics outside the child's experience. "Here and now" talk, then, is a result of selection of topics where goals are identifiable and where relevant responses can be made by the child. Given such topics, the interactions focus the child's attention on what is "new" in the here and now—what is noticeable and worthy of comment. For example, Sachs and Truswell (1978) have suggested that WH games (Where's your tummy? Where's your nose?) help infants to determine that simple variations in form signal differences in meaning. They also set the stage for learning that new information is likely to appear at the ends of utterances. At the same time, the child's perceptual system is activated by what is new and noticeable. As Greenfield and Smith (1976) have shown, "here and now" interactions allow for labeling of what is new.

L1 data often show a cooperative building of "sentences" through question prompts. An obvious, though perhaps unintended, instructional sequence obtains:

```
R=father; Brenda=child
Brenda:    (looking at a picture)
           cook
           say
R:         What'd the cook say?

Brenda:    something

Brenda:    Kimby
R:         What about Kimby?
Brenda:    close
R:         Closed? What did she close, hmmm?
```

Scollon (1979) and others have suggested, on the basis of a considerable number of examples such as those above, that syntactic structures grow as the child learns to do such conversations. Question prompts could also help establish an expectancy of a subject-verb-object word order for English.

Of course, the language of preschool children is not limited to the here and now. The literature on play shows that as early as 15 months, the caretaker may begin to lead the child into symbolic play. At first, the mother makes fantasy comments (e.g., "Oh, this is good" said as she sips imaginary coffee from a toy cup or "Is the dolly tired?" giving animate qualities to an inanimate object). By the time the child is 2, the mother makes requests that the child create an element in the fantasy (e.g., "Where is Big Bird going?" said as the child moves a toy figure, or "What'll we put in the pan?" said while pointing to a toy frying pan). While the mother still directs much of the play at the 20-month stage, by 38 months, the child is nominating and carrying out a variety of play scripts. Kavanaugh et al. (1983) suggest that fantasy play gives the child opportunities to understand how things feel and how objects work. They also show the child's understanding of family roles (mother, father, baby, pet) and the development of scripts for familiar events (i.e., themes center around caring for baby, meal preparation, the grocery store, going shopping, going to the doctor, driving the car, the birthday party). Since the scripts themselves are temporally ordered, such play gives practice in temporal ordering for narration, in the planning of activities through talk, and in using conversation structure (e.g., with play phones).

Teasing is another type of play experience. Observing 2-year-old Beth, Miller (1982) traces the development of ability to appropriately respond to and initiate teasing sequences. While the mother uses teasing to accomplish other purposes, such interactions focus on ownership rights that are linguistically marked. Most interesting, they give experience with emphatic stress, rapid delivery rate, and singsong intonation. In the first three samples of the 2-year study, Miller reports that Beth (25 months) displayed none of these prosodic features except rate. Once she began to use singsong intonation, she over-extended it to other contexts. She used the intonation with formulaic utterances (e.g., "yeayeayea") directed at no one in particular as she reveled in her own physical abilities. The self-displays are not all that different from asserting one's rights in "this is play" teasing sequences. Less frequently, Beth used this intonation for defiance while seizing possession of some object. At 28 months, Miller shows that Beth was beginning to narrow down the contexts in which she used this intonation. In final interactions, Beth and her mother used dispute tactics, emphatic stress and rapid delivery, appropriate voice quality (giggles and laughter to show "this is play" quality of the teasing), seizure of disputed objects, and fighting gestures.

Teasing exchanges give the learner experience in the use of intonation, rate, and pitch to express emotions of frustration and anger. Hopefully, the "instruction" also has the personal and social benefits intended by the mother: the development of independence, a way to control hurt feelings, a method of self-defense, and a way to speak up appropriately when angry.

Language play, play with language as language, can also provide special practice for the child in controlled production of difficult sounds. Many young children have difficulty with fricatives and with liquids, especially in clusters. In the example below (Gough 1984), the mother and child engage in sound play which includes both easy stops (/k, b/) and difficult fricatives and fricative + liquid clusters (/f, fr/).

```
J=mother; K=3:1 child; C=18-month child
K:      I said Fredded Wheat.
J:      You said what? (pretends surprise)
K:      I said, I said Fredded Wheat.
C:      (laughs)
J:      You think that's funny, Christopher, too?
K:      Mommy, could I have uh Fredded Wheat?
J:      (laughs)
C&K:    (laugh)
J:      I think it's in the buboard (cupboard), don't you?
K:      (laughs)
```

J: Shall we /look in the buboard for it?/
K: /Yeah. I think it's in the bu/board.
C: (laughs)
J: Let's get the yox (box) out and fee (see) if we have any Fredded Wheat.
K: What socks out?
J: The yox of cereal.
C: Yox oo cereal.
K: Yox of cereal.
C: Yox of cereal.
K: Mommy, can I pour the yox, the yix into my bowl?
J: Oh, I fink fo.
K: (laughs)
C: Fo.
J: I fink fo.
K: I fink fo. Fie foe fum. I smell a fum.
J, K, and C: (laugh)

Many children play with language when engaged in solitary play (cf. Weir 1962, Ochs 1974). As an example, Dana (age 5:4) played with the phrase "I don't care" in nap-time ramblings, while engaged in doll play, and while interacting with parents and peers. She varied the phrase, experimenting with rate, pitch, volume, and intonation, practicing how the phrase sounded. When she was interacting with others, the practice allowed her to understand the expression of "indifference." The practice gave her information on what circumstances (which frames) bring approving response to stated indifference and which do not.

Observations reveal the many possibilities for development open to the child in ordinary experiences and interactions. That is, experiences provide the child with a language learning syllabus of considerable interest. That syllabus grows throughout life as new experiences are met and new ways are developed to talk about them.

It is not difficult to find parallels for these child language examples in the data of second language learners. To summarize material presented in Hatch (1978, 1979), the L2 child Takahiro (Itoh's data) interacts in ways similar to those in Freedle and Lewis's study except that Takahiro, more sophisticated in language, not only vocalizes "aaahs" but rather imitates the phrases he hears, changing the intonation to make the vocalizing conversationally meaningful. Huang's data for Paul are rich in "here and now" talk, showing the many advantages of conversational interactions rooted in context for the development of basic word order syntax as well as for lexicon. Young's data show acquisition of suprasegmentals where increasing volume over a mixture of formulaic chunks and nonsense words serves as a defense in teasing and verbal fights. Peck(1978) shows language play situated in child-child social interaction and the opportunities it gives for phonological practice.

Solitary play with language also occurs in L2 data. Unlike the L1 example of the child practicing "I don't care," the L2 data do not show interacting social and language practice. For example, if Wes, the adult learner studied by

Schmidt (1983), practices/plays with r/l words like "Marilyn Monroe," it is not clear how this relates to social interaction. Rather, like the data on Eva (Kenyeres 1938) who loved to practice the "ui" sound in French, her second language, solitary language play may serve to make the code clear to oneself rather than to others. Since we have defined acquisition as the development of the ability to make experiences clear to oneself and to others, perhaps solitary language play, the language rehearsal that many adult learners claim they do, is geared toward the goal of making the code clear to oneself.

THE MODEL

The model within the framework makes a hypothesis about the internal work that is being done during these experiential encounters. The model is neither original nor completely articulated. Rather, we have combined our version of ideas proposed by Schank and Abelson (1977) and others with our version of Kempen and Hoenkamp's (1981) incremental procedural grammar. Since their ideas have been adapted, the descriptions given here should not be considered faithful representations of their work.

    Let us assume that during experiences, the acquirer begins to build a "knowledge structure" (using Schank's terminology). For example, in the Freedle and Lewis example, given in box 1, a knowledge structure, or script, of casual conversation is being constructed. It consists of information about conversational openings and closings, and the turn-taking system. Lexical formulas (e.g., hi, bye bye) that are part of that system are soon attached or interwoven into the framework, further defining and refining the shape of the system. As new information is encountered and recognized, it is checked against the knowledge structure. The new information may be rejected, it may be held in abeyance, it may be attached to the knowledge structure, or it may cause a reorganization of the structure so that the structure becomes more efficient by incorporating the new. The total knowledge structure evolves in both a top-down and a bottom-up manner as language, event, and social knowledge become interwoven. The total knowledge structure is thus made up of event structures (standardized into scripts) and the language attached to the script.

    However, if this language-building work is to be done, new elements must be recognized within experiences, as claimed, for example, in the WH-game example of "Where's your tummy?" The cognitive system must be alerted or activated to deal with the "new" and, eventually, to find the best way to accommodate the new into the internal system.

    Zernick (1984) provides an explicit example, relating this to second language learning. Assume an adult second language learner hears the new phrase "rip off" in a conversation where a friend complains, "Your mechanic ripped me off." The "car mechanic" experience is called up. Since the search shows no easy explanation of the term in that experience, the learner shifts to the next highest level, the "service encounter" event. The service encounter overlays the mechanic script. Some few cases of "rip off" are found at the service level, perhaps in the restaurant or the dentist or any of the other service encounters. Within "service" there are a series of normal actions such as arrange-service, do-service, pay-for-service, evaluate-service. In addition, there are cases of deviation from the norm such as service-not-done, bad-service, high-price, free-service, excellent-service. In trying to guess the meaning of "rip off," the learner is guided by intonation and other nonverbal clues to select from the negative examples that diverge from the norm. This narrows the scope of meanings to service-not-done, bad-service, and high-price. In this model, then, the learner would search for an already known phrase that might cover these meanings—for example, "cheat"—and test the scope and generalizability of "rip off" with those of "cheat." When divergences between "rip off" and "cheat" are found, they are identified and incorporated into the new knowledge structure.

To change the knowledge structure, estimates are made as to how the new differs and to what extent. The recognition of an estimate of degree of difference will, however, depend on frequency in the input, the scope of use, the perceptual saliency of a form (that is, how it is highlighted in the experience), and, of course, on the relationship of the form and function in the first and second languages. That is, are the form and function parallel in the learner's first language? Thus, natural perception and production factors along with the existence of similar knowledge structures for the first language should mediate the recognition and estimate of difference.

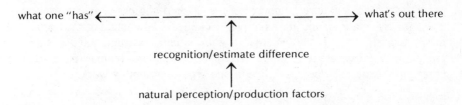

Many of these perception/production factors have been recognized as natural phenomena in languages and given the cover term "markedness." That is, the most unmarked form is likely to be of high perceptual saliency and be simpler or easier to produce. However, for many linguists, markedness is an internal theory. It should be obvious that in our account, markedness in an external phenomenon that has internal consequences. Forms that have high saliency, that differ most dramatically from each other should best be able to activate cognitive systems in initial learning. Once the cognitive system is on alert and assesses them (in)accurately, it builds a new structure, adapts an old one, or decides that the problem is not severe enough to warrant building anything. (The term "building" is only a metaphor to describe the growth of a system. No actual building may be going on.)

The first language, of course, also plays an important role in this model of second language learning. In broad terms, first language knowledge structures constitute much of what one has in the initial stages of L2 learning. For some learners, it may continue to be the base on which the second language is built. For other learners, this may not be efficient, so that as a foundation of L2 scripts is laid, the new language builds on and refines these knowledge structures rather than those of the first language.

The second part of the model has to do with the kind of abstract production system that is being developed to give language expression to knowledge structures. The system closest to what we believe is needed is incremental procedural grammar (IPG). In this grammar, sentences are not built in a single sentence-producing machine of phrase structure and transformational rules. Rather, the grammar has three parts: a *conceptualizer* that retrieves the knowledge structure frames and attached meaning fragments that are to be expressed in utterances; a *formulator* that takes the conceptual frame and lexical fragments, lexicalizes additional meaning fragments, and begins to build phrasal structures for them; and an *articulator* that is responsible for the saying of utterances.

The conceptualizer presents conceptual fragments from the frame to the formulator team that is charged with building a pragmatic and syntactic structure. To understand this, imagine a team of formulator specialists looking up meanings and selecting the best lexical candidates tied to the frame. Other experts begin working up candidate syntacticization for the lexical items to show the relationships among the conceptual units. The formulating teams may even work out organization for several synonyms and hold these in abeyance pending success or failure outcomes of the favored choices. Various experts check for pragmatic intent (for example, deciding on how much of the frame's information is shared and whether agent, patient, instrumental, or other pragmatic functions are to be emphasized). The formulator team is made up of procedure "experts" who specialize in one type of assembly work.

> For example, procedure NP knows how to build noun phrases; procedure PP can deliver prepositional phrases; procedure SUBJECT is responsible for the shape of subject phrases in main and subordinate clauses. Like the procedure or routines of ordinary computer programs, syntactic procedures are permitted to call on each other as subprocedures ("subroutines"). Procedure S, for instance, may decide to delegate a portion of its sentence-formation job to SUBJECT and OBJECT as subprocedures. OBJECT need not necessarily wait for SUBJECT to finish; they can get started simultaneously and run in parallel. (Kempen and Hoenkamp 1981: 11.)

Each conceptual fragment is handled piecemeal; NP experts may work simultaneously with S experts on some conceptual fragments. At the same time, other conceptual fragments are being set up by other specialists. The formulator builds a structure and sends it on the articulator. In many cases the work of the formulator will be eased by the use of already prefabricated (chunked, stereotypic, formulaic) phrases. That is, the search will bring up prepackaged phrases as well as lexical items. When phrases are already prefabricated, they can be shipped on out without much additional formulation. The output, each formulated package (whether only a single lexical item, a phrase, a clause, or a lexicalized sentence) is queued in the order received. Decisions are made on ordering according to the pragmatic properties of the package, its destination markers, source, and content. The ordering should work to unite the pragmatic and syntactic organization.

If the formulator is working on several conceptual fragments simultaneously and sending output to the articulator, you might wonder where choices are made regarding morphophonemic markers and phonological choices. We believe that this work is done at the articulator planning level, although IPG does not, because it would let us handle L2, as well as Broca's, problems with articulating bound morphology and phonology at the motor plan level.

This presentation of a three-level process—conceptualizer, formulator, articulator—is still very simplified. But perhaps it shows some of the advantages of an incremental grammar over a simpler sentence grammar. The model allows us to account for slips of the tongue, for repairs, for hesitation phenomena, and for the one-phrase or one-clause-at-a-time nature of extemporaneous talk. Slips of the tongue can be thought of as procedure failures and repairs as places where word searches have to be reinitiated. The model requires neither "complete-sentence" generation nor that we go back to a beginning S-node and run through phrase structures rules and T-rules again when trouble occurs.

A combination of the Schank and Abelson and IPG models allows us to predict strategies L2 learners might use in situations where formal instruction is not available. One such strategy is to select a script, such as "the bus trip" from the travel script, observe it in detail, and capture the high-frequency phrases and lexical entries for that script. While trying out these lexicalized phrases and words, supplemented with lots of nonverbal cues, the learner can begin to improve by selecting from the script whatever is most salient, formulating as much as possible (usually only short phrases in the beginning), and articulating that output however possible. As Lindblom has suggested in his "self-organizing" model of phonetics, this should provide enough syllables to begin organizing the phonemic system. Given the aid of the already-in-place L1 system, Lindblom would predict that those sounds with greatest social and perceptual benefit per articulatory cost would be produced first.

As work begins on other scripts, e.g., service scripts such as bargaining at vegetable markets or less observable service scripts such as getting the plumbing fixed, the formulator has more and more information as to what kinds of team "experts" will be needed and how they can best carry out their piecemeal work. The articulator also begins to refine the output (though, given most adult learners' problems with morphophonemic and phonological rules, it may never be very successful with these). If the model is correct, the early stages of L2 acquisition should be rich in chunks and high-frequency vocabulary tied to scripts, and short phrases linearly arranged to show pragmatic intent. The "basilang" studies (cf. Schumann 1984) show this to be the case. As the formulator has more and more material to work with, simple clauses (cf. Pawley and Syder's one-clause-at-a-time hypothesis) finally supplement the one-phrase-at-a-time and lexicalized sentence (chunk) output, and lexicon is generalized more appropriately across scripts. The problem then is to get the conceptual information and lexical choices into the pragmatic and syntactic frames that develop. Often, it is difficult to get both out of the articulator at the same time. That is, "empty boxes" appear. Even as native speakers, we begin "if—" and cannot find the material that is to go into the clause, or we begin a relative clause with "that's—" without the lexical material needed. Just then the articulator picks up a "backup box," usually a less complex but adequate phrase or clause. False starts and repairs of this sort occur in L1 data as well as in the speech of second language learners.

Since so much research in SLA has the syntactic system as its focus, we want to emphasize the fact that the organization of first language talk is often phrasal or, at most, clausal in nature and that it is also rich in repairs. Syntactic organization differs remarkably given time to plan and revise. The syntax of unplanned, spontaneous talk differs from that of highly organized, revised written discourse. Second language research must be sensitive to these differences. That is, oral data from L2 learners should be compared only with L1 data collected on very similar tasks. Our intuitions of what L1 learners say and write are simply not reliable. In addition, if learning takes place in an environment where opportunities to interact are rare, the type of syntactic structures and lexicon will be determined by experience with written text. If one is learning a foreign language via reading, the types of experience are quite different from those of oral language noted above. Consider Brown and Yule's "rainbow" example (1983:18). The written version is highly planned, shows dense syntax, and is richly lexicalized in comparison with the "one-clause-at-a-time" character of an unplanned talk version on the same topic.

normally after + very heavy rain + or something like that + and + you're driving along the road + and + far away + you see + well + er + a series + of + stripes + + formed like a bow + an arch ++ very very far away + ah + seven colors but ++ I guess you hardly ever see seven it's just a + a series of + colors + which + they seem to be separate but if you try to look for the separate (k ə z) – colors they always seem + very hard + to separate + if you see what I mean ++ (postgraduate student speaking informally.)
+ = pause, ++ long pause

And then, in the blowing clouds, she saw a band of faint iridescence colouring in faint shadows a portion of the hill. And forgetting, startled, she looked for the hovering colour and saw a rainbow forming itself. In one place it gleamed fiercely, and, her heart anguished with hope, she sought the shadow of iris where the bow should be. Steadily as the colours gather, mysteriously, from nowhere, it took presence upon itself, there was a faint, vast rainbow. (D. H. Lawrence, *The Rainbow*, chapter 16.)

Written language releases us from the stream of speech mode while lexical selection and syntactic organization take on more major roles. Hopefully, even the EFL learner who may only be able to interact with written text knows that it does not mirror the language of oral interaction. Scripts can be more elaborately composed using a full range of syntactic structures given time and inclination.

This very sketchy outline of our model draws freely on the work of Schank and Abelson and Kempen and Hoenkamp. Note that we speak of a production grammar rather than a comprehension grammar in this description. This is because in comprehending and coding experience we rely not on language alone but on a combination of social, cognitive, and language structures.

Rather than try to sketch the comprehension part of the model, we will attack two questions. First, what is the relationship of the three structures as internal, rather than external, knowledge systems? Second, given our hypothesis about the internal system, what is the relationship of external and internal systems—that is, what is the strength of the claim that is being made?

HOW SEPARATE ARE THE SYSTEMS?

No one denies that language acquisition, comprehension, and production are mental processes. Nor would anyone deny that cognitive and social systems are internal, mental systems. Since mental processes are not easily accessible for study, we may make whatever hypotheses we wish, and some of these may, rightly or wrongly, make more sense to us than others. Fortunately or unfortunately, the more we learn about neuroanatomy, the less convincing most models become.

Lewis and Cherry (1977) outlined three basic notions of the relationship of the internal system, diagraming them as shown in the figures.

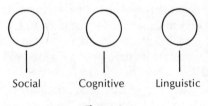

Social   Cognitive   Linguistic

Figure 1

In Figure 1 the three internal systems are separate. Since they are separate, the linguist need not consider social or cognitive structures when making hypotheses about the nature of language. In this view, sociolinguistics would not be the study of an interconnected social and language system but rather the study of modification rules that occur in a separate language system as

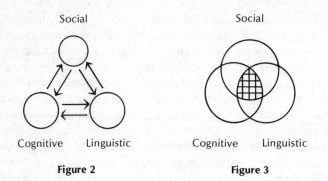

Figure 2   **Figure 3**

the result of membership in an external social group. Psycholinguistics would not be the study of an interconnected social, cognitive, and language system but rather the testing of linguistic theory against language performance.

In Figure 2, the three systems are still seen as separate but each has some connection with the other two systems. Some would claim causal direction for these connections. That is, language cannot develop without the appropriate cognitive structures being in place, or that language cannot develop without the appropriate social structures being in place. Some theorists have argued that once language structures are in place, they govern the cognitive system or even the social system. However, whatever the direction of causal claims, there is always evidence to show that parts of each system can still develop in the absence of the other two. (Cf. Yamada 1981 for a case study of a severely retarded woman with well-developed syntactic skills, and Blank et al. 1979 for a case study of a child with no apparent social skills but well-developed syntax.)

The interactive model (Figure 3) is the one that seems most plausible. It allows one to consider which parts of the systems build on those of the other systems. The construction of a piece of one system may offer a scaffolding for parts of other systems. For example, intonation seems to play a very large role in symbolic social play, in telling of jokes or funny stories, and in verbal "fights." Small children seem very much attuned to the intonation of jokes; they laugh at the appropriate time even though they do not understand the joke. It is as if they had developed a suprasegmental "envelope" for a joke and only needed to learn the story that goes into the joke. Young's (1974) two ESL kindergarten subjects acquired this suprasegmental envelope of accelerating rate and rising volume and pitch necessary for verbal threats. In fights, they used high-frequency chunks, e.g., "no way," "I can beat you up," and filled the rest of the sequence with nonsense.

The children are playing on swings.
N.S.:   I can beat your brother up. I can beat him up.
ESL Child: (Gradual build in volume over talk turn) You can beat him huh I can beat him to my party 'n you can beat him 'n you can beat my brother 'n he beat you up you (noises) it. I CAN BEAT YOU UP!!

Intonation thus gives a scaffolding on which to build the structures needed for such discourse. Not by chance, then, do neurolinguistic studies suggest that patients with certain types of lesions show deficits in both expressive intonation and the recognition of humor, jokes, teasing, and the like.

It is not just that a tremendous amount of borrowing goes on, though of course it is quite possible that procedures that work well for one system can easily be raided for others. Rather, one part may form a framework to which another system might attach its material. To continue the building metaphor, there may be a few general, powerful building basics for construction of knowledge structures. Yet there must also be infinite possibilities for variation around these basic procedures. The result would be that some learners construct more adequate and efficient systems than others. Each person builds a total system, however, that is both shared and unique, since it must result from an interpretation of both shared and unique experiences.

Using the interactive figure, one can account for the exceptional cases of Yamada and Blank et al. That is, under normal circumstances, the systems interact, but in abnormal cases it is possible to develop parts of systems without the third. The third figure provides for this by showing that parts of the systems do not overlap. So it is always possible to answer objections that some sets of procedures must be language-specific, social-specific, or cognitive-specific. The core can remain interwoven.

Just as the interpretation of experience evolves from the developing communication system, so the total communication system must evolve from the interpretation of our experiences for ourselves and others. What happens, then, when we want to incorporate new experiences that require large shifts within internal systems? Certainly this is the case when we consider adding new languages. When we find new material and want to add it in, how do we decide whether to just add on an addition or go back and remodel the complete system? Is it a matter of aesthetics (the old building looks okay), the high cost of total remodeling, or the need for efficiency of space and use? It would appear that it would be simpler to set up separate knowledge systems rather than try to constantly match to the L1 structures, copying identical elements and adding new rules where needed, or even to use the L1 system plus tags for L2 differences. Yet, from an interactive point of view, this does not seem efficient because of the effort needed to build a whole new addition. One could argue that all the basic procedures of the conceptualizer, formulator, and articulator remain the same—that only new "data files" are created. In a raw version this would view SLA as a relexification process. If the data files are rich, i.e., include not only scripts but also well-developed lexical rules, this seems fairly efficient. If, in addition, calling up data files triggers changes in formulator procedures, we get close to what L2 data look like. If you have worked with discourse data of noninstructed learners, you will probably want to argue that procedures in the conceptualizer as well as the formulator have to change to successfully handle L2 data. Somehow, the procedures of the articulator seem much less likely to change.

If only the files and not the processes change, what happens with third or fourth languages? Languages we do not know well or do not use often may be archived so long that we run into retrieval problems. When frames are pulled up, the same frames in several languages enter into similar simultaneous procedures. At least from our own tip-of-the-tongue phenomena and occasional mixing lapses, this seems to be the case. Somehow, the formulator gets confused in selecting lexical items or in developing structures around them. Or the articulator may get upset when "empty boxes" come down in one language, and take the next one in line even if it turns out to be from another language. And that language is not the first language but another partially known foreign language. Can we conclude that files for certain languages and experiences in them are more tightly grouped together?

Of course, no one can definitively say how systems interrelate internally. Decisions may be a matter of aesthetics. We all have our own aesthetics as to what is a pleasing hypothesis. While the clear, crisp lines of syntactic analysis are appealing, a model that sees SLA simply as a matter of building inter-language syntax should not be the central or only focus of research. We do not believe that language is a monolithic autonomous system centered around and controlled by syntax. Various subsystems of language may be more related to subsystems of the social system or other cognitive systems than to the syntax of language. How they all interrelate nobody knows; nevertheless, a messy, interrelated model rather than a neat and clean, syntax-centered language model is more viable. (What is aesthetically pleasing and what seems reasonable do not always turn out to be the same thing.)

STRENGTH OF CLAIM

The second question for the model is the relationship between external experience and internal knowledge structures. Let us consider the four classical claims: a contagion relationship, a causal, a triggering, and an interactive relationship.

It may appear that a contagion claim is being proposed. That is, if one is around here and now language, one catches here and now language, or if one is exposed to r's and l's, one inevitably catches them, just like the flu. In some ways the contagion claim makes sense, but, unfortunately, it sounds as though direct copies of the experience are being created, rather than a system of abstract knowledge structures. This is not a claim anyone would want to make.

The causal claim—i.e., that interaction *causes* language development—is also one we would not care to make. It is not the case that the opportunities for use cause a particular language form to develop (any more than one could say that social knowledge is acquired just because the learner has opportunities to display social-interaction forms). The acquisition of all mental systems is an internal neurological matter. We know that messages are transmitted electrically and chemically across cells, but what *causes* whatever structures there are (if there are any) to evolve in response to external stimulation is simply unknown.

The third position, triggering, is that held by many linguists. This view is that some outside influence is necessary to trigger what already lies present in the internal system, as an acorn already is an oak tree and needs only a shower or two to set it on its way. That is, a "universal grammar" already lies in place somewhere in the brain, along with an internal markedness theory. Only a bit of experience is needed to set it off. Development does take place; that is, the complete language system is not already present waiting to be set off. So experience is seen as necessary. The problem with this claim is that experience plays an almost irrelevant role. While the amount of experience needed is not specified, Chomsky clearly believes it to be minimal:

> If the system of universal grammar is sufficiently rich, then limited evidence will suffice for the development of rich and complex systems in the mind, and a small change in parameters may lead to what appears to be a radical change in the resulting system . . . . Endowed with this system and exposed to limited experience, the mind develops grammar that consists of a rich and highly articulated system of rules, not grounded in experience in the sense of inductive justification, but only in that experience has fixed the parameters of a complex schematization with a number of options. (Chomsky 1980: 66–67.)

The relationship claimed in the experience approach is an interactive relationship. Surely it is not just one bolt from the blue that sets the acquisition process in motion. Rather, there is a continuous interaction of the external and internal. Anyone who has worked with longitudinal data knows that the huge leaps predicted by the universal grammar model do not happen. Instead, thousands of infinitesimal additions occur and the systems are reorganized over and over as new additions accrue. Quantum leaps do not appear in the data. As Lindblom says, we should not underestimate the structure-forming power of the thousands of small changes. Those changes take place because experience is fed into self-organizing internal processes. As experience gives us new data, each new problem, new form, and new function triggers cognitive responses that get these experiences mapped into new or onto old knowledge structures through very small changes.

To conclude this section, we personally find the various hypotheses about internal systems fascinating. However, the arguments about these hypotheses and the models constructed to illustrate beliefs about mental systems result in a dead end if this is the sum of our work. The more we attribute the growth of the mental system to innate predetermined systems, the more speculative and less interesting our explanations become. If development is predetermined by the structure of innate networks, there is nothing left for us to explain, no role for experience as teacher, no role for the student as learner, and variability in learning is a minor problem to be handled by resetting some syntactic networks in slightly different ways.

Not surprisingly, even the strongest advocates of the innatist position, those most interested in language as a separate internal mental process, agree that language is acquired from "evidence," the external systems of language experience. The job of the applied linguist is to discover the links between experience and learning. Whether the links, once identified, lead to causal or merely triggering statements is of enormous theoretical interest to researchers but of little practical value to learners.

APPLICATION OF THE FRAMEWORK

To summarize the experience framework, in language acquisition it is assumed that learning is guided via interaction with a "teacher" in an associated set of experiences. These experiences differ for children and adults, for foreign language learners and immersion learners, and for instructed and uninstructed learners. The experiences serve many functions: they set preferred structures for discourse, for lexical boundaries and categorization; they highlight important information through suprasegmentals and pragmatic organization, clarify syntactic organization, and give data on accuracy at the morphophonemic and phonological levels as well. Basically, the focus of the framework is on external experience rather than the internal system—that is, it stresses the external and assumes the internal rather than vice versa.

Given the experience framework, how does it relate to second language teaching? If a teacher trainer or teacher wanted to use the framework, what might be done? For both the teacher and the teacher trainer, the task is to find those experiences that contribute most to learning and to work out ways to bring reasonable copies of those experiences, and the ways of dealing with them, into the classroom.

Not only should experiences be identified which bring rich possibilities for learning, but the experiences should directly involve the learner in discovery procedures. That is, the learner should be encouraged to become his own researcher. Most adults enjoy doing experiments. It is challenging but not frightening. Such experiences activate the system for discovery of the new in experience and promote an estimate of the degree of difference between what one already has (old knowledge structures) and the new. For examples of the types of activities we suggest, see Hatch, Flashner, and Hunt (1985). These activities could well be used by people who hold very different views of second language learning. What should be different is the relative importance given each of the subsystems in terms of number of activities. That is, syntax is not seen as central since, for the learner, the discourse system, the lexical system, and the suprasegmental system are of equal or greater importance in making experiences clear to oneself and to others. In contrast, while there are few activities that would be rejected as having no value to learning, the teacher should always be clear as to which experiences might best promote learning of particular parts of the second language.

CONCLUSION

The framework outlined in this paper is diffuse since the goals are broad. For some, the lack of a single focus is unattractive to say the least. They see no way of developing well-organized data collection, data description, and data analysis procedures when limits are not set. While, of course, we would like to derive an overall unified theory from the framework, it is not the case that all functions must be attacked simultaneously. What is important is that when pieces are investigated (or when pieces are taught separately) in the end the researcher returns to see how that piece is linked to the whole. We prefer a broad framework because it gives us freedom to look at any part of the total system without running the danger of believing that what we are looking at is disconnected from the rest of the system. The framework also ensures a direct link to language teaching and teacher training.

REFERENCES

Blank, M., M. Gessner, and A. Esposito. 1979. Language without communication: a case study. *Journal of Child Language*, 2: 329–352.

Brown, G., and G. Yule. 1983. *Discourse Analysis*. London: Cambridge University Press.

Chomsky, N. 1980. *Rules and Representations*. New York: Columbia University Press.

Freedle, R., and M. Lewis. 1977. Prelinguistic conversations. In M. Lewis and L. Rosenblum (ed.). *Interaction, Conversation, and Development of Language*. New York: Wiley.

Gough, J. 1984. Adult-child language play: a naturalistic study. Ph.D. qualifying paper, Applied Linguistics, UCLA.

Greenfield, P., and J. Smith. 1976. *The Structure of Communication in Early Language Development*. New York: Academic Press.

Grice, H. P. 1975. Logic and conversation. In P. Cole and J. Morgan (eds.). *Syntax and Semantics,* vol. 3, Speech Acts. New York: Academic Press.

Hatch, E. 1978. Discourse analysis, speech acts and second language acquisition. In W. Ritchie. Second Language Acquisition Research. New York: Academic Press.

Hatch, E., S. Peck, and J. Gough. 1979. A look at process in child second language acquisition. In E. Ochs (ed.). *Developmental Pragmatics*. New York: Academic Press.

Hatch, E., V. Flashner, and I. Hunt. 1985. *Linguistics for Language Teachers*. Third prepublication edition. ESL Department, UCLA.

Kavanaugh R., S. Whellington, and M. Cerbone. 1983. Mothers' use of fantasy in speech to young children. *Journal of Child Language,* 10: 45–55.

Kempen, G., and E. Hoenkamp. 1981. A procedural grammar for sentence production. Internal Report 81. Vakgroep Psychologische Functieleer, Psychologisch Laboratorium, Katholieke Universiteit, Nijmegen, the Netherlands.

Kenyeres, A. 1938. Comment une petite Hongroise apprend le francais.*Archives de Psychologie, 26: 321–366.*

Lewis, M., and L. Cherry. 1977. Social behavior and language acquisition. In M. Lewis and L. Rosenblum (eds.). *Interaction, Conversation and Development of Language.* New York: Wiley.

Lindblom, B. Undated. Can the models of evolutionary biology be applied to phonetic problems? Paper, Linguistics Department, Stockholm University.

Miller, P. 1982. Teasing sequences. In Bulletin of Cross-cultural Human Cognition and Development. University of California, San Diego.

Ochs Keenan, E. 1974. Conversational competence in children. *Journal of Child Language,* 1: 163–183.

Pawley, A., and F. Syder. 1977. The one clause at a time hypothesis. Paper, Linguistics Department, University of Auckland.

Pawley, A., and F. Syder. In press. Natural selection in syntax. *Journal of Pragmatics.*

Peck, S. 1978. Child-child discourse in second language acquisition. In E. Hatch (ed.). *Second Language Acquisition.* Rowley, Mass.: Newbury House.

Richards, J., and R. Schmidt. 1983. Conversational analysis. In J. Richards and R. Schmidt. *Language and Communication.* London: Longman.

Sachs, J. and L. Truswell. 1978. Comprehension of two-word instructions by children at the one-word stage. *Journal of Child Language,* 5: 17–24.

Schank, R., and Abelson. 1977. *Scripts, Plans, Goals and Understanding: An Inquiry into Human Knowledge Structures.* Hillsdale, N.J.: Lawrence Erlbaum.

Schmidt, R. W. 1983. Interaction, acculturation, and the acquisition of communicative competence. In N. Wolfson and F. Judd (eds.). *Sociolinguistics and Language Acquisition.* Rowley, Mass. Newbury House.

Schumann, J. 1984. Nonsyntactic speech in the Spanish-English Basilang. In R. Andersen (ed.). *Second Languages: A Cross-Linguistic Perspective.* Rowley, Mass.: Newbury House.

Scollon, R. 1979. A real early stage: an unzippered condensation of a dissertation on child language. In E. Ochs and B. Schieffelin (eds.). *Developmental Pragmatics.* New York: Academic Press.

Weir, R. 1962. *Language in the Crib.* The Hague: Mouton.

Yamada, J. 1981. On the independence of language and cognition: evidence from a hyperlinguistic retarded adolescent. Paper presented at the International Congress of Child Language. University of British Columbia, Vancouver.

Young, D. 1974. The acquisition of English syntax by three Spanish-speaking children. M.A. thesis, UCLA.

Zernik, U. 1984. Rina: a program that learns English as a second language. Paper presented at the Southern California Conference on Artificial Intelligence, UCLA.

2

CONVERSATION AND INTERLANGUAGE DEVELOPMENT: RETHINKING THE CONNECTION[1]

Charlene J. Sato
University of Hawaii at Manoa

Since the late 1970s, a number of researchers have turned their attention to the relationship between conversation and second language acquisition (SLA). Some have viewed the issue in terms of the necessity and sufficiency of conversational interaction in SLA (e.g., Hatch 1978a, 1978b, 1983; Long 1980, 1981, 1983). The central question in this work, more specifically, is the extent to which the linguistic and conversational adjustments by native speakers to learners determine process, rate, and ultimate achievement in SLA (Long 1983: 188). Through an extensive review of the literature in this area, Long (1983) provides strong evidence that such adjustments are necessary, although not sufficient, for SLA to occur.

Another perspective on the issue has emerged from functionalist approaches to the study of interlanguage (IL) development (e.g., Andersen 1984; Flashner 1983; Huebner 1983; Kumpf 1981, 1983; Lynch 1983; Meisel 1985; Pfaff 1982; Schumann 1981, to appear). Research of this type has concentrated largely on describing the dynamics of function-to-form or form-to-function mapping in the development of ILs.

While the two perspectives differ from each other in their treatment of theory (and theory construction) and method in SLA research, they both adopt the position that the development of learners' ILs is extensively and systematically influenced by discourse-pragmatic principles. This chapter attempts to provide a unified treatment of the issue by addressing aspects of the "necessity/sufficiency" question in light of recent findings from a longitudinal, functionalist study of Vietnamese-English IL development. Evidence from an analysis of one semantic domain—past-time reference (PTR)—is presented to support the claim that conversational interaction selectively facilitates the acquisition of the linguistic devices that code various semantic and functional domains in learners' ILs.

A LONGITUDINAL ANALYSIS OF PTR IN IL DEVELOPMENT

Purpose

The analysis of PTR to be reported here was part of a larger investigation (Sato 1985) that broadened the scope of IL analysis by examining the relationship between discourse processes and the emergence of IL morphosyntactic structures. The study was undertaken within Givón's (1979a, 1979b) functional-typological framework for syntactic analysis, modified to allow a more interactionist treatment of spontaneous IL speech data.

The research questions concerning PTR were framed in terms of the concepts of *parataxis* and *syntacticization*, defined as follows:

1. Parataxis: Extensive reliance on discourse-pragmatic factors in face-to-face communication and minimal use of target language (TL) morphosyntactic devices in expressing propositions. Discourse-pragmatic factors include shared knowledge between interlocutors, collaboration between interlocutors in the expression of propositions, and the distribution of propositional content over a sequence of utterances rather than a single utterance.
2. Syntacticization: The process through which the targetlike use of morphosyntactic devices in IL increases over time, while the reliance on discourse-pragmatic context declines.

With respect to these concepts, the analysis sought to determine, first, the extent to which PTR in IL was characterized by parataxis and, second, whether evidence of syntacticization could be found over time.

Subjects

The learners in this study are brothers, Tai and Thanh, who were about 10 and 12 years old when they arrived in the United States as boat refugees from Vietnam. Since their arrival, they have lived with American foster parents in Philadelphia, Pennsylvania.

At the time of this study, both learners were enrolled in the same public school in their predominantly black, working/middle-class community. Tai was placed in a mixed third and fourth grade class and Thanh in the sixth grade. Neither received any ESL instruction during this period since no ESL classes or teachers were available in their school. Both recalled understanding very little of the classroom discourse during their first 2 months in school and, according to teacher reports, participated minimally in classroom interaction.

Data

The data for this study were collected through weekly audiotaping of visits over a 10-month period between the subjects and the researcher, primarily in the home context. The boys' foster mother, Mary, was present during most of these visits. Other occasional participants included their foster father, Bud, their peers, family friends, and friends of the researcher.

While data from a wide range of situations were collected, the analysis of PTR used only data from spontaneous conversation. Given approximately 1½ hours of recording per session, a total of about 60 hours of interaction was collected. From this corpus, conversational data from sessions at roughly 4-week intervals were selected for analysis, yielding a total of about 15 hours of taped interaction. In each sample, both the learners' speech and their interlocutors' speech were analyzed. The former was transcribed in the international phonetic alphabet, with some modifications, and the latter in English orthography.

Analysis

The data were first segmented into utterances, an utterance being defined as a sequence of speech under a single intonation contour bounded by pauses. The following features were then identified and quantified in each sample:

1. Obligatory contexts of past-tense marking in English
2. Past-tense marking on verbs, both inflectional (i.e., regular), as in "smashed," and lexical (i.e., irregular), as in "came" and "bought"
3. Temporal and locative adverbials (e.g., "yesterday" and "in Vietnam")
4. Unmarked past-time contexts
5. Discourse-pragmatic indicators of past-time reference:
   a. Learner's (self's) immediately preceding utterance (SIPU)
   b. Other's immediately preceding utterance (OIPU)
   c. Non-immediately preceding utterance (NIPU)
   d. Situational context (i.e., objects, actions, or events in the immediate physical setting)

The data were also examined for a more global view of each learner's expression of past time in conversation. Particular attention was given to instances of miscommunication and repair by the learners and their inter-locutors.

Evidence of parataxis was expected to emerge as (1) lower proportions of linguistically encoded than contextually indicated instances of PTR; (2) heavy reliance upon interlocutor establishment of PTR; and (3) low frequencies of lexical past verbs and inflectional past verbs with explicit coding for past time. With respect to syntacticization, it was anticipated that (1) the learners' reliance upon contextual indicators of PTR would decrease over time; (2) their reliance upon interlocutors for the establishment of PTR would lessen over time; and (3) their explicit encoding of past time on lexical and inflectional past verbs would increase over time.

Results

The results are presented here in the following sequence: first the quantitative findings for marked and unmarked past-time contexts, past-time markers, and discourse-pragmatic indicators; then the description of conversational sequences involving PTR.

Marked and unmarked past-time contexts   An initial breakdown of linguistically marked and unmarked past-time contexts (PTCs), given in Table 1 for Thanh and Table 2 for Tai, showed that neither learner marked PTR in the majority of contexts. Thanh, the older learner, produced his highest level of marked PTCs in sample 4, about 53 percent. In all other samples, 50 percent or less of the PTCs were coded linguistically. In Tai's case, the lowest percentage—16 percent—occurred in sample 2, and the majority of PTCs were unmarked in all but one of the ten samples. Only in sample 3 did he mark PTR in at least half of the contexts. Figure 1, in which the percentages for marked and unmarked PTCs given in Tables 1 and 2 are plotted, provides an alternative display of these findings.

Developmentally speaking, no consistent movement toward higher frequencies of marked PTRs was observed. While the percentage of marked PTR increased for Thanh from 20 percent in sample 5 to about 46 percent in sample 9, it went down to 33 percent in sample 10. This finding must be viewed as tentative, owing to the low frequencies of tokens for Thanh. While Tai generally produced more past-time markers, his developmental pattern was even more variable. From sample 5 until sample 7, the percentage of marked PTCs remained at roughly 25 percent, then increased to 40 percent in sample 8, dipped to 22 percent in sample 9, and, finally, rose to 38 percent in the last sample.

Distribution of past-time markers   The linguistically marked PTCs were examined to determine the relative frequencies of particular markers, i.e., lexical past verbs, inflectional past verbs, and adverbials, both temporal and locative. While the low frequencies of tokens do not allow any strong claims, a few patterns should be noted. As shown in Table 3 for Thanh and Table 4 for Tai, both learners tended to use verb forms more often than adverbials. Within the adverbial category, Thanh produced both temporal and locative expressions, while Tai used only one locative expression, this in sample 5:

TABLE 1 Marked and Unmarked Past Time Contexts (PTCs) for Thanh

	1	2	3	4	5	6	7	8	9	10
Marked										
Number	6	9	6	8	2	7	13	20	5	4
Percent	40.00	13.64	50.00	53.33	20.00	31.82	33.33	40.82	45.45	33.33
Unmarked										
Number	9	57	6	7	8	15	26	29	6	8
Percent	60.00	86.36	50.00	46.67	80.00	68.18	66.67	59.18	54.55	66.67
Total PTCs										
Number	15	66	12	15	10	22	39	49	11	12
Percent	100.00	100.00	100.00	100.00	100.00	100.00	100.00	100.00	100.00	100.00

TABLE 2 Marked and Unmarked Past Time Contexts (PTCs) for Tai

	1	2	3	4	5	6	7	8	9	10
Marked										
Number	5	4	3	7	9	9	19	23	15	6
Percent	23.81	16.00	50.00	14.00	23.68	25.71	25.33	39.66	22.06	37.50
Unmarked										
Number	16	21	3	43	29	26	56	35	53	10
Percent	76.19	84.00	50.00	86.00	76.32	74.29	74.67	60.34	77.94	62.50
Total PTCs										
Number	21	25	6	50	38	35	75	58	68	16
Percent	100.00	100.00	100.00	100.00	100.00	100.00	100.00	100.00	100.00	100.00

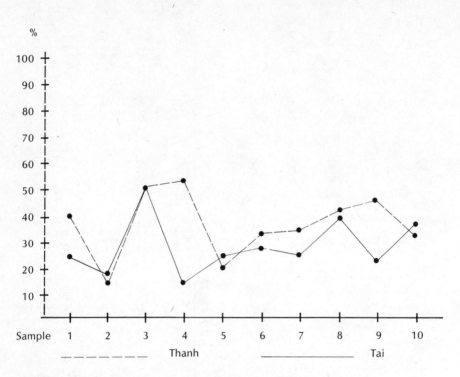

%

FIGURE 1 Marked Past Time Contexts for Thanh and Tai

[Context: Interlocutor has just asserted that Tai never has his picture taken with girls.]
  Tai: æ sku^w deį wan a-aį stæn∧p æn-wɪ g ǝlz
  at-school-they-want-I-stand-up-and-with-girls
  "At school, they wanted me to stand up [and take a picture] with [some] girls." (19.10)

The striking finding here was the lack of inflectional pasts in both learners' data. Although Tai did produce what could have been an inflectional past in sample 8: [peįnti] "painted" in the utterance   [hu ph-hu peįnti raį? ɪn deǝ] "who painted right in there?" only the vowel was discernible in the suffix. Aside from this instance, he produced no inflectional pasts. This finding thus confirmed predictions of low frequencies of lexical past and inflectional past verbs.

As for developmental changes in the production of past time markers, lexical past verbs increased only slightly in some of the later samples for both learners. Table 3 shows that Thanh used over twice as many lexical pasts in samples 6 and 7 as in any of the other samples; however, he produced only two and three tokens, respectively, in the last two samples. This decrease in later samples is difficult to interpret because of the low numbers involved.

A similar observation holds for Tai's production of lexical pasts, although a general tendency toward higher frequencies in the later samples is clearer in his data (see Table 4).

TABLE 3 Past Time Markers for Thanh

Markers	1	2	3	4	5	6	7	8	9	10
Lexical[a]	1	3	3	2	1	4	12	10	2	3
Lexical + temporal[b]	0	2	2	2	0	0	1	2	0	0
Inflectional[c]	0	0	0	0	0	0	0	0	0	0
Subtotal										
Number	1	5	5	4	1	4	13	12	2	3
Percent	16.67	55.55	83.33	50.00	50.00	57.14	100.00	60.00	40.00	75.00
Temporal[d]	3	4	1	4	0	2	0	6	1	1
Locative[e]	2	0	0	0	1	1	0	2	2	0
Subtotal										
Number	5	4	1	4	1	3	0	8	3	1
Percent	83.33	44.44	16.67	50.00	50.00	42.86	0.00	40.00	60.00	25.00
Total										
Number	6	9	6	8	2	7	13	20	5	4
Percent	100.00	100.00	100.00	100.00	100.00	100.00	100.00	100.00	100.00	100.00

[a]Lexical = lexical past verb, e.g., *bought, came*
[b]Lexical + temporal = lexical past verb plus temporal expression, e.g., *yesterday*
[c]Inflectional = inflectional past verb, e.g., *smashed*
[d]Temporal = temporal expression, e.g., *yesterday* ($\emptyset$-verb or with verb stem)
[e]Locative = locative expression, e.g., *in Vietnam* ($\emptyset$-verb or with verb stem)

TABLE 4 Past Time Markers for Tai

Markers	1	2	3	4	5	6	7	8	9	10
Lexical[a]	1	4	2	5	6	7	15	18	9	6
Lexical + temporal[b]	0	0	0	0	0	0	0	1	0	0
Inflectional[c]	0	0	0	0	0	0	0	1	0	0
Subtotal										
Number	1	4	2	5	6	7	15	20	9	6
Percent	20.00	100.00	66.67	71.43	66.67	77.78	78.95	86.96	60.00	100.00
Temporal[d]	4	0	1	2	2	2	4	3	6	0
Locative[e]	0	0	0	0	1	0	0	0	0	0
Subtotal										
Number	4	0	1	2	3	2	4	3	6	0
Percent	80.00	0.00	33.33	28.57	33.33	22.22	21.05	13.04	40.00	0.00
Total										
Number	5	4	3	7	9	9	19	23	15	6
Percent	100.00	100.00	100.00	100.00	100.00	100.00	100.00	100.00	100.00	100.00

[a]Lexical = lexical past verb, e.g., bought, came
[b]Lexical + temporal = lexical past verb plus temporal expression, e.g., yesterday
[c]Inflectional = inflectional past verb, e.g., smashed
[d]Temporal = temporal expression, e.g., yesterday (Ø-verb or with verb stem)
[e]Locative = locative expression, e.g., in Vietnam (Ø-verb or with verb stem)

TABLE 5 Unmarked Past Time Contexts for Thanh

	1	2	3	4	5	6	7	8	9	10
Discourse-pragmatic[a]										
Number	8	54	5	5	7	12	23	29	6	8
Percent	88.89	94.74	83.33	71.43	87.50	80.00	88.46	100.00	100.00	100.00
Situational[b]										
Number	0	2	0	1	0	0	2	0	0	0
Percent	0.00	3.51	0.00	14.29	0.00	0.00	7.69	0.00	0.00	0.00
No indicator										
Number	1	1	1	1	1	3	1	0	0	0
Percent	11.11	1.75	16.67	14.29	12.50	20.00	3.85	0.00	0.00	0.00
Total										
Number	9	57	6	7	8	15	26	29	6	8
Percent	100.00	100.00	100.00	100.00	100.00	100.00	100.00	100.00	100.00	100.00

[a]Discourse-pragmatic = discourse-pragmatic indicator   [b]Situational = situational context

The virtual absence of inflectional past markers motivated a subsequent phonological analysis of the learners' ILs. As this analysis is reported in greater detail elsewhere (Sato 1984), a synopsis of its findings is presented here. In essence, it was found that first language syllable structure transfer constrained the production of syllable-final consonant clusters. Since English past tense morphology frequently creates syllable-final consonant clusters, it was argued that the lack of use of inflectional pasts was due in part to phonological transfer.

Discourse-pragmatic indicators (DPIs) of PTR The second major aspect of the analysis examined all the past time contexts (PTCs) that were not marked linguistically for PTR. A similar dependence on context emerged in both learners' data. There were a few cases where nothing in either the situational context or the preceding discourse indicated that an event, act, or state was being referred to as past. The figures for Ø-indicator in Tables 5 and 6 display this finding. Such instances occurred slightly more often in Tai's data. That the temporal context was indeed past in such cases was indicated in subsequent discourse, either through confirmation checks by the interlocutor or through repairs of communication breakdowns.

The next stage of the analysis looked at interactional structure to locate the specific points at which PTR could be inferred. For each utterance in the learners' speech which contained an unmarked PTC, the closest preceding marking of PTR was identified, in either the learner's immediately preceding utterance (SIPU), his interlocutor's immediately preceding utterance (OIPU), or some non-immediately preceding utterance (NIPU).

For Thanh, PTR was mainly retrievable through NIPUs—in seven samples—and, less often—in two samples—through past-time marking in OIPUs (see Table 7).

For Tai, pastness was inferrable more frequently from OIPUs than from NIPUs in five of the ten samples (see Table 8). In the other five samples, the reverse occurred. To this extent, the data from Tai were more variable than those from Thanh, for whom the recoverability of past reference from NIPUs predominated from the third through the tenth samples. With respect to syntacticization, then, very little movement away from contextually embedded PTRs was discernible in either learner's data.

Communication breakdowns involving PTR Three conversational excerpts are now reviewed to illustrate the interactional nature of PTR—actually, the lack of PTR—in the learners' discourse. While communication breakdowns as well as unacknowledged miscommunications occurred occasionally, very few involved PTR specifically. Possible miscommunications are not retrievable through post hoc analysis without having the interlocutors themselves review the data (see Hawkins 1985 for an example of this procedure). However, actual breakdowns are amenable to analysis since the interlocutors explicitly attempted to repair them. The excerpts discussed here are taken from weeks 8, 13, and 31 of the study. The first involves Tai, the second both Tai and Thanh, and the third Thanh.

TABLE 6 Unmarked Past Time Contexts for Tai

	1	2	3	4	5	6	7	8	9	10
Discourse-pragmatic[a]										
Number	16	38	1	41	28	9	56	30	50	4
Percent	100.00	90.48	50.00	89.13	96.55	64.29	100.00	85.71	94.34	40.00
Situational[b]										
Number	0	4	0	1	1	0	0	2	1	2
Percent	0.00	9.52	0.00	2.17	3.45	0.00	0.00	5.71	1.89	20.00
No indicator										
Number	0	0	1	4	0	5	0	3	2	4
Percent	0.00	0.00	50.00	8.70	0.00	35.71	0.00	8.57	3.77	40.00
Total										
Number	16	42	2	46	29	14	56	35	53	10
Percent	100.00	100.00	100.00	100.00	100.00	100.00	100.00	100.00	100.00	100.00

[a]Discourse-pragmatic = discourse-pragmatic indicator   [b]Situational = situational context

TABLE 7 Discourse-Pragmatic Indicators (DPIs) of Past Time for Thanh

	1	2	3	4	5	6	7	8	9	10
NIPU[a]										
Number	3	23	3	3	6	6	18	21	5	6
Percent	37.5	42.59	60.00	60.00	85.71	50.00	78.26	72.41	83.33	75.00
OIPU[b]										
Number	4	31	1	1	0	6	4	8	1	2
Percent	50.00	57.41	20.00	20.00	0.00	50.00	17.39	27.59	16.67	25.00
SIPU[c]										
Number	1	0	1	1	1	0	1	0	0	0
Percent	12.50	0.00	20.00	20.00	14.29	0.00	4.35	0.00	0.00	0.00
Total	8	54	5	5	7	12	23	29	6	8

[a]NIPU = non-immediately preceding utterance in discourse   [c]SIPU = self's (i.e., learner's) immediately preceding utterance
[b]OIPU = other's (i.e., interlocutor's) immediately preceding utterance

TABLE 8 Discourse-Pragmatic Indicators (DPIs) of Past Time for Tai

	1	2	3	4	5	6	7	8	9	10
NIPU[a]										
Number	4	23	1	9	18	3	17	17	15	4
Percent	25.00	60.53	100.00	21.95	64.29	33.33	30.36	56.67	30.00	100.00
OIPU[b]										
Number	12	13	0	32	10	5	27	13	26	0
Percent	75.00	34.21	0.00	78.05	35.71	55.55	48.21	43.33	52.00	0.00
SIPU[c]										
Number	0	2	0	0	0	1	12	0	9	0
Percent	0.00	5.26	0.00	0.00	0.00	11.11	21.43	0.00	18.00	0.00
Total	16	38	1	41	28	9	56	30	50	4

[a]NIPU = non-immediately preceding utterance in discourse
[b]OIPU = other's (i.e., interlocutor's) immediately preceding utterance
[c]SIPU = self's (i.e., learner's) immediately preceding utterance

Excerpt 1: "The Fever Game." In this excerpt Tai (T) and his interlocutor (C), this researcher, have been chatting about a number of things. C nominates a new topic, believing that the boys have gone to see a professional soccer team, the Fever, play. In fact, they have not yet gone to see them.

Excerpt 1: "The Fever Game"

	T	C
1		Oh, Mary said that you went to
2		um–you went to a game by the
3		Fever?
4	noụ tan hi go yɛt no-Thanh-he-go-yet	
5		You didn't go yet? To the Fever?
6	wat? what?	
7		Did you go to see the Fever
8		play soccer?
9	yɛs yes	
10		When was that?
11	nat nat naụ not-not-now	
12		Oh uh-later? Oh I see. Who
13		else is going?
14	tan hi go ɪn də pɪʉ Thanh-he-go-in-the- [pɪʉ]	

In her topic nomination (line 1), C encodes what she takes to be a fact as a yes/no question. T attempts (it seems) to correct C's misunderstanding, although his response (line 4) is open to at least two interpretations, namely,

1. "Thanh has gone (already) but I haven't."
2. "*Thanh* hasn't gone yet (but I have)."

C checks on her understanding of T's response with two more confirmation questions (line 5). T then indicates noncomprehension (line 6), so C follows with a direct yes/no question (line 7) which renominates the topic, but this time without presenting any material as presupposed. Why T responds with "yes" to this question is not clear. Possibly, he did not understand it or interpreted it to mean: Did he *want* to go to see the Fever. In any case, C at this point has received contradictory answers to what she considers the same question. She next asks for a date (line 10) to settle the issue, but T responds with still another ambiguous statement (line 11). "Not now" could mean, of course, either earlier or later than the moment of speaking. C interprets it to mean "later" (line 12) and follows up with a subtopic nomination: "Who else is going?" T's response (line 14) is, again, problematic. Assuming the last word is "Fever," he seems to be saying that Thanh is going to see the Fever. However, as he could have answered C's question much more economically by simply saying "Thanh," it is curious that he produces a "complete" proposition, almost as an assertion.

Excerpt 2: "The Spelling Test." In the second instance of a communication breakdown, it is the learner, Tai (T), who apparently intends to establish PTR and is misinterpreted by C, the interlocutor. Eventually, the temporal reference problem is sorted out when first Thanh (Th) and later Mary (M, the boys' foster mother) intervene.

The session takes place at the boys' house with C attempting to sort out some of T's homework at the end of a visit. Th is doing some schoolwork nearby. T is showing C a list of words, apparently spelling words. Somewhat disconcerted by the seeming arbitrariness of the words—they have not been taken from a story or other discourse context—C begins to review the words with T to determine if he knows their meanings.

Excerpt 2: "The Spelling Test"

T and Th	C and M
1 ʔm ʔm aị tıŋ dæt aị hæb aa- [ʔmʔm]-I-think-that-I-have-uh	
2 lɔŋ dıs inʌʌ tunaịt learn-this-in-uh-tonight	
3 dæʔ aị hæb tu speɥlıŋ dæt that-I-have-to-spelling-that	
4	You have to spell all these words tonight?
6 yɛs tunaịt ɥm redi yes-tonight-um-ready	
	And tomorrow is your test?
7 nɥʔɥʔ [nɥʔɥʔ]	
8	When-
9 tunaịt redi hi dʌn tonight-ready. he-done	
10	You're done with your test?
11	For these?
12 mhm tunaịt mhm. tonight	
13 mhm ši seị yıt aị raị yɛt mhm. she-say-it-I-write-it	
14	Who? She said it-
15 nou ši ə seị-aị (xx) no-she-uh-say-I-(xx)	

(Th)16 (x) tɔk æn hi raɪt
(x)-talk-and-he-write

17   He has to write the words out?

18 mhm twanti eɪ̯?
mhm. twenty-eight

19   Tonight

20 rɛdi
ready

(Th)21 (xxx) naʊ̯
(xxx)-now

22   When is-
((in Vietnamese)) (xxx)

(Th)23 ɪn də mɔnin
in-the-morning

(Th)24 hi radi ɪn də mɔnin
he-(ready)-in-the-morning

25   Tomorrow in school you mean

26 nɔʔaa tunaɪ̯t
[nɔʔaa]tonight

(Th)27 tudeɪ̯ tudeɪ̯
today-today

28   You have to write these words

29 noʊ̯   tonight?
no

(Th)30 dɪs fo spɛulɪn yɛstudeɪ̯
this-for-spelling-yesterday

31 lɔɔŋ əgo
long-ago

32   Yesterday?

(Th)33 æn hi rædi ɪn də mɔnin
and-he-(ready)-in-the-morning

(Th)34 dɪs wan
this-one

35 noʊ̯ mæri tɛl (mɪs)=
no-Mary-tell-(miss)=

36   I'm-I don't understand

37 dɪ aɪ̯ lɔʊ̯rɛdi aʔ mm-
this-I-already-uh-mm-

38 æ skul Mæri=
at-school-Mary=

39   =these are

40   (M) =those are the words that

41   he had the spelling test on

42   today. Did you get new
words today?

43	Oooh, so you—these are
44	your old words
45	(M) Yeah they had a spelling
46	test today

In his first utterance in this exchange (line 1), T nominates a new topic: his need to learn the words. As indicated by her confirmation check (line 4) in the form of a paraphrase, C interprets [hæb aa-lɔŋ dɪs ɪnʌʌ tunaɪt] as "*have to learn* this *tonight*," i.e., a modal + verb construction encoding a to-be-realized obligation and an adverbial indicating a time after the moment of speaking. It is at this point that the breakdown occurs, and the subsequent interaction is devoted to repairing the trouble. Th attempts to clarify for C that T's spelling test for these words occurred that morning (lines 16, 21, 24, 27, 33, and 34). M eventually makes this point as well (line 40). What remains puzzling is what T meant by his very first utterance. If the test had indeed taken place prior to the present discussion, the utterance   [ai hæb aa-lɔŋ dɪs ɪnʌʌ tunaɪt]   and the next one, [dæʔ aɪ hæb tu spɛɟlɪŋ dæt], could not refer to an act—learning or spelling—following the conversation between T and C.

Excerpt 3: "The Rehearsal." The final excerpt contains a breakdown between Thanh (Th) and C. It occurs when Th attempts to express a future intention which C interprets as an instance of past time reference.

Excerpt 3: "The Rehearsal"

	Th	C
1		Okay. Just a second. Let me
2		give Tai this. Tai
3	oʷ bifɔ aɪ gɪb˥ əə ripɔrt	
	oh-before I-give-uh-report	
4	sačio ɛɛrɪk - æn mæri æn bʌd	
	Sachio-Erik-and-Mary-and-Bud	
5		And him? ((referring to Tai))
6	yʌp	
	yup	
7		As your audience?
8	yʌp aɪ gɪb dɛm ripɔrt	
	yup-I-give-them-report	
9		So this is the second time
		you'd—
10	noʷ wɛn aɪ gɪb - bifɔ aɪ gɪb	
	no-when-I-give-before-I-give	
11	ɪn də skuʷ	
	in-the-school	

12 æn ai̯-
and-I

13   Oh you mean-later=

14 =ɔn təˑsdei̯ ai̯ gɪb
on-Thursday-I-give

15   Ooh, okay. Oh that'll be good

Th has just rehearsed an oral report for school with C. He has been working on it for a couple of weeks and will present it to his class in a few days' time. The breakdown is triggered by Th's topic-nominating utterance (line 3), which C understands as "Before [i.e., earlier than the moment of speaking], I gave the report to Sachio, Erik, Mary, and Bud." She follows up on this understanding by asking if Tai had heard the report also as part of this captive audience (lines 5 and 7). Th, meanwhile, is unaware that C has misinterpreted the time reference and confirms C's "as your audience?" by repeating [yʌp ai gɪb dɛm ripɔrt] (line 8). Only in the next line does C reveal the miscommûnication, which then provokes Th's repair (lines 10 and 11), "before I give it in school . . . ."

What this excerpt reveals is variation in the use of temporal terms such as *before*. Returning to Th's initial remark, it can now be glossed as "before I give this report in school, I'll give it to Sachio, Erik, Mary, and Bud." From the native English speaker's perspective, *before* should immediately precede a clause or phrase expressing the temporal point of reference which, in turn, is accompanied by a (main) clause expressing the point in time prior to it, e.g., (1) "Before giving this report . . ." or (2) "before I give this report . . . ." Put more simply, Th's use of *before* did not relate two events or acts in time. C therefore used the moment of speaking as the point of reference and interpreted *give* as marking a past action.

Summary   With respect to parataxis and syntacticization, the findings presented above showed (1) lower proportions of linguistically encoded than contextually indicated PTR; (2) low frequencies of lexical past verbs and no inflectional past verbs; marked for past time; and (3) heavy reliance upon interlocutor establishment of PTR. Moreover, there were only minimal signs of movement over time toward extensive use of linguistic coding devices in the marking of PTR.

Discussion

The significance of these findings concerning PTR in IL speech is twofold. First, the present analysis adds to a small body of cross-linguistic research in this area of IL development and use. Second, it speaks to the question of how conversational interaction in a second language is related to IL development. Although the latter dimension is of greater interest in this discussion, some indication of the consistency of this study's findings with those of similar studies should be mentioned briefly.

While the design and analytical scope of related studies have varied somewhat, the parallels are clear. In an analysis of Spanish-German IL data elicited from 18 adults on an oral translation task, Dittmar (1981) found little evidence of morphological marking of temporal reference and extensive use of adverbials and various discourse strategies such as the linking of propositions to indicate a sequential relationship between events. Klein (1981) examined conversational narratives from a Spanish-German IL speaker, also noting a range of discourse strategies in the expression of temporality. In a third study of Spanish-German IL, in this case based on longitudinal data from a young adult, Meisel (1985) reported an absence of inflectional marking, an early preference for adverbials and connectives, and a number of discourse strategies that he termed interlocutor scaffolding, implicit reference, order of mention, and contrast of two or more events. Finally, in a study involving English as a second language, Schumann (1983) examined the expression of temporality in conversational data from five "basilang" adult learners (one Japanese, one Chinese, and three Spanish speakers). Again, a familiar array of features used to express temporality was identified: adverbials, serialization (Meisel's order of mention), calendaric reference, and implicit reference.

As Meisel's (1985) preliminary longitudinal analysis presented its findings in somewhat general terms—without quantification—the current study's inclusion of syntacticization was to have provided a more substantial account of developmental aspects of PTR. However, contrary to expectation, minimal syntacticization was observed in both learners' ILs. Clearly, this result does not indicate a movement away from parataxis toward systematic surface encoding of PTR. However, neither does it render invalid the concept of syntacticization per se. Instead, it must be argued that syntacticization was not observed in the data probably because of the short—10-month—period of study and an overestimation of the rate of development. Data collection for at least 2 or even 3 years seems necessary.

Rethinking the connection between conversation and IL development: In the analysis of PTR, both learners were shown to depend heavily on discourse and situational context for the establishment of PTR. While there was some use of lexical past verbs and adverbials, at least half the time PTR was not explicitly marked. Moreover, in the majority of past-time contexts—both marked and unmarked in the learners' speech—pastness was recoverable either from their interlocutors' utterances or from context. Thus, it is clear from the data that the contextual embedding of PTR lessened the interactional burden on the learners.

Put another way, it appears that excessive communicative pressure is not brought to bear upon learners' marking of PTR, mainly because such marking is usually not necessary for pastness to be inferred, however obligatory it may be in the L2's surface structure. Both learners in this study were able to communicate PTR satisfactorily as a result of much interactional support from their interlocutors. Hence, it might be argued that the expendability of past-time marking is one factor working against increased use of linguistic coding devices of PTR by learners.

Other constraints on the acquisition of inflectional pasts include: (1) the relative imperceptibility of such marking in the input to learners, and (2) the frequent phonological reduction of such marking by native speakers themselves, which also has the effect of making inflections less salient to learners (R. Andersen, personal communication). Together, functional and phonological constraints seem to have contributed to the very low frequencies of past time markers in both learners' data.

This tendency was countered to some extent by slight increases in lexical devices, i.e., lexical past verbs and adverbials. That the former slightly outnumbered the latter was perhaps to be expected. As Andersen (personal communication) points out, verbs are likely to occur, given their centrality in clauses; whereas temporal and locative adverbials are probably distributed at the level of "episode" or "discourse" topic and are thus less likely to occur in topic-maintaining discourse. In any case, since both verbs and adverbials, as content vocabulary, appear variably across different discourse contexts because of topic shift, repetition through repairs, and so forth, it should not be surprising to see this fact reflected in variable frequencies in the data examined here.

In short, the linguistic devices used to code PTR are probably differentially subject to constraints on their production by learners. There is, first, the overall functional constraint on marking PTR; second, the effect of phonological transfer on the production of inflectional suffixes that create consonant clusters; and third, the relative lack of clearly articulated, easily perceived instances of inflections in native-speaker input to learners. Finally, there is functional variation in the occurrence of still another coding device, lexical items with past reference.

A reasonable conclusion at this stage is that the compensatory nature of discourse-pragmatics enhances learners' participation in conversation, i.e., that conversational interaction facilitates their communicative *performance*. It is less easy to conclude, however, that conversational interaction facilitates *acquisition* of all the linguistic devices that encode PTR. In fact, it seems that aspects of face-to-face discourse, such as shared knowledge about the world, norms of social interaction, and the structure of conversation, foster the acquisition of some linguistic features of the L2 but not others. It may be, as Hatch (1978b) has suggested, that verb morphology, in particular, is not made salient by interlocutors' modifications:

Mistakes in the marking of verbs [in learner speech] . . . would not be caught by "when?" questions. Such question-corrections would more likely elicit a time adverb rather than a verb correction for morphology (p. 432).

This has proved to be exactly the case with the data from Thanh and Tai. In the three excerpts reviewed, for example, the interlocutor's many clarification requests elicited adverbials (e.g., *yet, not now, tonight, in the morning, on Thursday*) or nontemporal expressions (e.g., *what? yes, no*) rather than verbs marked for pastness. Instances of PTR that were lexically rather than inflectionally realized seemed more likely to be elicited from the learners during conversational repair sequences. Thus, while the structure of conversational interaction may help learners to focus on and use particular lexical items that encode PTR, some other mechanism must lead them to identify morphological PTR marking.

Recently, Hatch (1983) has advanced this argument at a more global level. While acknowledging that language acquisition proceeds through linguistic hypothesis-testing by learners and results in the creation of an "autonomous grammar," she points out that

other processes which are nonlinguistic may be critical to the learner's discovery of linguistic elements that make up that system. Such processes may make the formation of linguistic hypotheses possible (p. 187).

In the case of PTR, then, discourse processes such as clarification request-and-response sequences as well as expansions and reformulations by learners' (native-speaker) interlocutors may aid in the discovery of lexical but not morphological markers of pastness.

It is important to note also that the occurrence of such processes in the input to learners can vary. In the analysis of the points in discourse at which pastness could be inferred (see Tables 7 and 8), it was found that NIPUs predominated in Thanh's data, while OIPUs did so in Tai's data. What this means is that pastness was more often inferrable from some non-immediately preceding utterance in the discourse for Thanh but more often inferrable from the interlocutor's immediately preceding utterance for Tai.

At first glance, this difference seems to indicate a greater reliance by Tai on his interlocutor for the marking of PTR, i.e., a "disadvantage" for Tai. However, it may also reflect his greater access to "reruns" of input containing instances of linguistically marked PTR. The higher proportion of OIPUs in Tai's data, in other words, shows that his interlocutor provided almost turn-by-turn opportunities for the negotiation of meaning. Thanh's data, in contrast, suggest that he tended to have longer turns—multi-utterance turns and less alternation of turns with his interlocutor. Oddly enough, this apparent skill in producing longer sequences of speech may also have had the effect of depriving him of more frequent attempts by his interlocutor to resolve questions about temporal reference, which, in turn, would have emphasized particular lexical items—if not inflected verbs—that express PTR.

CONCLUSION

The conclusion that seems warranted by the evidence discussed here is that conversational interaction makes some markers of PTR more salient than others and thus probably contributes to variability in their patterns of acquisition. Adverbial expressions and lexical past verbs are favored by their distributional privileges, while verbal inflections are not. Of course, the fact that past time inflections pose a phonological problem as well for Vietnamese learners of English must also be assumed to influence the development of PTR in these learners' ILs. However, such a factor is arguably language-specific—or type-specific in typological terms—rather than universal. Of more general relevance are the discourse-pragmatic constraints on PTR that have emerged in the present study, namely, the contextual embedding of PTR and hence the redundancy of markers such as verb inflections, and the variably facilitative potential of interactional modifications by learners' interlocutors. The connection between conversational interaction and IL development is, unquestionably, a complex one. Certain aspects of conversational structure appear to facilitate the acquisition of some linguistic coding devices but not others.

Future work should examine semantic domains that are not as context-dependent as temporality seems to be to see if linguistic encoding proceeds faster and/or with fewer constraints than for PTR. Also in need of study is the relative utility of different conversational adjustments in accessing particular coding devices for learners' intake and subsequent hypothesis-testing.

NOTE

1. This paper reports on one aspect of my Ph.D. dissertation, "The syntax of conversation in interlanguage development" (Sato 1985), supervised by Roger W. Andersen at UCLA. I gratefully acknowledge Prof. Andersen's extensive and insightful feedback on this research.

REFERENCES

Andersen, R. 1984. The one-to-one principle of interlanguage development. *Language Learning,* 34:4. 77–95.

Dittmar, N. 1981. On the verbal organization of L2 tense marking in an elicited translation task by Spanish immigrants in Germany. *Studies in Second Language Acquisition*, 3:136–164.

Flashner, V. 1983. A functional approach to tense-aspect-modality in the interlanguage of a native Russian speaker. In C. Campbell et al. (eds.). *Proceedings of the Los Angeles Second Language Research Forum*, vol. II. Los Angeles: Department of English, ESL section, UCLA.

Givón, T. 1979a. From discourse to syntax: grammar as a processing strategy. In T. Givón (ed.). *Syntax and Semantics,* vol. 12, *Discourse and Syntax.* New York: Academic Press.

Givón, T. 1979b. *On Understanding Grammar.* New York: Academic Press.

Hatch, E. 1978a. Acquisition of syntax in a second language. In J. Richards (ed.). *Understanding Second and Foreign Language Learning.* Rowley, Mass. Newbury House. 34–70.

Hatch, E. 1978b. Discourse analysis and second language acquisition. In E. Hatch (ed.). *Second Language Acquisition: A Book of Readings.* Rowley, Mass.: Newbury House. 401–435.

Hatch, E. 1983. *Psycholinguistics: A Second Language Perspective.* Rowley, Mass.: Newbury House.

Hawkins, B. 1985. Is an "appropriate response" always so appropriate? In S. Gass and C. Madden (eds.). *Input in Second Language Acquisition.* Rowley, Mass.: Newbury House.

Huebner, T. 1983. *A Longitudinal Analysis of the Acquisition of English.* Ann Arbor, Mich.: Karoma Publishers.

Kessler, C., and I. Idar. 1979. The acquisition of English by a Vietnamese mother and child. *Working Papers on Bilingualism*, 18: 65–77.

Klein, W. 1981. Knowing a language and knowing how to communicate. In A. R. Vermeer (ed.). *Language Problems of Minority Groups.* Tilburg: Tilburg Studies in Language and Literature. 75–95.

Kumpf, L. 1981. An approach to tense/aspect/modality in the analysis of interlanguage. MS., University of California at Los Angeles.

Kumpf, L. 1983. A case study of temporal reference in interlanguage. In C. Campbell et al. (eds.). *Proceedings of the Los Angeles Second Language Research Forum*, vol. II. Los Angeles: Department of English, ESL Section, UCLA.

Long, M. 1980. Input, interaction and second language acquisition. Unpublished Ph.D. dissertation, UCLA.

Long, M. 1981. Input, interaction and second language acquisition. In H. Winitz (ed.). *Native Language and Foreign Language Acquisition. Annals of the New York Academy of Sciences*, 379: 259–278.

Long, M. 1983. Linguistic and conversational adjustments to non-native speakers. *Studies in Second Language Acquisition*, 5: 177–249.

Long, M., and C. Sato. 1984. Methodological issues in interlanguage studies: An interactionist perspective. In A. Davies, C. Criper, and A. Howatt (eds.). *Interlanguage.* Edinburgh: Edinburgh University Press.

Lynch, B. 1983. A discourse-functional analysis of interlanguage. In C. Campbell et al. (eds.). *Proceedings of the Los Angeles Second Language Research Forum,* vol. II. Los Angeles: Department of English, ESL Section, UCLA.

Meisel, J. 1985. Reference to past events and actions in the development of natural second language acquisition. In R. W. Andersen (ed.). *Second Languages.* Rowley, Mass.: Newbury House.

Pfaff, C. 1982. Functional approaches to interlanguage. Paper presented at the Second European-North American Workshop on Cross-Linguistic Second Language Acquisition Research, Jagdschloss, West Germany, Aug. 22–28.

Sato, C. 1984. Phonological processes in second language acquisition: another look at interlanguage syllable structure. *Language Learning*, 34:4.

Sato, C. 1985. The syntax of conversation in interlanguage development. Unpublished Ph.D. dissertation, UCLA.

Schumann, J. 1981. Non-syntactic speech in the Spanish-English basilang. Paper presented at the first European-North American Workshop on Cross-Linguistic Second Language Acquisition Research, Lake Arrowhead, California, September.

Schumann, J. 1983. The expression of temporality in basilang speech. Paper presented at the Los Angeles Second Language Research Forum, University of Southern California, Nov. 11–13.

Schumann, J. To appear. Utterance structure in basilang speech. In G. Gilbert (ed.), *Pidgin and Creole Languages: Essays in Memory of John E. Reinecke.* Honolulu: University of Hawaii Press.

Section Two

IN THE CLASSROOM

INTRODUCTION

Richard R. Day

The five chapters in this section all treat the role of conversation in the classroom. This is of particular interest to those of us involved with second language learning and teaching, for it has been claimed, and widely assumed, that instruction in the target language makes a difference (e.g., Long 1983). One of the key elements in the successful learning of a second or foreign language is reported to be the input the learner receives in the target language—the input hypothesis (cf. Krashen 1982). It has been claimed that the adjustments native speakers make when talking with nonnative speakers provide them with comprehensible input that is the key factor in the development of interlanguage (cf. Hatch 1983, Long 1981).

The chapters by Strong, Chaudron, Pica and Long, and Schinke-Llano are concerned with what is generally regarded as the major source of input for second language learners—teacher talk in the second or foreign language classroom. These four chapters examine teacher talk and its role in language learning.

Strong's chapter compares 10 teachers in bilingual classrooms with 10 in submersion classrooms, looking at their use of English versus the minority language (Spanish or Cantonese), the proportion of teaching time they talk versus remain silent, and the way they structure activities. Strong also examines individual differences in the teachers, regardless of classroom type.

His results are somewhat unexpected, if we regard a bilingual classroom as an environment where two languages (the children's and the target—in this case, Spanish or Cantonese and English) are used. Strong finds that the teachers in bilingual classrooms use as much English as teachers in all-English submersion classrooms and, as a group, spend much less time talking in the minority language than was to be expected from previous studies. Strong also finds that teacher silence proves to be a factor that has not been adequately measured in previous research, yet in his investigation it accounts for between 30 and 86 percent of the teaching time. He also finds that teachers are more likely to vary individually than as a group.

Strong's work has important implications for our understanding of the bilingual classroom and its role in the maintenance of minority languages and the teaching of English. Classrooms designated as bilingual may not be bilingual, as commonly understood by the use of the term. Strong suggests that previous reports on teachers' use of the minority language in bilingual settings may have overestimated that behavior.

Chapter 4, by Chaudron, is similar to Strong's work in that the focus is teacher talk, but in an immersion classroom. For Chaudron, the subjects are the teachers of English-speaking Canadian children learning French as a second language. Chaudron's purpose is to determine if and how immersion teachers set priorities between classroom performance of linguistic skills and subject-matter knowledge. He finds that the priorities that the three teachers said they had were indeed the ones they followed in their classrooms; namely, instruction in the French language is subordinated to teaching the subject matter. Chaudron finds that all three teachers consider linguistic errors to be of less importance than content errors made by their students. The teachers suggested that they would usually correct linguistic errors when they were concerned in some primary way with the content of the lesson (e.g., the pronunciation of new vocabulary).

In the next chapter, Pica and Long compare the teacher talk of experienced and inexperienced teachers. They examine the characteristics of teacher talk and of teacher-student conversation. Pica and Long also attempt to determine if teacher talk is learned over time (i.e., if there is a difference between the teacher talk of beginning vs. experienced teachers). They report finding differences between informal, noninstructional NS/NNS conversations and ESL classroom conversations in the amount of negotiation for meaning; however, the complexity of the linguistic input to the NNSs from teachers and native speakers was similar. Pica and Long conclude that this difference in the amount of negotiation for meaning might indicate that there is less comprehension of input by students in the ESL classroom.

In looking at teacher talk of beginning and experienced teachers, Pica and Long find some differences; however, they conclude that the similarities are greater than the differences and that the "influence of the classroom context is strong enough to outweigh the effects of teaching experience."

Pica and Long suggest that their findings provide little comfort for those who look to the ESL classroom as the major source of comprehensible input and subsequent interlanguage development. This state of affairs could be modified, they note, if the nature of the tasks in ESL classrooms were to involve more opportunities for a two-way exchange of information, probably combined with small group work.

In Chapter 6, Schinke-Llano treats the differences in speech between native speakers and nonnative speakers. She focuses on the organization of the speech of teachers as they explain a specific task to each of two students, a native speaker and a student with limited English proficiency (LEP). She discovers that the teacher interactions with the LEP students are more teacher-regulated, and the steps of the task made more explicit for them than for the NS students. Thus, the task situation for the LEP students is structured differently both linguistically and, as a result, cognitively than the task situation for the NS students.

Schinke-Llano points out that while the teachers' talk to their NNS students was different, all of the LEP students performed the task as directed. This forces her to question if the differential treatment was necessary. Schinke-Llano advances the possibility that teachers, because of an assumption that LEP students cannot fully participate in an instructional situation, may make their speech more explicit and their tasks more teacher-regulated than necessary.

Schinke-Llano claims that successful second language acquisition by LEP students might be hindered if their teachers modify their input based on inaccurate perceptions of their linguistic abilities. If this claim is true, she concludes that the cognitive development of LEP students might be adversely affected as well. Schinke-Llano observes that these possible negative cognitive consequences are speculative but are serious enough to merit investigation. She says that we need to investigate what the relationship is between modified input and interaction and second language acquisition and cognitive skills development in a second language.

The final chapter in this section focuses on the speech of young children who are learning English as a second language. In Chapter 7, Cathcart shows us that there is a great deal of variation in the speech of young ESL students, and she tries to account for it by looking at situational differences and at differences in input.

Cathcart examines the linguistic interactions of NNS students in a school setting and the situational variables that motivate or constrain them. Speech samples were collected from several types of formal and informal classroom and research situations from eight Spanish-speaking children learning English in a Spanish-English bilingual kindergarten. An analysis of the data reveals that there are four situational variables that seem to influence a different aspect of language behavior. Conversational control affects the number and overall variety of communicative acts or functions. Interlocutor differences (whether child-child or child-adult) seem to affect relative frequency of control and information-sharing behavior. In addition, the choice of some individual communicative acts seems related to task stage. Finally, other acts and language structures are influenced by the nature of the task or activity in progress. Cathcart then organizes the variables into a hierarchical model.

Cathcart suggests that her findings call into question the notion that the most natural representations of children's speech are those taken while they are at play. She also claims that her results indicate ways to improve naturalistic settings for investigating children's speech and for establishing naturalistic situations for language learning in young children.

REFERENCES

Hatch, E. M. 1983. Simplified input and second language acquisition. In R. W. Andersen (ed.). *Pidginization and Creolization as Language Acquisition.* Rowley, Mass.: Newbury House. 64–86.

Krashen, S. D. 1982. *Principles and Practice in Second Language Acquisition.* Oxford: Pergamon Press.

Long, M. H. 1981. Input, interaction, and second language acquisition. In H. Winitz (ed.). *Native Language and Foreign Language Acquisition. Annals of the New York Academy of Sciences,* 379: 259–278.

Long, M. H. 1983. Does second language instruction make a difference? *TESOL Quarterly,* 17: 359–382.

3

TEACHER LANGUAGE TO LIMITED ENGLISH SPEAKERS IN BILINGUAL AND SUBMERSION CLASSROOMS[1]

Michael Strong[2]
University of California San Francisco
Department of Psychiatry
Center on Deafness
San Francisco

Twenty elementary school teachers whose classes included Spanish or Cantonese speakers were observed over a period of one school year. The ten teachers in "bilingual" classrooms were compared with the teachers in "submersion" classrooms with respect to their use of English versus the minority language, the proportion of teaching time they talked versus remained silent, and the way they structured activities. Individual differences were also examined, regardless of classroom type. It was found that teachers in bilingual classrooms used as much English as teachers in all-English submersion classrooms and, as a group, spent much less time talking in the minority language than was to be expected from previous studies. Teacher silence also proved to be a factor that had not been adequately measured in previous research, and yet it accounted for between 30 and 86 percent of the teaching time of these subjects. The teachers were more likely to vary individually than as a group. The findings suggest that classrooms designated as bilingual may not be bilingual in a way that would be commonly understood by the term, that previous reports on teachers' use of the minority language in bilingual settings may be overestimating this behavior, and that the study of individual variation among teachers is possibly of more consequence than the hunt for similarities among particular groups.

Teacher language has been the focus of a number of studies of second language acquisition in recent years. Researchers have taken two approaches, the most common of which has been to examine aspects of teacher language as "foreigner talk" (Ferguson 1975, Long 1980). That is, they have studied how ESL teachers modify their English for nonnative speakers (e.g., Gaies 1977; Henzl 1973, Long 1981), and they have looked at the frequency of occurrence of certain syntactic structures in speech addressed to learners of English (Larsen-Freeman 1976, Wagner-Gough and Hatch 1975). Snow and Hoefnagel-Hoehle (1982) have since extended this line of research to children. A second approach has been to look at bilingual teachers and to focus on their differential use of L1 versus L2 (e.g., Fisher et al. 1982, Wong-Fillmore 1982, Legaretta 1977, Nystrom 1984, Schulz 1975, Townsend 1974).

Such study of teacher language to nonnative speakers from either of these perspectives is necessary, as we need to establish the importance of the role that teacher language plays in providing input for learners. For young children, in particular, teacher language is frequently their first encounter with English. They speak their native language at home and, depending on the makeup of the class, continue to speak it with their peers (Schulz 1975). In bilingual classrooms, teachers not only provide English input but also are responsible for educational input in the child's first language (what Cummins 1979 has called "cognitive academic language"). This academic language (in the children's L1 and/or English) is necessary for all aspects of scholastic achievement.

Because of the role the language of the classroom teacher plays both in providing academic language input, in some cases in two languages, and also as a fundamental element in the distinction between bilingual and nonbilingual programs, researchers are interested in finding out how crucial this aspect of non-English-speaking children's language experience may be for their ultimate level of fluency in English and their success in school. Differences in teacher language patterns, if they exist, will cause their students to have differential access to English and their first languages, and this may have significant effects on their progress through school.

The most familiar distinction with regard to teachers' linguistic output concerns the use or not of the children's first language. Since the Lau Remedies and Title VII, many bilingual-bicultural programs have emerged in the United States, and an extensive literature on their relative effectiveness (both in this country and abroad) now exists (for example, see Paulston's 1978 review.) The findings from this research are diverse and inconclusive, largely because of the many variables that affect such comparisons, such as the status of the minority language group, the socioeconomic level of the students, the motivation to learn the majority language, the number of years the students have been in the country, features of the particular programs, and many more. In general, it may be concluded that bilingual-bicultural education is advantageous for certain populations under certain conditions but that alternative approaches might be preferable in other situations. In a summary of such research, Rotberg suggests:

initial learning in the native language might be more desirable, both academically and psychologically, for children who come from low-income families and who are not proficient in their native language; in communities where the home language has a low status; for students likely to leave school in the early grades; and where teachers are not members of the same ethnic group as the students and may be insensitive to their values and traditions. (1982:159)

Even when these conditions are met, a bilingual program may be unsuccessful because of inadequacies in its execution. Teachers may fail to provide acceptable language input either because their abilities in the target or minority language are poor, or because they fail to use the native language in such a way as to facilitate learning. Epstein (1977) reports on a study of 136 randomly chosen bilingual teachers in New Mexico, of whom only 13 were able to read and write Spanish at the third grade level. Such a situation clearly undermines any attempts to implement a successful bilingual program.

However, fluency is irrelevant if the teacher does not use enough of the native language. Nothing is really known about what constitutes the ideal proportional use of English to native language in a bilingual classroom. A UNESCO monograph published in 1953 and cited by Legaretta (1977) states that, as a "rule of thumb," the objective should be a ratio of 50:50 between the two languages. Researchers rarely report instances of bilingual classroom language use that approximates this balance. In her own study of five Spanish bilingual classrooms Legaretta found teacher talk in Spanish ranging from 16 to 47 percent. The teacher who used the most Spanish was in an "alternate day program," where language use was essentially predetermined by the system. Schulz (1975) described the instruction in his single-classroom study as being about 70 percent in English and 30 percent in Spanish. Fisher et al. (1981) report the teachers in their very large sample as averaging 60 percent English talk, 25 percent L1 talk, 5 percent mixed language, and 10 percent silence. Across the six sites in this study the proportion of teacher talk in L1 ranged from 2 to 87 percent. Even allowing for different methodologies in these studies, the figures suggest that few teachers conform to the UNESCO rule of thumb, and it is indicated that children in bilingual classrooms receive L1 input in amounts that vary considerably from teacher to teacher.

This leads one to question exactly to what degree and in what ways so-called bilingual classrooms differ from English submersion classrooms with regard to the quantity and nature of teacher language. Furthermore, previous research has not focused on how teachers vary from one another in the overall amount of linguistic input they provide, or to what extent they dominate conversation in the classroom. This study aims to examine these issues.

SUBJECTS

The subjects for this study were 20 elementary school teachers (15 at third grade and five at fifth grade), 10 of whom were teaching in classrooms described as bilingual, and 10 whose students included a significant number of limited English speakers but who used only English when teaching. These may be described as submersion classrooms with pull-out ESL for the limited English speakers. Cantonese was the minority language in 10 of the classrooms and Spanish in the others. The classrooms were located in schools in northern California chosen at random from those whose districts had originally agreed to participate in a major study on language learning in bilingual classrooms.[3] The percentage of monolingual English-speaking children as a proportion of the total enrollment varied from zero to 44 percent, with an average of 14.5 percent in bilingual classrooms and 30.7 percent in the submersion classes. There were higher numbers of English speakers in the Spanish classes than were to be found in the Cantonese sample. The teachers themselves had all been teaching for at least 3 years (with one exception, a replacement for an original subject who quit early in the study.) Nine of the ten bilingual teachers were native speakers of the minority language, and the tenth was a fluent advanced Spanish speaker, having lived for some time in a Spanish-speaking country, in addition to formal study of the language.

PROCEDURES

Samples of classroom language were collected on video and audio tape at regular intervals over one school year. The coding of the teachers' language use was thus performed from the taped data rather than in real time, permitting a more detailed and a more accurate analysis. A simple coding system was developed whose aim was to obtain details of the amount of teacher language to which the children were exposed and the degree to which the bilingual teachers used English or the minority language. Teachers' use of different classroom activity structures was also measured, with a distinction drawn between whole class activities, small group work, and individual instruction. The kind of structuring is important, as it determines the size of the audience for the teachers' remarks, and variation in this aspect of their teaching will affect the amount of exposure to teacher talk enjoyed by any particular child (Wong-Fillmore 1982).

It was imperative that coders be able to record the necessary information at one presentation because of the many hours of tapes. To achieve this, the coder performed the following tasks:

1. Timed each event
2. Timed the teacher's use of English
3. Timed the teacher's use of the minority language

At the end of the event, the coder recorded the total times in minutes for teacher language and event, and noted a brief description of the event and activity structure.

An event was defined as a lesson or transition period whose boundaries were determined by a change either in content matter (e.g., from math to reading) or in activity structure (e.g., from whole class to small group). Timing was effected by the manipulation of three stopwatches. One watch measured the elapsed time of the event. A second was activated when the teacher began an utterance in English and stopped at the end of a dialogue or after 3 seconds of silence. The third stopwatch registered time spent using Spanish or Cantonese, and was operated according to the same principles. The difference between elapsed time and the teachers' English plus Spanish/Cantonese talk was computed as a measure of teacher silence. Teacher silence is thus a measure of the time the teacher is in the classroom but not involved in lecturing or conversing with the students. During these periods of teacher silence, students may themselves be silent, or some may be involved in conversations with peers.

From the many hours of tapes an average of 344 minutes was coded for each teacher on the language use dimensions, and 365 on the activity structure dimension. Four different coders worked on the data, and a 5 percent reliability sample involving two or more coders showed the following ranges of agreement:

Elapsed time of event: 100% (+ or – 10 seconds)
Time speaking English: 100% (+ or – 24 seconds)
Time speaking L1:   100% (+ or – 12 seconds)
Identifying structure: 94%

This subsample covered 16 events ranging in duration from about 4 to 24 minutes. The figures show an impressive level of agreement with regard to the identification of event and language parameters. The single disagreement over the type of activity structure involved a lesson in which the teacher instructed a group of about 16 students (class size was 28). Two coders defined this as a small-group activity and one as a whole-class event.

RESULTS

The object of the study was to compare teacher language use in submersion and bilingual classrooms to see how the two groups differed and how they varied individually. Thus three major hypotheses were tested:

1. Teachers in submersion classrooms use more English than teachers in bilingual classrooms.
2. Teachers in submersion classrooms structure their activities differently than teachers in bilingual classrooms.
3. Teachers vary individually in their language use and their use of different activity structures.

In addition, comparison was made with previous reports of teacher language use in bilingual classrooms.

Table 1 shows the percentage of time teachers spent using English, Spanish, or Cantonese, or not talking at all. A t-test comparing the submersion

TABLE 1   Percentage of Time Teachers Used English, L1, and Silence

	English	L1	Silence	Minutes observed
Bilingual teachers:				
3c1b	54	1	45	283
3c2	30	0	70	375
3c3b	46	6	48	215
3c4	30	1	69	493
5c1	42	11	47	487
3s1	60	8	32	487
3s2	44	23	33	179
3s3	53	8	39	270
3s4	58	2	41	496
5s1	52	8	40	177
Submersion teachers:				
3c1a	64		36	246
3c3a	59		41	235
3c5	55		45	439
3c6	14		86	455
5c2	54		46	533
3s5	69		31	462
3s6	62		38	251
3s7	63		37	255
5s2a	49		51	280
5s2b	51		49	269

and bilingual groups for English use resulted in a nonsignificant difference (t = 1.20, at the .05 level). The bilingual teachers' use of L1 ranged from 0 to 23 percent and was thus much lower than found in previous studies referred to above. Hypothesis 1 is thus rejected.

Table 2 shows the percentage of time classroom activities were organized as whole-class, small-group, or individual. A t-test comparing the submersion and bilingual classrooms in their use of whole-group activities resulted in a nonsignificant difference (t = 0.78, at the .05 level). The second hypothesis is thus rejected.

In order to measure individual variation among the teachers in their use of language and activity structures, attempts were made to fit log-linear models to the two three-dimensional tables. It was revealed that the model with the best fit was the fully saturated one, implying that the three variables of teacher, type of classroom, and the language or activity structure *and* their interactions are required to account for the distributions of the data. Even then, a certain amount of variation is left unexplained. The third hypothesis is thus accepted.

TABLE 2 Percentage of Time Spent in Different Activity Structures

	Whole class	Small group	Individual	Minutes observed
Bilingual teachers:				
3c1b	30	45	25	283
3c2	24	30	46	310
3c3b	36	28	36	215
3c4	30	22	48	424
5c1	25	35	39	487
3s1	22	37	36	487
3s2	37	43	20	482
3s3	43	12	45	270
3s4	44	31	25	496
5s1	38	28	34	485
Submersion teachers:				
3c1a	39	19	42	246
3c3a	17	51	32	235
3c5	49	32	19	439
3c6	22	12	66	455
5c2	37	24	39	533
3s5	48	30	22	462
3s6	35	48	17	255
3s7	26	14	60	255
5s2a	35	26	39	280
5s2b	65	24	11	207

DISCUSSION

The finding that teachers in bilingual classrooms used as much English as teachers in all-English classrooms is unexpected and has far-reaching implications for educators, parents, and researchers. As can be seen from Table 1, the extremely low amounts of L1 talk by bilingual teachers clearly account for this finding, as there are no apparent differences between the groups in their use of silence. Those who are dedicated to the bilingual approach for educating non-English-speaking children are suffering a distortion of their model in such classrooms, which might result in unjustified criticisms of their educational ideals. This is not to say, however, that there is any evidence that the children in these classrooms suffered setbacks in their school performance, simply that they probably did not represent the bilingual model advocated by proponents of that approach. Parents who feel strongly that their children should advance academically in their first language as well as English, and who are expecting a genuinely bilingual education, are likely to be disappointed with these findings. Researchers who make assumptions about classrooms described as bilingual might be faced with surprising if not misleading findings. Opponents of bilingual education are also likely to be surprised, as the basis of their opposition frequently centers around the fact that the children are not being exposed to enough English.

The question arises as to why the levels of L1 use among the bilingual teachers in this sample are so low compared with those in previous studies. One explanation is that teacher habits may have changed over the years as more opposition has been leveled against bilingual education. This does not account for the Fisher et al. findings, however, as their study was conducted around the same time as these data were collected. A second explanation is that the teachers in this study were simply an unusual group, and that they do not represent teachers in general. Certainly they were all drawn from one geographical location (albeit the same that Legaretta used in her study), and one might expect more L1 use in certain areas, such as parts of New York with large Puerto Rican populations (this is supported to some extent by the Fisher et al. data). It is more likely, however, that most of the other studies were less representative, as they examined much smaller samples of teachers. The Fisher et al. study, which had a larger sample, showed a wide range of native language use, with many teachers below the 10 percent level. Nystrom (1984) concluded in her study of high school teachers that all minority language input was provided (largely as a function of administrative policy) by teachers' aides. Aides' language was also included in Legaretta's study but was not an element in this research because aides were used only part of the day to tutor one or two of the lowest functioning students. If their language had been coded in addition to the teachers', the measures of L1 use would have been increased, although their talk was not available as input to most of the class.

A more promising explanation rests in the comparison of methods used to measure language use in the various studies. Schulz's (1975) study was based on self-reports of language use by the teacher. Such reports are notoriously inaccurate, as a bilingual frequently is unaware which language he or she is using (Legaretta 1977:9, Gumperz 1970:6–7). Even estimates by visitors to a classroom are likely to be inaccurate unless they take detailed notes over a long period of time. It is also common to make extrapolations on the basis of a single visit to a classroom (Legaretta relied on one visit of 2½ hours in each class). A single visit may chance on an atypical day, or the teacher may behave differently when an outsider is present. In contrast, the present study's samples were drawn from several days of observation at different times by researchers who visited the classes two days a week throughout the school year.

The large body of observations (about 6 hours of contact time per teacher drawn from different school days over the year) contributed considerably to the validity of these data.

Neither Schulz nor Legaretta took the overall quantity of teacher language into account. Teachers in this study all spent more than 30 percent of their teaching time in silence (for one of them this was as much as 86 percent). If such a factor is ignored, estimates of amounts of teacher talk are inflated, thereby giving a false impression of the amount of language the children hear. The Fisher et al. study did include a measure of teacher silence, but a close examination of their coding procedure reveals that the quantity of teacher talk was probably overestimated. Their approach involved time-sampled observations over a period of one or two days, during which the researcher coded teacher language in the following manner: When the teacher began to talk in English, the time of day was noted; when a switch was made to another language, the time was noted again. The teacher was considered to have been speaking English during this period, and L1 until the next switch. Silence was recorded only after a full 30 seconds of no language. Such a method would inevitably result in an underestimation of teacher silence and an exaggerated measurement of both English and L1 use. The coder also suffers the disadvantage of having to work in real time, making on-the-spot decisions that are not verifiable by replaying a tape.

No difference was determined between bilingual and submersion teachers in the organization of their classroom activities, indicating that children's access to teacher talk was not affected by program type. At the individual level, however, teachers do vary considerably from one another, both in the way they structure activities and in the amount of time they talk or are silent. Thus there are wide differences between teachers, but they cannot be predicted from the fact that they are in bilingual or submersion programs.

CONCLUSION

The data presented here indicate that classrooms designated as bilingual may not be bilingual in a way that would be commonly understood by the term. Not only can we expect an unbalanced use of the two languages by the teacher, but we cannot even assume the 70:30 proportion reflected in most previously published research. The reasons for this are unclear. It is possible that the teachers themselves, while apparently committed to the idea of bilingual education, feel instinctively that they really should be using English as much as possible. This feeling may be engendered by the low status of the minority languages in the local society. It is perhaps not by chance that the only nonnative speaker of the minority language among the bilingual teachers was the one who used the most L1 (23 percent). The teachers also clearly felt under no pressure from the administration to increase their use of the minority language, reflecting an apathy toward bilingual education at all levels in the schools. At one site the teachers actually complained to the investigator that their school adminstrators were not in favor of the bilingual program and would like to see it discontinued.

The second major finding is that teachers vary radically in their individual use of language in the classroom and in the way they structure activities. This suggests that research reports which focus on similarities between teachers, extrapolations from very small samples of teachers, or mean estimates of teacher language use should be viewed with some caution, unless they also publish the range across teachers in their sample.

The findings presented here suggest issues that might be pursued in future research. The relationship between teacher language patterns and academic performance in English and other subjects should be explored. Is there an ideal ratio of English to L1 that should exist in a bilingual classroom? Do students benefit when teachers talk more? Are there certain ways that teachers can use language that are more beneficial for their students than others? Some of these questions have already been addressed. Snow and Hoefnagel-Hoehle (1983), for example, with a tiny sample found that measures of quantity and directedness of speech input (both teachers' and peers') did not predict very well the subsequent improvement in language ability of second language learners. This led the authors to reason that, rather than look for a linear relationship between quantity and success, maybe one should seek a threshold above which more input does not produce more learning. They also suggest that quantity of language has differing effects on different language skills. Long (1982) in his review of the literature on input and second language acquisition has suggested that second language learners who can carry on interesting conversations with native speakers experience the optimal situation for hearing and understanding new structures and expressions. A more content-oriented analysis of teacher language (along the lines being pursued by Wong-Fillmore in her current research) might yield useful insights into the way teachers use both the first and second languages of their students. Last, and perhaps most important of all, further study of bilingual programs will determine whether the teachers in this study were anomalous, whether their language patterns are restricted to a particular age group or geographical area, or whether bilingual educational practices are really becoming indistinguishable from regular programs and thus no longer address the principles of the Lau Remedies and Title VII.

NOTES

1. Earlier versions of this paper were presented at the NABE Conference, Feb. 16, 1983, in Washington, D.C., and at the TESOL Convention, Mar. 18, 1983, in Toronto.

2. The author is grateful to Kevin Delucchi of the University of California, Berkeley for help with the statistical analysis, and to Mary Yu, Wai Lin Chang, and Teresa Austin for help with coding many hours of tapes.

3. The data for this study were collected as part of a research project funded by NIE (OE04008000–30) and awarded to Lily Wong-Fillmore and Paul Ammon at the University of California, Berkeley.

REFERENCES

Cummins, J. 1979. Cognitive/academic language proficiency, linguistic interdependence, the optimal age question and some other matters. *Working Papers in Bilingualism*, 19: 197–205. Toronto: Ontario Institute for Studies in Education.

Epstein, N. 1977. *Language, Ethnicity, and the Schools*. Washington, D.C.: Institute for Educational Leadership.

Ferguson, C. 1975. Towards a characterization of English foreigner talk. *Anthropological Linguistics*, 17: 1–14.

Fisher, C., W. Tikunoff, E. Gee, and M. Phillips. 1981. *Bilingual Instructional Perspectives: Allocation of Time in the Classrooms of the SBIF Study*. Part I of the Study Report, vol. III.2. San Francisco: Far West Laboratory for Educational Research and Development.

Gaies, S. 1977. The nature of linguistic input in formal second language learning: linguistic and communicative strategies in ESL teachers' classroom language. In H. D. Brown, C. A. Yorio, and R. H. Crymes *On TESOL '77: Teaching and Learning English as a Second Language*. Washington, D.C.: TESOL.

Gumperz, J. 1970. Sociolinguistics and communication in small groups. University of California, Berkeley, Working Paper 33, Language Behavior Laboratory.

Henzl, V. 1973. Linguistic register of foreign language instruction. *Language Learning*, 23 (1): 207–222.

Larsen-Freeman, D. 1976. An explanation for the morpheme acquisition order of second language learners. *Language Learning*, 26 (1): 125–134.

Legaretta, D. 1977. Language use in bilingual classrooms. *TESOL Quarterly*, 11 (1): 9–16.

Long, M. 1981. Questions in foreigner talk discourse. *Language Learning*, 31 (1): 135–157.

Long, M. 1982. Input, interaction and second language acquisition. In H. Winitz (ed.). *Native Language and Foreign Language Acquisition. Annals of the New York Academy of Sciences*, 379. New York.

Nystrom, N. 1984. Policy implications of teaching behavior in bilingual and ESL classrooms. Paper presented at the Seventh Annual Colloquium on Classroom Centered Research, Nineteenth Annual Convention of the Teachers of English to Speakers of Other Languages, Houston, Tex., Mar. 6–9.

Paulston, C. B. 1978. Bilingual/bicultural education. In L. Shulman (ed.). *Review of Research in Education*. Itasca, Ill.: Peacock Publishers. 186–228.

Rotberg, I. 1982. Some legal and research considerations in establishing federal policy in bilingual education. *Harvard Educational Review*, 52 (2): 149–168.

Schulz, J. 1975. Language use in bilingual classrooms. Paper presented at the Tenth Annual Convention of the Teachers of English to Speakers of Other Languages, Los Angeles.

Snow, C., and M. Hoefnagel-Hoehle. 1983. School-age second language learners' access to simplified linguistic input. *Language Learning*, 32 (2): 411–430.

Townsend, D. 1974. A comparison of the classroom interaction patterns of bilingual early childhood teachers. Ph.D. Dissertation, University of Texas, Austin.

Wagner-Gough, J., and E. Hatch. 1975. The importance of input data in second language acquisition studies. *Language Learning*, 25 (2): 297–308.

Wong-Fillmore, L. 1982. Instructional language as linguistic input: second language learning in classrooms. In L. Cherry Wilkinson (ed.). *Communicating in the Classroom*.

4

TEACHERS' PRIORITIES IN CORRECTING LEARNERS' ERRORS IN FRENCH IMMERSION CLASSES[1]

Craig Chaudron
University of Hawaii at Manoa

Research on the effectiveness of second language (French) immersion programs has been directed toward determining whether the students achieve greater proficiency in the L2 than comparison students in regular L2 instruction; whether the immersion students' achievement in other subject matter taught using the L2 as the medium of instruction is comparable with that of students taught using the L1 as the medium of instruction; and whether immersion students show any detrimental effects on their L1 (here, English) proficiency as a result of the immersion context.

Results of immersion research indicate that various types of immersion programs are successful in developing L2 without sacrificing achievement in either L1 or other subjects (Stern, Swain, McLean, Friedman, Harley, and Lapkin 1976; Edwards and Smyth 1976; Swain and Bruck 1976; Barik and Swain 1976a, 1976b). These results are largely based on summative evaluations comparing immersion program students with regular English program students.

However, research on issues concerning in-class instruction in immersion programs has been virtually nonexistent. The "communicative" use of the L2 might in some ways be a hindrance to complete L2 development if students' utterances are too often accepted for their *content* when the grammatical form is slightly aberrant. This complex field of inquiry is not readily clarified by results of end-of-the-year standardized tests.

In order to provide a focus from which to develop further research into this issue, the author undertook a pilot study of classroom interaction in an immersion program at the grades 8 and 9 levels in conjunction with the Bilingual Education Project of the Ontario Institute for Studies in Education.[2] The intent of the study was to determine whether, and in what ways, immersion teachers established priorities between classroom performance of linguistic skills and of subject matter knowledge. More precisely, the questions asked were: (a) How much are learners' L2 linguistic errors corrected in either French or other subject classes, relative to errors of other sorts? (b) In what ways are errors corrected—that is, how insistent are teachers in their reaction to errors, and what sorts of information do they provide to inform the students of the nature of the errors?

It was believed that answers to these questions would help to: (1) indicate the teachers' instructional priorities, (2) ascertain whether a predominance of language instruction was taking place during instruction about other topics, (3) suggest some possibilities for a comprehensive model of teachers' corrective reactions, and (4) reveal some of the strategies students use in rectifying their errors.[3]

The results of the pilot study suggest some answers to question a, and thus to points 1 and 2 above, but only partially, since other indicators of priorities need investigation (e.g., *amount of time* spent on different grammatical topics, procedural necessities, pronunciation drills). Question b and point 3 have also been answered in some detail, and the results are reported in Chaudron (1976, 1977). Point 4 remains for the most part unanswered; some provocative possible answers are suggested by, for example, Mehan (1974) and Naiman, Fröhlich, Stern, and Todesco (1978). The use of a model for corrective reactions (Chaudron 1977) may aid the investigation of this point.

METHODOLOGY

Procedure

Tape recordings of actual ½-hour lessons were made at each of two separate times in the school year. Time 1 was early in the year (October) and time 2 was late in the year (April), in order to detect changes that might have occurred in the course of the year. The same three teachers' lessons were recorded at each time, according to the schedule shown in Table 1. Transcripts of each lesson were typed, and citations or references to them will be made according to the codes in parentheses.

Following the recordings at time 2, all three teachers were asked to listen to the tapes of their own lessons at that time and to indicate on special forms the errors made by their students and the purpose and structure of the corrections

TABLE 1 Immersion Lessons Observed

Grade	Teacher	Time 1 lessons	Student N
8	1	Science (Sci 8.1)	About 30
		Mathematics (Math 8.1)	About 30
		French (Fr. 8.1)	About 15—half of class
8	2	Geography (Geo 8.1)	About 30
9	3	Geography (Geo 9.1)	About 30
		French (Fr 9.1)	About 30
		Time 2 lessons	
8	1	Science (Sci 8.2)	About 30
		Mathematics (Math 8.2)	About 30
8	2	History (Hist 8.2)	About 30
		French (Fr 8.2)	About 15—half of class
9	3	History (Hist 9.2)	About 30
		French (Fr 9.2)	About 30

they provided, if any. It was believed that this would afford the investigator greater insight into the purposes and priorities held by each teacher.[4]

Before the above request, the teachers had not been informed of the exact focus of the recording and observation of their lessons. They had been led to believe that the investigator was merely interested in the general organization of lessons and materials presentation. It is believed that the presence of the investigator and the small tape recorder did not make any major difference in the frequency or kind of corrective strategies that occurred.

The analysis is therefore based on the *oral* correction both of *oral* errors and of some other behaviors judged inappropriate by the teachers (to be described below). Nonverbal types of corrections (i.e., the teacher points to an underlined word on the blackboard) have been considered only when the observer's memory or the recordings allow a reconstruction of the event. Very few of the correcting interactions in the present study are excluded by this limitation.

Definition of Corrections

There are several conceptions or definitions of a "correction" (see Politzer 1965, Brooks 1964, Allwright 1975, and summary in Chaudron 1977). The conception employed here is that a corrective reaction is any reaction by the teacher which transforms, disapprovingly refers to, or demands improvement of, a student's behavior or utterance. No judgment has been made in the first analysis concerning the psychological reality (the "explicitness" or "implicitness") of the correction, nor have corrections been limited to occurrences in which the student responds with a correct utterance. This conception allows the broadest range of possibilities for any subsequent analysis of the effect of teachers' reactions on the students' learning.

Definitions of Errors

Errors were identified according to two basic criteria, and they then were classified according to type of error (no attempt has been made to determine the source of errors by error analysis). The two criteria are: (1) an objective evaluation of linguistic or content errors according to linguistic norms or evident misconstrual of facts, and (2) any additional linguistic or other behavior that the teachers reacted to negatively or with an indication that improvement of the response was expected (cf. Fanselow 1977 for a similar approach). The attempt was made to locate *all* errors, whether or not they were reacted to, so that both absolute (how much the teacher corrects) and relative (which types of errors are corrected) priorities in correction could be determined.

Instances of errors were then classified according to the following types.[5]

Phonological Errors

Pronunciation errors are very common and to be expected in the performance of beginning students of a L2. Clearly, virtually everything uttered in the teacher's reaction could be considered a correction of the student's pronunciation. Therefore, only an approximate count of phonological errors was made, based on clear "interference" from English, for example, the use of /u/ for French /y/.[6] The discussion of linguistic errors below will disregard phonological errors.

Morphological Errors

Some gradual shading of phonological errors into morphological errors is inevitable. In the present analysis morphological errors include the failure to "elide" articles (*le* and *la* with nouns beginning with vowel sounds); omission or incorrect use of articles (*le* for *les*, etc.) and the partitive (*de* for *du*, etc.); incorrect or omitted prepositions; and the incorrect omission or addition of bound morphemes (e.g., conjugation for tense (*est, sont*), inflection for number or gender (*cheval, chevaux*), and nominal suffixation (*marche, marcheur*).

Syntactic Errors

There are few syntactic errors evident in the students' production, owing, for the most part, to their simple sentence constructions. The classification here includes errors of word order (adjective preceding noun, object pronoun following verb, misplaced negation). Another type, which is not strictly "syntactic," rather one of "coherence" in discourse, pertains to the proper identification of pronominal referents (to events in the classroom context). For example, students will occasionally use a subject pronoun without any clear referential antecedent or they will inappropriately use, or omit, the presentatives *c'est* and il y a. This has been included as a type of syntactic error.[7]

Syntactic errors and morphological errors together are henceforth termed "linguistic" errors.

Content Errors

These errors consist of those for which student responses show incomplete (e.g., a student's failure to state the units of measurement in science or math) or incorrect expression of the concepts relevant to the subject. This applies equally to grammatical *knowledge* in French (e.g., the classification of words in grammatical categories), to measurement in science, calculation in mathematics, and facts in history. Some content errors may be manifested in a single word, but they show evidence of misunderstanding of concepts:

Hist 9.2   S: Les prisonniers étaient venus parce que le roi a dit qu'ils, uh, qu'ils pouvaient venir.
   T: Qu'ils *pouvaient* venir?
   [Teacher's emphasis; i.e., "qu'il fallait qu'ils viennent" would be correct.]

Content errors may also simply be inappropriate answers that do not supply the information expected in the teacher's question. However, since most student responses could be expanded upon or qualified more than is actually demanded, the teachers' implicit or explicit expectations for precision have set the limits for the classification of content errors.

Discourse Errors

It has been useful to regard certain corrective interactions in these immersion classrooms as appeals to the rules of interaction or classroom procedure, rather than as linguistic or subject-matter corrections. Nonetheless, there is a strong possibility that the teachers' reactions to discourse errors contain a good deal of linguistic information for the students. For example, since late immersion classrooms demand the exclusive use of French as soon as the students can manage, numerous exchanges occur in which the teachers must discourage the use of English (with typical phrases such as "Ça, c'est anglais") or provide French translations. The occurrence of this type of discourse error was noticeably more frequent at time 1 than at time 2. Other discourse errors include the failure of the student to answer or to speak loudly enough; speaking without recognition or taking up a question or response out of its order in the lesson; unrequested repetition of answers previously supplied by other students; and the use of incomplete, but semantically clear, phrases.

This last type of discourse error is a particularly difficult one to identify, for these teachers will only occasionally insist on the use of full sentences. After such a correction, change in lesson focus will usually again allow a more elliptical language. Such errors have been counted only when they were reacted to, and in contexts immediately following such reactions. Since numerous discourse errors have not been isolated as such, the frequency of discourse correction will be seen to be relatively high; but a high frequency might also be expected, considering the importance of consistent classroom procedures.

Lexical Errors

This classification was initiated only for the second set of recordings at time 2. Previously, such errors were classified as either morphological, content, or discourse. However, with the increased number of communicative ventures attempted by the students later in the year, their need for specific vocabulary had begun to play a greater role in their classroom participation. For example, whereas in the beginning of the year the students' use of English would often involve entire sentences that the teacher would admonish and/or translate (a discourse error), at the later time there are numerous instances of the students asking (in French) how to say a particular English word in French (not an error), or using an English word in the midst of a French sentence (and the teacher would merely provide the correct French word as a lexical correction). Again, a gradual shading exists between lexical errors and "content" errors. The context determined the classification, i.e., if the student erred in his expression of subject-matter knowledge, or if he merely failed to remember the appropriate French word. For example, see the Hist. 9.2 exchange above as a content error, contrasted with the following exchange:

Hist 8.2 T: Qu'est-ce que (Lord Carleton) fait en 1786 . . .
          S: Il uh, aide de trouver une solution de problème . . . des population . . .

Here, the student meant to say *essaie de trouver*. The meanings (as well as the sounds) of the two words are rather close in this context, so there is little question of this being a content error—rather, it appears more to be a "slip of the tongue," confusing two lexical items.

Summary

The determination of errors is clearly a difficult process that depends on the immediate context of the utterance in question as well as on an understanding of the content of the lesson, the intent of the teacher or student, and at times, the prior learning of the students.

Any further work in this area may require a more detailed categorization of different types of errors. Discourse errors, for example, are largely procedural, but the one type discussed above, that of incompleteness of a sentence, might be included in a category of "referential" errors, in which one could also include some of the kinds of errors included here under syntactic errors (lack of coherence, or incorrect presentatives). This possibility, and the separation of lexical from content errors, or phonological from morphological errors, and so on, may all require a much larger corpus of observations.

Nonetheless, the type of decision, such as whether *il* used in referring to a woman or a feminine noun is a referential or simply a morphological (even in some cases a phonological) error, will have to be made in some arbitrary but consistent manner.

RESULTS

Frequencies of Correction of Different Error Types

Tables 2 and 3 show the frequencies of teachers 1, 2, and 3 for correcting different errors at time 1 and at time 2. The error counts shown are of the total number of instances of error. That is, if the student repeats the same error after an attempted correction or if it occurs twice in the same utterance, it counts as two errors, a counting that decreases slightly the proportion corrected, for the teacher rarely will correct the duplicated error twice. Errors that students self-correct are not included.

If the teacher responded in the sense described above in the definition of corrections, it was counted as a correction. Corrections sometimes occurred where the nature of the error is uncertain from the author's point of view, but where the teacher clearly reacts negatively to, or reformulates, the student's reply.[8] This has resulted in some cases in the tables of more than 100 percent frequency of correction, which have been rounded off to 100 percent. The types of errors are those described above.

Many factors could account for the variation between Tables 2 and 3 (i.e., between times 1 and 2), between teachers, and between lessons. The factors that are suggested are reasoned on the basis of the particular lessons and contexts on the recording days, the teachers' own comments following the lessons, and other evidence from the transcripts.

Differences in number of errors from time 1 to time 2

1. The increase in the number of *morphological errors* in some classes from time 1 to time 2 (Sci 8.1 and Sci 8.2, Math 8.1 and Math 8.2, and Fr 8.1 and Fr.

TABLE 2 Frequency of Correction (% Corrected) versus Frequency of Different Error Types (No. of Errors) by Lesson—(Time 1)

	Teacher 1			Teacher 2	Teacher 3		
	Sci 8.1	Math 8.1	Fr 8.1	Geo 8.1	Fr 9.1	Geo 9.1	Totals
Phonological:							
No. of errors	23	1	21	46	23	4	118
No. of corrections	18	0	14	27	16	1	76
% corrected	78	0	67	59	70	25	64
Morphological:							
No. of errors	20	8	7	39	35	35	144
No. of corrections	8	4	6	13	33	9	73
% corrected	40	50	86	33	94	26	51
Syntactic:							
No. of errors	1	2	0	6	2	4	15
No. of corrections	1	1	0	4	3	2	11
% corrected	100	50		67	100	50	73
Content:							
No. of errors	17	18	17	3	3	12	70
No. of corrections	15	15	18	4	3	10	65
% corrected	88	83	100	100	100	85	93
Discourse:							
No. of errors	9	12	13	14	9	0	57
No. of corrections	9	5	6	4	8	0	32
% corrected	100	43	46	28	89		56
Linguistic (morph + syn):							
No. of errors	21	10	7	45	37	39	159
No. of corrections	9	5	6	17	36	11	84
% corrected	43	50	86	38	97	28	53

8.2) might be explained by the increase in amount of participation in French by the students at time 2. This did not occur in one situation, where the difference between morphological errors at the two times *decreased* from Geo 8.1 to Hist 8.2, possibly owing to the fact that in Hist 8.2 a great deal of time was devoted to reading from worksheets in the particular class observed.

2. The increase in *content errors* from Fr 8.1 to Fr 8.2 may be attributable to the change in teacher (teacher 1 at time 1 and teacher 2 at time 2); the tasks in both classes were similar, but teacher 2 tended to elicit more responses exemplifying grammatical knowledge (see brief discussion below on teacher 1's priorities).

3. The marked decrease in *discourse errors* for all classes (except from Geo 9.1 to Hist 9.2) is mainly explicable by the students' more extensive use of French. Also important is the students' apparent growth in familiarity with interactional requirements.

TABLE 3 Frequency of Correction (% Corrected) versus Frequency of Different Error Types (No. of Errors) by Lesson—(Time 2)

| | Teacher 1 | | Teacher 2 | | Teacher 3 | | |
	Sci 8.2	Math 8.2	Fr 8.2	Hist 8.2	Fr 9.2	Hist 9.2	Totals
Phonological:							
No. of errors	41	11	37	22	18	7	136
No. of corrections	14	3	27	11	5	0	60
% corrected	34	27	73	50	30	0	44
Morphological:							
No. of errors	55	19	29	21	33	36	193
No. of corrections	22	6	21	11	17	11	88
% corrected	40	32	72	52	52	31	46
Syntactic:							
No. of errors	2	1	7	1	5	4	20
No. of corrections	0	0	6	1	5	1	13
% corrected	0	0	86	100	100	25	65
Lexical:							
No. of errors	8	2	3	2	2	7	24
No. of corrections	5	2	3	2	2	4	18
% corrected	63	100	100	100	100	57	75
Content:							
No. of errors	14	24	32	10	8	7	95
No. of corrections	13	24	23	10	7	6	83
% corrected	93	100	72	100	88	86	87
Discourse:							
No. of errors	2	4	3	5	3	1	18
No. of corrections	1	4	3	4	2	0	14
% corrected	50	100	100	80	67	0	78
Linguistic (morph + syn):							
No. of errors	57	20	36	22	38	40	213
No. of corrections	22	6	27	12	22	12	101
% corrected	39	30	75	55	58	30	47

Differences in the teachers' frequency of correction (no. of corrections divided by no. of errors) from time 1 to time 2

1. Teacher 1 (columns 1 to 3, Table 2, and 1 and 2, Table 3) appeared to maintain the same relative frequency of corrections (percent corrected) for *content* versus *linguistic errors* (morphological plus syntactic errors), with some apparent shift in favor of content errors: Sci 8.1, 88 versus 43 percent; Sci 8.2, 93 versus 39 percent; Math 8.1, 83 versus 50 percent; Math 8.2, 100 versus 30 percent. In teacher 1's Fr 8.1 class, where both content and language are important, approximately equivalent concern for content and linguistic errors is indicated (100 versus 86 percent).

2. Teacher 2 (column 4 in Table 2, and columns 3 and 4 in Table 3) also consistently shows less concern for *linguistic errors* in subjects other than

French: Geo 8.1 shows 100 percent content corrected versus 38 percent linguistic corrected, and Hist 8.2 shows 100 percent content corrected versus 55 percent linguistic corrected. Teacher 2's Fr 8.2 class shows approximately equal concern (72 versus 75 percent).

3. Teacher 3 (columns 5 and 6 in Tables 2 and 3) showed somewhat similar differentials between *content* and *linguistic* corrections at both times 1 and 2. Fr 9.1 and Fr. 9.2 show 100 versus 97 percent and 88 versus 58 percent corrections, respectively. Fr 9.1 was exceptionally high, in that it was almost uniquely pattern drills, while Fr 9.2 has a relatively low frequency of correction for linguistic errors, in part because the *content* of a reading passage was being discussed and the students' linguistic errors were not important to the intent of the lesson. Geo 9.1 and Hist 9.2 show 85 versus 28 percent, and 86 versus 30 percent, respectively.

Summary

The maintenance of this linguistic-content differential distinction for French versus other lessons is shown clearly in the following combined tabulation of all three teachers' frequency of corrections at times 1 and 2, for French versus other lessons. The corrections totaled in Table 4 are only for *linguistic* and *content* errors.

TABLE 4   Frequency of Linguistic and Content Errors Corrected by All Three Teachers in French and Other Lessons

	% linguistic errors corrected (morph + syn)	% content errors corrected
French:		
Time 1	95	100
Time 2	66	75
Other subjects:		
Time 1	37	88
Time 2	37	96

The French lessons show much closer balance between the two kinds of corrections at both times 1 and 2 (95 and 100 percent at time 1, and 66 and 75 percent at time 2), than the balance evident in other lessons at either time (37 versus 88 percent at time 1, and 37 versus 96 percent at time 2). The marked decrease in percentage of corrections of either kind for French classes from time 1 to time 2 (from 95 to 66 perecent linguistic, and from 100 to 75 percent content) seems to be a result of the increased amount of student participation in conversation in the two French classes at time 2.

Both teachers 2 and 3 encouraged a greater amount of discussion of various topics at time 2 in their French classes, and they did not confine themselves to the material in the textbook. In particular, teacher 2 in Fr 8.2 posed several extra questions regarding knowledge about morphology and

TABLE 5   Teacher 1's Selection of Errors and Freqency of Correction*

		Phon	Morph	Syn	Lex	Cont	Totals
Sci 8.2:							
No. of errors		5 (41)	10 (55)	1 (2)	3 (8)	3 (14)	
No. of corrections		4 (14)	2 (22)	0 (0)	2 (5)	2 (13)	10
% corrected		80 (34)	20 (40)	0 (0)	67 (63)	67 (93)	
Correct responses	No.	3	2	0	1	1	7
by student	%	75	100	0	50	50	70
Math 8.2:							
No. of errors		1 (11)	2 (19)	0 (1)	1 (2)	0 (24)	
No. of corrections		0 (3)	0 (6)	0 (0)	0 (2)	0 (24)	0
% corrected		0 (27)	0 (32)	0 (0)	0 (100)	0 (100)	
Correct responses	No.						
by student	%						

*Figures in parentheses are from Table 3.

phonology. The students offered many more responses than the teacher could react to. This also explains the relatively high number of content errors for Fr 8.2 in Table 3.

Teachers' Priorities

The obvious question that follows from this analysis concerns the teachers' general awareness of the differences that have been seen above. In particular, what are their criteria for correctness of student participation, and what are their reasons for applying these criteria at any point during the course of a lesson?

The problem of variability in correction for a given type of error was illustrated in Mehan (1974). Correcting an error at one point, and omitting correction at another, may create misunderstanding. If teachers' professed criteria do not complement their actual performance, the chances for providing effective corrections are decreased.

The teachers were asked, following time 2, to list their students' errors on a special form, while listening to the recordings of their respective lessons. They were to indicate the type of error, whether or not they had corrected it, the intention of the correction (or lack of correction), the form of the correction, the importance of the error, and whether another form of correction would have been more effective. They were additionally asked to submit comments regarding their priorities.

For several reasons, the teachers did not select all instances of error that are now apparent from the transcripts: (1) One teacher indicated that, owing to the quantity of errors, only a representative few were selected. (2) The teachers' selections were also limited by their insufficient awareness of what the investigator understood as errors. They were not given any examples of categories, out of the concern that the investigator's suggestions would bias their subjective criteria. (3) Finally, close listening to the tapes during transcription revealed errors that would not be evident during a one-time-through listening. Despite these reasons, the teachers selected a wide range of errors (except discourse errors, which are therefore excluded from the following discussion).

Teacher 1's Priorities Teacher 1 maintained that correction of linguistic difficulties should be relegated to French lessons, that interruptions for such corrections in mathematics or science (Math 8.2 and Sci 8.2) would frustrate other students' attempts to express themselves. Only when faulty pronunciation or inaccurate vocabulary and syntax would lead to misunderstanding of the lesson material has she noted the need for interventions. One instance, however, illustrated the teacher ignoring both linguistic *and* content accuracy, which she reported was for the sake of supporting the student's effort to attempt a complex response.

Teacher 1's stated priority is also evident in the tabulation of her selection of students' errors and in her frequency of corrections for these selected instances, shown in Table 5.

TABLE 6 Teacher 2's Selection of Errors and Frequency of Correction*

		Phon	Morph	Syn	Lex	Cont	Totals
Fr 8.2:							
No. of errors		20 (37)	2 (29)	1 (7)	1 (3)	12 (32)	
No. of corrections		18 (27)	2 (21)	1 (6)	1 (3)	11 (23)	33
% corrected		90 (73)	100 (72)	100 (86)	100 (100)	92 (72)	
Correct responses	No.	13	2	1	1	8	25
by student	%	72	100	100	100	89	76
Hist 8.2:							
No. of errors		3 (22)	3 (21)	1 (1)	2 (2)	2 (10)	
No. of corrections		3 (11)	3 (11)	1 (1)	2 (2)	2 (10)	11
% corrected		100 (50)	100 (52)	100 (100)	100 (100)	100 (100)	
Correct responses	No.	3	1	0	2	0	6
by student	%	100	33	0	100	0	55

*Figures in parentheses are from Table 3.

TABLE 7 Teacher 3's Selection of Errors and Frequency of Correction*

		Phon	Morph	Syn	Lex	Cont	Totals
Fr 9.2:							
No. of errors		8 (18)	8 (33)	1 (5)	2 (2)	2 (8)	14
No. of corrections		4 (5)	6 (17)	0 (5)	2 (2)	2 (7)	
% corrected		50 (30)	75 (52)	0 (100)	100 (100)	100 (88)	
Correct responses	No.	4	5	0	2	1	12
by student	%	100	83	0	100	50	86
Hist 9.2:							
No. of errors		3 (7)	10 (36)	2 (4)	8 (7)	3 (7)	17
No. of corrections		1 (0)	4 (11)	1 (1)	8 (4)	3 (6)	
% corrected		33 (0)	40 (31)	50 (25)	100 (57)	100 (86)	
Correct responses	No.	1	2	0	3	3	9
by student	%	100	50	0	38	100	53

*Figures in parentheses are from Table 3.

(The Math 8.2 lesson was primarily one of review of work done on homework sheets, and teacher 1 did not select any of the content errors that actually occurred in that lesson.) The figures in parentheses in Tables 5 through 7 are taken from Table 3 for comparison of the teachers' *selection* of instances with the *total* instances of error and correction as determined by the analysis of the transcripts. (In Table 5, there are no entries for number of corrections or correct responses by student when the teacher neglected to select any instances of error or to provide correction.)

The two lower rows in Tables 5 through 7 for each lesson (No. and percent correct responses by student) are counted from the transcripts to indicate to what degree the correcting instances of the teacher's selection were "successful," in the sense that the students responded again, this time with a correct response. To maintain uniformity with the other data presented here, the teachers' categorizations of types of errors have not been used; the types used are those described above in the definitions of errors.

Teacher 2's Priorities   Teacher 2 commented that few of the errors he perceived in his grade 8 History lesson (Hist 8.2) stem from lack of understanding of history. Most were linguistic errors which he said required repetition of the correct model, or explanations. He perceives the study of history in French as a supplemental opportunity to expand the students' knowledge of French. He classified the errors he selected largely into those of pronunciation, vocabulary, grammar, "reading" (i.e., several instances of students' misreading their notes or their books—these have been categorized by type as if they were errors in normal pronunciation), and confusion in knowledge of (grammatical) terms. The rather large number of content errors and corrections in Fr 8.2 were primarily of this last type. Most of the "reading" errors were phonological. Table 6 shows the tabulation of teacher 2's selection of occurrence of errors and corrections.

Teacher 3's Priorities   Comments by teacher 3 show that her concern for the progression of the lesson in grade 9 history (Hist 9.2) overrode her concern for strictly linguistic errors. She meant by this that pronunciation and grammatical errors could be better treated in French class (Fr 9.2), while only errors of subject-matter content or new vocabulary were important in Hist 9.2. She compared Hist 9.2 to a history lesson in the L1, where nongrammatical language would also be "tolerated (as long as comprehension is retained)."

These reflections are borne out to a degree in the tabulation (Table 7)[9] of teacher 3's selection of corrections of different errors in Fr 9.2 and Hist 9.2, where her percentage of correction for content and lexical errors is high. Again, the frequency and percentage of her corrections that students actually responded to with the correct response are shown, and comparison is made with the frequencies from Table 3.

Comparison of Tables 5 through 7   Despite the three teachers' actual differences in rate of correction, the results shown in Tables 5 through 7 indicate some similarities in their selections from the transcripts.

TABLE 8 Ratios of "Success" in Correction Related to Teachers' Selection of Errors

	Sci 8.2	Math 8.2	Fr 8.2	Hist 8.2	Fr 9.2	Hist 9.2
Phonological:						
No. of corrections	14	3	27	11	5	0
No. of correct responses	7	0	14	5	4	0
% correct responses	50	0	52	45	80	
% teachers' selection	75		72	100	100	100*
Morphological:						
No. of corrections	22	6	21	11	17	11
No. of correct responses	3	0	6	2	7	3
% correct responses	14	0	29	18	41	27
% teachers' selection	100		100	33	83	50
Syntactic:						
No. of corrections	0	0	6	1	5	1
No. of correct responses	0	0	2	0	0	0
% correct responses			33	0	0	0
% teachers' selection	0		100	0	0	0
Lexical:						
No. of corrections	5	2	3	2	2	4
No. of correct responses	3	0	0	0	2	3
% correct responses	60	0	0	0	100	75
% teachers' selection	50		100	100	100	38
Content:						
No. of corrections	13	24	23	10	7	6
No. of correct responses	6	12	11	4	5	3
% correct responses	46	50	48	40	71	50
% teachers' selection	50		89	0	50	100

*Represents teacher-perceived error types that were not classified as such in analysis.

1. All three teachers have primarily selected those instances of errors which they "corrected" or reacted to in some way, instead of ignoring them. Of those selected that were not corrected, especially linguistic errors in subjects other than French, teachers 1 and 3 indicated that they *consciously* avoided correction in order not to distract from the progress of the lesson.

2. In proportion to their actual occurrence, morphological errors appear to be those least selected by these teachers (35 out of 193 = 18 percent)—that is, they are possibly the least noticed, and the teachers indicated several times that such errors were not generally important.

3. It is furthermore noticeable that of the instances of error selected by all three teachers, those which were followed by a correction tended to be corrections that elicited correct responses from the students. The ratio for all teachers (adding the Totals columns) of such "successes" to the number of corrections is 69 percent. As in 1 above, this selection of successful corrections may be due to the added salience on the recordings of those teacher-student exchanges in which the teacher reacts and the student is led to reply again.

The actual ratio of "success" in correction for all these classes was 39 percent, which is shown broken down in Table 8, presenting data from the analysis of the transcripts. For most of the corrections, the rate of students' correct responses is influenced either by the teachers' persistence in obtaining a correct response or by the students' voluntary attempts to recapitulate the teacher's correction. (The relationship between the teacher's persistence and the student's voluntarism is of course a very complex one that requires investigation beyond the present study.)

The "No. of corrections" in Table 8, representing the total number of teacher corrections, are from Table 3; the "No. of correct responses" are counted from the students' replies to the teachers' reactions; the "% correct responses" equals "No. of correct responses" divided by "No. of corrections"; and the "% teachers' selection" are the same as the "% correct responses by student" from Tables 5 through 7.

Comparison of the rows for "% correct responses" and "% teachers' selection" of correct responses shows that, although the teachers may have selected more corrective exchanges with successful outcomes, the actual frequencies of correct responses to correction of different types, relative to each other within a given lesson, are somewhat comparable with the teachers' selections. This is to say that when correct responses to, e.g., phonological errors were high, the teacher also tended to perceive and select them more from the recordings. Numerous factors, among them those mentioned above in the section on teachers' priorities, interact to keep this relationship from being systematic.

Summary of teachers' stated priorities

All three teachers had expressed a concern for linguistic development through subject-matter discussions, and teacher 2's professed subordination of history study to the learning of French is not borne out in his actual performance in correction—he, too, tends to neglect linguistic errors more in Hist 8.2 and Geo 8.1 than in Fr 8.2 (comparing Tables 2 and 3). In *rating* types of errors, moreover, all three teachers considered content errors to be more important than linguistic and phonological errors. Many of their corrections of phonological errors are only brief modeling of correct pronunciation, with no insistence on a correct response from the student. Occasionally, however, certain phonological errors were considered important and were insisted upon.

Regarding linguistic errors, all three teachers commented on the varying importance of some types of linguistic errors over others, depending on the level of their students' knowledge of French, the amount of time already spent in exercises on particular items, and recurrent individual problems with specific errors, such as gender and tense. The teachers suggested that they preferred to correct those items which are focal points of lessons, especially the use of new vocabulary or, for example, synonym and antonym contrasts in French class. Difficult idioms or grammatical points that surpassed the knowledge and experience of the students were to be ignored.

CONCLUSION

The questions raised in the introduction concerned general instructional priorities, where the teachers' rate of correction and proportion of corrections of various types of errors were considered as indicators of their priorities. The present results show a reasonable degree of agreement between the teachers' stated priorities and their classroom practice. Language instruction is indeed subordinated to the subject matter—even in French class, where factual communication about stories and narratives often is the subject of discussion, as well as grammatical content.

The beginning use of a second language at a later age is unavoidably beset with misunderstandings and uncertainties, but the evident L2 communicative growth of these students within the 5 months between observations attests to their involvement in learning and to their comprehension of the challenges posed by an immersion learning context. If the teachers persist with a high rate of correction of content errors, concern for the students' general academic achievement is not justified without some evidence of poor achievement.

On the other hand, the initial question concerning immersion students' growth in L2 skills is not totally clarified. When, as often seems to be the case in these classes, the *communicative* use of French takes precedence over correct linguistic use, one must ask in what ways the teachers' reactions (correcting or not) guide the learners' sensitivity to linguistic correctness. [L1 acquisition appears to be successful despite parents' inattention to syntactic and linguistic errors in their children's language (Brown and Hanlon 1970), but the case of later L2 learners is not necessarily equivalent.]

Although immersion students at the grade 8, 9, and other levels show significantly higher achievement in French than comparison students who take French as a subject (Barik and Swain 1976a, 1976b), there is still a need to determine which behaviors on the part of the teachers can help their students improve linguistic performance, and which behaviors tend to confuse or to inhibit the development of performance. This chapter has attempted to describe what teachers do quantitatively with different error types. In Chaudron (1977) the teachers' corrective strategies have been described, and an indication of some more effective ones has been outlined. A further report investigates some of the linguistic problems resulting from the use of the L2 as a medium of instruction (Chaudron 1978).

EPILOGUE

I have only revised this paper by updating some of the references and making one or two slight stylistic changes. It is surprising how little the issues touched on here have been elaborated on in the intervening 7 years. The role of corrections in the classroom has been more or less neglected by researchers, if not in fact discredited by theories of second language acquisition that emphasize natural acquisitional processes (e.g., Krashen 1982). The subsequent evaluation of immersion education programs has shown that the immersion students' achievement in French relative to native speaker peers is very high (cf. Genesee 1983, Swain and Lapkin 1982). Thus they did not suffer linguistically from the emphasis on communication of other subject matter that is evident in this study.

In regard to the study of feedback on error in classrooms, however, a few more recent studies have followed up on the work of Fanselow (1977), Allwright (1975), and Chaudron (1977). Both Salica (1981) and Nystrom (1983) adapted Chaudron's descriptive framework (1977), while Courchêne (1980) adapted Fanselow's categories. Kasper (in press) adopts the ethnographic tradition of Schegloff, Jefferson, and Sacks (1977). These researchers have found great variability in different teachers' corrective behaviors; so they have not been able to establish clear relationships between correction and outcomes. Some recent studies of nonclassroom corrective feedback have also aimed toward determining the interactive processes, priorities, and outcomes of error correction (Day, Chenoweth, Chun, and Luppescu 1984; Brock, Crookes, Day, and Long, this volume; Wren 1982), yet the difficulty of following the learners longitudinally renders an explicit connection virtually impossible to establish.

Despite the lack of evidence that feedback on linguistic error in classrooms or outside them is consistently effective in stimulating learners' interlanguage progress, the possibility remains that certain learners, especially those with a formal learning style, can derive benefit from error correction. Yet the characteristics of successful correction, surely involving both linguistic and affective components, are far from clear. This area deserves continued serious research and experimentation.

NOTES

1. Reprinted from Working Papers on Bilingualism/Travaux de recherches sur le bilinguisme, No. 12, 22–44, with the permission of the author and publisher.

This chapter is a significantly revised version of a qualifying research paper prepared for entrance into a doctoral program at the Ontario Institute for Studies in Education. The author wishes to thank Merrill Swain for her constant comments and encouragement during the execution and analysis of the study, and during the subsequent writing of various versions of the present chapter. The data and opinions presented are, however, the responsibility of the author.

2. The study, conducted in the 1975–1976 school year, was funded by a grant-in-aid from the Ministry of Education, Province of Ontario, to the project director, Dr. Merrill Swain. The students in the present study had had grade 7 French for 20 minutes a day. For those grade 7 students who will enter the immersion program in grade 8, French lessons are increased to 1 hour a day for the final 2 months of grade 7.

3. Various kinds of measurement of classroom interaction and of educational achievement might be attempted to clarify these issues; the present study is only one type of investigation, which itself needs replication in different settings, with perhaps more teachers for longer periods of time.

4. Teachers 1 and 2 are native European French speakers and teacher 3 is a native English-speaking Canadian with an excellent command of French.

5. Not everyone will agree with what has been included in each type of error. Other more general or more specific classification schemes might be appropriate. The present one developed somewhat naturally out of the data, and I have attempted to be as explicit as possible about what was included in each type, so that readers can make their own interpretation about the importance of error correction in each of the categories.

6. The occasional difficulty of discerning the precise sound quality of some utterances on the tapes complicated the location or description of phonological errors.

7. Other instances of lack of coherence are so deficient that they are difficult to analyze. These have mostly been ignored in the analysis; if the teachers did react with a request for a repetition of the student's response, (especially when the volume of the response was in question), the "error" could be judged as a discourse error.

8. For example, the following student statement was followed up by the teacher's syntactic reconstruction. However, given the sometimes disjointed nature of student utterances (with pauses, implicit references, etc.), it is difficult to say that this student's response was incorrect syntactically:

Hist 9.2   S: Elle dit que, les Volkswagens ici, il y a le même quantité de Mercedes là.
　　　　　 T: En Suisse, qu'il y a de Volkswagens ici.

9. In Hist 9.2 teacher 3 typified a number of errors as "vocabulary," which according to the present analysis would be content errors, but the quantity of them has justified placing them under "lexical" errors in this case. Also, one error in pronunciation was perceived by teacher 3 which was not considered so by the investigator. This accounts for the greater number of these two types of errors and their corrections in Table 7, compared with Table 3.

REFERENCES

Allwright, Richard L. 1975. Problems in the study of the language teacher's treatment of learner error. In M. K. Burt and H. C. Dulay (eds.). *On TESOL '75: New Directions in Second Language Learning, Teaching and Bilingual Education.* Washington, D.C.: TESOL. 96–109.

Barik, Henri C., and Merrill Swain. 1976a. A Canadian experiment in bilingual education at the grade eight and nine levels: the Peel study. *Foreign Language Annals,* 9: 465–479.

Barik, Henri C., and Merrill Swain. 1976b. A Canadian experiment in bilingual schooling in the senior grades: the Peel study through grade ten. *International Review of Applied Psychology,* 25: 99–113.

Brock, Cynthia, Graham Crookes, Richard R. Day, and Michael H. Long. The differential effects of corrective feedback in native speaker-nonnative speaker conversation. (This volume.)

Brooks, Nelson. 1964. *Language and Language Learning: Theory and Practice.* 2d ed. New York: Harcourt, Brace and World.

Brown, Roger, and Camille Hanlon. 1970. Derivational complexity and order of acquisition in child speech. In J. R. Hayes (ed.). *Cognition and the Development of Language.* Toronto: Wiley. 11–53.

Chaudron, Craig. 1976. Teacher strategies in handling student errors in French immersion classes. Paper presented at the Linguistic Circle of Ontario, Toronto, Mar. 6.

Chaudron, Craig. 1977. A descriptive model of discourse in the corrective treatment of learners' errors. *Language Learning,* 27: 29–46.

Chaudron, Craig. 1978. Grammatical development and communication in FSL immersion classes: the case of the French article. Paper presented at the Fifth International Congress of Applied Linguistics, Montreal, Aug. 23.

Courchène, Robert. 1980. The error analysis hypothesis, the contrastive analysis hypothesis, and the correction of error in the second language classroom. *TESL Talk*, 11/2: 3–13; 11/3: 10–29.

Day, Richard R., N. Ann Chenoweth, Ann E. Chun, and Stuart Luppescu. 1984. Corrective feedback in native-nonnative discourse. *Language Learning*, 34: 19–45.

Edwards, H. P., and F. Smyth. 1976. Alternatives to early immersion programs for the acquisition of French as a second language. *Canadian Modern Language Review*, 32: 524–533.

Fanselow, John. 1977. The treatment of error in oral work. *Foreign Language Annals*, 10: 583–593.

Genesee, Fred. 1983. Bilingual education of majority language children: The immersion experiments in review. *Applied Psycholinguistics*, 4: 1–46.

Kasper, Gabriele. In press. Repair in foreign language teaching. In G. Kasper (ed.). *Learning, Teaching and Communication in the Foreign Language Classroom*. Arhus, Denmark: Arhus University Press.

Krashen, Stephen D. 1982. *Principles and Practice in Second Language Acquisition*. Oxford: Pergamon.

Mehan, Hugh. 1974. Accomplishing classroom lessons. In A. Cicourel, et al. (eds.). *Language Use and School Performance*. New York: Academic Press. 76–142.

Naiman, Neil, Maria Fröhlich, H. H. Stern, and A. Todesco. 1978. *The Good Language Learner*. Toronto: O. I. S. E.

Nystrom, Nancy Johnson. 1983. Teacher-student interaction in bilingual classrooms: four approaches to error feedback. In H. W. Seliger and M. H. Long (eds.). *Classroom Oriented Research in Second Language Acquisition*. Rowley, Mass.: Newbury House. 169–188.

Politzer, Robert L. 1965. *Teaching French: An Introduction to Applied Linguistics*. Waltham, Mass.: Blaisdell Publishing Company.

Salica, Christine. 1981. Testing a model of corrective discourse. M. A. in TESL thesis, University of California at Los Angeles.

Schegloff, Emanuel A., Gail Jefferson, and Harvey Sacks. 1977. The preference for self-correction in the organization of repair in conversation. *Language*, 53: 361–382.

Stern, H. H., M. Swain, L. D. McLean, R. J. Friedman, B. Harley, and S. Lapkin. 1976. Three approaches to teaching French. Toronto: Ontario Ministry of Education.

Swain, Merrill, and Maggie Bruck (eds.). 1976. Special Issue of the *Canadian Modern Language Review*, 32.

Swain, Merrill, and Sharon Lapkin. 1982. *Evaluating Bilingual Education: A Canadian Case Study*. Clevedon, England: Multilingual Matters.

Wren, Debora. 1982. A case study of the treatment of oral errors. *Selected Papers in TESOL*, vol. 1. Monterey, Calif.: Monterey Institute of International Studies. 90–103.

5

THE LINGUISTIC AND CONVERSATIONAL PERFORMANCE OF EXPERIENCED AND INEXPERIENCED TEACHERS

Teresa Pica
University of Pennsylvania
Michael H. Long
University of Hawaii at Manoa

Theoretical claims have been made concerning the importance of comprehensible input for second language acquisition (SLA) (e.g., Krashen 1980, Larsen-Freeman 1983) and the roles of linguistic and conversational adjustments in achieving comprehensibility (e.g., Hatch 1983, Long 1981a). Thus, samples of the target language that are *comprehensible* to learners and that contain items one step ahead of their current SL abilities are claimed to be the driving force behind interlanguage development. Linguistic and/or conversational adjustments made by NSs talking to learners are believed to be a major way in which comprehensibility is achieved.

The studies reported here set out to address, in turn, two questions that arise when these ideas are applied to SLA in a classroom setting:

1. What are the characteristics of teacher speech as modified linguistic input to the classroom learner, and of teacher-student conversation in classroom discourse as samples of modified conversation?
2. Is the ability to modify input and conversation appropriately part of any teacher's competence, or must it be developed through experience over time?

STUDY 1: THE ESL CLASSROOM AS AN ACQUISITION ENVIRONMENT

Method

Subjects   Subjects for the study were 10 ESL teachers (1 male and 9 females) and their students. Some of the teachers had several years of classroom experience, while others (trainees) had little experience or none at all. Four teachers were teaching their regular elementary-level classes in the Philadelphia area, while six were teaching those same students for the first time, following one hour's observation of the classes concerned. The classes were either in a preacademic intensive university program or in a conversational program offered as a community service. Class size ranged from 7 to 16 students, who were from a variety of first language backgrounds.

Baseline data on native speaker-nonnative speaker (NS–NNS) conversation came from two previous studies of foreigner talk discourse (Long 1980, 1981b), parts of which had involved 16 and 36 NS–NNS dyads, respectively, engaged in informal (noninstructional) conversations. Subjects in those studies were strangers, meeting for the first time for the purpose of the research. The NSs varied widely in the amount of prior foreigner talk experience they possessed (zero to several years). The NNSs in both cases were of elementary ESL proficiency, from a variety of first language backgrounds in the first study, and NSs of Japanese in the second.

Data collection   Teachers were given a small cassette recorder and asked to tape at least 10 minutes of a lesson with their regular class of students. The lessons ranged from discussion of reading assignments to vocabulary review, conversation games, and other communication activities. They all involved the teacher's giving directions, and all were predominantly oral-aural and teacher-fronted.

Data from the informal (noninstructional) NS–NNS conversations were collected according to the following procedure. Subjects, who had had no prior acquaintance with each other, were introduced by first name by the researcher and asked to have a 5-minute conversation about anything they liked. The researcher then left the room, leaving a small cassette tape recorder running. All participants knew that their lessons or conversations were being recorded.

Hypotheses and Results

Input   Previous research (Long 1980) has found the linguistic complexity of speech to NNSs not to differ significantly from that to other NSs provided comparisons involve dyads made up of speakers who are comparable on such other relevant variables as age, status, and SL proficiency, and provided both

TABLE 1 Words per T-unit and S-nodes per T-unit in Teacher Speech and in Native Speaker Speech to Nonnatives in Informal Conversations

	T-units in words		S-nodes per T-unit	
	Teachers (n=10)	NS-NNS (n=32)	Teachers (n=10)	NS-NNS (n=32)
$\bar{x}$	6.94	7.03	1.44	1.30
s	1.06	1.84	0.23	0.32
	t=0.23, df=40, p>10		t=0.70, df=40, p>.10	

sets of dyads are working on the same task. Consequently, it was hypothesized that there would be no significant difference in either (1) the mean length of T-unit in words of (2) the syntactic complexity of T-units (number of tensed or tenseless verb forms per T-unit) when ESL teacher speech was compared with other NS speech to NNSs in the informal conversations. As shown in Table 1, both hypotheses were sustained, with neither the average length nor the syntactic complexity of T-units differing significantly across settings.

Following previous findings to this effect (Long and Sato 1983), it was further hypothesized that ESL teacher speech and NS speech in informal NS–NNS conversations would contain significantly different frequencies of questions, statements, and imperatives. (Imperatives in this analysis included *let's* constructions and modal and infinitival imperatives.) The teacher speech was expected to show proportionately higher frequencies of statements and imperatives (and consequently, fewer questions), owing to the use of statements for providing feedback in approximately one-third of all teacher moves, and the use of imperatives for many classroom management functions, respectively. This hypothesis was also supported by the data, as shown in Table 2.

TABLE 2 Questions, Statements, and Imperatives in T-units in Teacher Speech and in Native Speaker Speech to Nonnatives in Informal Conversations*

		Questions		Statements		Imperatives		
		n	%	n	%	n	%	Total
Teachers	(n=10)	206	24	535	63	112	13	853
NS-NNS	(n=32)	121	48	133	52	0	0	254
		χ^2=73.37, df=2, p<.001						

*Percentages rounded to nearest whole number in this and subsequent tables.

It was further predicted that the proportions of Wh and yes/no questions would differ, with the relative frequency of Wh forms being higher and of yes/no forms lower in the classroom talk than in the informal conversations. It was supposed that teachers would employ more Wh questions because of their apparent value as devices for management functions, for eliciting specific information, and for checking students' understanding and knowledge of the SL.

TABLE 3 Wh and Yes/No Questions in Teacher Speech and in Native Speaker Speech to Nonnatives in Informal Conversations

		Wh questions		Yes/no questions		
		n	%	n	%	Total
Teachers	(n=10)	85	43	111	57	196
NS-NNS	(n=32)	36	39	56	61	92
		χ^2=0.30, df=1, p<.75				

As shown in Table 3, the prediction was not borne out. There was merely a slight but nonsignificant trend in that direction.

Conversational adjustments The fourth hypothesis concerned another dimension of questions, namely, their referential or display functions in the two types of discourse. *Referential* questions are those to which the speaker does not know the answer; *display* questions are those to which he or she does and which are frequently used by teachers as a means of checking students' knowledge (What's the opposite of "up" in English?) as opposed to as a way of obtaining information unknown to the questioner. Following previous findings (Long and Sato 1983), it was hypothesized that the frequency of display questions would be higher in the classroom talk than in the informal conversations. This hypothesis was sustained, as shown in Table 4, in which it can also be seen that fully 91 percent of these 10 teachers' questions were display questions, confirming the results of the earlier study.

TABLE 4 Display and Referential Questions in Teacher Speech and in Native Speaker Speech to Nonnatives in Informal Conversations

		Display		Referential		
		n	%	n	%	Total
Teachers	(n=10)	105	91	11	9	116
NS-NNS	(n=36)	2	0	999	100	1001
		χ^2=473,806.11, df=1, p<.000				

The last three hypotheses also addressed the issue of conversational adjustments in the two varieties of NS–NNS discourse. Teacher talk was expected to contain fewer confirmation checks and clarification requests than NS speech in the informal conversations because of the predominantly one-way flow of information in classroom conversation. SL teachers are rarely in any doubt about what a student is trying to say, given that students are generally responding to display questions the teacher has asked, to which he or she already knows the answer. Such new information in lessons of this type generally comes from the teacher, who then needs to ensure that students have understood. Hence, it was predicted that teacher talk would also contain a higher frequency of comprehension checks than NS speech outside the

TABLE 5 Confirmation Checks, Clarification Requests, and Comprehension Checks in Teacher Speech and in Native-Speaker Speech to Nonnatives in Informal Conversation

	Confirmation checks		Clarification requests		Comprehension checks		
	n	%	n	%	n	%	Total
Teachers (n=10)	13	14	18	19	63	67	94
NS-NNS (n=36)	206	72	50	18	27	10	283
χ^2=139.95, df=2, p<.001							

classroom. (Operational definitions of confirmation checks, clarification requests, and comprehension checks were those described in Long 1980). As shown in Table 5, all three hypotheses were sustained. Presumably because of the two-way flow of unknown information in the informal conversations, NS speech therein contained significantly higher frequencies of confirmation checks and clarification requests, and significantly fewer comprehension checks than the instructional talk.

Discussion

The results reported above confirm findings of the earlier study by Long and Sato (Long and Sato 1983, Long 1983a). ESL classroom conversation, in lessons for elementary-level students, at least, is different from informal, noninstructional NS–NNS conversation in several ways relevant to its potential as an acquisition environment. While the complexity of *linguistic input* to learners in the two contexts is similar, the amount of *negotiation for meaning* that occurs in the classroom setting is much smaller, as measured by the significantly lower number of *conversational* adjustments by teachers, *presumably* indicating a lesser degree of comprehension on the students' part of the input that is available. ("Presumably" is stressed because actual student comprehension was not measured in this study.) The reason for the lesser amount of negotiation work is probably to be found in the other confirmed finding, namely, the far higher frequency of display questions in the instructional talk, and the lack of two-way information exchange this indicates.

STUDY 2: SPEECH ADJUSTMENTS AND TEACHING EXPERIENCE

Method

Subjects Subjects for the second study were 14 elementary ESL classroom teachers and their students. Six of the teachers were from the first study, had two or more years of ESL experience, and were observed teaching their regular classes. Two additional experienced (EXP) teachers were observed teaching two of those elementary classes for the first time. The remaining six teachers were inexperienced (INX) ESL practice teachers from a master's degree program in ESL. They had had no or minimal ESL teaching experience, and were observed teaching the six experienced teachers' classes for the first time following a 1-hour period of observation of the classes concerned.

The rationale for including the two additional EXP teachers as controls was to check on the possibility that any differences found between the other six EXP teachers and the six INX teachers might be due to differences in the level of familiarity with the particular ESL students in the classes used in the study. Since the six EXP teachers were teaching their regular classes, it was necessary to have a sample of EXP teacher performance with a class of students unfamiliar to them in order to replicate the teaching task confronting the INX teachers as closely as possible. The confound of teaching experience with familiarity with particular students could of course be avoided by having all teachers, EXP and INX, teach new classes, but the disruption involved (to 12 classes in this case) precluded that option in this study.

For the purpose of discussion, the subjects of the study are referred to henceforth as follows: six experienced regular (EXR) teachers, two experienced visiting (EXV) (control) teachers, and six inexperienced (INX) teachers.

Data collection Data were collected in the same way as for the ESL classroom data in the first study. The six EXR teachers were given a cassette recorder and asked to tape at least 10 minutes of a lesson with their regular class of students. On the same day or the following day, the six INX teachers and the two EXV teachers representing the control group observed one of these classes for at least an hour. They then presented a 10-minute lesson based on a task comparable with that which the regular teacher had used.

The lessons in this second study were similar in scope, materials, and presentation to those described in the data-collection section for the first study. As in that study, all participants knew they were being tape-recorded.

Hypotheses and Results

Input As in the first study, and for the same reasons, no differences were predicted in either the length in words or the syntactic complexity of T-units in the different teachers' speech. These hypotheses were additionally motivated by the null findings on these measures in an earlier laboratory study comparing EXP teachers and nonteachers explaining to nonnative speakers (who were not physically present) how to locate an object in a picture of a room (Dahl 1981). As shown in Tables 6a and 6b, both hypotheses were sustained across EXR and INX, and EXR and EXV teachers.

TABLE 6a   Words per T-unit in EXP and INX Teachers' Speech

	EXR teachers (n=6)	INX teachers (n=6)	EXR teachers (n=2)	EXV teachers (n=2)
$\bar{x}$	7.30	7.93	6.32	5.92
s	0.71	1.43	0.12	0.16
	t=1.47, df=10, p<.10		t=2.77, df=2, p<.10	

TABLE 6b   S-nodes per T-unit in EXP and INX Teachers' Speech

	EXR teachers (n=6)	INX teachers (n=6)	EXR teachers (n=2)	EXF teachers (n=2)
$\bar{x}$	1.48	1.52	1.33	1.32
s	0.23	0.23	0.56	0.06
	t=0.07, df=10, p<.10		t=0.06, df=2, p<.10	

It was further predicted that there would be significantly different distributions of questions, statements, and imperatives in the speech of EXP and INX teachers, with the INX ones using more questions. It was reasoned that the INX teachers would be less "socialized" into the classic exchange structure of classroom discourse—teacher initiation (usually a question), student response, and teacher feedback—documented by so many studies (e.g., Sinclair and Coulthard 1975). As a result, the feedback moves, usually encoded as statements, and the management directives, usually encoded as imperatives, might be less prevalent in the INX teachers' speech. In addition, Long and Sato (1983) had found that ESL teacher speech contained fewer questions than native speaker speech to nonnatives in informal conversations. As shown in Table 7, questions, statements, and imperatives were differentially distributed in the speech of both groups of teachers. The distributions themselves, however, were remarkably similar. Questions made up 20 and 26 percent of EXP and INX teachers' speech, respectively, statements 66 and 64 percent, and imperatives 13 and 10 percent.

A fifth hypothesis concerned the forms that teacher questions took. It was predicted that INX teachers would utilize more yes/no and fewer Wh questions than EXP teachers. This was expected because of the known native speaker preference for uninverted and yes/no questions in conversations with nonnative speakers outside classrooms, probably because of the relatively easier conversational role such questions leave the nonnative compared with Wh questions (see Long 1981b for discussion). The INX teachers would not have had time to develop the full range of classroom questioning strategies the experienced teachers would employ. This hypothesis was supported, as shown in Table 8.

TABLE 7 Questions, Statements, and Imperatives in EXP and INX Teachers' Speech

	Questions		Statements		Imperatives		
	n	%	n	%	n	%	Total
EXR Ts (n=6)	117	20	386	66	78	13	581
INX Ts (n=6)	100	26	244	64	36	10	380
χ^2=7.07, df=2, p<.01							
EXR Ts (n=2)	50	20	165	67	30	12	245
EXV Ts (n=2)	56	33	79	47	32	19	167
χ^2=16.52, df=2, p<.001							

TABLE 8 Wh and Yes/No Questions in the Speech of EXP and INX Teachers

	Wh	Yes/no	Total	
EXR Ts (n=6)	57	56	113	χ^2=10.51 df=1
INX Ts (n=6)	26	69	95	p<.005
EXR Ts (n=2)	20	27	47	χ^2=3.61 df=1
EXV Ts (n=2)	31	22	53	p>.05

TABLE 9 Disfluencies in EXP and INX Teachers' Speech

	Disfluent	Fluent	Total	
EXR Ts (n=6)	62	852	914	χ^2=21.87 df=1
INX Ts (n=6)	81	500	581	p<.001
EXR Ts (n=2)	36	390	426	χ^2=2.86 df=1
EXV Ts (n=2)	12	243	255	p<.10

The final characteristic of classroom input examined was the relative fluency of the EXP and INX teachers' speech. It was hypothesized that the INX teachers' lesser familiarity with classroom teaching would result in their speech being marked by more disfluencies, measured by the frequency of hesitations, false starts, and interruptions of an utterance by any interlocutor. This hypothesis was supported, as shown in Table 9.

Conversational adjustments It was predicted that EXP teachers, being more familiar with the apparently pervasive conventions of classroom discourse, would employ more display and fewer referential questions than INX teachers.

TABLE 10 Display and Referential Questions in EXP and INX Teachers' Speech

	Display	Referential	Total	
EXR Ts (n=6)	52	9	61	$\chi^2=0.27$ df=1
INX Ts (n=6)	53	8	61	p<.50
EXR Ts (n=2)	21	2	23	$\chi^2=0.00$ df=1
EXV Ts (n=2)	36	5	41	p>.99

TABLE 11 Frames in T-units and Fragments in EXP and INX Teachers' Speech

	Frames	T-units and fragments	Total	
EXR Ts (n=6)	210	704	914	$\chi^2=1.14$ df=1
INX Ts (n=6)	124	457	581	p<.50
EXR Ts (n=2)	89	337	426	$\chi^2=16.95$ df=1
EXV Ts (n=2)	89	166	255	p<.001

This hypothesis found no support in the data, however, as shown in Table 10. Display questions were used almost exclusively by all teachers, experienced or not. If these teachers were typical, it seems that even neophytes understand their role in terms of what Barnes (1976) has called the "transmission" model of education. Teachers are "knowers," whose primary function is to give information and to test whether students have received it by asking them to display their new knowledge. Although lacking experience as teachers themselves, perhaps they have learned this aspect of teacher behavior from their own experiences as students.

The INX teachers' lessons were expected to be less clearly structured than those of EXP teachers. Thus, it was expected, for example, that INX teachers would use fewer conversational "frames," such as *Right, OK, Now,* and *So.* As shown in Table 11, this turned out not to be the case. EXV teachers, on the other hand, did use significantly more frames than EXR teachers. We can see no obvious explanation for this apparently anomalous finding.

It was predicted that there would be fewer self-repetitions (complete or partial, exact or semantic) on the part of INX teachers, owing to their lesser familiarity with this device as a strategy for avoiding communication breakdowns (see Long 1983b for discussion of such strategies). In fact, however, no differences were found in this behavior between EXR and INX, or between EXR and EXV teachers, as shown in Table 12.

Because of their greater use of the conventionalized exchange structure, and the frequency of repetition (with or without reformulation and other

TABLE 12   Self-Repetitions in EXP and INX Teachers' Speech

	Self-repetitions	T-units and fragments	Total	
EXR Ts (n=6)	153	761	914	$\chi^2=1.65$ df=1
INX Ts (n=6)	82	499	581	p<.25
EXR Ts (n=2)	59	367	426	$\chi^2=0.93$ df=1
EXV Ts (n=2)	28	227	255	p<.50

TABLE 13   Other-Repetitions in EXP and INX Teachers' Speech

	Other-repetitions	T-units and fragments	Total	
EXR Ts (n=6)	103	811	914	$\chi^2=5.63$ df=1
INX Ts (n=6)	43	538	581	p<.025
EXR Ts (n=2)	51	375	426	$\chi^2=5.19$ df=1
EXV Ts (n=2)	16	239	255	p<.025

changes—see Chaudron 1977 for details) as the teacher's react move, it was predicted that EXR teachers would utilize more other-repetitions (complete or partial, exact or semantic) than INX teachers. This hypothesis was confirmed, as shown in Table 13. The finding should be treated cautiously, however, since, as the table shows, EXR teachers also used more other-repetitions than EXV teachers.

Still in the realm of conversational adjustments, it was hypothesized that INX teachers would use more confirmation checks and clarification requests than EXP teachers, because of their relative lack of experience in dealing with more or less comprehensible student interlanguages. As shown in Tables 14 and 15, the number of confirmation checks and clarification requests in all lessons, regardless of teacher experience, was tiny, further confirmation of the predominantly one-way flow of information in all the classes already noted in the analyses of display and referential questions. The fact that EXV teachers used more confirmation checks than EXR teachers (Table 14), and both INX and EXV teachers used more clarification requests than EXR teachers (Table 15) suggests that *both* groups were simply reflecting their unfamiliarity with the particular students they were teaching for the first time, and not that either was departing from the transmission model, with its minimal requirements for strategies and tactics to avoid and repair communication breakdowns.

INX teachers were expected to use more comprehension checks than EXP teachers, because of their lack of familiarity with typical levels of comprehension to be expected of ESL students. As Table 16 shows, there was

TABLE 14 Confirmation Checks in EXP and INX Teachers' Speech

	Confirmation checks	T-units and fragments	Total	
EXR Ts (n=6)	9	905	914	$\chi^2=0.47$ df=1
INX Ts (n=6)	3	578	581	p<.50
EXR Ts (n=2)	1	425	426	$\chi^2=5.93$ df=1
EXV Ts (n=2)	4	251	255	p<.025

TABLE 15 Clarification Requests in EXP and INX Teachers' Speech

	Clarification requests	T-units and fragments	Total	
EXR Ts (n=6)	8	906	914	$\chi^2=4.76$ df=1
INX Ts (n=6)	12	569	581	p<.05
EXR Ts (n=2)	0	426	426	$\chi^2=5.93$ df=1
EXV Ts (n=2)	5	250	255	p<.025

TABLE 16 Comprehension Checks in EXP and INX Teachers' Speech

	Comprehension checks	T-units and fragments	Total	
EXR Ts (n=6)	31	883	914	$\chi^2=3.31$ df=1
INX Ts (n=6)	30	551	581	p<.10
EXR Ts (n=2)	22	404	426	$\chi^2=0.30$ df=1
EXV Ts (n=2)	10	245	255	p<.75

in fact no difference in the frequency of use of comprehension checks across the teacher groups, although there was a clear, but nonsignificant, trend in that direction.

The final hypothesis concerned the amount of classroom talk (measured as the total number of T-units and fragments in teacher speech) used by the EXP and INX groups. It was predicted that INX teachers would talk less because they were less familiar with the power associated with their position, and also because their lesser use of the three-part exchange structure described earlier might involve omitting the feedback, or evaluative component in that exchange, thereby leaving more speaking turns for students. As shown in Table 17, this hypothesis was not supported by the data, although there was a nonsignificant trend in the predicted direction.

TABLE 17 Volume of EXP and INX Teachers' Speech (T-units and Fragments)

	EXR Ts (n=6)	INX Ts (n=6)	EXR Ts (n=2)	EXV Ts (n=2)
x̄	152.33	96.83	213.00	106.50
s	65.74	46.05	56.56	31.81
	t=1.69, df=10, p<.10		t=2.32, df=2, p<.10	

Discussion

In general, the similarities outweighed the differences found between EXP and INX teachers in this study. Certain conventions of classroom discourse, such as the centrality of the teacher's position and the communicative dominance this provides, appear to be present from the outset. Reflections of this power include the sheer quantity of teacher talk, the use of the solicit—response—react exchange as the dominant discourse structure, and the heavy reliance on display questions as a means of initiating such exchanges. EXP and INX teachers performed as one population in all these areas, as well as in the linguistic complexity of the input they provided.

There were some differences between the two groups of teachers, however. Experience seems to be necessary for becoming proficient in the use of some of the conventions surrounding second language classroom talk. EXP teachers, for example, learn to encode questions in a wider range of forms, employing notably more Wh forms as a way of checking students' comprehension and ability to formulate answers in the target language. And the fluency of teachers' classroom performance also appears to increase with time.

Nevertheless, the conclusion drawn from this study is that the influence of the classroom context is strong enough to outweigh the effects of teaching experience. Consequently, even those with little or no previous experience immediately exercise the power when given the opportunity. Perhaps this is the result of long years of experiencing teaching vicariously—as students.

CONCLUSION

If one accepts the claims of Krashen and others concerning the importance of comprehensible input in SLA, the two studies reported here are not very encouraging for learners whose primary acquisition environment is the SL classroom. As was the case in an earlier study (Long and Sato, 1983), the lessons examined here were found to provide less opportunity for the negotiation for meaning that is necessary if learners are to obtain comprehensible input than did informal NS-NNS conversations outside classrooms.

The reason for this state of affairs is not hard to appreciate: it is difficult for learners to negotiate if they have nothing to negotiate with. Their most obvious potential bargaining chip—information unknown to the teacher that he, she, or other students need in order to do something—is not available to them so long as teachers structure discourse such that information flows in one direction only, *from* teacher *to* students. That this was the case in these lessons was clear, among other things, from the pervasiveness of display questions and the relatively high frequency of comprehension checks, in contrast with the tiny number of confirmation checks and clarification requests in the teachers' speech. This state of affairs prevailed, furthermore, in both EXP and INX teachers' lessons, suggesting that the dominant role is "natural" for teachers, and perhaps inevitable unless something is done about it.

It is not being suggested that teachers should stop exercising their power to manage learning. *If* provision of opportunities for learners to negotiate input is a concern, however, supplements to the teacher-fronted "lockstep" mode of instruction appear to be desirable, with interlanguage talk in small-group work being one obvious alternative of proved efficacy (see Long and Porter 1985 for review). *Some* methodological innovations, at least, seem necessary if the SL classroom is to provide a more productive conversational context for SLA.

REFERENCES

Andersen, R. W. (ed.). 1983. *Pidginization and Creolization as Language Acquisition.* Rowley, Mass.: Newbury House.

Barnes, D. 1976. *From Communication to Curriculum.* Harmondsworth: Penguin.

Chaudron, C. 1977. A descriptive model of discourse in the corrective treatment of learners' errors. *Language Learning,* 27 (1): 29–46.

Dahl, D. A. 1981. The role of experience in speech modifications for second language learners. *Minnesota Papers in Linguistics and Philosophy of Language,* 7: 78–93.

Hatch, E. M. 1983. Simplified input and second language acquisition. In R. W. Andersen (ed.). *Pidginization and Creolization as Language Acquisition.* Rowley, Mass.: Newbury House. 64–86.

Krashen, S. D. 1980. The input hypothesis. In J. E. Alatis (ed.). *Current Issues in Bilingual Education.* Washington, D.C.: Georgetown University Press. 168–180.

Larsen-Freeman, D. 1983. The importance of input in second language acquisition. In R. W. Andersen (ed.). *Pidginization and Creolization as Language Acquisition.* Rowley, Mass.: Newbury House. 87–93.

Long, M. H. 1980. Input, interaction, and second language acquisition. Ph.D. dissertation, University of California, Los Angeles. (University Microfilms No. 81–11, 249.)

Long, M. H. 1981a. Input, interaction, and second language acquisition. In H. Winitz (ed.), *Native Language and Foreign Language Acquisition. Annals of the New York Academy of Sciences,* 379: 259–278.

Long, M. H. 1981b. Questions in foreigner talk discourse. *Language Learning,* 31 (1): 135–157.

6

FOREIGNER TALK IN JOINT COGNITIVE ACTIVITIES[1]

Linda Schinke-Llano
Northwestern University

That the phenomenon of foreigner talk exists has been documented repeatedly in recent years.[2] While some researchers have concentrated on describing the characteristics of foreigner talk in different settings, others have speculated on the relationship between speech modifications and second language acquisition. Krashen (1982: 21), for example, has formulated the input hypothesis, which states that "we acquire by understanding language that contains structure a bit beyond our current level of competence (i+1)." Long (1980, 1981), on the other hand, argues that input is a necessary, but not sufficient, factor in second language acquisition; modified interaction is the factor that is both necessary and sufficient.

Still other researchers and theoreticians have concerned themselves with the relationship between second language acquisition and cognitive skills development in a school setting (Cummins 1980, Wong Fillmore 1982, Saville-Troike 1984). Cummins (1980), for example, has posited the notion of CALP (cognitive-academic language proficiency) and BICS (basic interpersonal communicative skills), indicating that the former is critical to the advancement, if not the survival, of second language learners in the school system.

In order for the relationship between speech modifications and second language acquisition to be understood, more information needs to be known about the nature of those modifications addressed to second language learners. Further, because of the large numbers of limited-English-proficient (LEP) students in U.S. schools, it is imperative that we study the specific nature of speech adjustments in an academic setting. Thus, a two-part study was designed that would characterize the linguistic environment experienced by LEP students in all-English-content classes.

One portion of the study — that devoted to classroom observations — has been reported elsewhere (Schinke 1981, Schinke-Llano 1983). The observations revealed that teachers interact significantly less frequently with LEP students than with their native English-speaking (NS) counterparts. Further, when interactions do occur with LEP students, they are significantly different in functional type. Finally, the more crucial the functional type of interaction to the learning process, the more differential the treatment of LEP and NS students with respect to interaction length.

Although the observations conducted in the classroom yielded valuable information regarding such things as interaction patterns and functional mix of language, a more controlled instructional setting was necessary in order to identify characteristics of foreigner talk specific to joint cognitive activities. Specifically, do teachers utilize language to structure joint cognitive activities differently for LEP students than for NS students? If so, what are the nature and extent of those differences? Further, if differential language use exists, what are the possible ramifications for LEP students? These questions are the focus of the experimental portion of the study presented here.

SUBJECTS

The study was conducted at the end of the academic year in the public school system of a large industrial town in the Chicago area. The school system is highly integrated, both linguistically and racially. Subjects were twelve monolingual English-speaking classroom teachers situated in four schools. Four were fifth-grade teachers, four were sixth-grade teachers, and four taught fifth- and sixth-grade combination classes. All had classroom populations consisting of native speakers of English, nonnative speakers of English fluent in their second language, and LEP students.

Twenty-four students participated in the experimental study, two from each teacher's class. Twelve students were native speakers of English; twelve were LEP students. All LEP students observed were Spanish-speaking; all participated in the district's bilingual education program. Students categorized as LEP fell into the first three levels of language fluency as defined by the state "Rules and Regulations for Transitional Bilingual Education" (1976, pp. 3–4).[3] In all, five students from fluency level I, four from level II, and three from level III participated.

DATA COLLECTION

A situation was devised in which identical demands were placed upon the teacher communicating with a LEP student and with a student who is a native speaker of English (NS). The task selected for the situation was one that was academic in nature, yet not associated with a specific content area: the filling out of a catalog order blank. The twelve teachers had been informed during the first portion of the study that observations were being made of classroom language. In addition, for this portion of the study, the teachers were told that observations would be made of them as they explained a task to each of two students. At the onset of the task, each teacher was given a catalog page, an order blank (see Appendix A), and the following typed instructions:

Using the accompanying pages, explain to the student how to fill out an order blank. Then, with your assistance if necessary, have the student fill out an order blank by ordering the two items circled. This is *not* a test; completion of the task is not essential.

Each student involved (one LEP and one NS student per teacher) was asked in his or her native language by the researcher if he or she would agree to assist in an exercise with the teacher. Each was informed that the activity was not a test and would not be graded, and that it was not important if the task were finished or done correctly.

Teacher-student dyads were audiotaped for approximately 10 to 15 minutes each. Taping was done during the school day at a time when students not involved in the experiment had individual seatwork. Taping was conducted in private rooms near or adjacent to the participating classrooms. Field notes were kept on any pertinent comments the teachers may have made outside of the taping sessions. The tapes were then transcribed in preparation for analysis.

CODING AND ANALYSIS

The data were analyzed to ascertain if there were any variation in the way teachers utilize language to structure the task for the two groups of students. Both quantitative and qualitative features were considered. First, to ascertain any differences in total amount of language used with the two groups, lines of teacher talk in the transcript were counted, and tapes timed. A chi-square analysis was used to determine if the differences were significant, both for the total groups and for the three language fluency levels involved.

Next, in order to characterize the nature of the instructional interactions, the concept of abbreviation was utilized. In order to do this, the task at hand, filling out a catalog order blank, was conceived of as a single task having many substeps, or as a directive having many subdirectives (see Appendix B). Sections II-C and III-C, filling in the catalog number, were then chosen for more detailed analysis for several reasons. Most importantly, it is a relatively difficult step, since it is the only step of the task involving both the picture of the item and its written description on the catalog page, as well as the order form. In addition, II-C and III-C involve observable behaviors that can be measured objectively. Finally, since each student had to order two items, this step occurred four times

101

for each teacher. Thus, more detailed comparisons both within and across teachers could be done.

In the coding and analyzing of these data, each substep of sections II-C and III-C explicitly mentioned by the teacher was identified. Explicit mention includes the utilization of:

1. Nonverbal directives (e.g., pointing)
2. Direct directives (e.g., "The number goes in this blank.")
3. Indirect directives (e.g., "Where does that number go?")

Recall that abbreviation refers to the degree to which subdirectives of the task are explicitly mentioned. In this case, the imperative "Fill in the catalog number" would be highly abbreviated since it entails five subdirectives (find the picture, the letter, the description, the catalog number, and the blank). One illustration of such highly abbreviated speech is the following interaction:

T: Okay. Do F first. And where's the catalog number? Do the catalog number first.
NS: (Writes the catalog number).

Only the substep "Find the catalog number" is mentioned; the other four are not.

If, on the other hand, each subdirective was actually stated by the teacher, the speech would not be abbreviated at all. The interaction below illustrates such lack of abbreviation.

T: ... Okay. Now. This is a table. (Points.) What letter?
LEP: M?
T: M. Can you find M right along here? (Points to description.)
LEP: (Points to description.)
T: ... Okay. Catalog number. That's the number that we'll find right here. (Points to number.)
      Copy that whole thing along here. (Points to blank.)
LEP: Here? (Points to blank.)
T: Uh-huh. Why don't you put this closer. Okay. Numero. Write the numbers: two-two ...
LEP: (Writes number.)

In this instance, the teacher specified all five substeps for the student.

Related to the question of abbreviation is that of regulation. The same sections of transcript were coded concurrently to determine whether the steps were teacher-regulated or student-regulated. In short, which person — the teacher or the student — is responsible for the proceedings of the task? In this case, for example, does the teacher or the student locate the catalog number? If it is the student, does he do it through mediation (assistance) by the teacher?

Relating the coding of regulatory behavior to that of abbreviation, both nonverbal and direct directives are labelled as teacher-regulated behavior. Statements such as "This would be our number" (teacher points to catalog number) and "The catalog number will be down below: seven-ten-G-M-B" are regarded as teacher-regulated substeps. Indirect directives fall into the category of student-regulated behavior that is mediated. Examples of mediated student-regulated behavior are "Can you find the letter?" and "Where's the description?" Finally, pure student-regulated behavior occurs only if the substep is not mentioned (either explicitly or implicitly) by the teacher. Recall that abbreviation and regulation are inversely related. The more abbreviated the language used to direct the task, the more student-regulated it is. The less abbreviated the directions, the more teacher-regulated the task.

Results of the abbreviation and regulation coding were reported in grid form, weighted, and tabulated in order to ascertain any differences in treatment of the two groups of students. A Mann-Whitney U Test was utilized to determine the significance of differences obtained.

In summary, the purpose of the portion of the study reported here is to compare the instructional interactions between teachers and LEP students with those between teachers and native English-speaking students. Specifically, is there variation in the way teachers utilize language to structure the task situation for the two groups of students?

RESULTS

As stated previously, the analysis of the instructional dyads focused on how teachers utilize language to organize the instructional task for the two types of students. One organizational aspect examined was the quantity of speech used.

TABLE 1   Number of Lines of Teacher Talk in Transcripts

Teacher	NS	LEP	Ratio of NS to LEP
T1, 2, 3, 6, 11	488	500 level I	.98
T4, 8, 9, 10	343	472 level II	.73
T5, 7, 12	161	235 level III	.69
Totals	992	1207	

A summary of the number of lines of teacher talk in the transcripts is given in Table 1. Findings are presented according to the language fluency level of the LEP students engaged in interaction.

Chi-square calculations reveal that the amount of language utilized with LEP students as a group is significantly more than the amount used with non-LEP students as a group (p < .001). Looking at the three language fluency levels involved, we find significant differences (p. < .001) at both levels II and III. At level I, however, the difference between the two groups is not significant, a finding totally out of line with the others. This deviation is attributable to T3, who did not request the LEP student to order a second item. If the frequency counts for T3 are removed from the calculations, the difference in the amount of language used with NS and LEP students is also significant (p < .05). Thus, teachers talked significantly more to LEP students, regardless of fluency level, in the task situations.

When an analogous analysis of the amount of time used in each dyad is done, results are not significant. This finding is examined in the discussion section.

Not only did teachers in the study talk to LEP students more, they organized the task quite differently for them with respect to abbreviation. Recall that the following steps from the task were studied in the transcripts:

II. Fill out order blank for first item
    C. Write catalog number
      1. Find picture of item
      2. Find letter
      3. Find description
      4. Find catalog number
      5. Find blank

III. Fill out order blank for second item
    C. Write catalog number
      1. Find picture of item
      2. Find letter
      3. Find description
      4. Find catalog number
      5. Find blank

TABLE 2 Summary of Instructional Tasks—Steps Specified and Persons Responsible*

Strategic Step	T1						T2					
	T	*M*	*NS*	*T*	*M*	*LEP*	*T*	*M*	*NS*	*T*	*M*	*LEP*
Intro 1:												
II.C.1												
2												
3												
4												
5												
Intro 2:												
III.C.1												
2												
3												
4												
5												
Item 1:												
II.C.1	X			X			X			X		
2		X	X					X			X	
3		X	X					X			X	
4		X	X					X	X			
5		X	X				X	X				
Item 2:												
III.C.1	X			X			X			X		
2		X				X		X				X
3		X				X		X	X			
4	X					X				X	X	
5		X				X		X				X

*Placement of X's indicates which of the task steps were specified, as well as who was responsible for them. An X in the T column shows that the step was teacher-regulated. An X in the M column indicates a student-regulated step that was mediated by the teacher. An X in either the LEP or NS column shows that the step was student-regulated.

Table 2 (continued)

Strategic Step	T3						T4					
	T	M	NS	T	M	LEP	T	M	NS	T	M	LEP
Intro 1:												
II.C.1								X		X		
2								X		X		
3								X		X		
4							X					
5							X				X	
Intro 2:												
III.C.1								X				
2								X				
3										X		
4								X				
5								X				
Item 1:												
II.C.1		X		X			X			X		
2	X			X				X	X			
3	X			X				X				X
4	X			X			X					X
5		X		X				X		X		
Item 2:												
III.C.1		X					X			X		
2			X					X	X			
3		X						X				X
4	X							X			X	
5			X					X		X		

Strategic Step	T5						T6					
	T	M	NS	T	M	LEP	T	M	NS	T	M	LEP
Intro 1:												
II.C.1		X		X				X		X		
2		X		X			X					X
3	X			X			X				X	
4	X			X			X				X	
5	X			X								
Intro 2:												
III.C.1								X				X
2							X			X		
3										X		
4										X		
5												
Item 1:												
II.C.1		X			X					X	X	
2		X			X		X					X
3		X			X					X	X	
4		X			X		X				X	
5		X			X					X		X
Item 2:												
III.C.1		X		X				X	X			
2		X			X		X			X		
3		X	X							X		X
4		X	X							X	X	
5		X	X							X	X	

Table 2 (continued)

Strategic Step	T7						T8					
	T	M	NS	T	M	LEP	T	M	NS	T	M	LEP
Intro 1:												
II.C.1										X		
2										X		
3										X		
4										X		
5												
Intro 2:												
III.C.1										X		
2												
3												
4												
5												
Item 1:												
II.C.1		X		X				X		X		
2	X				X			X				X
3		X		X			X					X
4		X		X			X				X	
5		X			X				X		X	
Item 2:												
III.C.1		X		X			X					X
2			X	X						X	X	
3			X	X						X		X
4			X	X			X				X	
5			X			X				X		X

Strategic Step	T9						T10					
	T	M	NS	T	M	LEP	T	M	NS	T	M	LEP
Intro 1:												
II.C.1												
2	X											
3												
4	X											
5												
Intro 2:												
III.C.1												
2												
3												
4												
5												
Item 2:												
II.C.1		X		X			X			X		
2		X	X				X			X		
3		X	X					X		X		
4	X		X					X			X	
5		X				X			X		X	
Item 2:												
III.C.1		X		X				X	X			
2			X			X	X		X			
3			X			X				X	X	
4		X	X				X				X	
5		X				X				X		X

106

Table 2 (continued)

Strategic Step	T11						T12					
	T	M	NS	T	M	LEP	T	M	NS	T	M	LEP
Intro 1:												
II.C.1												
2												
3												
4												
5												
Intro 2:												
III.C.1												
2												
3												
4												
5												
Item 1:												
II.C.1	X			X			X			X		
2	X			X			X			X		
3	X		X					X				X
4	X		X				X			X		
5	X		X				X			X		
Item 2:												
III.C.1	X			X			X			X		
2	X		X				X			X		
3	X			X						X		X
4	X			X			X			X		
5		X		X						X		X

A summary of these strategic steps is presented in Tables 2 and 3. In Table 2, the Roman numerals and numbers at left correspond to the steps just listed. X's indicate which step of the task was specified. Further, placement of X's in different columns indicates whether the step was teacher-regulated (T), student-regulated with mediation (M), or student-regulated (NS or LEP). Five of the teachers gave an overview of the forms before proceeding to the ordering of items. Since such introductions affect subsequent ordering, they are included in the chart as well.

To illustrate how the summaries in Table 2 were arrived at, let us look at a portion of the transcripts from three teachers. T12, for instance, had the following exchange with a LEP student when directing the ordering of the first item:

T: Okay, (student's name), I've got an order blank here. Two things here I'd like for you to order. One is letter F (points to item). Let's see, it's a wall blackboard . . .

       Okay, see if you can find the catalog number yourself. Ah, this is the board. See if you can find the letter F. Write the catalog number down. You see the letter F?

LEP: (Nods yes.) Like this?

T: We're going to put it on one line here. See if you can find the letter F.

LEP: Oh. (Points to description of item. Writes "F" on form.)

TABLE 3 Composite Abbreviation Scores Reflecting Explicitness and Regulation of Tasks

	T1		T2		T3		T4		T5		T6	
	NS	LEP	NS	LEP	NS	LEP	NS	LEP	NS	LEP	NS	LEP
Intro. 1*							-2	-4	-3	-5	-3	-2
Intro. 2								-4			-1	-2
Item 1*	+2	-3	0	-3	-3	-4	+3	-1	+5	+5	+3	-1
Item 2	+3	+3	+4	+1	+1		+4	0	+5	+1	+4	-2
Composite dyad score†	+5	0	+4	-2	-2		+7	-1	+10	+6	+7	-3
Difference score‡	+5		+6				+8		+4		+10	

	T7		T8		T9		T10		T11		T12	
	NS	LEP	NS	LEP	NS	LEP	NS	LEP	NS	LSP	NS	LEP
Intro. 1				-4	-2							
Intro. 2				-1								
Item 1	-1	-3	-1	+1	+2		-1	-3	0	-3	-4	-4
Item 2	+4	-2	+3	+2	+4	+3	+2	-1	+1	-1	0	0
Composite dyad score	+3	-5	+2	+3	+6	+2	+1	-4	+1	-4	-4	-4
Difference score	+8		-1		+4		+5		+5		0	

*Scores for introductions 1 and 2 and items 1 and 2 result from adding the values assigned to the X's in Table 7. X's in the T column receive -1; in the M column, zero; and in the NS or LEP column, +1.

†The composite dyad score is the sum of the scores for items 1 and 2.

‡The difference score is the LEP score subtracted from the NS score.

In this case, although the teacher specifically mentions each step, the responsibility for finding the information or determining where to put it rests with the student. In the chart, then, five X's are marked in the M column.

While Table 2 illustrates trends in the differential treatment of NS students, quantification of the data is essential to focus on the degree and direction of those differences. Thus, values were assigned to the behaviors manifested: -1 for any X in the T column, zero for an X in the M column, and +1 for an X in the NS or LEP column. Scores were tabulated by teacher for each catalog item ordered. Thus, abbreviation scores per item could range from a minimum of -5 (for highly explicit, teacher-regulated interactions) to a maximum of +5 (for nonexplicit, student-regulated interactions). Further, scores from the two items ordered were added so that a composite abbreviation score could be had for each dyad. These scores, then, can range from -10 to +10, with the latter value again representing the most abbreviated interaction. Finally, difference scores for each teacher were calculated by subtracting the LEP dyad score from the NS dyad score. Potentially the scores can range from -20 to +20. The larger the score, the more extreme the difference in treatment of the two groups. Direction is indicated by positive and negative numbers: positive numbers represent more abbreviated interactions with NS students; negative values, more abbreviated interactions with LEP students. Table 3 summarizes these tabulations.

One finding obvious from these data is the large variations in strategic style among the teachers. With respect to the composite dyad scores (item 1 plus item 2), for example, teachers in interaction with NS students had scores ranging from −4 to +10 (T12 and T5, respectively). In interaction with LEP students, teachers showed a score range of −5 to +6 (T7 and T5, respectively). Difference scores (NS minus LEP) reflect this variation as well. Differences range from zero (T12) to +10 (T6). Another variation was in the use of introductory explanations.[4] Five of the teachers utilized this technique: three with both types of student, one with the NS only, and one with the LEP only.

Despite the degree of variation in instructional strategies among the teachers, very strong patterns are evident. One such pattern is the shift in abbreviation from the first item ordered to the second. In the NS dyads, eleven of the twelve teachers were more abbreviated in their organization of the instructions when ordering the second item than when ordering the first item. T5 showed no increase; however, the scores (both +5) already represent the maximum in nonexplicit, student-regulated behaviors. In the LEP dyads, nine teachers showed increased abbreviation of the instructional task when progressing from the first to the second item ordered. Two (T5 and T6) showed decreased abbreviation. (T3 could not be evaluated since the LEP student was not requested to order a second item.) Thus, with both types of students involved in the instructional interaction, there is a consistent pattern of increased abbreviation as the task situation progresses. That is, fewer steps of the task were specified, and less teacher regulation was utilized for both NS and LEP students when ordering the second item.[5]

In spite of this common trend in interactions with both NS and LEP students, important differences emerge when one compares speech to the two groups per item ordered. Regarding the first item, ten of the twelve teachers were more abbreviated in their speech to native speakers. Two (T5 and T12) evidenced speech to the two types of students that was no different. For the second item, nine NS interactions were more abbreviated than the corresponding LEP interactions; two (T1 and T12) were no different. (Again T3 was not included.)

When the abbreviation scores for the dyads are ranked, and the Mann-Whitney U test is used to analyze the data, the differences are found to be significant ($p=.0028$). Thus, as a group, teachers structure the instructional task situation in a significantly more abbreviated manner for NS students than for LEP students. That is, the interactions with LEP students are more teacher-regulated, and the steps of the task made more explicit than for the NS students.

DISCUSSION

The results of the analysis of the data presented here are particularly interesting when viewed from the perspective of other classroom-centered findings. Take, for example, the finding that a significantly larger amount of speech occurs with LEP students, although the time spent with them in the task situation is not significantly greater. The notion has been presented that some teachers may not interact with LEP students in their classes because of a belief that such interaction would be too time-consuming (Schinke 1981, Schinke-Llano 1983). If this is true for a number of teachers, as is believed, the results of this phase of the study indicate that this assumption is ill-founded. Given equally demanding task situations, teachers do not spend significantly more time with LEP students than with NS students.

Another explanation offered for the lack of interaction with LEP students in class is the belief on the part of teachers that LEP students are not capable of participating in the interaction (Schinke 1981, Schinke-Llano 1983). Again, the results presented here do not support this supposition. All LEP students performed the task as directed. Granted that the speech to the LEP students was found to be less abbreviated, i.e., more teacher-regulated and more explicit, than that to native speakers, these characteristics raise an intriguing question. Given the fact that all LEP students performed at whatever the level of abbreviation directed to them, was the differential treatment necessary?

We have already seen that the LEP students did not take significantly longer to perform their tasks. That they took longer at all may have been due precisely to the teachers' speech being greater in amount, more teacher-regulated, and more explicit. Only two teachers (T5 and T6) felt it necessary to lessen abbreviation between the first item ordered and the second. In the case of T5, that change seemed totally unnecessary since the LEP student had already ordered the first item completely without assistance from the teacher. In the case of T6, the shift was more warranted since the student was having difficulty; yet the change was slight—from a score of −1 on the first item to −2 on the second. Thus, out of an assumption that LEP students cannot fully participate in an instructional situation, teachers may be making their speech more explicit and their tasks more teacher-regulated than necessary.

Certainly there is evidence, albeit anecdotal, that teachers in the study were unaware of the ability of the LEP students to perform in an instructional task situation or that they anticipated problems with them. Prior to beginning the task with the LEP student, T3 said, "This is going to be difficult." T5 sighed deeply at the onset of the taping. T6 asked incredulously, "I've got do to this with him?" T8 stated, "It's going to take me longer to explain." (Actually, T8 took exactly the same amount of time with each student.) T9 asserted, "This is going to be hard." "This is going to be fun," T11 commented, rolling her eyes heavenward. Only T12 positively acknowledged the LEP student: "She speaks English pretty well." After the task, however, several teachers expressed surprise or pleasure with the performance of the LEP students. T3, for example, stated, "I wish I could talk to her more. She seems so bright." T5 looked pleasantly surprised at the completed order form. T6 and T11 offered comments to the observer of "Not bad" and "Nice job." Such comments coupled with the fact that LEP students did perform the task as directed certainly lend credence to the notion that teachers' perceptions of LEP students' abilities may be inaccurate.

The preceding comments are not intended to dismiss that fact that the students in question are, indeed, limited in their command of English. Further, it is apparent from the data that the teachers utilize language differently to structure cognitive activities of LEP students than for their native-speaker counterparts. The most important question, however, remains unanswered: What are the ramifications of such modified interactions for LEP students?

IMPLICATIONS

Before we discuss the implications of the interaction patterns observed, it is important to comment on the issue of perceptions. It has already been stated that foreigner talk is used because of perceptions on the part of the speaker that the interlocutor cannot function adequately in his second language. Therefore, a crucial question, especially in the context of a school setting, is whether these perceptions are accurate. In a general conversational context, misperceptions would not be serious. In an instructional situation, however, they may have consequences. Thus, experimental studies are needed that would relate teachers' perceptions of LEP students' abilities on a given task to the speech adjustments evidenced and to the students' subsequent performances.

If teachers' perceptions of LEP students' linguistic and cognitive skills are inaccurate (i.e., if teachers underestimate LEP students' abilities as these data suggest), what are the possible consequences for the students? First, of course, is the issue of second language skills. Second language acquisition may suffer if teachers modify their input based on inaccurate perceptions of the LEP students' linguistic abilities, particularly their receptive skills. The data presented here do not constitute evidence for this claim. However, if one accepts Krashen's theory of optimal input (1982) and Long's position on the role of modified interaction (1980, 1981), it is then reasonable to conclude that overly modified input will serve to impede the students' progress in English, in the domains of both BICS and CALP (Cummins 1980). Empirical studies are, of course, needed to investigate these questions.

If one accepts the conclusion just stated that second language development may be negatively affected by unnecessarily modified input, it is then logical to conclude that cognitive development may be negatively affected, as well. Once again, the data reported here do not provide support for this statement. Nonetheless, Cummins (1980) claims that academic achievement (i.e., cognitive skills development) relies upon the development of CALP. Thus, if CALP is not sufficiently developed—owing, in this case, to inappropriately modified input—then desired academic achievement on the part of LEP students will not result. While the cognitive consequences suggested here are speculative, they are sufficiently serious to warrant further investigation.

Now that the possible negative consequences of modified input and interaction based on inaccurate perceptions of students' abilities have been discussed, it is appropriate to examine the opposite situation. If one were to assume that the teachers in the study adjusted their language in ways appropriate for interaction with the LEP students, one certainly could not claim that either linguistic or cognitive development would be affected. Interestingly, however, the same basic research questions remain unanswered. That is, what is the relationship between modified input and interaction and second language acquisition and cognitive skills development in a second language? If one assumes that modifications can be either facilitative of or detrimental to linguistic and cognitive skills development, what, then, is the nature—and extent—of these adjustments that facilitate L2 acquisition and cognitive development?

CONCLUSION

It has been shown that teachers utilize language differently to structure task situations for LEP students than for native English-speaking students. Thus, LEP students in joint cognitive activities experience a different linguistic environment than do their NS counterparts. Such differential treatment, especially if based on inaccurate perceptions of the LEP students' abilities, may have negative consequences for second language acquisition and cognitive skills development. The nature of the relationship between modified input and interaction and the development of both second language and cognitive skills is, of course, yet to be determined.

APPENDIX A

MAIL ORDER FORM

Send to: _____
Name

_____
Street Number & Name

_____
City   State   Zip

Telephone: _____

Form of payment:

Check   Money   Credit
          Order   Card

Quantity	Catalog Number	Color or Size	Page	Name of Item	Weight	Price	Total

TOTAL AMOUNT ENCLOSED

APPENDIX B

Steps Necessary to Complete Catalog Order Form

I. Fill out top
   A. Write name
   B. Write address
      1. Write street number and name
      2. Write city
      3. Write state
      4. Write zip code
   C. Write telephone number
   D. Mark form of payment
      1. Credit card
      2. Check
      3. Money order

II. Fill out order blank for first item
   A. Select item
   B. Write quantity
      1. Decide how many
      2. Find blank
   C. Write catalog number
      1. Find picture of item
      2. Find letter
      3. Find description
      4. Find catalog number
      5. Find blank
   D. Write color or size
      1. Find color or size
      2. Find blank
   E. Write page number
      1. Find page number
      2. Find blank
   F. Write name of item
      1. Find name of item
      2. Find blank
   G. Write weight
      1. Find weight
      2. Find blank
   H. Write price
      1. Find price
      2. Find blank
   I. Write line total
      1. Do any necessary calculations
      2. Find blank

III. Fill out order blank for second item (same as II)

IV. Fill in grand total
   A. Add prices for two items
   B. Fill in blank

NOTES

1. I would like to express my appreciation to James V. Wertsch for his invaluable assistance in establishing the data analysis procedures for this study. Any errors or misinterpretations are, of course, my own.

2. Ferguson (1971: 143) first described "a kind of 'foreigner talk' which is used by speakers of a language to outsiders who are felt to have very limited command of the language or no knowledge at all." Long (1980) provides a detailed summary of findings of foreigner talk studies.

3. It should be noted that the procedure for the identification of LEP students in Illinois has changed since these data were collected. However, at the time of the study, the language fluency levels were defined according to the following:

I. The student does not speak, understand, or write English, but may know a few isolated words or expressions.

II. The student understands simple sentences in English, especially if spoken slowly but does not speak English, except isolated words or expressions.

III. The student speaks and understands English with hesitancy and difficulty. With effort and help, the student can carry on a conversation in English, understand at least parts of lessons, and follow simple directions.

IV. The student speaks and understands English without apparent difficulty but displays low achievement, indicating some language or cultural interference with learning.

V. The student speaks and understands both English and the home language without difficulty and displays normal academic achievement for grade level.

VI. The student (of non-English background) either predominantly or exclusively speaks English.

4. The use of introductions appears to be correlated with the degree of abbreviation in the subsequent ordering of items. The four NS dyads in which overviews were used manifested the four highest abbreviation scores (T4, 5, 6, 9). Two of the four LEP dyads utilizing overviews evidenced the highest LEP abbreviation scores (T5 and T8).

5. This pattern also manifests itself in progressing from the introductions to the first item ordered.

REFERENCES

Cummins, James. 1980. The exit and entry fallacy in bilingual education. *NABE Journal*, 4: 25–60.

Ferguson, Charles. 1971. Absence of copula and the notion of simplicity: A study of normal speech, baby talk, foreigner talk, and pidgins. In *Pidginization and Creolization of Languages*. Cambridge: Cambridge University Press. 141–150.

Illinois State Board of Education. 1976. Rules and regulations for transitional bilingual education. Springfield, Ill.: author.

Krashen, Stephen. 1982. *Principles and Practice in Second Language Acquisition*. Oxford: Pergamon Press.

Long, Michael. 1980. Input, interaction, and second language acquisition. Unpublished Ph.D. dissertation, University of California at Los Angeles.

Long, Michael. 1981. Input, interaction, and second language acquisition. *Annals of the New York Academy of Sciences*.

Saville-Troike. 1984. What *really* matters in second language learning for academic achievement? *TESOL Quarterly*, 18 (2, June): 199–219.

Schinke, Linda. 1981. English foreigner talk in content classrooms. Unpublished Ph.D. dissertation, Northwestern University.

Schinke-Llano, Linda. 1983. Foreigner talk in content classrooms. In H. W. Seliger and M. H. Long. (eds.). *Classroom Oriented Research in Second Language Acquisition*. Rowley, Mass.: Newbury House. 146–165.

Wong Fillmore, Lily. 1982. Language, minority students and school participation: What kind of English is needed? *Journal of Education*, 164: 143–156.

7

SITUATIONAL DIFFERENCES AND THE SAMPLING OF YOUNG CHILDREN'S SCHOOL LANGUAGE

Ruth Cathcart
Monterey Institute of International Studies

Since the work of classroom discourse analysts and ethnographers documented the existence of interaction patterns unique to elementary school settings (e.g., Sinclair and Coulthard 1975, Mehan 1979a), educational researchers have shown considerable interest in the description and facilitation of conversational competence in children's classroom interaction. Researchers in second language acquisition are also interested in variation in classroom language, especially since it has been shown that second language learners who become competent in some conversational settings still may not succeed in other, more academic, types of communication activities (Cummins 1979, 1981).

Although the study of variation in classroom language is an important area of sociolinguistics, with both theoretical and pedagogical implications, there is presently very little data available on "within-school" language contrasts (Mehan 1979a). The goal of the present study is to provide some information on the nature of language differences across different classroom settings or activities and to construct a model for future study of the relationships of situational variables to classroom language.

STUDIES OF SITUATIONAL VARIATION AND LANGUAGE ACQUISITION

Studies of situational variation in second language acquisition have generally focused on levels of competence, demonstrating that learners perform differently or appear to have varying degrees of competence depending on the task that is used to evaluate them. For example, Dickerson and Dickerson (1977) found that a group of Japanese second language learners appeared to be at different levels of acquisition of a phoneme depending on whether their pronunciation was measured by list reading, dialogue reading, or free speech. Tarone (1983) suggested, based on research such as Dickerson's and others', that learners' interlanguage systems are not a single uniform package of rules and hypotheses. Rather, they include variable rules based on the different contexts in which language is being used and learned.

A very different approach to the study of situational variation in language use is reported by Ervin-Tripp (1977), who has been interested not so much in competence across situations as in the nature of syntactic realizations of one speech act, directives, in several different social settings. Her findings concern such issues as how differences in interlocuters influence the directness or indirectness of command forms.

Still another type of study of situational variation in language use has been done by Cole, Dore, Hall, and Dowley (1978). These researchers compared groups of 3- and 4-year-old preschool children in two situations (a supermarket trip and a discussion of the same trip in the classroom with their teacher). In the market, discussion centered on available objects and ongoing activities, whereas in the classroom, the discussion of the same activities was displaced in time and space. Even though most of the conversations involved adults' eliciting information from the children and the topic in both places was "supermarket," the different physical situations (especially the presence or absence of the referent objects of the discussion) caused very different interactional demands and corresponding differences in language. For example, since adults realized the greater cognitive demands that classroom discussion (displaced reference) exerts on younger (3-year-old) children, they adjusted their language, thus influencing the children's language production. Adults asked more yes/no questions of 3-year-olds and more wh- questions to 4-year-olds. Since yes/no responses were shorter for all children, 3-year-olds who answered more of these questions produced shorter and less elaborated utterances.

DEFINING TERMS

Existing studies that discuss situational variation in language use cover a wide range of topics. Thus, in designing a study, researchers must (1) define the scope and type of variation in question and (2) characterize the situations involved. That is, one may choose to focus on production of a single item (such as a phoneme), a group of items (such as directives), or all the language found in a given setting (e.g., a field trip, a classroom). The situation itself may vary from a simple experimental task to a complex setting such as a school.

The present study resembles that of Cole et al. in that the goal is to document the overall nature of language likely to occur in a group of situations or settings, to compare the differences across them, and to identify, where possible, whatever situational variables might contribute to the differences. The basic unit of analysis is the communicative act,[1] although some attention is also directed to syntactic realizations of these acts. The study is set in a kindergarten classroom, and the comparisons are of subsettings of that classroom and the playground (described by Mehan as "within-school" contrasts). In addition, two experimental tasks are included, tasks that are sometimes used in research on young children to stimulate spontaneous language.[2]

The within-school settings are as defined by the participants. Using participant-designated social settings, variously called "contexts" (Erickson and Schultz 1977), "activity structures" (Bossert 1977), or "participant structures" (Phillips 1972), is traditional in classroom ethnography. Mehan (1979b) describes participation structures as those units of interaction which are, or can be, overtly identified by the participants. For example, teachers in the present classroom explicitly described the events of the day as "free play," "recess," "ESL," etc. In addition, these situations could be and were identified by observers based on bounding by ritual utterances such as "OK, who is ready for recess?" and "Mrs. G.'s group to the rug for ESL." Although the present study is not an ethnography, it did begin with extensive observation and participation in the classroom, and thus it was possible to identify interaction structures as is done in classroom ethnography. This is desirable since, if participant-defined situations are found to be "linguistically real" (i.e., if there are in fact identifiable differences in language across these real school situations), the study is likely to be of more direct use to classroom teachers. In this study, the neutral terms "situation," "setting," and "activity" are used interchangeably to refer to the participant-designated activities and experimental tasks under examination. This study is deliberately observational and nonstatistical because it is felt that too little is presently known about the nature and motivation of classroom conversation to allow appropriate selection and control of variables. The aim of the study is to raise plausible issues for further examination in the study of the discourse of young language learners.

THE SUBJECTS

The study was carried out in the kindergarten class of a bilingual school situated in a northern California suburban industrial community of about 33,000 people. The data for the study were collected from eight Spanish-speaking children in the Spanish-English bilingual class. The eight learners included four girls and four boys, ranging in age from 5.0 to 5.6 at the beginning of the study. The subjects were the only children classified as non-English-speaking (NES) at the beginning of the school year. There were also approximately 40 other children in the team-taught class (both bilinguals and monolingual English speakers).

THE DATA

The data used in this study are part of a larger sample of data collected for a study on individual differences.[3] The contexts or situations examined provided a fairly complete sample and overview of the activities the children engaged in every day. The only type of activity that was excluded involved the "whole-group" structure where 40 children were singing or listening to announcements. Under these conditions it was virtually impossible to collect data on individual children. The classroom settings identified by teachers and researchers included:

1. Recess: outdoor free play; all children together
2. Seatwork: a drawing or cut-and-paste activity; all children at long tables
3. Free play: indoor educational play with a choice of toys set out by the teachers; all children together
4. ESL: the time designated for limited English proficient (LEP) children to work in a group with the English-speaking teacher

The two situations established by the researchers were:

1. Playhouse: a play setting designed by the researchers to allow observation of a subject playing with one other child who spoke only English (c.f. Wong-Fillmore 1976)
2. Interview and storytelling: sessions in the experimentation room with the subject and the observer sitting at a small table having a discussion.

The corpus of data included a total of 3275 communicative acts collected from the six situations. The number of acts from each situation ranges from 138 in free play to 1822 in the playhouse.

DATA ANALYSIS

The major steps in the collection and analysis of data were:

1. Subjects were observed throughout an academic year in observation periods running from about 15 to 20 minutes (see Table 1 for schedule).
2. All the utterances of the subjects were transcribed and codes for language functions using the taxonomy of communicative acts seen in the appendix. Coding was done by the author, another researcher, and a classroom teacher not otherwise involved in the study. Average agreement between coders on a sample set of transcripts was .82.
3. The number of individual acts seen in each of the situations was tabulated and more detailed analysis of certain acts performed.
4. The incidence of various acts and concurrent situational variables was discussed.[4]
5. A hierarchy of setting variables and communicative acts was created as a framework for future research.[5]

TABLE 1 Display of the Language Sampling Time Line*

Date Situation	Sept./ Oct.	Nov.	Dec.	Jan.	Feb.	Mar.	Apr./ May	Total	Approx. time, hr.
Recess	30	15	1	11	10	3	1	71	17.8
Free play	13	7		2	2	2		26	6.5
Seatwork	24	12	3	4	3			46	11.5
Playhouse				8	8	8		24	10.0
Interview		8					8	16	6.7
Storytelling		8					8	16	2.6
ESL							1	1	0.5
								N=200	55.6

*Numbers indicate number of separate samples.

RESULTS

Most Frequent Acts Within Research Settings (See Table 2)

Recess The most frequent acts used at recess were requests for action (26 percent), calls for attention (8 percent), protests/prohibits (6 percent), and refusals (7 percent). These all fall within the category of control acts, and their frequency at recess provides evidence that much of the children's communication behavior at recess is involved with manipulation or attempting to manipulate the behavior of others, and responding to such attempts.

Free Play Free play is characterized by calls for attention (18 percent), requests for action (11 percent), and refusals (6 percent). The general picture of act frequency differs from that of recess in that requests for objects composed (10 percent) of the data and requests for information another (10 percent). In addition, an unusual behavior (by one child), pretend reading, made up 7 percent of the data.

Seatwork Seatwork was characterized, as was free play, by calls for attention (18 percent), requests for objects (11 percent), and requests for information (10 percent). However, requests for action were less frequent (below 5 percent), and two additional information-sharing acts comprised more than 5 percent of the corpus. These were "give information" and "imitate." In addition, boundary markers (especially "I finished") made up 5 percent of the data in this setting.

Playhouse In the playhouse, as at recess and free play, calls for attention and requests for action are common, 10 percent and 7 percent, respectively. Requests for information also made up 7 percent of the data. In addition, four other acts that did not reach criterion frequency in other samples made up significant portions of the playhouse data: label objects, label actions (including self-accompanying statements), label attributes, and expressions of intent. Thus, while resembling other play and work situations in some ways, the

122

TABLE 2   Characterization of the Situations by Most Frequent Acts* (in % of Total Acts)

	Recess	Free play	Seatwork	Interview and storytelling	Playhouse	ESL
Control acts:						
Initiate						
Call attention	8	18	18		10	
Request object		10	11			
Request action	26	11			7	
Protest, prohibit	6					
Respond						
Refuse	7	6				
Social/play acts:						
Boundary markers			5			
"Reading"		7				
Information-sharing acts:						
Announce or initiate						
Describe						31
Label object					5	
Label action					5	
Expressive						
Express intent					7	
Request and respond						
Request information		6	10		7	
Give information			6	38		41
Shift, avoid				11		
Imitate			6			
Confirm				30		
n=	191	138	212	354	1822	236

*Table entries represent percentages; n=frequency of act tokens.

playhouse is unique both in the wider variety of acts and in the use of descriptive information-sharing acts.

   Interview and storytelling   The major portion of the subjects' language in the interview samples is made up of giving the information solicited by the interviewer (38 percent) or confirming her suggestions (30 percent). In addition, a certain percentage of the children's acts serves to shift attention or avoid answering the interviewer's questions (11 percent). Storytelling language raises an interesting issue for data collection and the definition of language proficiency in general. By the current "social" coding system, nearly all storytelling acts, being responses to elicitations such as "and what happened here?" consisted of "give information" acts. However, the forms of these acts were unusual in that they could also resemble labels of actions, statements of intent, etc., depending on what type of story the elicitor chose. A researcher with a syntax-focused research question such as "Can children produce future tense forms?" could effectively use storytelling samples for a quick measure of this language ability. However, working within a social-interactional definition of communicative acts, one cannot accept these utterances simply as equal to "expressions of intent," the other act that motivated future tense markings. The issue of interest is one familiar to testers: Can the elicitation of (or failure to elicit) syntactic forms of a given type in a test situation represent appropriate use of these forms or acts in the situation where they would normally be produced spontaneously?

Control Acts

In this section a subset of the children's communicative acts is discussed in detail. This subset consists of those acts used to control or manipulate behavior, control acts. In the interest of space it was necessary to focus on one portion of the children's communicative acts; the category of control acts was chosen arbitrarily over the other major category, information sharing. (For a detailed analysis of information-sharing acts, see Cathcart 1983.)

Two questions are posed in this examination of the children's use of control acts: (1) Can the nature and distribution of the individual control acts shed light on the question of which situational variables seem to influence them? (2) Are the main differences across situations to be found in the frequency of occurrence of the acts or in the grammatical realization of the acts and the forms that result from them?

Most of the control acts were found in four situations: recess, free play, seatwork, and playhouse. Their distribution, expressed in percentages of the acts within each situation, can be seen in Table 3.

Calls for Attention   The percentages of calls for attention are similar in free play and playhouse samples (30 and 29 percent), but rather large differences in relative quantity are seen in the recess (10 percent) and seatwork (43 percent) samples. The differences between recess calls for attention and others are clear. Most of the calls at recess are of the form: "Lookit!" "Lookit, J." or "Hey!" These one-word imperatives do not seem to meet with much success in engaging other children's attention. The calls for attention that make up 43 percent of the control acts in the seatwork sample, on the other hand, consist mostly of attempts to solicit compliments, especially from the teacher. The children hold up their papers and call out:

"Mrs. P.!"   "Lookit mine!"   "Lookit pretty!"   "Lookit, Mrs. A.!"

Most of the attention calling for compliments is directed toward the teacher, and direct address is common. So are object complements, directing attention to the objects to be praised: "Lookit a nose!"

Although the percentages of control acts used to call attention in free play and the playhouse are similar, their uses and resulting forms are not the same. In the free play samples, calls seem to consist of two main types: calls similar to those seen to children at recess (e.g., "Hey!") and calls for compliments on achievements (bragging?) like "lookit mine!" similar to those seen in seatwork,

TABLE 3 Percentage of Total Control Acts That Each Control Act Represents* (within situations)

Control acts	Recess	Free play	Seatwork	Playhouse
Initiate				
Call attention	10	30	43	29
Request object	3	17	27	8
Request action	35	18	7	20
Invite, offer	4	1		4
Warn, threaten	4	1	3	
Request permission	5	2	2	4
Protest, prohibit	8	6	7	2
Claim possessions	1	8	1	8
Claim roles	3	2		6
Complain	3		2	
Support				
Repeat, confirm	7	4	1	7
Add, expand		1		
Clarify			1	
Intensify	2			1
Respond				
Comply	3		1	4
Refuse	9	10	4	6
Ignore	1			
n=	147	84	90	633

*Table entries represent percentages; n=frequency of act tokens.

but directed to other children rather than the teacher. The playhouse samples, however, show a large number of calls specifically directing the interlocutor to focus on a certain play object (e.g., "lookit this!") in addition to calls to the playmate ("Hey, F.!").

Calls for attention, then, are normally simple imperatives. The general use for them, as their name implies, is to get attention, but their secondary functions are difference in different situations. While at recess the children called out frequently to attract another child to a game, many seatwork calls attempted to solicit compliments on academic achievements and a fair portion of the calls in the playhouse setting directed interlocutors to a potential play object.

Requests for objects The requests for objects in seatwork samples differ from other settings in two ways: first, a much larger percentage of control acts here are requests for objects (27 percent as opposed to 17 percent in free play, 8 percent in playhouse, and 3 percent in recess). Second, "need" statements and indirect requests occur here and are rare or nonexistent in other samples. For example, children say "I don't have a color" and "me no tail" and "I need yellow".

The finding that indirect directives occur exclusively in seatwork samples is consistent with descriptions of types of control acts used by L1 learners (Ervin-Tripp 1977). Ervin-Tripp states that young children are able to use

125

nonimperative request forms like "I want juice," and an adult will interpret the utterance as a directive and supply the juice. In the same way that children come to expect parents to supply food and drinks, the necessitites of life, teachers are expected to supply paper, paste, and other classroom tools. Thus the nature of the seatwork task, being assigned and required by the teacher, includes a role for a supplier of necessities. Children expect to present their needs to this person and have them fulfilled without insisting or negotiating.

The situation is quite different in play settings, where children may desire to obtain objects that are in the temporary possession of other children and where they know that obtaining these things may require force ("Gimme . . . ") or polite negotiation ("Lemme have it please."). In the playhouse, requests for objects include mainly imperatives with "Lemme," "Gimme," and "I want," as seen in these examples:

```
Lemme + put it please
        use da keys
        see
Gimme + one
        dis
        my necklace
I wan' + dis
        tea
        dis motorcycle
```

These constructions also appear occasionally in the other situations. "Gimme" requests are seen especially in attempts to get objects from other children in free play, while "I want" statements occur in recess and seatwork samples (especially when children attempt to obtain objects from adults). "Lemme" is less common, produced by only one child in recess and seatwork in what seems to be a "formulaic" or "chunked" expression, "Lemme see." Nonformulaic "Lemme" constructions may be acquired later by language learners since they require verb complements rather than nouns or noun phrases.

Requests for action Requests for action consist of the directives typically used to manipulate the behavior of others ("Get out!" "Come here!") as well as indirect requests and suggestions. In the seatwork samples, there were very few requests for action (7 percent of all the control acts). One of these ("I dunno how to write my name") is the same sort of indirect request as was seen in requests for objects in the seatwork (compare with "I don't have yellow" from the same sample). Again, the child seems to assume that someone will provide the required assistance if he simply states the problem since namewriting is a necessary (teacher-assigned) part of completing the task.

The other requests for action in the seatwork sample are all task-related requests for action given by one child to another on the topic of placing pieces of paper on a cut-and-paste owl ("down here," "ober here," "the eyes is over here").

126

In the playhouse and free play samples, the requests for action percentages were similar (20 and 18 percent), but they were considerably higher in recess (35 percent). These requests were dissimilar in other ways across the three situations. In the recess samples, the requests were nearly all simple one- or two-word imperatives, for example:

> Push! (on the swings)
> GO! (on the slide)
> Come on! (during running games)
> Get out! (on the bikes)

The free play sample revealed that two of the three children who used requests for action used the same types as were most often found at recess:

> Here! Here!
> Come on!
> Go play!

One child, however, became very involved in building houses from blocks with another child and produced some very different-looking (longer and more complex) requests for action during this interaction:

> Hafta make it big!
> We hasta geda big big.
> We need to make a door.
> High!

Comparison of recess and free play directives, then, shows that much control behavior is a result of the subjects' trying to get other children to participate in an activity, or to get them out of one where they are not wanted. The physical factors of space and fluid groupings seem to motivate the short, often shouted, imperatives found at recess and in the language of some of the children at free play.

The contrast is striking in the free play example where a child's control acts were devoted to organizing steps for an ongoing (block-building) activity. His requests for action are longer, with more complex syntax, and focused on manipulation of objects rather than of other children. This atypical behavior gives insight into how a task within a setting can change the nature of the language behavior observed there.

In all the classroom settings discussed above, then, two factors seem to be influencing the length and complexity of the requests for action: task and interlocutors. First, the requests for action that are made to an adult tend to exceed in length and complexity those which are made to children. Second, when the length and complexity of requests for action are increased during peer interaction, it is among task-related directives during the execution of tasks with a joint goal.[6]

This information might lead us to expect longer and more complex requests for action in the playhouse setting, since the two children have ample opportunity for joint, task-focused play. However, while vocabulary and syntax were more varied in these samples, length and complexity of requests for action were no greater. For example, "we can . . . " and "we're gonna . . . " were used to suggest play, and the direct address form "you" was used in many imperatives ("you fix that," "you cut this").

These patterns might occur because a great deal of time in the playhouse is spent, not in joint play as might be expected, but in negotiation of what type of play should take place. This may be a result of the fact that, only in the playhouse, where space and interlocutors are restricted, do the non-English speakers have equal negotiation status with English speakers, giving rise to large numbers of negotiation directives. That is, in other situations such as free play, where the limited English speakers are at a sociolinguistic disadvantage, their requests for action tend to be simple directives to move other children in or out of their play space. Only if they somehow get into an ongoing joint task with English speakers do more complex, task-directed requests for action appear.

Offers/Invitations and Requests for Permission These functions occurred rather rarely and almost exclusively in the playhouse, but they deserve brief mention for two reasons: first, a large percentage (46 percent) of the invitations and offers were of the interrogative form, "You wanna . . . ?" or "Wanna . . . ?" These were among the rare instances of interrogative forms in the data and almost the only interrogatives addressed to other children. Second, requests for permission also revealed certain information about interrogative forms. When requesting permission from other children, learners used "I wanna . . . " or "Lemme . . . " while, when asking permission from adults, they often used subject-verb inversion, usually with "can" ("Can I eat one?" "Can we open this?") or noninverted forms with interrogative intonation ("Tomorrow I can play again?"). It is notable that statements with question intonation (except "you wanna . . . ?") or subject-verb inversions are rarely used with peers. If this finding is supported by data on other functions of interrogative forms, it might provide a situational clue as to where most question forms are used (i.e. mainly with adults) and thus to why and how they are acquired.

Complaints Functionally, complaints seem to be an indirect request for action, a request that an adult control some behavior of another child. However, the forms they take are unique among the control act data: third person singulars ("He say me stupid," "We change and now he want it back," "Da girl, she not let me use da bike"). "Errors" were common here, as none of the verbs is properly inflected and negatives are incorrectly formed. On the other hand, these utterances are longer and more "analyzed" (nonformulaic) and thus provide evidence of more linguistic development than most other control acts used by the children. It seems possible that it is in making these complaints that some of the children are using their knowledge of English to its fullest. Thus, it could be that observing or eliciting complaints in a realistic situation could help a researcher identify the upper level of a child's syntactic competence.

In terms of sociolinguistic boundaries of complaints, it is notable that, as with requests for permission, the more complex and atypical forms of the acts are used to adults in child-initiated interactions.

Refusals and compliances These acts occurred in nearly all the situations. Compliances were largely of the form "OK," occasionally accompanied by a permission statement, as in "OK, you be the doctor." Refusals were often of the form "No!" especially at recess and free play.

In the playhouse and seatwork samples, other forms of refusals occurred. Seatwork refusals were limited to: "That not mine!" (after being asked to pick up something) and "Hey, I'm not finished!" (when someone tried to collect his paper). Playhouse refusals, however, tended to be "No" plus a justification or expansion, as in "No, I'm da mommy," "No, I want it." There were also several occurrences of fully negated utterances like "I don't want some" or "I no talk to you." The playhouse refusals are among the few instances of sentence-internal negation in the data.

Overall, negative forms are low in frequency. It seems that children do a lot of requesting objects or actions, and much less refusing or complying with these requests. This implies that the children around the learners may use fewer control acts than the learners themselves. Without further analysis it may only be speculated that this situation arises because getting attention and getting others to respond in concrete ways (e.g., by performing actions or giving objects) are social strategies (Wong-Fillmore 1976) for getting one-to-one interactions in an attempt to obtain comprehensible, contextualized language input.

It may also be that, in the playhouse, the subjects are in a position of power relative to their interlocutors since they are nominated by the researcher and have the choice of which English speaker they will invite to play. Ervin-Tripp et al. (1984) have shown that more control acts are addressed to subordinates and fewer to those in power in children's play interactions. Thus, for this general social reason as well, the learners would be expected to direct the behavior of the native speakers more than the native speakers would direct theirs.

SUMMARY

Detailed examination of control acts revealed several facts:

1. Calls for attention, while occurring with similar frequency across some situations, may differ in length and complexity. In addition, the same acts may have different secondary functions. In recess samples, for example, calls for attention are used to manipulate the children's participation in games, and in seatwork they are used to solicit compliments.

2. A large number of indirect requests for objects are included in the control acts used by children during seatwork. This use of indirectness seems to be a result of the children's assumption that adults (teachers) will supply the goods and services necessary for them to complete assigned tasks.

3.   Similarly, indirect requests for action often occur during seatwork activities. Differences in length and complexity of requests for action can be seen in various play samples. These differences seem to depend on differences in interlocutors, and whether a task is in progress or under negotiation.

4.   Complaints, used mainly at recess, provide most of the obligatory contexts for use of third person singulars in the data. It is possible that, in this setting, learners are often stretched to the fullest use of their knowledge of English syntax.

5.   Refusals were found in several situations but were especially notable in the playhouse, causing much of the sentence-internal negation in the data as well as a number of utterances composed of "No!" plus an assertion.

CONTINUA OF SITUATIONAL VARIABLES

The foregoing analysis suggests that four major situational variables affect certain aspects of language behavior: conversational control, interlocutors, task stage, and task type. These variables can be represented on the four continua as shown in Figure 1.

The endpoints of the first continuum, conversational control, are control of the interaction by the subject, and lack of control by the subject. The interlocutor may be adult or child. The interview and ESL lessons exemplify control of conversation by adults, while at recess conversation is often controlled by other children for different reasons. Situations where subjects have control are characterized by a wide variety of communicative acts and syntactic structures. In contrast, noncontrol situations seem to produce single-word utterances, short phrases, and many formulaic chunks.

The second continuum represents the variety of age and authority relationships that may characterize the interlocutor. Situations in which an adult was interlocutor tend to give rise to more information sharing, while child interlocutors inspire more control acts.

The third continuum concerns task stage, or the degree of joint involvement of the learner in a task and/or conversation topic. At one extreme there is no task or conversation topic, such as when a child is wandering around the playground. At the next stage a task or topic may be under negotiation, for example, when a child asks someone a question, requests permission, or makes an introductory statement or suggestion. The third point on the continuum represents joint task involvement. This may take place when the two interlocutors have agreed upon the work or game at hand, and their communication topic pertains to this task. At the other extreme lies routine or ritual involvement in a well-established task for which negotiation is unnecessary. Different task stages involve the selection of different individual communicative acts. For example, more requests for objects are used where tasks are already established and work on the task is proceeding. This is also true for complaints about violation of task

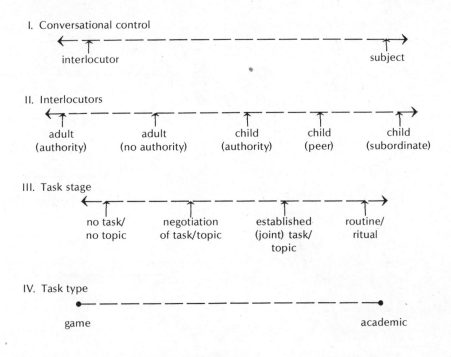

I. Conversational control

interlocutor   subject

II. Interlocutors

| adult | adult | child | child | child |
| (authority) | (no authority) | (authority) | (peer) | (subordinate) |

III. Task stage

no task/	negotiation	established	routine/
no topic	of task/topic	(joint) task/	ritual
		topic	

IV. Task type

game   academic

FIGURE 1 Continua of Situational Variables

or game rules, insults, and imitations. For negotiation of tasks, however, children choose expressions of intent, labels of objects and ongoing actions, and claims or assignment of possessions. Ervin-Tripp et al. (in press) also report use of different functions related to task stage, especially that refusals, denials, and prohibitions are more common during the "stage-setting" or negotiating phase. Where no task is established, calls for attention and certain requests for action seem to typify the learner's production data.

The last continuum concerns task type, or the idea that the specific task seems to govern the selection of certain communicative acts and the surface forms of many utterances. For example, some of the language produced in games is different from that produced in academic tasks, and pretend play may involve different language from that used during a block-building project.

An integration of these variables can be seen in the hierarchical model in Figure 2. This display indicates more clearly which language was found in conjunction with each variable configuration (including the information-sharing acts discussed in Cathcart 1983). The model provides a summary of the present findings and a basis for future examination of the relationship of setting variables and language in young second language learners. The supercategory of this model is the overall conversational structure of a situation, specifically whether or not it allows the learner to control the conversation (e.g., nominate and establish topics, solicit information).

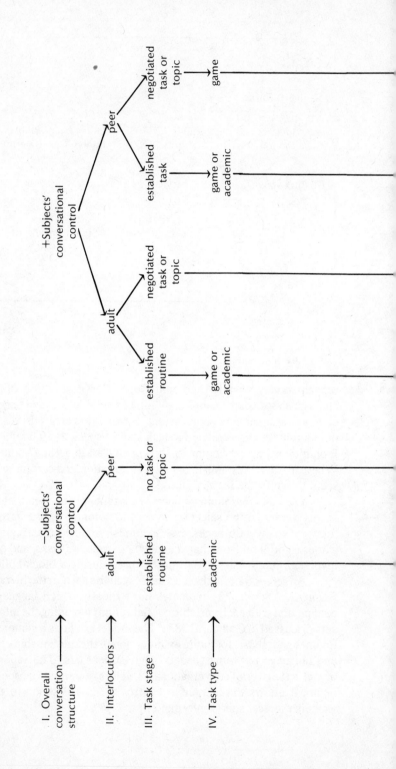

Communicative acts Control		call attention protest request action	complain request object	request permission	request object request action	call attention request permission offer claim
Information	give information confirm shift/avoid	(brag)* (exclaim)		request information	request information (insult) (imitate)	request information express intention deny/contradict label action label object
Examples	"feaders" "yeh" "I dunno."	"Come on!" "Stop it!" "Lookit!" ("No hands!")	"I don't have red." "He not let me play."	"Can I do it?" "This is yours?"	"We can put dis." "We got to make it big." ("Yous ugly.")	"Hey, Jesse," "You wanna ..." "Dis is mine." "This is for play?" "No. I'm the doctor." "I'm gonna cook." "I'm going ..."

*Items in parentheses were frequent for one or a few subjects in this situation.

FIGURE 2 Hierarchy of Situational Variables

A possible combination of variables allowed by following a row of arrows in this figure will be called a variable configuration. (For example, one variable configuration beginning at the top left and moving down would include subject conversational control, adult interlocutor, established task.) The first level of that configuration represents the lack of learner control that occurs when an adult or authority figure assumes control of the settings and imposes a conversational structure and a task upon it (as in the ESL lesson in this study). The language accompanying such a configuration of variables is generally restricted to the minimal forms that will meet the requirements of the controlling adult, here short phrases or single words.

Another conversational structure where there can be a lack of learner control occurs where peers are present and available but the subject is unable to enter into any task or topic collaboration because of either the nature of the activities, his own reticence, or lack of social or linguistic ability. In this case, no topic collaboration is established, as exemplified by most of the recess data and parts of the free play samples. Such a configuration leads to many unsuccessful calls for attention, and manipulation of the physical positioning of others through requests for action and prohibition ("Come here!" "Stop!"), but few other types of utterances.

On the right side of the figure (columns 3 to 6) are the factors related to general conversational structures where subjects can or do control the conversations. There are two cases where children can control conversations with adult interlocutors. First is where an established or ritualized routine is taking place among children (e.g., a game with certain rules or an academic task with certain prespecified procedures). The adult is present or nearby but not in control of the conversation. Thus the child may initiate interactions with her at will, particularly concerning objects or actions necessary for completing the task, or violation of the rules (e.g., complaints like: "He no let me play").

Another similar configuration occurs when an adult is present but not in control of the conversation, but there is no particular established (school) routine underway. This is seen in the playhouse sample, where children negotiate with adults, requesting information and permission related to possible play activities ("Can we play with dis?").

Finally, there are the variable configurations where the child is or may be in conversational control and the interlocutor is a peer. One configuration involves "established task," as in the teacher-designated seatwork, joint building projects in free play, and some joint projects in the playhouse. Here ritual insults occur as well as complex imperatives of various sorts including suggestions. The other ("negotiated task/topic") is exemplified by most of the playhouse interaction. Here the children do most of their topic nomination (related to pretend play, role play, or toy manipulation), including assigning of objects and roles, expressing of intent, and self-accompanying language.

Although syntax is not a major focus of this study, the reorganization of the findings within the model in Figure 2 does illustrate certain things about the children's syntax. First, it can be seen that there is very little syntactic speech accompanying variable structures where others control the conversation. Most of the negation, interrogation, and tense marking occur under "+ subject control" conditions. It also appears that much of the syntax subjectively described as complex or "analyzed" (e.g., indirect requests, third person singular inflections) occurs with adults in the "+ subject control" column.

These findings indicate that both form and function may vary systematically across classrooms settings. If data from other studies can be integrated into this model, relationships found here will be confirmed and a predictive model will have been established for future research.

IMPLICATIONS

In an observational study such as this, care must be taken not to overinterpret or overgeneralize results. However, some cautious suggestions can be made regarding the idea of "natural" or "spontaneous" language and the elicitation and sampling of that language.

1. The notion implicit in some studies of children's language that play samples provide the most "natural" language is questionable. On one hand, the present playhouse sample provides the greatest quantity and variety of language, and might be interpreted as support for that view. However, a simple conclusion that those data are therefore the "best" would overlook the purpose for which communicative competence is often being measured, especially in school: successful and mature interaction with adults. If we were to take the teacher's point of view, perhaps the best samples would be those which include the most complex language, syntactically, or those where the learners' "errors" can be observed, as in the recess samples here. An extreme version of either approach cannot be expected to provide a realistic estimate of children's conversational competence.

In addition, there are major differences between the playhouse language and that seen in the most similar classroom setting, "free play." Thus a warning must be issued to researchers attempting to set up "spontaneous" interaction between children that will then be treated as identical to what children are doing on their own. Small differences in variable configurations, such as more restricted space or different power relationships between children, may alter language samples in important ways. Clearly, both naturalistic and experimental samples must be collected with careful attention to all the situational and interactional variables of the specific situations in which the learners will need to use their skills.

2. This study offers information on how better to construct or select naturalistic settings for answering more limited research questions. If a study has a functional or syntactic focus, such as the examination of intention

135

statements or future tense forms, it seems that the subject should be paired with one child in a restricted space and supplied with toys that lend themselves to role play and pretend play (as in the playhouse). Or if the researcher is interested in indirect requests, a challenging academic task will be needed where an adult is available but not controlling the children's interactions (as in the seatwork setting from this study).

3. If the results of this study are replicated with native speakers, the model of setting variables and language use could also be used as a guide to setting up naturalistic situations for language learning in young children. For example, if language teachers wished to induce children to produce third person inflections "spontaneously," they could set up a configuration of situational variables where subject control of conversation, adult interlocutors, and a violation of a routine or ritualized task are likely to coincide (such as at recess in this sample).

In summary, this study confirms Tarone's (1983) notion of language competence as multifaceted. Any complete description of language or communicative proficiency will need to define and describe situational variables of the data-collection setting. In addition, any teacher who hopes to provide realistic language acquisition for learners will need to consider the individual situational variables that constrain or motivate spontaneous language use.

APPENDIX

Taxonomy of Communicative Act Functions*

Control:
    Initiate
        Call attention   "Hey, lookit"
        Request object   "Gimme that"
        Request action   "Come here"
        Invite, offer   "Do you want some?"
        Warn, threaten   "If you do, I'll ..."
        Request permission   "Can I go?"
        Protest, prohibit   "Don't touch it."
        Claim, assign
            Possessions   "This is mine."
            Roles   "You're the daddy."
        Complain   "He hit me."
    Support
        Repeat, confirm   "Go on. Go on."
        Add, expand   "Yes, and you too."
        Clarify   "That means dog."
        Intensify   "I did!"
    Respond
        Comply   "OK"
        Refuse   "No."
        Ignore

Information:
Announce, format,   "Guess what?"
initiate or
describe support
        Label object   "That's a cowboy"
        Label action   "He's singing."
        Location   "It's over there."
        Attribute   "Mine's green."
        Function   "It's for writing."
        Reason   "Because I found it."
        State intent/prof.   "He's gonna do it."
        Clarify   "I said, 'He's it.' "
    Express
        Express opinion   "I like boys."
        Internal state   "I feel sick."
        Accompany self   "Now, I'm making tea."
        Express intent   "I'm gunna fix it."
        Personal experience   "We went to Mexico."
        Insult, compliment   "You're ugly."
        Brag   "I'm bigger."
        Exclaim   "Oh, no."

* Developed with reference to the taxonomies of Wells (1975) and various rough drafts of taxonomies from the research project of Wong-Fillmore and Ervin-Tripp (Ervin-Tripp, personal communication).

```
Request
    Request information
        Instruction            "How do you do it?"
        Description            "What does a bug look like?"
        Intent                 "What are you gonna do?"
    Request clarification      "What?"
Respond
    Give clarification         "Yeh, a green one."
    Give information
        Label object
        Label action
        Location
        Attribute
        Function
        Reason
    Deny, contradict           "I won't do it."
    Evaluate                   "That's a good book."
    Shift, avoid, ignore       "I dunno."
    Imitate                    "Yeh."
    Confirm

Social routine:
    Boundary markers           "Recess time"
    Politeness markers         "Thanks"
    Greetings                  "Hi"

Play with language:
    Sound effects              "rrrrrr"
    Word play, chants          "woo woo goo goo daa"
    "Reading"                  "once upon a time . . ."
```

NOTES

1. "Communicative acts" is a term used here to describe any behavior of a speaker that represents an attempt to express or encode a meaning or message through linguistic or paralinguistic channels. While the communicative act is a functional unit in some ways similar to the "speech act" described by Searle (1969), Dore (1973), etc., the term communicative act is preferred for two reasons. First, since the term "speech act" is in such common usage to describe the units suggested by Searle, it carries with it the expectation of a similar taxonomy of acts. The communicative acts used in this child language study are different and are organized into different types of categories. Second, the notion of communicative acts includes acts that clearly intend to convey messages but do not involve speech (such as grunts, sounds, and nods).

2. The two experimental settings, "interview" and "playhouse," are included in the comparison because they are the sort of elicitation activities that have sometimes been described in the literature as "natural" or capable of eliciting "spontaneous" language from children. For example, see Oller's (1979:18) discussion of the interview test as a pragmatic language task or Wong-Fillmore (1976:156) for a discussion of a "playhouse" setting as spontaneous interaction. It is important to include such so-called naturalistic experimental settings in a documentation of variation in children's spontaneous language so that researchers will be able to determine to what extent they are indeed similar to the types of natural interactions they are intended to simulate.

3. National Institute of Education Grant NIE–79–0118 to L.W. Fillmore and S. Ervin-Tripp, University of California, Berkeley.

4. Since data could not be sampled at the same time from each setting and from each subject, a comparison was also made of longitudinal and individual differences within situations (Cathcart 1983). The findings demonstrated: (a) Language was more stable longitudinally in some situations than in others. (b) There were some differences among the subjects in which of the acts they produced within a setting. However, no patterns were discovered which *contradicted* the main findings of the study on situational differences.

5. More detail on the procedures involved in data collection and analysis can be found in Cathcart (1983).

6. However, it should be noted that Ervin-Tripp et al. (1984) found more elliptical requests in construction play than in other types of play, a finding that suggests that the issue may be more complex than can be ascertained from this one example.

REFERENCES

Bossert, S. 1977. Classroom structure and peer associations. Unpublished ms. cited in Mehan 1979b.

Cathcart, R. L. 1983. Situational variability in the second language production of kindergartners. Doctoral dissertation, University of California, Berkeley.

Cole, M., J. Dore, C. Hall, and R. Dowley. 1978. Situation and task in young children's talk. Working paper No. 7, Rockefeller University Laboratory of Comparative Human Cognition and the Institute for Comparative Human Development.

Cummins, J. 1979. Cognitive/academic language proficiency, linguistic interdependence, the optimal age question, and some other matters. *Working Papers in Bilingualism*, 19.

Cummins, J. 1981. The role of primary language development in promoting educational success for language minority students. In *Schooling and Language Minority Students: A Theoretical Framework.* Los Angeles: Evaluation, Dissemination and Assessment Center, California State University, Los Angeles.

Dickerson, L. and W. Dickerson, 1977. Interlanguage phonology: current research and future directions. In S. P. Corder and E. Roulet (eds.). The Notions of *Simplification, Interlanguages, and Pidgins: Actes du 5eme Colloque de Linguistique Applique de Neufchatel*, 18–30. Cited in Tarone 1983.

Dore, 1973. The development of speech acts. Doctoral dissertation, City University of New York.

Erickson, F., and J. Schultz, 1977. When is a context? *Quarterly Newsletter of the Institute for Comparative Human Development*, 1(2): 5–10.

Ervin-Tripp, S. 1977. Wait for me roller skate! In S. Ervin-Tripp and C. Mitchell-Kernan (eds.). *Child Discourse*. New York: Academic Press. 165–189.

Ervin-Tripp, S. 1984. Activity structures as scaffolding for children's second language learning. In J. Cook-Gumperz and W. Corsaro (eds.). *Children's Language and Children's Worlds*. New York: Cambridge University Press.

Ervin-Tripp, S., C. O'Connor, and J. Rosenberg. 1984. Language and power in the family. In M. Schultz and C. Kramerae (eds.). *Language and Power*. Beverly Hills: Sage Publications.

Mehan, H. 1979a. *Learning Lessons.* Cambridge, Mass.: Harvard University Press.

Mehan, H. 1979b. Participation structures. Ms. Far West Laboratory for Educational Research, San Francisco, Calif.

Oller, J. 1979. *Language Tests at School.* London: Longman.

Phillips, 1972. Participant structures and communicative competence. In C. Cazden, V. John, and D. Hymes (eds). *Functions of Language in the Classroom.* New York: Teachers College Press.

Searle, J. 1969. *Speech Acts.* London: Cambridge University Press.

Sinclair, J.M., and R.M. Coulthard. 1975. *Towards an Analysis of Discourse.* New York: Oxford University Press.

Tarone, E. 1983. The variability of interlanguage systems. *Applied Linguistics*, 14(2): 143–163.

Wells, G. 1975. *Coding Manual for the Description of Child Speech.* Bristol: University of Bristol.

Wong-Fillmore, L. 1976. The second time around. Doctoral dissertation, Stanford University.

Section Three

TASK, TALK AND LEARNING

INTRODUCTION

Richard R. Day

The three chapters in this section, like those in Section Two, focus on language in the classroom, but from a different perspective: the role of task type in the second language acquisition process. Tasks have been traditionally assigned to second language learners in the belief or the hope that these activities might result in an increase in proficiency in the second language. Unfortunately, until recently, there has been little empirical evidence to determine if tasks in general, and what types of tasks in particular, do indeed aid in the successful acquisition of a second language. These three chapters address aspects of this question.

Duff, in Chapter 8, examines the effect of two different types of tasks, problem-solving tasks and debates, and of two task types, convergent and divergent, on the input and interaction of NNS-NNS dyads, using native speakers of Japanaese and Mandarin learning ESL. Duff notes that these small-group, so-called teacherless tasks have pedagogic interest since they allow students to work in pairs on their own and since they can be adapted to suit the particular interests and needs of students in a wide variety of situations.

While both types of tasks may be considered two-way, in the sense that there must be a two-way exchange of information between the members of the dyads, Duff claims that there is a crucial difference. She characterizes a debate as a "divergent" task and a problem-solving situation as a "convergent" task. She predicts that the two different task types will produce different kinds of language use.

Duff's predictions are supported by her data. She finds that debates reduce the opportunities for negotiation of input because of the long turns they involve. Since there are reduced opportunities for the negotiation of input, debates thus reduce and constrain the amount of comprehensible input the learners receive. Problem-solving tasks, on the other hand, seem to allow a great deal of clarification of meaning, both syntactic and lexical, because of the relatively greater frequency of questions asked in doing them. However, because of the limitations of the investigation, Duff does not want to rule out the use of debates in the ESL classroom. She concludes that the two task types are complementary in "pedagogic and psycholinguistic value, and therefore *both* have a role in second language instruction and SLA."

In Chapter 9, Rulon and McCreary examine the difference between small-group and teacher-fronted activities, focusing on aspects of negotiated interaction. Like Duff, Rulon and McCreary make a distinction between two types of small-group tasks. Unlike Duff, however, they differentiate tasks that call for a focus on meaning versus tasks that are "contextualized — given to the students as an integral part of the lesson or unit as a whole." They believe that the latter are more desirable since contextualized tasks result in less time spent negotiating meaning and more time spent discussing the content of the task. Thus in their investigation, Rulon and McCreary compare the speech of ESL students working on a contextualized task in small groups and in a traditional teacher-fronted classroom.

Their results are mixed. There seems to be little difference in the two situations on the variables of length of student utterance, syntactic complexity, and various interactional features. They do find, however, that the subjects in the small-group situation use more content confirmation checks and more content clarification requests than do the subjects in the teacher-fronted situation. They conclude from this that the contextualized two-way task leads to significantly more negotiation of content than the teacher-fronted format.

Rulon and McCreary also learn that the discussion in the small-group format covers the same information — the same content — as does the teacher-led discussion. They infer from this that ESL students working on contextualized two-way tasks may cover as much content as teacher-led discussion groups.

In Chapter 10, Porter describes the results of a study into the language used by adult ESL subjects and NS of English in task-centered discussions. There are three aspects of her study: differences in input to the ESL subjects by the NS and by other ESL learners; differences in production by learners in speaking to others with varying degrees of English proficiency; and the appropriateness of the language used by the ESL subjects with each other.

Porter's investigation shows that the input that the NNSs receive from ESL subjects is just as comprehensible as input from a NS, and that NSs and intermediate and advanced ESL students provide similar repair and prompting strategies. Porter notes that the findings on input indicate that ESL teachers need not be concerned about their students learning each other's errors or miscorrecting one another. Her findings also indicate that the subjects receive more and better quality input from advanced learners than from intermediates.

This suggests to her that teachers should consider pairing students of different proficiencies in the target language.

In terms of production, Porter finds that her ESL subjects produce more speech when talking to each other than when talking to native speakers. She claims that more advanced students might benefit from talking with less proficient students since they would have numerous opportunities to produce comprehensible output (Swain 1985) and to practice negotiation of meaning.

Finally, Porter finds that her subjects are not adequate sociocultural models for each other in terms of expressing opinions, agreements, and disagreements. This suggests that teachers should either make sure that their ESL students have contacts with native speakers or that they make explicit classroom presentations on sociolinguistic topics.

REFERENCE

Swain, M. 1985. Communicative competence: Some roles of comprehensive input and comprehensible output in its development. In S. M. Gass and C. G. Madsen (eds.). *Input in Second Language Acquisition*. Rowley, Mass.: Newbury House. 235–253.

8

ANOTHER LOOK AT INTERLANGUAGE TALK: TAKING TASK TO TASK[1]

Patricia A. Duff
The University of Hawaii at Manoa

It is the purpose of this chapter to examine the effect of task type on the input and interaction in nonnative speaker – nonnative speaker (NNS–NNS) dyads. The study we report analyzes the speech generated by dyads of Japanese and Mandarin Chinese speakers enrolled in English as a second language (ESL) classes at the University of Hawaii at Manoa. Two types of pedagogic tasks, problem-solving tasks (PS) and debates (D), and two examples of each, are the focus of this study.

Many claims are prevalent in the literature regarding the validity and effectiveness of certain tasks in second language acquisition classroom instruction and second language classroom acquisition (SLA). However, there have been few studies of an experimental nature that substantiate such claims. In this chapter, therefore, we investigate the potentially differential role that types of tasks play in the SLA process. We empirically validate the notion that some task types are more conducive to SLA than others with data that clearly show qualitative and/or quantitative differenes across tasks in the speech of the ESL subjects.

In our analysis, the *quantity* of input is measured in terms of the number of words and communication units (c-units) produced. The *quality* of input is measured by calculating the total values for the following features: turns, types of questions, and syntactic complexity (S-nodes). Unfortunately, it is beyond the scope of this study to analyze repetitions and reformulations, which would otherwise be useful measures of interaction.

The organization of the chapter is as follows. In the first section, we review the literature related to the topic of NNS-NNS interaction, paying particular attention to the variable of *task* and some of the problems associated with operationalizing types of tasks. Next, we provide the rationale for defining PS as "convergent" or shared-goal tasks, and D as "divergent" or independent-goal tasks. This distinction is made on the basis of the interaction each type of task produces, and the focus of one dyad member relative to the other in performing the task.

In the second section, we outline our study and present our general research question, hypotheses, tasks, methods, measures and analyses. This is followed by a discussion of the results not only in terms of the original research question but also in light of possible confounding variables. In conclusion, we offer some preliminary pedagogical and psycholinguistic implications and suggestions for further research.

BACKGROUND TO THE STUDY

Interlanguage Talk

The studies that have looked at "interlanguage (IL) talk" have consistently shown that speech modifications found in the discourse directed at NNSs by either native speakers (NSs) or other NNSs are instrumental in the SLA process for both pedagogical and psycholinguistic reasons (see Long and Porter 1985 for a review of this literature). Furthermore, the research to date suggests that in small-group and pair work, there are more opportunities per learner for this kind of negotiation to take place than in teacher-led discussion. Although it is still premature to make strong generalizations, because it also appears that pair work might be even more conducive to increased interaction than small-group work (cf. Doughty and Pica not dated), we limit the focus of our study to dyadic interaction.

Task

Along with the studies looking at group size and IL talk, researchers have also examined the degree to which *task type* influences interactional outcomes within groups. Examples of task types often referred to in the literature are as follows: one-way versus two-way tasks (Long 1981); optional versus required exchange of information, information gap, and decision-making tasks (Doughty and Pica not dated); problem-solving tasks (Porter 1983), negotiation of meaning versus negotiation of output (Young 1984), and other nominal categories (e.g., Butler-Wall 1983). While it is not possible to discuss and

148

compare each of these classifications of task types here, they are relevant insofar as they have in part motivated our distinction of PS and D as convergent and divergent task types.

Although the task-based research has been largely conducted in the interest of more effective second language instruction, from the point of view of teachers, there are three potential problems with the work that has been done. First, the tasks that have received the most attention tend to be "spot-the-difference" and "odd man out" (Long 1981), and more recently, "plant the garden" (Doughty and Pica not dated). On the one hand, the linguistic and cognitive operations required of learners performing these tasks are basic to the education process, such that most children in first language classes perform similar operations. However, to develop the communicative competence of adult learners (often in higher education), we propose that higher-level linguistic, social, and cognitive operations be integrated into pedagogic tasks. For this reason, we include PS and D in this study, both of which can be easily adapted, in terms of content and processes involved, to intermediate and advanced classes (e.g., in English for Specific Purposes).

The second problem with some of the tasks currently used is that they seem to require more teacher preparation and materials (e.g., felt boards, unmatching pictures, and classroom management necessary for "two-way" informational exchange) than equally productive "teacherless tasks" such as PS and D might involve.

Third, although many of these classifications have been operationalized experimentally, there is overlap between some of the categories. For example, the distinction between one-way/two-way and optional/required seems to reflect the effect of group size on interaction, and not task type per se; second, the proposed distinction between negotiated meaning and negotiated outcome does not involve mutually exclusive categories.

In short, there is a narrow but productive vein of research looking at the role of task in SLA, but there exists outside of this realm a wider body of empirically unsupported literature promoting "task-based," "interactional," "communicative," "negotiative," and "learner-centered" instruction. In the research undertaken in the present study, we observe and quantify characteristics of two task types in order to speak more confidently to issues related to the pedagogic and psycholinguistic suitability of certain tasks and the type of interaction ESL teachers can expect from them.

Task Type and This Study

For the purpose of the present study, we selected two types of pedagogic tasks that are commonly prescribed for use in first language (L1) and second language (L2) classrooms: PS and D (e.g., Christison and Bassano 1981, Ur 1981, Sadow 1982, Spaventa 1980, Rooks 1981, Alexander 1968, Pifer and Mutoh 1977).

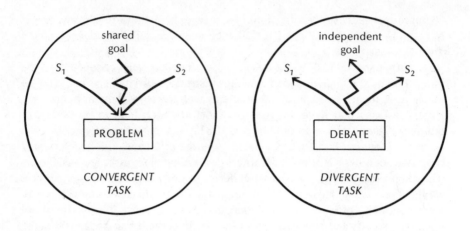

FIGURE 1 Convergent and Divergent Tasks

In PS, pairs of learners are asked to solve a given problem together, that is, to agree on a justifiable solution to it. Because the shared goal of learners in PS is to reach a mutually acceptable solution, we characterize it as a "convergent task type," and predict a certain degree of recycling of language related to the problem in order to achieve this goal. PS tasks cover a very broad range of topics and operations, but fairly typical ESL examples include the theme of survival tactics (Task 1, "Desert Island," from Sadow 1982; see Appendix A) and the ranking of individuals' moral fortitude (Task 2, "Sad Story," adapted from Spaventa 1980; Appendix A).

In D, the same pairs of learners are assigned different viewpoints on an issue, and they are asked to defend the given position and refute their partner's with as many arguments as possible. Because this task has implicitly opposite or independent goals for each member, we characterize it as a "divergent task type." Examples include discussions of the pros and cons of television (Task 3, "Television," Appendix A) and the controversial relationship between age and wisdom (Task 4, "Age and Wisdom," Appendix A). Both debate topics are adapted from Alexander (1968) and Pifer and Mutoh (1977).

The distinction between PS and D is shown in Figure 1.

OUTLINE OF THE PRESENT STUDY

Purpose

Based on many of the trends established in the task literature (cf. Long and Porter 1985), it is our primary purpose to answer the following research question: What are the qualitative and quantitative differences in the input and interaction that occur in PS and D (i.e., convergent and divergent) tasks?

We expect that there will be some similarities between the two tasks, since both, we believe, require the two-way exchange of ideas and opinions. Thus, for either task type to be successfully completed (problems solved or divergent views expressed), interlocutors must somehow acknowledge and/or incorporate the other's output in order to produce a coherent response.

At the same time, however, we predict that problems to be solved together by pairs generate significantly more negotiation than D, simply because *both* parties in a convergent task have vested interest or responsibility in the ultimate decision or solution that is rendered. Consequently, PS and D systematically produce distinctive patterns of IL interaction.

To be more specific, our first five hypotheses below concern the *quantitative* differences between the two task types, and hypotheses 6 and 7 deal with *qualitative* differences. Hypothesis 8 does not compare task types but rather looks at the role of *ethnicity* on qualitative and quantitative measures across tasks.

Hypotheses

1. There is no significant difference across tasks of total number of words produced by pairs of subjects per task, or of the number of individual subjects' words. We propose the null hypothesis here because we have no reason to predict differences in total language production based on task type.

2. There are more total turns taken in PS than in D, and thus more subject turns as well. This stems from the notion that a convergent activity lends itself to frequent turn exchange, in order that both parties can systematically monitor and negotiate the decision-making process before deriving a mutually acceptable solution.

3. There are more words per turn in D than in PS. That is to say that D turns contain more extended discourse than PS, because it takes longer for a speaker in a typically divergent task to state an opinion and also provide sufficient argumentation; each speaker is thus independently responsible for conveying a point of view that the partner is not expected to support.

4. There are more c-units (Loban 1966) in PS than in D, in terms of both total values per task and each subject's values. In line with the prediction that more negotiation takes place in PS than in D, this expects a general measure of amount of communication to favor PS over D.

5. There are more words per c-unit in D than in PS. Because it takes longer per turn to make a point in D than in PS (hypothesis 3) and because of the cooperative nature of interaction in convergent tasks, D c-units are less condensed than those in PS.

6. The syntactic complexity (S-codes per c-unit) of discourse in D is greater than that of PS, primarily owing to the kind of verbal reasoning that occurs in D.

7. The features listed below often associated with increased interaction occur with greater frequency in PS than in D:

    a. Comprehension checks
    b. Clarification requests
    c. Confirmation checks
    d. Collaborative checks
    e. Referential questions
    f. Expressive questions
    g. Rhetorical questions
    h. Total questions
    i. Subject questions

Most of the above features are defined and discussed in Long and Sato (1983). In this study, however, because of the number of requests for agreement or feedback, we have also added category d, in which explicit feedback or agreement or disagreement is sought (e.g., "Agree?"). We predict that the process of problem solving in dyads encourages subjects to interact more with their partners to clarify opinions and ensure mutual understanding and cooperation.

8. There is an effect for *ethnicity* on the interaction within dyads. Based on ESL classroom experience, we predict that Chinese (CH) speakers produce more speech and more interaction than (J), both quantitatively (as measured by number of words, turns, words per turn) and qualitatively (determined by the total number of questions soliciting responses).

METHOD

Subjects

The subjects in the study were four Mandarin (CH) speakers and four Japanese (J) speakers, all enrolled in ESL classes at the University of Hawaii at Manoa. Each subject was part of one CH/J dyad only; thus, there were four dyads total (see Figure 2).

GENDER	CH/J DYADS
M/M	2
F/F	2

FIGURE 2 Dyads

To reduce the number of sociolinguistic factors that might confound the discourse patterns within dyads, we controlled for the following variables as much as possible (summarized in Table 1): (1) *L1 background* (2) *length of residence* in United States (3) *proficiency level* (4) *familiarity* (all pairs were acquainted as ESL classmates) (5) *age* (6) *class standing* and (7) *gender.*

Procedure

After subjects were matched for the variables mentioned above, they were asked to take part in discussions of four separate tasks: two PS and two D. A written set of instructions and tasks was given to each subject, as well as an oral explanation of the procedure.

Dyads were randomly assigned a sequence of the same four tasks in counterbalanced order, with 2 minutes of reading time and 8 minutes of discussion time allocated for each task. Subjects were assured that they were not being tested; this was simply a chance for them to discuss some topics of potential interest with another student. Each dyad was audio-recorded in the researcher's office, with the researcher out of the room. Of the total of recorded discourse, only the first 5 minutes of discussion for each task was then transcribed and coded.

Measures

Measures included in this study have been reasonably well described and utilized elsewhere in the literature, with the possible exception of c-units. Therefore, we will not list and define each selected measure here. Rather, we cite the appropriate references: *turns* (e.g., Allwright 1980, Sacks et al. 1974, Goodwin 1981); *S-nodes* (e.g., Brock 1985), and *questions* (i.e., a to g above; see Long and Sato 1983); see also Duff 1985.

With regard to *c-units*, however, we needed to adapt an operationalizable definition of a minimal unit of communication not based on syntax or phonology from that used by Loban (1966) or Brock (1985), so that as much IL data and interaction as possible could be included in our analysis. This entailed establishing a semantic base potentially more inferential than other units of analysis. Rather than just "an independent grammatical prediction," a c-unit could be a word, phrase, or sentence that in some way contributed pragmatic or semantic meaning to a conversation.

Interrater Reliability

Because of time constraints, it was not possible to test for interrater reliability on every measure; however, those measures considered most highly inferential

TABLE 1 Subjects' Biodata and Pairing

Dyads 1–4: CH/J

Partners' background	Dyad 1	Dyad 2	Dyad 3	Dyad 4
Initials of name	JLJ	XT	XW	HZ
Country	PRC	PRC	PRC	PRC
Age	30	32	27	23
Sex	F	M	M	F
Length of residence	3 months	3 years	3 months	3 months
Years English studied before arrival	5	3	4	14
TOEFL	483	460	483	Mich. Test 75
ELI classes fall 1984	70, 100	72, 80, 100	70, 72, 73	70, 72, 73
Major	TIM	Electr. Eng.	Meteorol.	Mech. Eng.
Class standing	Undergrad.	Grad. (Ph.D.)	Grad. (Ph.D.)	Grad. (M.A.)
Initials of name	HG	MU	HI	YS
Country	JPN	JPN	JPN	JPN
Age	27	29	26	20
Sex	F	M	M	F
Length of residence	1 year 3 months	4 months	8 months	1 year 9 months
Years English studied before arrival	6	7	8	6
TOEFL	493	487	480	473
ELI classes fall 1984	70, 72	72, 80, 83	70, 72, 73	70, 72, 100
Major	Math	Ocean Eng.	Resource Econ.	Undergrad.
Class standing	Uncl. Grad.	Grad. (Ph.D.)	Grad. (Ph.D.)	

TABLE 1 (continued)

Partners' background	Dyads 5–6: J/J		Dyads 7–8: CH/CH	
	Dyad 5	Dyad 6	Dyad 7	Dyad 8
Initials of name	EK	KM	CC	YSC
Country	JPN	JPN	PRC	PRC
Age	18	22	18	18
Sex	F	M	F	M
Length of residence	3½ years	3 months	4 years	5 years
Years English studied before arrival	2	10	3	3
TOEFL	500	487	507	
ELI classes fall 1984	72, 73, 80	70, 100	72, 73, 80	72, 100
Major	Poli. Sci.	English Ed.	A & S	A & S
Class standing	Undergrad.	Unclass. Grad.	Undergrad.	Undergrad.
Initials of name	MK	KJS	SWC	CYL
Country	JPN	JPN	Taiwan	PRC
Age	19	38	23	18
Sex	F	M	F	M
Length of residence	1¾ year	14 years	4 years	4 years
Years English studied before arrival	5	10	3	3
TOEFL	530	457		437
ELI classes fall 1984	72, 73	72, 80, 83	70, 72	70, 72, 73
Major	A & S	Philos.	Fine Arts	Electr. Eng.
Class standing	Undergrad.	Grad. (M.A.)	Undergrad.	Undergrad.

	CH/J	CH/CH	J/J
M/M	2	1	1
F/F	2	1	1

FIGURE 3 Dyads for Hypothesis 9

(i.e., types of questions and c-units) were tested with an independent rater. For all questions and for c-units, there was 90 percent agreement in coding, and for words per c-unit, the level of agreement was above 95 percent. After interrater reliability was achieved, all transcripts were coded by this researcher only.

Analyses

To test hypotheses 1 through 7, we did a paired t-test (one-tail), which compared dyads 1 through 4 for all measures for PS1 and PS2, together, against those for D1 and D2, together. Owing to the number of tests we were making, we set our criterion level for significance at $p < .005$.

In order to test the effects of a subject's *ethnicity* (whether CH or J) and the ethnicity of a subject's *interlocutor* (same or different), four additional dyads were included in the study (see Table 1): two CH/CH dyads (one M-M, one F-F) and two J/J dyads (one M-M, one F-F). Therefore, in the analysis of hypothesis 8, the construction of the dyads was as shown in Figure 3.

Using the data from dyads 1 through 8, we did an ANOVA to determine main effects for the independent variables *ethnicity* and *interlocutor*, as well as the two-way interaction of the same. For these tests only a subset of dependent measures was selected, namely, words per task, questions (at turn boundaries soliciting responses), turns, and words per turn. In interpreting our ANOVA results, we were less conservative than we were with the t-tests; our criterion level for significance was $p < .05$.

RESULTS

The results of calculations and statistical analyses are found in Tables 3 through 11. We now report these results in terms of our eight hypotheses, and summarize them in Table 2.

Hypothesis 1

As predicted, there was no significant difference in the total number of words or subject words generated by PS and D, which means that in terms of the total volume of words produced by individual subjects of dyads, PS and D are

TABLE 2 Summary of Results

Hypothesis		Measure	Prediction	Supported?	Significance
1		Total/subject words	PS=D	Yes	
2		Total/subject turns	PS>D	Yes	ǂ
3		Words/turn	D>PS	Yes	†
4		Total/subject c-units	PS>D	Yes	ǂ
5		Words/c-unit	D>PS	Yes	ǂ
6		S-nodes/c-unit	D>PS	Yes	ǂ
7		Questions	PS>D		
	a.	Comprehension check		No	
	b.	Clarification required		No	
	c.	Confirmation check		Yes	†
	d.	Collaboration check		No	
	e.	Referential Q		Yes	†
	f.	Expressive Q		No	
	g.	Rhetorical Q		No	
	h.	Total Q		No	
	i.	Subject Q		Yes	
8	a.	Total words	CH>J	Yes	*
	b.	Subject words	CH>J	Yes	ǂ
	c.	Questions	CH>J	Yes	ǂ
	d.	Total turns	CH>J	Yes	*
	e.	Subject turns	CH>J	Yes	*
	f.	Subject words/turn	CH>J	No	
	g.	Turns stolen	CH>J	Yes	*

*p<.05   †p<.005   ǂp<.001

comparable. As we see in Table 3, the values for the mean number of words for each task type are approximately: *total words* PS 426/D 415; and *subject words* PS 213/D 207.

Hypothesis 2

From Table 3, we learn that PS generated a significantly greater number of total turns per task and individual subject turns ($p < .001$); thus, our prediction is supported. The total number of words represented in hypothesis 1 were distributed over about twice as many turns in PS as in D. The means in Table 3 are approximately: *total turns PS 47/D 23; subject turns PS 23/D 12.*

Hypothesis 3

The hypothesis that there would be more words per turn in D than in PS is also confirmed by our analyses (see Table 3). That is to say that while the total number of words is about the same for D and PS, because the number of turns taken is about half, each turn must contain about twice as many words as the

TABLE 3 Paired t-Tests (One-Tail) Comparing PS and D (4 Dyads): Quantitative Differences

Measure	Mean	SD	T value	DF	Significance
Total words:					
PS	426.00	107.60	0.44	3	
D	414.75	98.21			
Subject words:					
PS	213.00	89.95	0.34	7	
D	207.31	108.79			
Total turns:					
PS	46.88	7.94	14.43	3	†
D	23.25	6.74			
Subject turns:					
PS	23.25	4.51	15.17	7	†
D	11.63	3.47			
Words/turn:					
PS	9.56	4.77	−3.64	7	*
D	17.34	8.47			
Total c-units:					
PS	85.50	17.60	16.70	3	†
D	53.25	18.36			
Subject c-units:					
PS	42.75	13.80	12.14	7	†
D	26.63	12.56			
Words/c-unit:					
PS	4.19	1.38	3.50	7	†
D	7.21	2.04			

*p<.005   †p<.001

turns in PS do. D turns therefore involve more extended discourse than PS; the mean number of words per turn is approximately: D 17/PS 10.

Hypothesis 4

The number of total c-units and subject c-units per task type are, as we expected, greater in PS than in D. The difference in values is nearly double, and is highly significant ($p < .001$). These results are also shown in Table 3. The mean values for c-units are approximately: *total c-units* PS 86/D 53; and *subject c-units* PS 43/D 27.

Hypothesis 5

The hypothesis that there would be more words per c-unit in D than in PS (see Table 3) is supported ($p < .001$). In this case, D contains c-units that are almost twice as long as those in PS, i.e., approximately: *words/c-units* D 7/PS 4.

TABLE 4 Paired t-Test (One-Tail) Comparing PS and D (Four Dyads): Qualitative Differences

Measure	Mean	SD	T value	DF	Significance
S-nodes/c-unit:					
PS	0.72	0.28	−4.98	7	†
D	1.26	0.49			
Comprehension check:					
PS	0.06	0.18	−1.10	7	
D	0.56	1.24			
Clarification request:					
PS	0.50	0.54	−0.39	7	
D	0.63	0.74			
Confirmation check:					
PS	2.06	1.55	3.53	7	*
D	1.06	1.66			
Collaboration check:					
PS	1.63	2.42	1.60	7	
D	0.31	0.37			
Referential Q:					
PS	5.38	2.81	3.63	7	*
D	1.38	1.51			
Expressive Q:					
PS	0.25	0.38	0.42	7	
D	0.19	0.26			
Rhetorical Q:					
PS	0.44	1.05	0.27	7	
D	0.31	0.59			
Total Q:					
PS	19.38	5.14	5.28	3	
D	8.88	5.25			
Subject Q:					
PS	9.69	4.64	4.49	7	*
D	4.44	3.65			

*p<.005   †p<.001

Hypothesis 6

With regard to the syntactic complexity of c-units, our hypothesis predicting more complicated discourse in D than in PS is borne out, as can be seen in Table 4. This significant difference ($p < .001$) is reflected in the means, which are approximately: *S-nodes/c-unit* D 1.3/PS 0.7. In short, D discourse is almost twice as syntactically complex as PS discourse.

Hypothesis 7

Our results for the categories of questions listed in hypothesis 7 and summarized in Table 2 are less supportive of our general prediction when considered item by

TABLE 5 Summary of Means on Dependent Measures According to the Effects of Independent Variables: Ethnicity and Interlocutor (Eight Dyads): Dependent Measures

Independent variables	Total words	Subject words	Questions	Total turns	Subject turns	Words/ turn	Stolen turns
Ethnicity:							
CH	486.00	281.03	7.31	40.28	20.56	15.91	2.2
J	423.19	173.78	3.69	30.97	14.97	14.78	0.8
Interlocutor:							
Same	488.81	244.66	5.75	36.19	18.09	17.24	1.6
Different	420.38	210.16	5.25	35.06	17.44	13.45	1.4

item, as in Table 4. However, there are significant differences for the number of confirmation checks, referential questions, and the total number of subject questions generated ($p < .005$), favoring PS with about twice as many questions as D.

To be more specific, our hypothesis regarding comprehension checks and clarification requests was *not* supported, as there was a general tendency for D to produce more of each than PS (though not significantly). A nonsignificant trend in the opposite direction, however, was that there were more collaboration checks, expressive and rhetorical questions, and total questions asked in PS than in D.

Hypothesis 8

This hypothesis predicted that regardless of task type, CH would dominate conversations with J and would also produce greater values on selected measures in dyads with other CH. Because of the large amount of data generated by the eight dyads, we were able to test the hypothesis according to a subset of measures only: total words and subject words, total turns and subject turns, words per turn, and questions (here, those at a turn boundary directly soliciting a response). Another feature that was examined was turn stealing (i.e., completing or usurping another's turn when not encouraged to do so).

The results, presented in Tables 5 through 11, and graphically displayed in Figures 4 through 9, indicate quite convincingly that there is an overall main effect for ethnicity. We first present our findings for negotiation in the CH/J dyads (1 to 4) only. Then using the data from all eight dyads, we will be able to analyze the two-way interaction of *ethnicity* (CH versus J) and *interlocutor* (performance of subject with interlocutor of same versus different ethnicity).

Indeed, in CH/J conversations (dyads 1 to 4), CH subjects dominated approximately 66 percent of the total number of words, compared with the J 33 percent (see Tables 5 through 7, Figures 4 and 5), which is a highly significant difference ($p < .001$). Likewise, CH subjects took more turns than J ($p < .01$; see

Two-Way Interaction Effects of *Ethnicity* and *Interlocutor*:
Cell Means for Selected Dependent Measures

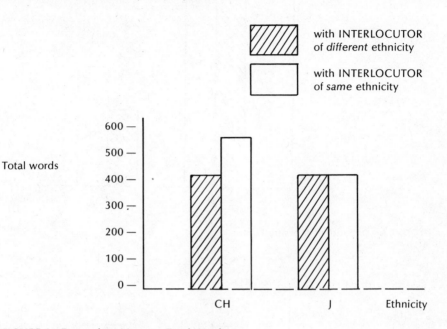

FIGURE 4 Dependent Measure Total Words

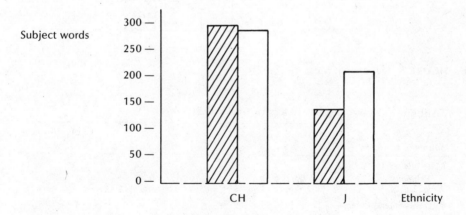

FIGURE 5 Dependent Measure Subject Words

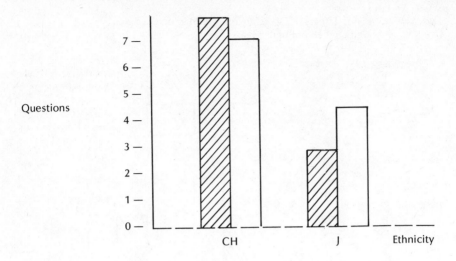

FIGURE 6 Dependent Measure Questions

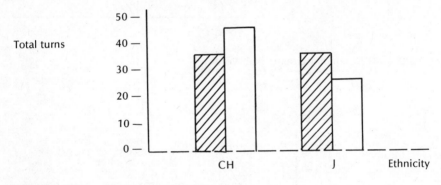

FIGURE 7 Dependent Measure Total Turns

TABLE 6 ANOVA Dependent Measure Total Words

Source of variation	SS	DF	MS	F	Significance of F
Main effects:					
Ethnicity	63,126.56	1	63,126.56	4.70	*
Interlocutor	74,939.06	1	74,939.06	5.58	*
Two-way interactions,					
ethnicity, interlocutor	63,126.56	1	63,126.56	4.70	*
Residual	805,723.25	60	13,428.72		
Total	1,006,915.44	63	15,982.79		

*p<.05

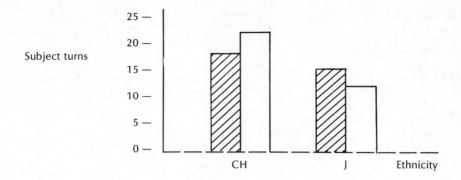

FIGURE 8 Dependent Measure Subject Turns

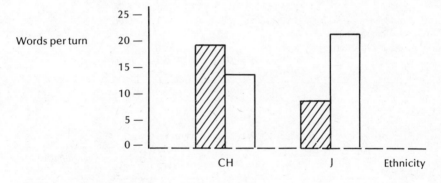

FIGURE 9 Dependent Measure Words per Turn

TABLE 7 ANOVA Dependent Measure Subject Words

Source of variation	SS	DF	MS	F	Significance of F
Main effects:					
Ethnicity	184,041.00	1	184,041.00	23.21	†
Interlocutor	19,044.00	1	19,044.00	2.61	
Two-way interactions,					
ethnicity, interlocutor	30,888.06	1	30,888.06	4.23	*
Residual	438,068.38	60	7,301.14		
Total	672,041.44	63	10,667.32		

*p<.05   †p<.001

TABLE 8 ANOVA Dependent Measure Questions

Source of variation	SS	DF	MS	F	Significance of F
Main effects:					
Ethnicity	210.25	1	210.25	11.82	*
Interlocutor	4.00	1	4.00	0.23	
Two-way interactions,					
ethnicity, interlocutor	20.25	1	20.25	1.14	
Residual	1067.50	60	17.79		
Total	1302.00	63	20.67		

*p<.001

TABLE 9 ANOVA Dependent Measure Total Turns

Source of variation	SS	DF	MS	F	Significance of F
Main effects:					
Ethnicity	1,387.56	1	1,387.56	5.74	*
Interlocutor	20.25	1	20.25	0.08	
Two-way interactions,					
ethnicity, interlocutor	1,387.56	1	1,387.56	5.74	*
Residual	14,495.63	60	241.59		
Total	17,291.00	63	274.46		

*p<.05

TABLE 10 ANOVA Dependent Measure Subject Turns

Source of variation	SS	DF	MS	F	Significance of F
Main effects:					
Ethnicity	500.64	1	500.64	8.12	*
Interlocutor	6.89	1	6.89	0.11	
Two-way interactions,					
ethnicity, interlocutor	221.27	1	221.27	3.59	*
Residual	3698.69	60	61.65		
Total	4427.48	63	70.28		

*p<.01

Tables 5, 9, 10; Figures 7 and 8). Finally, in the CH/J conversations, CH stole (i.e., completed) a significantly greater number of J turns (p <.01) than the reverse (see Table 5).

In the two-way analysis of variance we found that both independent variables influenced outcomes on some dependent measures; however, *ethnicity* was, generally speaking, the more robust variable. The interaction of *ethnicity* and *interlocutor* (see ANOVA Tables 6 through 11) is graphically displayed in Figures 4 through 9.

TABLE 11 ANOVA Dependent Measure Words per Turn

Source of variation	SS	DF	MS	F	Significance of F
Main effects:					
Ethnicity	2,036.27	1	2,036.27	0.23	
Interlocutor	22,990.14	1	22,990.14	2.54	
Two-way interactions,					
ethnicity, interlocutor	127,359.77	1	127,359.77	5.62	*
Residual	542,683.69	60	9,044.73		
Total	695,069.86	63	11,032.86		

*p<.01

In short, we can summarize the ANOVA results as follows. In terms of total words, both *ethnicity* and *interlocutor* are responsible for a significant amount of variation (p <.05). For this reason, we see that a CH subject interacting with another CH produces many more total words than other combinations of subjects (see Table 6, Figure 4). On the measure of subject words, however (see Table 7, Figure 5), the main effect of *ethnicity* accounts for more of the variation (p <.001) than the two-way interaction of *ethnicity* and *interlocutor* (p <.05). Thus CH produce more words than J, regardless of the ethnicity of their interlocutors. Similarly, *ethnicity* accounts for most of the variation in questions asked (p <.001); in other words, CH ask more questions than J (see Table 8, Figure 6).

For total turns and subject turns, our hypothesis is again supported (see Tables 9 and 10, Figures 7 and 8). We find that there is a significant main effect for *ethnicity* on the values for these measures across tasks (p <.05 and p <.01, respectively). In the former case, there is also a significant two-way interaction effect (p <.05). CH tend to take more turns in conversation than J, particularly when interacting with other CH. Words per turn, however (see Table 11, Figure 9), do not show a main effect for either *ethnicity* or *interlocutor*, although the interaction of the two variables yields highly significant results (p <.001)

Lastly, we report that the main source of systematic variation in turn stealing is *ethnicity* (see Table 5). Thus, CH steal about three times as many turns as J, regardless of their interlocutor's ethnicity (p <.005).

In summary, hypothesis 8 is strongly supported. CH contribute more words, questions, and turns than J do to the kinds of conversations generated by our four tasks; furthermore, they steal more of their interlocutor's turns as well.

DISCUSSION

In discussing the results presented above, we focus on four important aspects of our analyses: (1) *quantitative differences* between task types, (2) *qualitative differences*, (3) *between/within-task variation*, and (4) confounding variables (e.g., ethnicity). We also illustrate some of our findings with excerpts for our data (see Appendix B). The four discourse samples, which we have selected from the transcripts of dyad 1, exemplify the verbal interaction for each of the four tasks in the study.

Quantitative Differences

The most obvious and significant quantitative differences between task types were the number of total turns and subject turns taken, and inversely, the number of words per turn. The established interactional patterns thus reveal that in PS, the rhythm of turn taking is much faster than in D. By way of analogy, the exchange in PS is more like a tennis match than, say, a football game in which each side has more than one opportunity per turn to take the offensive and advance.

This pattern is displayed in the discourse samples (Appendix B). In PS, for example, we observe shorter turns with more immediate feedback about the other speaker's preceding utterance. In effect, many of these turns contain nothing more than simple phrases. In the D excerpts, too, we have included instances in which the turn-taking exchange is quite frequent (in fact, probably greater than it is on average for D), thereby showing the range of turn taking in D. On the other hand, extended discourse like that of the first half of the "television" text and the second half of "age and wisdom" (see Appendix B) is probably more representative of the bulk of discourse generated by D. Indeed, many D "turns" elsewhere in the transcripts lasted more than one page each, upon the completion of which they were often followed by a "Pardon?" or "I don't understand" from the overwhelmed partner.

Qualitative Measures

In this section, we discuss the syntactic complexity and other characteristics of PS and D discourse. As was seen in the results, there were more S-nodes per c-unit in D than in PS. This difference can be attributed to several factors. Since the topics in PS were "given" in the instructions, it was natural and quite adequate for subjects to assert "new information" in topic-comment constructions without syntacticized verbal elements (for a linguistic discussion of this phenomenon in CH and J discourse, see Rutherford 1983).

This occurred with predictable regularity in PS1, in particular, for which a list of objects was provided, and subjects were to choose a subset of objects that would be most useful to them on a desert island. For example, in the discourse sample for PS1 (see Appendix B), we have the following phrases without S-nodes: "MATCH important" and "Battery no *ne*," which reflect this discourse-functional strategy. Because we do not have L1 baseline data for this task type, it is unclear to what extent this is a result of L1 language typology, IL talk, task (cf. Butler-Wall 1983), or a combination of factors.

Conversely, in D it was often necessary for subjects to repeat or reformulate their own or their partner's viewpoint for the purpose of clarification or rebuttal. As a result, the c-units tended to be not only longer but complete with more complex syntactic constructions as well.

Examples from the discourse samples for D1 and D2 (see Appendix B) are as follows (the symbol — signifies a short pause): "Of course if you are a robber — you can be skillful through your experience to rob or to steal something" (four S-nodes); and "I think with the time passed and you can get some more information you can __ know something more __ understand something __ what's good what's not good" (seven S-nodes). Obviously, there is a common problem of run-on sentences in D, which are, presumably, taxing on the listener's short-term memory and psycholinguistic processing abilities.

For the same reason mentioned above, that is, that there was seemingly more reformulation in D than in PS, it is regrettable that we could not quantify that feature in this study. One of the main pedagogic and psycholinguistic benefits of D may well be that it requires or stimulates a great deal of self- or other-paraphrasing (see e.g., Discourse Sample 3 in Appendix B, where both CH and J attempt to restate their partner's opinion). In this respect, there may be another important qualitative difference between the two task types that remains unexplored.

Another intriguing feature of D discourse, in particular, concerns other-completions, in which both speakers contribute to a single proposition or utterance across two or more turns. Unfortunately, we cannot document this phenomenon of cooperative interactional behavior in greater detail here, although it is illustrated in Discourse Sample 3; e.g., J: "And if you live in USA—"/ CH: "—You just receive the USA's ideas."

With regard to the feature of questions, we found that there were more subject questions in PS than in D, the main contributing subcategories being referential questions and confirmation checks. Indeed, in PS, there were many requests for definitions, e.g., "Battery — What's this?" (PS1, Appendix B), which in most cases the interlocutor was able to satisfy; e.g., "Battery uh (2) causing uh- produce uh electric energy no?"

In D, however, we found that comprehension checks (e.g., "You know what I mean?") and clarification requests (e.g., "What do your meaning?") predominated; depending on the subject, rhetorical questions appeared as well (e.g., "Why he drinking? Because his wife love another man"). Again, this reflects the nature of the task and the complexity of input from one speaker to another, which either caused speakers to ensure that listeners were following them, or listeners to express uncertainty when necessary.

In D, contrary to what some might expect, most subjects did more than simply express the same opinion over and over again (cf. Higgs and Clifford 1982, who report this problem with D). We found that there was negotiation of the meaning of D partners' views through questioning, paraphrasing, and commenting, and subjects generally constructed various arguments and examples in favor of their own view or in opposition to their opponent's.

On the other hand, for psycholinguistic reasons grounded on the comprehensible input hypothesis (Krashen 1982), it is apparent that there are more opportunities in PS than in D for input to be either "predigested" for learners or at least made more easily processible for them. At this point, we cannot speculate on the value of a "comprehensible output" hypothesis and its possible bearing on our results (cf. Swain in press). Therefore, operating within the "comprehensible input" framework, we conclude that for qualitative reasons, PS tasks are on the whole more conducive to SLA than D.

Between/Within Task Type Variation

We have already documented some of the main differences between PS and D. Moreover, many of the differences established on the basis of four dyads also appear with consistency across all eight dyads eventually tested, although we coded for words, turns, and a general category of questions only for the latter four dyads. While differences between PS and D on the measures of total words and subject words increase slightly when values for four extra dyads are included in the analysis, this does not bear on our results, since the differences are not significant.

Within-task type differences are rather interesting, although it is important to point out that there is a great deal of consistency in the values on all measures for PS1 and PS2, on the one hand, and D1 and D2, on the other. Nonetheless, differences that emerge within task types can be linked to several factors.

First, the kind of verbal reasoning involved in individual tasks may vary. For example, we could claim that in PS2 less information is given to the learners than in PS1; perhaps more importantly though, the line of reasoning necessary to argue that one character is more responsible than another for the unfortunate chain of events is quite advanced. That is, while in PS1 a subject might say "You catch fish? You need gun right? You shoot fish right?" (i.e., If you want to catch fish, you'll need a gun to shoot them with), in PS2 we have what might be considered a more elaborate argument: "If Jim not drink so much, he not get this accident, then he don't get his leg cut off right?" (i.e., If Jim had not drunk so much, he wouldn't have had this accident and he wouldn't have needed to have his leg amputated).

Although both tasks require some suspension or abstraction from the "here and now," PS2 generates a slightly different kind of discourse, and this is reflected by greater syntactic complexity and length of turns, relative to PS1.

For much the same reason, D2 seems to require a slightly more advanced level of verbal reasoning, because a relationship or correlation between man's age and wisdom is being disputed, rather than the advantages and disadvantages of an activity (i.e., television viewing). Again, both require a certain degree of abstraction and thus are also accompanied by many conditional constructions;

in relative terms, however, D2 generates more syntactically complex discourse and longer turns than D1 as a result.

The kind of within-task type differences discussed above are, of course, based on just two tasks per task type in this study. A more authoritative treatment of differences between- and within-task types would require a research design with more tasks of each type.

Confounding Variables

Although the primary focus of this chapter is the effect of task type on interlanguage patterns, by controlling for certain other variables we were able to pinpoint some sources of variation that might otherwise have been obscured. Among those variables singled out in our ANOVA for the eight dyads were *ethnicity* and *interlocutor*, which have been reported above. A third variable, of lesser interest but which we were able to isolate as well, is that of *gender*. Below we discuss each of these potentially confounding variables in order.

Ethnicity and interlocutor CH, we found, are indeed "dynamic" subjects, and tend to participate much more actively in pedagogic tasks than J, even when global proficiency is comparable. Consequently, CH not only speak more in terms of words, they also take more frequent turns and ask more questions to encourage their partners to participate in the discussion with them. Of course, because of the different sociolinguistic orientations of CH and J speakers, the CH interactional patterns may be considered "face threatening" (Brown and Levinson 1978) for J. Similarly, the rate of speech for the former group tends to be faster than for the latter (as measured by total number of words per minute) and the turn boundaries shorter (in seconds), and this could also be a source of consternation for interlocutors from different backgrounds (cf. Scollon and Scollon 1983).

CH, however, maintain the same interactional tendencies with other CH, thus accentuating these cross-ethnic differences; likewise, J maintain the same sort of reservations (in terms of speech output, turn taking, and question asking) when interacting with other J. Perhaps with some sociolinguistic intervention by a teacher (cf. Porter 1983), it would be more beneficial for reticent speakers, in particular, to pair up learners from different L1s in classrooms and thereby provide opportunities for as much interaction and negotiation as possible.

Varonis and Gass (not dated) have also suggested that dyads be composed of subjects from different L1s, although for different reasons. They maintain that there is more interaction and thus a psycholinguistic advantage when learners are paired with other learners with less familiar IL accents. While this is most likely true, we were surprised to observe in our same-L1 dyads (5 to 8) that there was no oral recourse to the subjects' L1 while performing the assigned tasks. In both different-L1 and same-L1 dyads, however, learners occasionally jotted down Chinese characters for one another to avoid communication breakdown resulting from a lexical void.

Gender   Gass and Varonis (this volume) report on the variable of gender and its effect on subjects' performance in dyadic conversations. While we purposely did not structure our dyads so as to match subjects of different genders, we were able to test the overall differences between male and female interaction patterns with an ANOVA.

The results showed that there was no significant difference across genders on the measures tested. However, we found that *female* subjects tend to produce more total and subject words (481 and 241 for F, 427 and 214 for M), to produce more words per turn (17 for F, 14 for M), and to steal more turns (1.9 for F, 1.2 for M). Conversely, *males* asked a slightly greater number of questions (5.7 for M, 5.3 for F) and took slightly more total turns and subject turns (36 and 18 for M, 35 and 17 for F).

In sum, males and females produced comparable results on most measures, and none were significantly different. Therefore, gender was apparently not a confounding variable as a significant main effect.

SIGNIFICANCE OF THE STUDY AND PEDAGOGICAL IMPLICATIONS

The importance of this research is that it shows how pedagogic tasks of various types can be studied to determine their relative effectiveness in SLA.

We chose two so-called teacherless tasks, PS and D, which have pedagogic appeal because (1) they allow learners to work on their own (here, in pairs) and (2) they can be adapted to suit the particulars of learner interests and needs, especially at the intermediate and advanced levels. We type-cast PS and D as convergent and divergent tasks, and derived testable hypotheses based on the implicit interactional characteristics of the two. The results allow us to make the four following general observations, which address issues ranging from task design to classroom management.

1. The extended discourse (long turns) in D reduces opportunities for negotiation of input, since turn boundaries arise less frequently than in PS; coupled with the greater syntactic complexity of D, this reduces and constrains the amount of comprehensible input available for the purpose of SLA.
2. In PS, owing to the relatively greater frequency of questions asked, there is a constant source of clarification of meaning, whether syntactic, pragmatic, or semantic. This confirms the usefulness of PS in SLA. In D, there are fewer questions asked overall, and less importance paid to details. Consequently, it would seem there are fewer opportunities for input that is orginally incomprehensible to be rendered more comprehensible, which would theoretically facilitate the acquisition of new forms.
3. The patterns of interaction that occur are, in part, a function of the ethnicity of speakers, such that speakers from different ethnolinguistic backgrounds may not share the same sociolinguistic rules for speaking (and Porter 1983 suggests they are not good sociolinguistic role models for each other, as a result). Teachers should therefore identify the characteristics of ethnically

influenced patterns and be prepared to assist in the modification of inappropriate ones; moreover, they might group learners accordingly.
4. A considerable amount of negotiation takes place within dyads, especially when performing (interactionally) convergent tasks.

While a number of pedagogical implications could conceivably be drawn from the present study, we offer a last challenge to teachers and materials developers regarding the development of pedagogically and psycholinguistically sound tasks for classroom use. We contend that this educational principle is illustrated and supported by PS tasks.

Widdowson (1983) claims that what is probably most important in the second language classroom is that learners be given an opportunity to become *better learners*, that is, to develop their language learning "capacity" alongside the development of other cognitive skills and processes. Thus, from this perspective, tasks not only need to generate appropriate *linguistic* input and interaction between learners, they also need to stimulate the development of learners' general *cognitive* capacity through the same process.

According to Widdowson,

Education ... seeks to provide for *creativity* whereby what is learned is a set of schemata and procedures for adapting them to cope with problems which do not have a ready-made formulaic solution .... (1983:19) ... The ability to realize particular meanings [and] solve particular problems, by relating them to schematic formulae stored as knowledge, constitutes what I [call] capacity ... [And] capacity ... is the driving force behind both the acquisition and the use of language (1983:106).

In sum, this view favors the development and use of creative PS tasks in L2 classrooms, as in L1 classrooms, because they require learners to make use of world knowledge and previous experience, both linguistic and nonlinguistic (cf. Collins and Stevens 1982, Glaser 1984, Johnson-Laird and Wason 1977, Klahr 1976, Mayer 1983).

LIMITATIONS

In this final section, we outline the limitations of this study and make suggestions for further research in this area. The limitations were primarily due to time constraints but must be noted as they may bear on the results presented above.

First, levels of interrater reliability could not be established for all the features coded in the data. There is, even with interrater reliability, the possibility of inconsistency, which in turn might bias the results one way or another.

Second, owing to the low number of dyads in this study, there were low degrees of freedom in the statistical analyses, and possibly low generalizability. Similarly, by matching our subjects to form dyads, rather than assigning them randomly, we also reduce the generalizability of our findings to other populations.

Third, the experimental context in which the tasks took place may have influenced the outcomes to some extent and moreover may not represent what goes in the classroom. Nonetheless, it appeared that subjects' conversations were quite spontaneous and unreserved, such that many dyads exceeded the time allotted for individual tasks.

Lastly, it would seem to be an obvious limitation of this study not to have also examined other interactional features, such as self- and other-repetitions, reformulations, and other-completions.

SUMMARY AND CONCLUSION

In this chapter we set out first to motivate a new distinction between types of pedagogic tasks and second to collect and quantify data to test our predictions about the effect of task type on the interactional patterns generated by one or the other type of task.

To summarize our findings, we differentiated problem-solving tasks and debates according to the focus of the interaction and the direction or goal of the negotiation produced. We felt that both PS and D could be considered two-way tasks in the sense that in order to complete the task, there must be a two-way exchange of information (ideas, opinions) between subjects; this was also a requirement of the task. However, by characterizing them as "convergent" and "divergent" tasks, respectively, we were able to predict differences between these task types, which were later supported in our analyses.

As hypothesized, PS generated more turn-taking, more c-units, and more questions than D. Conversely, D produced longer turns, more syntactically complex discourse, and more extended discourse (cf. Brown and Yule 1983), which was also predicted.

Both tasks could be rightly considered "teacherless tasks," as they have been termed in some of the literature (e.g., Spaventa 1980), because even without the intervention of a teacher, negotiation does indeed take place between learners. Both task types are accompanied by various clarification techniques, such as questions, repetitions, reformulations, and explanations of different kinds. Furthermore, both seemed to generate the level of verbal and logical reasoning that we had hoped for.

In spite of these shared features and functions, however, we observed in PS, more than in D, the kind of interaction associated up until now with the production of comprehensible input and, theoretically, the possibility for acquisition of new structures. These differences were in most cases highly significant, and confirm our notion that PS tasks are useful vehicles of instruction and language practice in second language classrooms.

It is, however, beyond the scope of this study to decide which task type generates more linguistic structures at the appropriate level for SLA to occur. Moreover, we are not in a position to discredit the role of language production in the same SLA process. For this reason, it is perhaps wiser to suggest that PS and D are somehow complementary in pedagogic and psycholinguistic value, and therefore *both* have a role in second language instruction and SLA.

Lastly, we found that ethnicity, and in some cases the interaction of ethnicity and interlocutor, was in part responsible for variation in our study; gender was not a significant main effect though. CH produced more words in performing the tasks and asked more questions than J. In both CH/CH dyads and CH/J dyads there was a considerable amount of discussion; in J/J dyads, however, there seemed to be less interaction. In CH/J dyads, it appeared that J were somewhat frustrated by their interlocutors' discourse strategies, and this indicates an area for the sensitive intervention of teachers.

As a result of these findings, we encourage further research of the type undertaken here, but with a slightly broader focus. For example, it would be interesting to look at the degree of recycling of topics and reformulations of utterances that accompany certain task types, and also the *kind* of syntactic structures that task types generate in addition to general measure of complexity. Furthermore, the minimal unit of analysis used (e.g., here, c-unit) needs to be further refined so that results can be compared across studies in the future.

We also suggest that future research examining tasks control for ethnicity as we did, thereby yielding ethnolinguistically determined patterns of interaction for other specific groups. Furthermore, we encourage teachers and researchers to continue to observe and quantify the differences within and across task types. In this way, we will eventually produce a clearer picture of the relative contributions of tasks and task types to linguistic and interactional behavior. This, in turn, will ultimately facilitate curriculum and materials development, and provide a means by which to evaluate classroom instruction and task effectiveness.

Lastly, there must be more experimental work done in the area of SLA to determine the degree to which a balance is needed between comprehensible input and comprehensible output (cf. Swain 1985, Brown and Yule 1983).

In short, researchers and teachers, like their students, have many more tasks ahead of them.

APPENDIX A

Instructions

You and your partner will be asked to take part in two "problem-solving" tasks and two "debates." For each of the four activities, you will need to work with your partner to agree on a solution to a problem or to take a different point of view from your partner in debating a topic.

Please discuss every topic as much as possible, as though you felt the topic was very important. This is not a test, though, so you can say whatever you like without worrying about being "graded." This is simply a chance for you to discuss a topic in English with another student like yourself.

For each activity you can read the page in your booklet for *TWO* minutes before discussing it with your partner. Then you will have *EIGHT* minutes to do the task. *Even if you have not finished at the end of eight minutes, please stop and turn to the next page.*

Good luck and have fun! *THANK YOU VERY MUCH FOR YOUR HELP!*

PROBLEM SOLVING

The Desert Island You are on a sinking ship. There are rubber boats available for your rescue. The boats could hold only a limited amount of supplies and people, though. You can see a small desert island in the distance. If your boat makes it there safely, you will need things to help you survive until you are rescued.

Look at the *list of items* you have been given. You can take only *THREE* items from *each group*. Together you must decide (and agree completely) on *which things to take* and *which things to leave behind.*

GROUP 1	GROUP 2	GROUP 3
large flares	pillows	fresh water
matches	sleeping bags	7-up
flashlights	tent	coffee
oil lamps	blankets	canned juices
oil	sheets	beer
batteries	coats and jackets	tea
can opener	extra clothes	whiskey
utensils		

GROUP 4	GROUP 5	GROUP 6
salt	bows and arrows	frozen meat
flour	set of knives	dried fruits
sugar	gun	fresh fruits
yeast	bullets	dried vegetables
dry milk	fishing pole	fresh vegetables
water-purification tablets	small chairs	canned beans
	dishes	dry soup
	first-aid kit	
	ropes	

A Sad Story Jim's wife had just walked out on him (she loves another man). Jim rushed out of the home, pedaled unsteadily to the local bar, and started drinking.

A couple of hours later, he staggered out of the bar and somehow got on his bike.
He was wobbling from side to side down High Street when a car knocked him down, crushing his leg.
The driver went straight on without slowing down at all.
He was rushing his wife to the maternity hospital.
When they finally got Jim to the hospital, he had to wait three hours in the emergency waiting room.
The doctor who finally examined him, amputated (cut off) the wrong leg.
This doctor had been on duty for over 27 hours (he was a student doctor).

There are five people in the story. Together with your partner, decide which of the people was *most to blame* for what happened, and then in order, from *most* to *least* responsible. Thus, you should rank each person in order, from most guilty to least guilty. Your decision will be used by insurance company people and by lawyers in settling this case.

DEBATE

Television   You must defend the view that *"television has a terrible influence on people and society in general; it is thus an evil invention."* Your opponent does not believe this. Think of all the *problems* associated with TV viewing, and give examples that prove that *YOU* are right. You must not agree with the other person. Take a few minutes to gather your thoughts that support the point of view that TV is a very destructive thing.

Whenever your opponent gives an example of something *good* about TV, try to think of reasons why it is at the same time a bad influence, and mention alternative means of accomplishing the same things as TV provides.

You must defend the view that *"television is the greatest invention of all time."* Your opponent thinks that television is not useful, even worse, that it is an *evil* and terribly destructive machine.

Think of all the *benefits* that people can gain from TV, and give examples that prove that *YOU* are right. You must not agree with the other person. Take a few minutes to gather your thoughts that support the point of view in favor of TV.

Whenever your opponent gives an example of something *bad* about TV, try to think of reasons for explaining the same thing in a way that puts the blame not on TV, but on people, society, etc.

Age and Wisdom   You must defend the view that *"Older is not necessarily wiser, that is, that there is no direct relationship between how old someone is and how wise or intelligent he or she is."* You know that this excuse is often used for forcing youths to obey their parents (even though the children know what is better for themselves) and for forcing young employees to hold lower positions in companies than older (but not as intelligent) employees. Your partner thinks that an older person has "the voice of experience." Well, that just isn't enough nowadays.

Think of all the things that young people can teach their elders! Think of the benefits that the younger generation have compared with previous generations: technology, education, travel . . . . Give examples that show that *you* are right. You must not agree with your opponent. Take a few minutes to gather your thoughts on this subject.

Whenever your opponent gives an example of the strengths (mental, spiritual) that come with age, remind him or her of the tremendous weaknesses that also come.

You must defend the view that *"With age comes wisdom; that is, the older a person is, the wiser, or more, intelligent he or she is."* Your opponent thinks that your idea is old-fashioned and untrue. Your partner does not see any relationship between age and wisdom.

Think of all the things that young people can learn from their elders. Isn't this why children should obey their parents; because "parents know best"? Think of the benefit that older people have in terms of the amount of experience they have already gained in life. Give a few examples that show that *you* are right. You must not agree with your opponent. Take a few minutes to gather your thoughts on this subject.

Whenever your opponent gives an example of the weakness that comes with age, remind him or her that the weakness is only physical, not mental or spiritual.

APPENDIX B

Discourse Sample 1

TASK: PS1 "DESERT ISLAND"

CH: What-what? This one? Flare (2) Do you think it's important?

CH: I don't think so

CH: Match? Will you can know the time? (laugh) Oh __ match yeah

CH: Match? Yeah, yeah, yeah

CH: Bat-bat-battery What's this?

CH: Oh oh yeah I see

CH: Elec-electro-electricity

CH: So should __ flashlight __ Flashlight do you think it's important? Because may-be you should uh ask some ship to help

CH: But-but-but I think you can burn a fire It's the same function

J: Flare __ is used to __ signal

J: Mmmm

J: MATCH important

J: Match

J: Battery no *ne*?

J: Battery uh (2) causing uh__ produce uh electric energy no?

J: Battery
You can in the car battery

J: Yeah uh large flare __ flashlight

Discourse Sample 2

TASK: PS 2 "SAD STORY"

CH: Divorce? With Jim's-xx-Jim's wife will divorce with him? Wha-what-what do your meaning?

J: But-but I-I feel Jim and Jim wife (2) yeah (3) will be-will divorce __ even without him

CH: Yeah __ her boyfriend

CH: Yeah

J: Oh (2) uh (2) what I mean uh __ even if her boyfriend-

J: -Her boyfriend isn't (2) is NOT-

CH: Yeah

J: -Jim and Jim wife (3) Jim-uh-the relationship between Jim and Jim wife-

CH: You-you-you think uh he is a bad man?

J: -Is not goo-will be __ bad

CH: No not bad man?

J: No no no

CH: But wh-wh-wha-who is the most should be blamed person inside it?

J: Yeah

CH: Jim is a __ victi-victim I think

J: Jim and Jim wife

CH: I think his wife __ and her wife's boyfriend __ I think __ because __ they caused this serious __ result

J: Yeah

Discourse Sample 3

TASK: D1 "TELEVISION"

CH: OK I think TV is good because it's a __ you see __ you can let people know __ more things about the world This is very useful very helpful people So they can just sit at home and know everything __ happened in their state in their country __ even in the world __ SPACE! What do you think of?

J: Ah (3) it seems like ah your opinion seems right but ah (2) the information from TV is sometimes um __ very (3) mm (5) not always right uh

CH: Uhhuh

J: One event can __ can be seen from a lot of point of view So (5) uh we sometimes believe TV's scene __ is right but that is one of the __ one of the (2) reality

CH: But your meaning is __ mm the program on TV __ 's a lot of __

J: -No no no no About uh I am speaking about your opinion You can-you say you can __

CH: -Can get some more information from the TV

J: All of the world

CH: Yeah

J: But um (3) but (4) mass media is not always (2) uh (4)

CH: Balance?

J: Um sometimes unbalanced

CH: Unbalanced? For what?

J: I-if one uh about one-

CH: Yeah

J: -Event __ USA __ TV program and Soviet Union TV __ Soviet . . TV program s-uh (2) said __ different way

CH: Oh I see uh

J: And if you live in USA __

CH: -You just receive the USA's ideas

Discourse Sample 4

TASK: D2 "AGE AND WISDOM"

J: . . . Bad bad influence (3) . . . Experience sometimes uh worked for people-for people as a MAL influence

CH: Influence?

J: Yeah __ mal

CH: More?

J: Bad-bad influence __ mal influence

CH: Oh (2) I don't know what do you meaning

J: Mal means bad.

CH: M-A-L? (looks in dictionary) . . . Oh I see __ mal oh MAL influence Your meaning isa

J: Even if the same experience-

CH: Yeah

J: -One person uh-

CH: -Can get some useful idea but other can get some bad idea from that

J: Yeah

CH: Do you think so?

J: Yeah I think so

CH: Mmm but this __ not __ I don't think
this is will affect the decision of the-oh
yeah you think like this but this depends
I think (2) Of course everyone will-not
everyone is the same __ so some of them
are good __ and some of them are bad
(2) But you see I think the world is
developing __ so everyone will improve
no matter how improve he will __ and
(2) of course if you are a robber __ you
can be skillful through your experience
to rob or to steal something But this is
not necessary I think (2) I think with the
time passed and you can get some more
information you can __ know something
more __ understand something __
what's good what's not good

NOTE

1. I am grateful to the following people for their assistance in this project: Dr. Craig Chaudron, for his comments and help with statistical analyses; Dr. Michael Long, for discussions related to task types; Prof. Jason Alter, for kindly allowing me access to the students in his ESL classes; Carla Deicke, for her patience in interrater reliability testing; and Jan McCreary and Kathy Rulon for discussions concerning coding and analysis of the data. I am also indebted to Dr. Richard Day for his useful editorial comments and suggestions on earlier drafts of this paper.

Needless to say, the above individuals do not necessarily share my views, and I alone am responsible for any remaining errors, oversights, and faulty interpretations.

REFERENCES

Alexander, L. G. 1968. *For and Against*. London: Longman.
Allwright, R. L. 1980. Turns, topics, and tasks: patterns of participation in language learning and teaching. In D. L. Larsen-Freeman (ed.). *Discourse Analysis in Second Language Research*. Rowley, Mass.: Newbury House.
Brock, C. A. 1985. The effects of referential questions on ESL classroom discourse. *Occasional Papers* 1. Honolulu: Department of English as a Second Language.
Brown, G., and G. Yule. 1983. *Teaching the Spoken Language*. London: Cambridge University Press.

Brown, P., and S. Levinson. 1978. Universals in language usage: politeness phenomena. In E. Goody (ed.), *Questions and Politeness: Strategies in Social Interchange.* London: Cambridge University Press.

Butler-Wall, B. 1983. Optional syntax in oral discourse: evidence from native speakers of English. In C. Campbell, V. Flashner, and J. Lubin (eds.). *Proceedings of the Los Angeles Second Language Research Forum,* 2: 18–47.

Christison, M. A., and S. Bassano. 1981. *Look Who's Talking!: a Guide to the Development of Successful Conversation Groups in Intermediate and Advanced E.S.L. Classrooms.* San Francisco: Alemany Press.

Collins, A., and A. L. Stevens. 1982. Goals and strategies of inquiry teachers. In R. Glaser (ed.). *Advances in Instructional Psychology,* vol. 2. Hillsdale, N.J.: Lawrence Erlbaum Associates.

Doughty, T., and T. Pica. Not dated. Information gap tasks: Do they facilitate second language acquisition? Manuscript.

Duff, P. A. 1985. Another look at interlanguage talk: Taking task to task. ESL 750 Term Paper. The University of Hawaii at Manoa.

Gass, S. M., and E. M. Varonis. 1985. Sex differences in nonnative speaker–nonnative speaker interactions. (This volume.)

Glaser, R. 1984. Education and thinking: the role of knowledge. *American Psychologist,* 39/2: 93–104.

Goodwin, C. 1981. *Conversational Organization: Interaction between Speakers and Hearers.* New York: Academic Press.

Higgs, T. V., and R. Clifford. 1982. The push toward communication. In T. V. Higgs (ed.). *Curriculum, Competence, and the Foreign Language Teacher.* Skokie, Ill.: National Textbook Company. 57–79.

Johnson-Laird, P. N., and P. C. Wason (eds.). 1977. *Thinking: Readings in Cognitive Science.* Cambridge: Cambridge University Press.

Klahr, D. (ed.). 1976. *Cognition and Instruction.* Hillsdale, N.J.: Lawrence Erlbaum Associates.

Krashen, S. D. 1982. *Principles and Practice in Second Language Acquisition.* Oxford: Pergamon.

Loban, W. 1966. *Language Ability: Grades Seven, Eight, and Nine.* Washington, D.C.: Government Printing Office.

Long, M. H. 1981. Input, interaction, and second language acquisition. In H. Winitz (ed.). *Native Language and Foreign Language Acquisition. Annals of the New York Academy of Sciences,* 379: 259–278.

Long, M. H., and P. Porter. 1985. Group work, interlanguage talk, and second language acquisition. *TESOL Quarterly,* 19:2.

Long, M. H., and C. J. Sato. 1983. Classroom foreigner talk discourse: forms and functions of teachers' questions. In H. W. Seliger and M. H. Long (eds.). *Classroom Oriented Research.* Rowley, Mass.: Newbury House.

Mayer, R. E. 1983. *Thinking, Problem-Solving, Cognition.* New York: W. H. Freeman & Company.

Pifer, G., and N. W. Mutoh. 1977. *Points of View.* Rowley, Mass.: Newbury House.

Porter, P. 1983. How learners talk to each other: input and interaction in task-centered discussions. Paper presented at TESOL '83, Toronto.

Rooks, G. 1981. *The Non-Stop Discussion Workbook: Problems for Intermediate-Advanced Students of English.* Rowley, Mass.: Newbury House.

Rutherford, W. 1983. Language typology and language transfer. In S. Gass and L. Selinker (ed.). *Language Transfer in Language Learning.* Rowley, Mass.: Newbury House. 358–370.

Sacks, H., E. A. Schlegloff, and G. Jefferson. 1974. A simplest systematics for the organization of turn taking for conversation. *Language.* 50(4): 698–735.

Sadow, S. A. 1982. *Idea Bank: Creative Activities for the Language Class.* Rowley, Mass.: Newbury House.

Scollon, R., and S. B. K. Scollon. 1983. Face in interethnic communication. In J. C. Richards and R. W. Schmidt (eds.). 1983. *Language and Communication.* New York: Longman.

Seliger, H. W., and M. H. Long (eds.). 1983. *Classroom Oriented Research.* Rowley, Mass.: Newbury House.

Spaventa, L. (ed.). 1980. *Towards the Creative Teaching of English.* London: George, Allen and Unwin.

Swain, M. 1985. Communicative competence: some roles of comprehensible input and comprehensible output in its development. In S. Gass and C. Madden (eds.). *Input in Second Language Acquisition.* Rowley, Mass.: Newbury House.

Ur, P. 1981. *Discussions That Work: Task-Centred Fluency Practice.* London: Cambridge University Press.

Varonis, E. M., and S. M. Gass. Not dated. Non-native/non-native conversations: A model for negotiatation of meaning. To appear in *Applied Linguistics.*

Widdowson, H. G. 1983. *Language Purpose and Language Use.* London: Oxford University Press.

Young, R. 1984. Negotiation of outcome and negotiation of meaning. *TESOL Quarterly.* 18(3): 525–526.

9

NEGOTIATION OF CONTENT: TEACHER-FRONTED AND SMALL-GROUP INTERACTION[1]

Kathryn A. Rulon and Jan McCreary
University of Hawaii at Manoa

The purpose of this chapter is to examine selected aspects of negotiational interaction in small-group and teacher-fronted activities in the ESL classroom. A teacher-fronted activity refers to interaction controlled and directed by the teacher and is contrasted with a small-group activity in which no teacher is present and no designated member of the group is responsible for the control or direction of interaction taking place.

The focus of the investigation is the negotiation of both meaning and content. According to Young (1984), the negotiation of meaning refers to "the process of spoken interaction between a native speaker (NS) and a nonnative speaker (NNS) whereby the meaning of an unclear or misunderstood word or phrase is clarified to the satisfaction of both parties" (1984:1). In this chapter, the definition has been expanded to also include the interaction between two NNSs. The negotiation of content is the process of spoken interaction, whereby the content of a previously encountered passage (aural or written) is clarified to the satisfaction of both parties, either NSs or NNSs.

Although the teacher-fronted classroom continues to be the norm, there is a growing emphasis on group and pair work, with a resultant increase in the opportunities for the learner to use the target language. One of the advantages of the small-group setting appears to stem from the fact that the more intimate setting provides students with the opportunity to negotiate the language they hear, free from the stress and rapid pace of the teacher-fronted classroom. (For a more detailed review of the pedagogical rationale for small-group work, see Long and Porter 1985).

The increasing use of small-group work in the language classroom is supported by findings of a number of studies showing that the amount and variety of negotiation is greater in small groups than in the teacher-fronted classroom (Long, Adams, McLean, and Castanos 1976; Pica and Doughty 1984; Doughty and Pica not dated). It has been shown that given the opportunity to negotiate new input, NSs and NNSs alike modify both their language (e.g., simplified vocabulary, slower rate of speech, less complex utterances) and the interactional patterns of their conversations (e.g., asking more questions to clarify what has been said and what is being said) (see Long and Porter 1985). Long (1981:24) claims that these modifications help to make the conversation more comprehensible for the learner, thereby creating an environment more conducive to the acquisition of the second language.

In order to generate negotiation in both the small groups and the teacher-fronted classroom, these IL talk studies used two-way tasks (see Long and Porter 1985 for a description of this task type). However, in reporting these studies there was no mention of the relationship between the task and the lesson as a whole. That is, the task was not necessarily related to previous classwork, nor were the students necessarily familiar with the topic or vocabulary of the task. Consequently, the analysis of the negotiation generated by these tasks focused on the meaning, in terms of not only what the interlocutor has just said but also what was meant by various expressions used in the description of the task itself. For example, if a class of foreign students were given a task of deciding which five items to take with them to survive a shipwreck, much of the lesson might be taken up with explaining the meaning of flares or shark repellent before the students could even begin the task. The discussion that followed might still involve trying to recall those explanations rather than discussing the task itself.

If, on the other hand, the task was contextualized (i.e., given to the students as an integral part of a lesson or unit as a whole), the students' background knowledge of the topic would be activated, making them more familiar with the concepts and vocabulary of the task. Thus, the time spent negotiating meaning would be reduced and the possibility of discussing the content of the task would be increased, resulting in an effective use of discussion time.

PURPOSE

As noted above, previous studies have shown that there is more negotiation in small groups than in the teacher-fronted classroom. However, it appears that these studies looked at the task in isolation rather than as part of the lesson as a whole, resulting in an analysis focused on the negotiation of meaning, while ignoring the negotiation of content. The purpose of the present study, therefore, is to compare teacher-fronted and small-group interaction as generated by a task used within the context of a lesson.

HYPOTHESES

Both teacher and learning in the teacher-fronted classroom can be an extremely stressful experience. The teachers feel pressured to maintain a rapid pace to prevent the students from becoming bored and the students are under stress at having to speak in front of the authoritative figure of the teacher and their peers (Long et al. 1976). The stress students feel when they are called on to speak in class is a result of "audience effect" (Barnes 1973, as cited in Long et al. 1976). Stress created by the pace of the lesson and the "audience effect" pressures students to produce short, syntactically correct sentences (Long et al. 1976). On the basis of these considerations, the following hypothesis was generated:

H1: Longer units of speech (as measured by the number of words per communication unit) are produced by students when they are in a small-group situation than when they are in a teacher-fronted class.

In order to investigate the question of the syntactic complexity (as measured by the number of sentence nodes per communication unit) of the speech produced in the teacher-fronted classroom and in small groups,[2] hypothesis 2 was generated. Note, however, that as syntactic complexity of the speech has not been previously investigated, the direction of hypothesis 2 cannot be predicted.

H2: The language produced by the subjects in the small groups is of the same syntactic complexity as the language produced by subjects in the lockstep.

Previous studies have shown that the more negotiation of meaning (e.g., confirmation checks, clarification requests) takes place in small groups than in the teacher-fronted classroom. It is predicted, therefore, that the results of the following two hypotheses will support the findings of previous studies.

H3: A greater number of confirmation checks is produced by the students in the small groups than by both the teachers and the students combined in the teacher-fronted classes.
H4: A greater number of clarification requests is produced by the students in the small groups than by both the teachers and the students combined in the teacher-fronted classes.

Considering the nature of negotiation itself, there is reason to think that the negotiation of content might parallel the negotiation of meaning. Although this speculation is not based on previous research, the following hypotheses were generated:

H5: Content confirmation checks occur more frequently in small-group situations than in teacher-fronted classes.

H6: Content clarification requests occur more frequently in small-group situations than in teacher-fronted classes.

Of interest is the question of the coverage of content in the discussion in the teacher-fronted situation and the small-group format. In order to investigate this issue, the following hypothesis was formulated:

H7: The coverage of the informational content supplied in the lecture by the subjects in the small groups is quantitatively equivalent to the coverage of informational content in the teacher-fronted classes.

METHOD

Subjects

The subjects for this study were NNSs enrolled in two sections of the same advanced academic listening class in the English Language Institute (ELI) at the University of Hawaii. The students were mainly from East Asian countries (e.g., Philippines, Thailand, Hong Kong, People's Republic of China) and were pursuing either an undergraduate or graduate degree at the university. The length of time the subjects had been in Hawaii ranged from 3 months to 11 years. Despite the difference in length of residence (LOR), the subjects were considered to be of similar proficiency levels with regard to their academic listening ability. Their TOEFL scores, however, ranged from 450 to 560.

Three students from each section were randomly selected to form two groups of three. The three students forming the first small group (SG1) were from: the Philippines (LOR = 11½ years), Hong Kong (LOR = 1½ years), and Thailand (LOR = 7 years). There were two females and one male in the group, between the ages of 26 and 29. The second small group (SG2) was made up of three females between the ages of 18 and 26; one was from the Philippines (LOR = 10 years), one from Thailand (LOR = 4 months), and the third from Hong Kong (LOR = 1 year). The fact that each group contained students from the same three countries was coincidental.

The sections from which these students were selected form the comparison groups for the study. The first teacher-fronted classroom (TF1) consisted of 13 students and the second (TF2) was made up of 15. Both teachers had a considerable amount of TESL experience and were teaching their own classes. The following is a summary of the groupings made for the purposes of this study:

SG1: 3 students randomly selected from TF1
SG2: 3 students randomly selected from TF2
TF1: Female teacher and 13 students
TF2: Male teacher and 15 students

Data Collection

As we did not want to disrupt the classes unnecessarily, we used the material and the format used by the teachers in the class. Before seeing a video of a lecture on the American Revolution, the students were given a prelistening exercise (see Appendix A). The purpose of the exercise was to familiarize the students with the vocabulary and the concepts of the lecture and relate these concepts to similar events with which they were familiar. These exercises were carried out with the class as a whole.

Two days later, the students viewed the 14-minute videotape of a lecture on the American Revolution. The students were told to take notes on the lecture. Immediately following the lecture, the three students who had been randomly selected were asked to go to another classroom to complete the assigned task. This procedure was performed twice, first with TF1 and then with TF2.

Both the small groups and the teacher-fronted classes were given the task of completing an outline by listing and discussing the advantages and disadvantages of the colonists and the British during the American Revolution (see Appendix B). All the students were allowed to use their notes during the discussion. So that the data could be collected as unobtrusively as possible, the researchers did not observe the classes nor did they remain in the same room with the small groups after instructions were given. Both the small groups and the teacher-fronted classes were given 20 minutes for the discussion and were tape-recorded for that period of time. The teachers were aware that the class was being recorded for a study, but neither of them was aware of its purpose.

The tapes were later transcribed; each transcription was verified by a second person. As one of the group's discussions ended after 18 minutes, only the first 18 minutes of the other three discussions were used in the analysis.

Analysis

To test hypothesis 1, the mean number of words per communication unit (c-unit) was calculated. Loban's definition of a c-unit (1966) as well as Brock's adaptation of it (1985) was considered too limited for the purposes of this study. Analyzing NNS conversation necessitated a definition that was based not on syntax or phonology but rather on meaning. Thus, for the purposes of this study, a c-unit is defined as a word, phrase, or sentence which communicates pragmatic or semantic meaning regardless of grammaticality.

After coding the transcripts for c-units, the mean number of words per c-unit was calculated. A comparison was then made between the students in the SGs and those in the TF classes with regard to the mean length of c-units produced.

Hypothesis 2 was tested by measuring the mean number of sentence nodes (s-nodes) per c-unit. The transcripts were coded for s-nodes, and the mean number of s-nodes per c-unit for the students in both the SGs and the TF classes was calculated. A t-test was performed to establish the difference in syntactic complexity between the two.

To test hypothesis 3, the transcripts were coded for confirmation checks. Confirmation checks were defined as:

either Yes/No or uninverted questions spoken with rising intonation that involve exact or semantic, complete or partial repetition of the previous speaker's questions, and serve either to elicit confirmation that their user had heard and/or understood the previous speaker's previous utterance correctly or to dispel that belief (Long and Sato 1983:275).

The total number of confirmation checks calculated for the SGs was compared with the total number calculated for both the teachers and the students in the TF classes.

To test hypothesis 4, the transcripts were coded for clarification requests that were identified and defined as being:

designed to elicit clarification of the interlocutor's preceding utterance . . . They require that the interlocutor either furnish new information or recode information previously given (Long and Sato 1983:276).

The total number of clarification checks that occurred in the SGs was compared with the total number produced by both teachers and students in the TF classes.

To test hypotheses 5 and 6, modifications of the two repair types described above were made. The *content* confirmation check (CC) is exactly the same as the confirmation check except that rather than confirming the previous *speaker's* previous utterance, the speaker is confirming the *lecturer's* utterance. In other words, the speaker is trying to confirm that what he or she understood was said in the lecture that took place before the discussion task began was indeed what was said and/or what was meant by the lecturer. The following exchange from the data illustrates a CCC:

CCC S1:   The war is fight in England yeah?
         S2:   Huh? NO! The war is fight in the US in the colonies That's why the um- the um- the English xx but they cannot yeah But

Student 1's utterance is an uninverted question with rising intonation. It implies that the speaker thought she heard the lecturer say that the war was fought in England. Not entirely certain, however, she sought *confirmation* of this fact from one of the participants.

The same distinction is made for the content clarification requests (CCR). A CCR is designed to elicit clarification of a point made by the *lecturer* from one of the other task participants. The following excerpt from the data illustrates this repair type:

CCR S1:   Where did the internal supplies from?
         S2:   From the other colonies

Student 1 heard the lecturer refer to the internal supply routes, but he didn't understand what the lecturer meant by this. His Wh-question is designed to elicit *clarification* of this point from one of the other participants.

The CCC and CCR differ in the same manner that the confirmation checks and clarification requests differ. The CCC is either a yes/no or uninverted question spoken with rising intonation that involves exact or semantic, complete or partial repetition of something mentioned by the lecturer. The hearer is being requested to *confirm* the speaker's understanding of what took place in the lecture. The CCR, on the other hand, is used when the speaker does not understand a point made by the lecturer and is asking one of the participants to explain or *clarify* the lecturer's utterance. CCR's usually take the form of a Wh-question or may begin with utterances such as "I don't understand why . . . " or "I don't know how . . . "

The total number of CCCs calculated for the SGs was compared with the total number for both the teachers and the students in the TF classes in order to test hypothesis 5. The same comparison was made with CCRs to test hypothesis 6.

To test hypothesis 7, the transcripts were coded according to subjects' coverage of the informational content supplied in the lecture. Prior to coding the transcripts, the two researchers agreed on the information essential to the successful completion of the task. The procedure was similar to that of a teacher devising an answer sheet to be used in correcting an exam that included essay or short-answer item formats. The transcripts were then coded for coverage of these topics. The total number of topics covered by the two SGs combined were tallied and compared with the total number of topics covered by the teachers and the students in both TF classes.

Interrater reliability checks were conducted on random samples of the data before the actual coding began. These samples were recoded after acceptable levels of agreement for each measure were attained. Using simple percentage nominal agreement, each conducted on two raters working independently, the following levels of agreement, which were considered acceptable, were produced.

Measure	% agreement
Words per c-unit	92
S-nodes per c-unit	89
Confirmation checks	90
Content confirmation checks	100
Clarification requests	80
Content clarification requests	92

In addition to the interrater reliability checks conducted on the above measures, the subjects' coverage of the informational content supplied in the lecture was also verified.[3] Cases of disagreement were equally distributed between both the SGs and the TF classes; that is, there were six cases of disagreement in the SGs and the same number of disagreements in the TF classes. The following results were obtained and considered adequate.

RESULTS

Hypothesis 1: Longer units of speech are produced by students when they are in a small-group situation than when they are in a teacher-fronted class. The subjects in the two small groups produced a total of 478 c-units in an 18-minute period. The mean length of c-units measured by words per c-unit was 4.66. The students participating in the teacher-fronted classes, on the other hand, produced a combined total of 232 c-units over the same period of time. Their mean length was 4.39 words per c-unit. Table 1 presents a comparison between the SGs and the TF classes with respect to the number of c-units produced and the mean number of words per c-unit. Since there is no statistically significant difference (t = .86, df = 708, n.s.) in the length of c-units produced by the students in either the SGs or the TF classes, hypothesis 1 was not supported.

Main topic number	Subtopics possible points	% agreement
1	4	100
2	2	100
3	2	100
4	4	100
5	2	100
6	2	100
7	2	91
8	3	94
9	2	83
10	3	81
11	3	88
12	3	88
13	3	100
14	2	83
15	4	100
16	3	100

Hypothesis 2: The language produced by the subjects in the small groups is of the same syntactic complexity as the language produced by students in the teacher-fronted classes. Table 2 presents the mean number of s-nodes per communication unit for both the SGs and the TF classes. The mean number of s-nodes per c-unit was .67 in the SGs and .79 for the students in the TF classes. As predicted, the syntactic complexity of the language produced by students in the SGs was not significantly different (t = 1.2, df = 708, n.s.) from the language produced by the students participating in the TF classes.

TABLE 1 Mean Number of Words per Communication Unit: Comparison of SGs and TF Classes

	Students in SGs	Students in TF classes
n	478	232
x	4.66	4.39
s	3.88	3.96
t	.86	df=708, n.s.

TABLE 2 Syntactic Complexity (Mean Number of s-nodes per Communication Unit): Comparison of Students in SGs and TF Classes

	Students in SGs	Students in TF classes
n	478	232
x	.67	.79
s	.76	1.47
t	1.2	df=708, n.s.

Hypothesis 3: A greater number of confirmation checks are produced by the students in the small groups than by both the teachers and the students combined in the teacher-fronted classes. The total number of confirmation checks made by the two SGs was 10. The TF classes produced eight confirmation checks, 67.5 percent of which came from the teachers. The difference between the two groups was not statistically significant ($X = .5$, df $= 1$, n.s.). Thus, hypothesis 3 was not supported by the data. Table 3 presents the raw frequencies of confirmation checks.

Hypothesis 4: A greater number of clarification requests are produced by the students in the small groups than by both the teachers and the students combined in the teacher-fronted classes. The total number of clarification checks made by the subjects in the two small groups was 13 and by those in the TF classes was 8. The teachers were responsible for 67.5 percent of the clarification requests in the TF classes. The difference between the SGs and the TF classes was not statistically significant ($X = 1.19$, df $= 1$, n.s.). Table 3 also presents the raw frequencies of clarification requests.

TABLE 3 Raw Frequencies of Confirmation Checks and Clarification Requests: Comparison of All Teachers' and Students' Turns in SGs and TF Classes

	Confirmation checks	Clarification requests
SGs	10	13
TF classes:		
Ts	5	5
Ss	3	3
	X=.5	X=1.19
	df=1, n.s.	df=1, n.s.

Hypothesis 5: Content confirmation checks occur more frequently in small-group situations than in teacher-fronted classes. A total of 40 CCCs were made by students in the SGs. The TF classes produced a total of 16 CCCs, 75

TABLE 4 Raw Frequencies of Content Confirmation Checks and Content Clarification Requests: Comparison of All Teachers' and Students' Turns in Small Groups and Teacher-Fronted Classes

	Content confirmation checks	Content clarification requests
SGs	40	36
TF classes:		
Ts	12	0
Ss	4	1
	X=9.44	X=31.24
	df=1, p<.005	df=1, p<.001

percent of which were made by the teachers. The difference between the two groups was statistically significant ($X = 9.44$, df $= 1$, p $<.005$). This hypothesis was therefore supported by the data. Table 4 presents the raw frequencies of CCCs for both groups.

Hypothesis 6: Content clarification requests occur more frequently in small-group situations than in teacher-fronted classes. A total of 36 CCRs were made by students in the SGs. Only one CCR occurred in the TF classes, and as is shown in Table 4, it was made by a student. The difference between the two groups was statistically significant ($X = 31.24$, df $= 1$, p $<.001$), thereby providing support for this hypothesis.

Hypothesis 7: The coverage of the informational content supplied in the lecture by the subjects in the small groups is quantitatively equivalent to the coverage of informational content in the teacher-fronted classes. The total number of topics fully covered by the learners in the SGs was 19; the total for the subjects in the TF classes (this includes points mentioned by either the teacher or the students) was also 19. The number of topics that were only partially covered in the SGs was nine and in the TF classes was eight. The SGs neglected to disuss four of the topics that were deemed essential for completion of the task, whereas the TF classes neglected to mention five of these topics. Table 5 indicates the percentage coverage of each of the topics for each of the four groups separately. As is evident from the table, there is no topic that is not mentioned by at least one of the four groups.

Table 6 presents a comparison of the total content coverage of the two SGs combined and the two TF classes combined. The table shows that the data support hypothesis 7. A test for significance was thought to be unnecessary, since both groups covered exactly the same number of topics.

A summary of the results comparing the length and complexity of c-units as well as features of negotiation and the informational content coverage between the SGs and the TF classes is presented in Table 7.

TABLE 5 Informational Content Coverage: Comparison of Percentage Coverage of Each of the 16 Topics Among the Four Groups

	Point value	SG1	SG2	TF1	TF2
1	4	100	100	100	100
2	2	100	100	100	100
3	2	100	100	0	100
4	4	50	100	75	100
5	2	0	100	100	100
6	2	100	50	100	100
7	2	100	100	100	100
8	3	67	0	67	100
9	2	100	0	50	0
10	3	100	33	67	100
11	3	100	67	100	67
12	3	100	100	100	0
13	3	0	67	100	0
14	2	100	100	0	50
15	2	25	50	100	25
16	3	100	67	100	67

TABLE 6 Informational Content Coverage Summary: Comparison of Percentage Coverage of Each of the 16 Topics between the SGs and the TF Classes

Content covered, %	SGs	TF classes
100	19	19
75	0	1
67	4	4
50	3	2
33	1	0
25	1	1
Not covered	4	5

TABLE 7 Summary of the Differences between SGs and LS

The small groups produced	p level
Longer units of speech	n.s.
Less syntactically complex units of speech	n.s.
More confirmation checks	n.s.
More clarification checks	n.s.
More content confirmation checks	0.005
More content clarification checks	0.001
The same informational content coverage	No test performed

DISCUSSION

The results of the investigation seem to suggest, at first glance, that few clear-cut differences exist between the small group and teacher-led discussions. There seemed to be little difference in the two settings with respect to the length of student utterance, the syntactic complexity of the speech, or the interactional features.

This interpretation, however, is misleading for two reasons. First of all, hypotheses 5 to 7 were supported by the data and they provide substantial evidence, as have previous studies, that there are significant differences between small discussion groups and teacher-fronted classes. In addition, the lack of support for the differences between SGs and TF classes with respect to the other features investigated should be considered in light of the unit of analysis and the subjects' level of proficiency.

In terms of the unit of analysis, it could be argued that our definition of a c-unit was too broad. Minimal expressions of assent such as "mhm" and "yeah" were counted as one unit of analysis, that is, a c-unit. Such expressions were much more prevalent in the SG discussions than they were in the TF classes because of the very nature of the interaction that takes place in a small group opposed to a large one. In calculation of the mean length of c-unit, these one-word expressions lowered the average length of the c-units produced by the students in the SGs. Narrowing the definition of the c-unit to exclude these one-word utterances and then reanalyzing the data could conceivably reverse the findings of this investigation. In other words, a reanalysis may support the hypothesis that students participating in small groups produce longer units of speech than students participating in teacher-fronted discussions.

In addition, these one-word expressions do not contain an s-node. The number of s-nodes per c-unit was the measure of syntactic complexity (hypothesis 2); so a group containing a large number of these expressions is likely to have proportionately fewer s-nodes per c-unit. If the c-unit were changed to exclude these utterances, the results of not only hypothesis 1 but hypothesis 2 as well may be altered.[4]

More negotiation of meaning was expected to take place in the SGs. A higher frequency of confirmation checks and clarification requests, the features generally associated with negotiation of meaning (hypotheses 3 and 4) did occur in the SGs, but the difference was not statistically significant. This is not entirely unexpected. Brock (1985) reported a very low number of clarification requests occurring in classes with learners of high proficiency levels. "It seems likely that the generally high level of proficiency of the learners involved resulted in far fewer instances of unintelligible speech necessitating clarification than might have been the case with students of lower proficiency" (Brock 1985:55). Not many confirmation checks or clarification requests were produced by the students in either the SGs or the TF classes. As the participants in this study were of a comparable level of proficiency to those in the Brock study, the overall low production of these features could be attributed to proficiency level. An additional explanation for these results may be that since the task was contextualized and required the students to discuss the *content* of the lecture, it follows that the greater percentage of negotiation will be concerned with *content* rather than *meaning*.

As predicted by hypotheses 5 and 6, the difference in the number of content confirmation checks and content clarification requests occurring in the SGs and the TF classes was significant. The SGs produced more than twice the number of CCCs and 36 times the number of CCRs. Recall that the SGs and the TF classes were given exactly the same task, to discuss the lecture and complete the chart (Appendix B). The participants in the SGs conferred and communicated with each other so as to arrive at an agreement concerning the factors that played a part in the American Revolution while the students in the TF classes, were, for all intents and purposes, listening to "Lecture 2," the topic of which was "Lecture 1." Very little *negotiation* of either content or meaning was actually taking place in these TF classes.

An additional observation concerning the pronounced differences between the two groups investigated should be mentioned. This concerns the degree to which the students in the TF classes understood the initial lecture. Perhaps the teacher's "discussion" following the lecture cleared up any misunderstandings they might have had about the lecture's content and so there was no need to request clarification. On the other hand, perhaps misunderstandings continued to exist, but the students did not, as a result of the "audience effect" (Barnes 1973), feel confident enough to make their need for clarification known in such a large "audience." A test covering the content of the lecture would have been a worthwhile follow-up to the discussion task. This could have provided data in support of one or the other of the above speculations. In addition, the quiz could have been readministered several weeks later, in order to ascertain the degree to which the students who participated in the study retained the content of the lecture and the discussion that followed it.

Perhaps the most surprising finding was that which supports hypothesis 7 — that there was no difference between the amount of informational content covered by the students in the small groups and by the class that was led by the teacher. This finding implies that students in a small group, without assistance from the teacher, are able to cover as much content as are students working in a large group in which the teacher is acting as a facilitator.

While the results reported and discussed above are of interest to teachers because of the implications they may have for the ESL classroom, verification with larger numbers is essential if confidence in these findings is to be established. The small number of groups involved in this investigation is undoubtedly a limiting factor.

CONCLUSION

With the limitations of this study in mind, a discussion of the implications these findings may have for the ESL classroom is in order. It has been shown that when students are placed in a group situation and asked to complete a contextualized, two-way task, significantly more negotiation of content takes place than when the teacher leads the discussion. This negotiation of content, like negotiation of meaning, may be essential to the promotion of interaction necessary for successful second language acquisition (Long 1981:24). If such is the case, working in small groups after the completion of listening and/or reading comprehension passages may not only promote an atmosphere essential to successful second language learning but may enhance the students' comprehension of the passage as well.

Although the qualitative substance of the two groups' discussion was not formally dealt with in this chapter, the researchers did note that one of the small groups was convinced that the American Revolution took place in England. This is the only misconception that never received clarification within the group. It is impossible to say whether such misconceptions were held by students participating in the teacher-fronted classes.

The fact that the students spent 18 minutes discussing the American Revolution with the belief that it was fought on British soil leads one to believe that teachers have an important role in the classroom when students are working in small groups. That role, we believe, is to act as a consultant. However, further research is necessary to determine exactly what that role should entail.

Despite the limitations of this study, the results have laid the groundwork for further investigation into the negotiation of content. Research in this area is becoming more and more essential as there is a continual increase in the number of nonnative speakers attending universities where English is the medium of instruction. Since the tasks these students are ordinarily requested to perform focus primarily on content and are integrated into the lesson as a whole, it is important to ascertain the most effective means of discussing this content. As language teachers we would like to be able to promote the students' understanding and use of the language and at the same time afford them the opportunity to increase general background knowledge in a given content area.

APPENDIX A

Prelistening Activity: The American Revolution

Discuss each of the following questions in your groups and write down the important points.

1. In a war between a colony and its mother country, what advantages would you expect the mother country to have?

2. Can you think of any wars in which a colony won its independence from the mother country? How long did the fighting last? Were any nations other than the colony and the mother country involved in the war?

3. The lecture you will be hearing on Friday is about the American Revolution. State five things you think the lecturer will discuss.

APPENDIX B

Postlistening Activity: The American Revolution

As in every war, both sides have advantages over each other. The lecturer discusses both the advantages and disadvantages that the English and the Colonies had in their fight against each other. Using your notes, discuss these points. Be sure to explain why you consider a particular point to be an advantage or a disadvantage. Then, list the advantages and disadvantages for both sides on the chart below.

ENGLISH

ADVANTAGES	*DISADVANTAGES*
1.	1.
2.	2.
3.	3.
4.	4.
5.	5.

COLONIES

1.	1.
2.	2.
3.	3.
4.	4.

NOTES

1. We would like to thank the following people: Professor Craig Chaudron for his help with the statistical analysis of the data; Professor Michael Long for his suggestions on the design of the study; and Professor Richard Day for his helpful comments on earlier versions of this chapter. We are also grateful to the teachers and their students for allowing us to use their classes for the study. Finally, we would like to thank Patricia Card and Philip Pinsent for their help with this project and Patsy Duff and Michael Harrington for their comments during discussions of this chapter. The authors are solely responsible for any misinterpretations or mistakes.

2. Pica and Doughty (1983), for example, in their initial study comparing teacher-student and student-student interactional patterns, investigated the grammaticality of input. However, the present study is investigating the syntactic complexity of the speech produced in small groups of students and the teacher-fronted classroom.

3. The following procedure was used to verify the subjects' coverage of the informational content supplied in the lecture. The 16 main topics that were deemed essential to the completion of the task had from two to four subtopics. One point was scored for each subtopic that appeared in the transcript. A five-point scale was used to score items worth four points, since the items could be given a point value of 0 to 4. If the raters were in total agreement as to the degree of coverage of a particular topic, in other words, if the same number of points were awarded by both raters, five points were assigned. If their scores differed by one point, four points were assigned, and so forth. Values were assigned to each score, from which the percentage agreement was calculated.

4. A post hoc analysis of the data, excluding such one-word expressions as "mhm" and "yeah," supports the assumption that the basic unit of analysis, the c-unit, should be redefined. With the exclusion of these utterances, hypothesis 1 was supported. That is, significantly longer units of speech were produced by the students in the SGs than by those in the TF classes ($t = 2.97$, df$= 584$, p $<.005$). The students in the SGs produced a total of 369 c-units with a mean length of 5.82 words, whereas the students in the TF classes produced 217 c-units with a mean length of 4.81 words, on the average one word less than the students in the SGs.

The results of hypothesis 2 were also affected by the reanalysis. While we are unable to report a significant difference ($t = 1.40$, df$= 584$, n.s.) between the SGs and the TF classes with respect to syntactic complexity, there is a trend toward more syntactically complex units of speech being produced by the students in the SGs. The mean number of s-nodes per c-unit for the students in the SGs was .89. The students in the TF classes produced a mean of .79 s-nodes per c-unit.

REFERENCES

Barnes, D. 1973. *Language in the Classroom.* London: Open University Press.

Brock, C. A. 1985. The effects of referential questions on ESL classroom discourse. *Occasional Papers* 1. Honolulu: Department of English as a Second Language. University of Hawaii.

Doughty, C., and T. Pica. Not dated. Information gap tasks: do they facilitate second language acquisition?

Freed, B. F. 1978. Foreigner talk: a study of speech adjustments made by native speakers of English in conversation with non-native speakers. Ph.D. dissertation, University of Pennsylvania.

Hatch, E., and H. Farhady. 1982. *Research Design and Statistics for Applied Linguistics.* Rowley, Mass.: Newbury House.

Loban, W. 1966. *Language Ability: Grades Seven, Eight, and Nine.* Washington, D.C.: Government Printing Office.

Long, M. H. 1981. Questions in foreigner talk discourse. *Language Learning*, 31(1).

Long, M.H., L. Adams, M. McLean, and F. Castanos. 1976. Doing things with words — verbal interaction in lockstep and small group classroom situations. In R. Crymes and J. Fanselow (eds.). *On TESOL '76.* Washington, D.C.: TESOL.

Long, M. H., and C. J. Sato. 1983. Classroom foreigner talk discourse: forms and functions of teachers' questions. In H. W. Seliger and M. H. Long (eds.). *Classroom Oriented Research in Second Language Acquisition.* Rowley, Mass.: Newbury House.

Long, M. H., and P. A. Porter. 1985. Group work, interlanguage and second language acquisition. *TESOL Quarterly.* 19:2.

Pica, T. and C. Doughty. 1983. Native and non-native input in the ESL classroom. Paper presented at the 10th University of Michigan Conference on Applied Linguistics: Input in Second Language Acquisition, Oct. 28 – 30, 1983, Ann Arbor.

Pica, T., and C. Doughty. 1984. The role of group work in classroom second language acquisition. Paper presented at the Colloquium on Classroom-Centered Research at the 18th Annual TESOL Conference, Mar. 6 – 11, 1984, Houston.

Porter, P. A. 1983. How learners talk to each other: Input and interaction in task-centered discussions. Paper presented at the 17th Annual TESOL Conference, 1983, Toronto, Canada.

Young, R. 1984. Negotiation of meaning and negotiation of outcome in the reading classroom. Paper presented at the Tenth World Congress on Reading, July 30 – Aug. 2, Hong Kong.

10

HOW LEARNERS TALK TO EACH OTHER: INPUT AND INTERACTION IN TASK-CENTERED DISCUSSIONS

Patricia A. Porter
San Francisco State University

How learners talk to each other is important for both theoretical and pedagogical reasons. According to one current theory of second language acquisition — Krashen's input hypothesis (1978, 1982) — comprehensible input, i.e., the language that the learner is exposed to and can understand, is viewed as the critical ingredient for language acquisition. For language learners in school settings, much target language input comes from other learners, rather than from native speakers. If input is crucial, particularly that input provided in communicative exchanges, as Krashen suggests, then descriptions and evaluations of learner input are vital to an understanding of the role of input in second language acquisition.

But what should an adequate description of learner input include? Long (1981) hypothesizes that the crucial feature of native speaker input is not simplified language, as described in studies of teacher talk and foreigner talk, but the frequency of various conversational management devices that native speakers use when talking with learners. These devices, called interactional modifications, serve to prevent and repair breakdowns in communication and to sustain the conversation. They include confirmation checks, comprehension checks, clarification requests, repetitions, expansions, and questions. Knowing whether and to what extent learner input includes these crucial features can tell us how relevant and useful learner input is for language acquisition.

From a pedagogical perspective, the current focus in the language classroom on the teaching of communicative competence relates directly to the need to know how learners talk to each other. Increased learner-learner interaction and a concern for a wider variety of competencies demand answers to questions such as these: What happens when students engage in communicative tasks with their production unmonitored by the teacher? Is their grammatical accuracy less accurate than when monitored? Do they learn mistakes from each other? Do they carry over social interaction patterns from their native languages and cultures? Should we set up groups or pairs according to language abilities? According to social skills?

This chapter addresses these issues by describing the input that learners at two proficiency levels provided to each other and to native speakers during task-centered discussions and by comparing that input with native speaker input. Specifically, the chapter reports on a quantitative analysis of these features of learner and native speaker input: *quality of speech* (lexical errors, syntactic errors, and false starts), *amount of speech* (number of words), *monitoring* (self- and other-corrections of lexical and syntactic errors), *repairs* (comprehension checks, communication checks, etc.), and *prompts* (completions of other's utterances). A sixth variable, *ratings* of the speakers by ESL teacher judges, is a measure of accuracy and fluency. The chapter also reports on a qualitative analysis of the *appropriateness* of language used for expressing opinions, agreeing, and disagreeing.

A brief review of relevant studies of input shows clearly just how little is known about how learners talk to each other. Of the three main sources of input available to the learner, i.e., native speakers outside the classroom, teachers, and other learners, only the varieties of language common to the first two, labeled "foreigner talk" and "teacher talk," have been studied in depth in the last few years (e.g., Arthur et al. 1980; Chun et al. 1982; Day et al. 1984; Freed 1978; Gaies 1977; Hatch 1978, 1983; Henzl 1979; Long 1981; Scarcella and Higa 1982). This research has shown that foreigner talk is characterized by a number of modifications such as syntactic simplicity, a high frequency of questions, and a variety of interaction devices to maintain the conversation. Teacher talk in the second or foreign language classroom has also been found to be characterized by modifications in lexicon, syntax, phonology, and accompanying nonverbal behavior. All the modifications found in both these registers are thought to aid in communication with learners, but just how and whether such modifications aid the acquisition process is still undocumented.

The third source of input to learners, language produced by other learners in and outside the classroom, has not been extensively researched. One of the early quantitative studies of conversations between learners (Long, Adams, McLean and Castaños 1976) found that learner discussions in pairs promoted a greater quantity of speech and a greater variety of speech acts and social uses of language than did the teacher-led discussions. In a study of the ways learners are able to negotiate for meaning, Gaies (1983) examined learner feedback to teachers during referential communication tasks and found that learners used a variety of kinds of feedback and that learners varied considerably in the amount of feedback they provided. In a related study of learners in small-group work, Bruton and Samuda (1980) found that learners were capable of correcting each other successfully and were able to employ a variety of different error treatment strategies.

More recent studies of learner speech have been influenced by Long's 1981 classification of the language of foreigner talk into *input* features (such as length of T-units, type-token ratio) and *interaction* features (such as number of questions, confirmation checks, clarification requests, repetitions). Long found that in foreigner talk, modifications in interaction are more consistently observed than are modifications in input, and he hypothesized the following: "Participation in conversation with native speakers, made possible through the modification of interaction, is the necessary and sufficient condition for second language acquisition" (1981:24).

In line with this hypothesis, researchers have begun to examine the interaction features in learner conversations and how the variety and frequency of these features compare with those found in learner–native speaker conversations. For example, Varonis and Gass (1983) have studied "non-understanding routines" (indicators of a lack of comprehension leading to repair sequences and negotiation for meaning) and the influence of task type on negotiation of meaning. Pica and Doughty (1983, 1984) have studied grammaticality of learner production and interactional negotiation in small group vs. teacher-led discussions as well as the influence of group size and task type.

These studies are a beginning, but it is clear we need additional research not only for theoretical but also for pedagogical reasons. Rivers (1981: 83) describes current pedagogical practices in this way: "Much more time is now devoted than formerly to communicative interaction among students as an indispensable element in learning to use a language," adding that these practices are based on "a new realization of the active role of the language learner, as opposed to the teacher, in the language class." This focus on communicative interaction in the classroom reflects the current emphasis on the variety of competencies that are now seen to make up communicative competence (e.g., Canale and Swain 1980 define them as grammatical, sociolinguistic, and strategic competence). Although Krashen's input hypothesis minimizes the role of speaking in second language acquisition, many ESL educators agree that in order to promote communicative competence, learners must get practice speaking in communicative exchanges in the classroom. For example, Canale and Swain suggest that classroom activities should be characterized by "aspects of genuine communication such as its basis in social interaction, the relative creativity and unpredictability of utterances, its purposefulness and goal-orientation, and its authenticity" (1980:33).

202

In sum, both teachers and second language researchers need better descriptions of the input available to the learner as the raw material for language acquisition. We need to look at the input learners provide to each other during communicative activities: its grammatical accuracy, its interactional features, and its sociolinguistic appropriateness; and we need to see how this learner input differs across proficiency levels as well as how it differs from native speaker input. This is precisely the focus of a study made by the author (Porter 1983). The method and findings are presented below.

METHOD

Participants

Twelve learners of English and six native speakers participated in the study. The learners, all adult males, were native speakers of Spanish from five Latin American countries. They were enrolled in two different intensive English programs, and all but one planned to attend universities in the United States (three were undergraduates and eight were graduate students). They had been in the country an average of 4 months, and two-thirds of them were in the second term in their ESL programs. There were six learners at each of two proficiency levels, determined by their class placement in their ESL programs and by their scores on the Test of English as a Foreign Language (TOEFL): *advanced* (TOEFL mean = 497, range = 467–533) and *intermediate* (TOEFL mean = 415, range 360–453).

The native speakers, also adult males, were students at the two universities connected to the intensive programs (two were undergraduates and four were graduate students). Although two were foreign language teachers (French and Spanish), none had prior contact with the learners, extensive contact with nonnative speakers, or ESL teaching experiences.

Data Collection

The data collected were audio recordings of discussions based on problem-solving tasks. The tasks used were: "The Plane Crash," which involves ranking 10 individuals as survivors; "The Alligator River Story," which involves ranking five characters according to their moral behavior; and "Lost at Sea," which involves ranking 15 items for their usefulness for survival at sea. The discussions were done in pairs, with each participant speaking with three different interlocutors, *a native speaker*, an *advanced learner*, and an *intermediate learner*, discussing the three different tasks on three different days.

The orders of interlocutors were balanced, and the tasks were balanced as much as possible for order and pair combination. For clarity, the pair combinations and the number of discussions were as follows:

Pair combination	Number of discussions
Native–native	3
Native–advanced	6
Native–intermediate	6
Advanced–advanced	3
Advanced–intermediate	6
Intermediate–intermediate	3
Total	27

The 27 discussions averaged about 22 minutes in length, resulting in some 10 hours of data. The discussions were transcribed and the data were analyzed both quantitatively and qualitatively. For the quantitative analysis, the frequency of a number of features was tabulated. Counts were obtained for each participant for each discussion, as sampling was not deemed appropriate. The reliability of the counts for the more subjective of the measures was established by high percentage agreement scores and high correlations with counts obtained by a second rater on one-third of the data. The data format for the counts was a nine-cell matrix as seen in Figure 1. For each cell, $n = 6$.

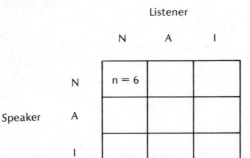

N = native speaker
A = advanced learner
I = intermediate learner

FIGURE 1 Data Matrix for Quantitative Analysis

Two research questions were addressed by the quantitative analysis: these concerned *input* to learners and *production* by learners. A third question concerned the *sociolinguistic appropriateness* of the learner language and entailed a qualitative analysis. In the following sections, the procedures and results for these three questions will be presented and discussed separately.

RESULTS AND DISCUSSION

Input to Learners

The first questions was: "How does input to a learner differ according to the proficiency level of the interlocutor?" An analysis of variance procedure was used in which listener level was taken as the between-subjects measure and speaker level as the repeated measure. Six planned comparisons were carried out, with F-ratios used to test for statistical significance. Figure 2 diagrams the two comparisons of special interest here, those examining speaker effects. (Note that since the concern here was the *speech addressed to learners*, the speech addressed to native speakers, represented in the diagram by the crosshatched area, was not analyzed.) These comparisons are: (A) Does native speaker input to learners differ from learner input? and (B) Does advanced learner input to learners differ from intermediate learner input? The six dependent variables examined are described in the following section.

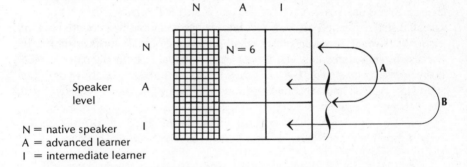

FIGURE 2 Diagram of Comparisons for Question 1, Input

 Rating Two native speaker judges, experienced ESL teachers, listened to each discussion and rated each speaker on a five-point scale on these criteria: comprehensibility, fluency, grammar, pronunciation, and vocabulary. Because of high interrater correlations (.84 or above) and high intercategory correlations (.96 or above), an average of the 10 ratings (5 categories, 2 judges) was used as a measure of quality of language for each participant.

 Quality As the result of a principal components analysis done on a number of tabulated measures for the purposes of simplifying the structure of the variables, an average of two variables, *error rate* and *false start rate*, was selected as an additional measure of quality of language. (The correlation between these two variables was .74.) These rates provide an indication of "faulty" input in terms of lack of grammaticality and disfluency. The error rate is based on the number of grammatical and lexical errors, and the false start rate is based on the number of words in false starts of various types: exact repetitions (e.g., *I*, I see him), unretraced false starts (e.g., *what about the*, maybe we should go the other way), and retraced false starts (e.g., *if he*, if you did that). Both measures were adjusted for amount of speech, resulting in the number per 100 words.

Total words This variable served as a measure of amount of speech and included all false starts and backchanneling expressions.

Monitor This is a composite variable made up of the average of the self-correction rate and the other-correction rate. It is a measure of attention paid to grammatical and lexical errors in the speaker's own speech (self-correction) and the interlocutor's speech (other-correction). Errors and corrections for pronunciation were not counted. The correction rates were computed by dividing the number of *successful* corrections by the number of errors made.

Self-correction and other-correction are both types of repair as the term is used by Schegloff, Jefferson, and Sacks (1977) but were dealt with separately from other types of repair (see below) because they are directly related to grammatical and lexical error. *Self-correction* includes both self-initiated correction [e.g., (1) my decisions was, *were* based; (2) so if you really love a people, a *person*] and other-initiated correction (e.g., A: . . . that is not his matter. B: His business? A: *His business*.) Note that both the examples of self-initiated self-correction also contain false starts and would be counted in that category as well. However, only a small proportion of false starts eventuate in successful self-corrections. *Other-correction* includes both overt, or direct, corrections (as in speaker B's "*His business?*" in the example above or in the following: A: You know the man, the male, the man, mans are uh- B: *Men.*) and more covert, or indirect, corrections which usually take the form of restatements (e.g., A: . . . maybe you don't have time in order to chose uh- the uh- the the order for the the importance in that moment. B: You *wouldn't* have time *right then*.)

Repair The frequencies of the following conversational interaction features were totaled to make up repair: confirmation checks, clarification requests, comprehension checks, verifications of meaning, definition requests, and lexical uncertainties. Examples are provided in Table 1. The repair rate was computed by dividing the number of repairs by the length of the discussion in minutes.

Prompt A prompt is a word, phrase, or sentence added in the middle of the other speaker's utterance to continue or complete the utterance. Examples are given in Table 1. As with the repair rate, the prompt rate reflects an adjustment for the length of the discussion in minutes.

Table 2 reports the means and F-ratios for these six variables for the input question. The findings are summarized in the following two sections according to the two comparisons.

TABLE 1 Examples of Repairs and Prompts

% of data	Type	Example
50	Confirmation check	L: ... he's better than Gregory N: *He's better than Gregory?*
18	Clarification request	L1: I think it's not too bad, not too bad. L2: *What?* L1: Bad, it's not too bad. L2: For me is terrible!
17	Comprehension check	L: To sin- uh ... to sink N: To sink. *Do you know what that is?* L: To go uh- N: To go under ...
15	Verification of meaning	L: ... *is for location?* N: Yeah, for finding your location
	Definition request	L: ... *what is the meaning of research?* N: Um, study? You study a problem and find an answer.
	Lexical uncertainty	L1: Yes, he's very simple one. Is, is very *how you say-* L2: I don't know, but he take advantage of the situation

Examples of prompts

1. N: ... because the other items uh- that are mentioned here
   L: *Is not useful for nothing.*
   N: Are not useful in this situation.

2. L1: ... but eh- we have to to get an agreement and for example the the the most important person
   L2: *Is the famous doctor.*
   L1: We agree is the famous doctor.

Native Speaker Input vs. Learner Input

Not surprisingly, native speaker input was significantly different from learner input on four variables: rating , quality, total words, and monitor. *Ratings* by ESL teachers showed native speaker input to be twice as good as learner input. In *quality*, native speaker input was about one-third as "faulty" as learner input. The means reflect an average of errors and false starts; another way to interpret the data is to add the variables and conclude that about 6 percent of the native speaker input was "faulty," compared with about 20 percent of the learner input. The native speakers did not use the kind of ungrammatical language sometimes found in foreigner talk; rather, their errors were those of performance, such as subject-verb agreement and pronoun reference.

Considering the differences in quality of input provided by native speakers and learners, the obvious question is "How much of a bad thing is truly a bad

TABLE 2 Means and F-ratios for Six Variables: Question 1 (Input: Speech Addressed to Learners)

Variable	Means				F-ratios (df=1, 20)	
	Native	Learner	Advanced	Intermediate	Native vs. Learner	Advanced vs. Intermediate
Rating (average of 10 ratings, 1–5)	5.0	2.4	2.7	2.1	203.12†	7.14*
Quality (average of errors and false starts per 100 words)	2.9	9.8	9.2	10.6	140.21†	4.18‡
Total words	1916	1455	1845	1065	7.60*	16.27
Monitor (average of self-correction and other-correction per error)	15.8	3.7	3.6	3.8	16.88†	0.00
Repairs (No./100 minutes)	37.6	28.6	26.6	30.6	1.47	0.22
Prompts (No./100 minutes)	16.9	16.9	20.9	12.9	0.00	1.95

p<.05   †p<.001   ‡Interaction effect for speaker by listener level, F=5.90.

thing?" While this study cannot presume to answer this important question, it can address the issue of comprehensibility from one perspective. The learner rate of 20 percent seems rather low, but it does not include errors in pronunciation. Had these errors been included, the difference between native speakers and learners on this measure would have been considerably greater. In this case, however, where learners were from the same language background, pronunciation errors did not make language incomprehensible to other learners: virtually no breakdowns of communication occurred in learner-learner discussions owing to phonological problems; in the native-learner pairs, on the other hand, native speakers occasionally had trouble understanding learner phonology as evidenced by clarification requests. The point is that learners from the same native language background may serve as better interaction partners for each other than learners from different language backgrounds on the basis that their similar interlanguage phonologies will be comprehensible.

Native speakers had significantly more *total words* than learners. When the total words were considered as a percent of the total conversation, it was found that native speakers averaged 62 percent of the talk in discussions with learners, with native speakers dominating in 11 of 12 pairs. In the 12 learner-learner discussions, the more talkative learner averaged 59 percent of the total words. The similarity of these figures suggests the need to look more closely at the significant differences between the natives and the learners for total words, which turns out to be due to the low mean for the intermediates (1065), which pulls down the overall learner mean: the amount of input provided by natives and advanced learners is very close (1916 and 1845 words respectively). If amount of input is the important consideration, learners may get comparable quantities of input from native speakers and advanced learners.

These findings are comparable with others reported in the literature. Prior studies of foreigner talk have reported that native speakers take on the role of conversational maintainer in conversations with nonnative speakers (e.g., Freed 1978, Hatch 1978), yet Scarcella and Higa (1982) found that native speakers produced fewer utterances than their adolescent nonnative partners (46 percent of all utterances) but more utterances than their child nonnative partners (72 percent of all utterances) on a block-building task. Parallel to this was their finding that the adolescents initiated more topics than the native speakers or children, and the researchers suggest that this topic initiation may have been a way for the adolescents to keep the conversation focused on familiar subjects that they could easily understand. Scarcella and Higa argue that the adolescents worked harder than the children to make the input comprehensible: the native speakers seems to expect more of older learners. It could be that the native speakers in this study expected more of the advanced learners and did not have to talk as much (e.g., by supplying questions, expansions, repetitions, etc.) to maintain the conversations with them as they did with the intermediates.

Native speakers *monitored* their own and their interlocutor's speech more closely than did the learners, this pattern being parallel for self-correction and for other-correction. It is not surprising that native speakers had higher rates for *self-correction* because they made far fewer errors to correct. (The self-correction rate was based on the ratio of number of successful corrections to number of errors.) Of greater interest is that both native speakers and learners made at least twice as many self-corrections for syntax as for lexicon. This differs from previous findings on native speaker speech (Maclay and Osgood 1959) and on learner speech (Fathman 1980), where lexical errors were found to be self-corrected more frequently. It is possible that the frequent correction of syntax and morphology by these adult learners can be accounted for by their cognitive maturity and by their attendance in an intensive English course with considerable focus on grammar.

Regarding *other-correction*, one finding was that native speakers corrected about 8 percent of learners' errors while learners accurately corrected about 1.5 percent of each other's errors. Both native speaker corrections and learner corrections were fairly equally distributed for grammar and lexicon. An important finding was that only about 0.3 percent of learners' errors were *miscorrected* by their learner partners. This extremely low frequency suggests that miscorrections are not a serious problem of learner input. Also, the low frequency of native speaker other-corrections, 8 percent, suggests that the native partners were not particularly helpful at providing corrective feedback to the learners. (Similar results have been found in other studies of foreigner talk, e.g., Freed 1978, Chun et al. 1982, Day et al. 1984.)

The most interesting findings for this comparison were the lack of significant differences between native speaker and learner input for the interaction variables *repair* and *prompt*. The findings are important in that they indicate that learners are capable of negotiation of repair and prompting like native speakers. The findings support Breen and Candlin's contention that teachers should not assume that just because learners have not mastered the target language they approach the task of communication in a naive and superficial way (Breen and Candlin 1980).

Not only were the repair frequencies similar for native speakers and learners, but the types were similar as well. The percentages of the various types are reported in Table 1. The last three types, which made up 15 percent of the total, were used more by learners than by native speakers, as would be expected. These three types can be described as communication strategies, falling under the special category "appeal for assistance" in Tarone's taxonomy (1981). The low frequency of these communication strategies suggests that learners *only rarely* took advantage of the opportunity to get help on vocabulary and grammar from native speakers (28 instances in 4¼ hours of discussion with native speakers and 21 instances in 4½ hours of discussion with other learners.) This suggests that the social constraints outlined by McCurdy (1980) which foster the simulation of understanding in native-nonnative conversations may have been in operation in these task-centered discussions: by using these particular communication strategies, the learner admits ignorance, and perhaps because of face-saving considerations, he or she is not likely to do so too often. Note that the first two types of repair, which constitute over two-thirds of the repair, are different in nature: they can be construed as a problem of hearing or a lack of attention rather than ignorance and they are thus not as face-threatening. (See the discussion by Day et al. regarding on-record vs. off-record repair, 1984.) The findings on repair cannot provide evidence on how much simulation of understanding was going on, but they do suggest that the more equal status of the learners in learner-learner discussions (as opposed to their unequal status in native-learner discussions) did not serve to loosen the social restrictions on repair dramatically.

Advanced Learner Input vs. Intermediate Learner Input

Advanced learner input to learners was found to be significantly different from intermediate learner input on two variables, rating and total words. The findings on *rating* show that the ESL teacher judges were able to distinguish two different levels of learners whereas the findings on *quality* did not show a significant difference between levels. These divergent findings could be accounted for by the possibility that differences in pronunciation and rate of speech were picked up by the judges; the variable quality measured only grammatical and lexical errors and false starts. (Note that the learners differed more in their error rates, 8.2 vs. 10.3 per 100 words, than in their false start rates, 10.1 vs. 10.8 per 100 words, advanced vs. intermediate respectively.)

The findings for quality revealed a moderately significant speaker-by-listener interaction effect: advanced learners had more errors and false starts when talking to advanced learners, whereas intermediates had more while talking to intermediates. Neither length of discussion nor proficiency of interlocutor seems to account for this finding. (For both groups, the means for input to native speakers were midway between those for input to advanced and intermediate for this variable.) The implication of these findings for rating and quality is that such slight differences in learner levels do not imply the advantage of one level over the other as input providers as far as accuracy of input is concerned.

The other significant difference between advanced and intermediate learner input was in amount of speech. As previously pointed out, the mean for *total words* for advanced learners was very similar to that for native speakers, suggesting that advanced-level learners are better input providers if quantity of input is the goal.

Of greatest interest in the findings on comparison B is the lack of significant differences between the two learner levels for the variables *monitor*, *repair*, and *prompt*. The means in Table 2 show that intermediates made fewer prompts than advanced learners, but this difference was not significant. The lack of differences on these three variables suggests that learners at these two levels bring comparable skills of interaction to their discussions and there is no clear advantage of one level over another.

Production By Learners

The second question was: "How does the speech the learner produces change depending on the interlocutor's proficiency level?" Here, in the analysis of variance procedure, speaker level was taken as the between-subjects measure and listener level as the repeated measure. Again a portion of the data was examined, this time only the speech produced by learners. Figure 3 diagrams the two comparisons of special interest, those examining listener effects: (A) Does learner speech to native speakers differ from learner speech to other learners? and (B) Does learner speech to advanced learners differ from learner speech to intermediate learners? The same six variables were examined for this question, and the means and F-ratios are presented in Table 3. As with question 1, the results will be presented in two sections, corresponding to the two comparisons.

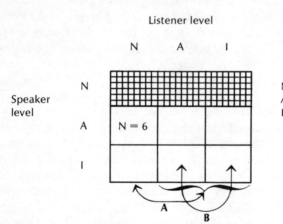

N = native speaker
A = advanced learner
I = intermediate learner

FIGURE 3 Diagram of Comparisons for Question 2, Production

Learner Speech to Native Speakers vs. Learner Speech to Other Learners

A surprising finding was that learners' speech to native speakers received a significantly lower *rating* than that to other learners, yet by the measure of *quality*, their production was no different in the two contexts. (Learners were also rated lower when they spoke to advanced learners than to intermediate learners, but the difference did not reach statistical significance.) These findings suggest a need for further research into the influence of speaking context on evaluators of learner speech. In classroom testing of communication skills, for

212

TABLE 3   Means and F-ratios for Six Variables: Question 2 (Production: Speech Produced by Learners)

Variable	Means				F-ratios (df=1, 20)	
	Native	Learner	Advanced	Intermediate	Native vs. Learner	Advanced vs. Intermediate
Rating (average of 10 ratings, 1–5)	2.1	2.4	3.2	2.5	4.47*	1.01
Quality (average of errors and false starts per 100 words)	9.7	9.9	9.8	10.1	0.28	0.11‡
Total words	1168	1455	1562	1348	7.19†	2.93
Monitor (average of self-correction and other-correction per error)	3.1	3.7	3.4	4.0	0.47§	0.34
Repairs (No./100 minutes)	33.0	28.6	22.4	34.8	0.73	4.42*
Prompts (No./100 minutes)	3.4	16.9	18.9	14.9	9.56†	0.65

p<.01   †p<.01   ‡Interaction effect for speaker by listener level, F=13.77.   §Interaction effect for speaker by listener level, F=6.89.

example, students are sometimes evaluated on the basis of speech samples collected in conversations or other interactive activities. A teacher's rating of a student may well be influenced by the ability of the speaker serving as the interlocutor. This study would predict that pairing with a competent speaker may result in lower assessment of a learner's skill than would pairing with a less competent speaker and vice versa.

As might be expected, learners talked significantly more to other learners than to native speakers. (See the means for *total words*.) Clearly if production practice is viewed as essential to acquisition, learners will benefit by practicing with other learners rather than with native speakers.

There was no listener-level effect for either the variables *monitor* or *repair*; learners monitored errors comparably and made similar repairs whether speaking with natives or with other learners. These findings suggest that both types of interlocutors are equally effective conversation partners. The finding for the other interaction feature, *prompts*, suggests that learners make better partners: learners prompted each other five times more than they prompted native speakers. Clearly the learners in this study did not need to rely on this prompting as a conversational resource with the native speakers (as suggested for the adolescent group studied by Scarcella and Higa 1982). They may have felt socially constrained from making prompts to native speakers, but they used them freely with each other.

Learner Speech to Advanced Learners vs. Learner Speech to Intermediates

On five of the six variables, there were no significant differences in the way learners talked to advanced as opposed to intermediate learners. The findings of comparable production across listener levels for *rating* and *quality* are not surprising as the variables reflect a speaker's linguistic competence and fluency, which, though subject to a certain amount of variability, will not change drastically across interlocutors when speakers are engaged in comparable tasks. The main implication for learner production in the language classroom is that it does not matter in terms of grammatical accuracy and fluency whether the learner practices with an advanced learner or with an intermediate learner.

A final point about errors concerns a finding regarding error incorporation: only 3 percent of learners' errors could be accounted for by their repetition of an error their interlocutor had made. In other words, learners repeated only a very small amount of the faulty input they received.

The findings on *total words*, while not reaching statistical significance, showed that learners talked more with advanced learners, mainly because the conversations lasted longer than conversations with advanced learners. In terms of level differences, then, intermediate learners stand to gain from talking to advanced learners from both an input perspective and a production perspective: they get to talk more because the discussions go on longer, and in comparison with their talk with native speakers, they get a slightly larger percent of the conversation (40 percent with advanced learners, 38 percent with native speakers). Advanced learners get more input from and production practice with other advanced learners than intermediates; however, they get only slightly less production practice with intermediates because they dominate the conversations.

The one significant difference for this comparison was for *repair*: learners made about one-third more repair with intermediates than with advanced learners. This expected finding suggests that talking with intermediates may be advantageous in that learners get more practice in negotiation for meaning than they get with advanced learners.

Language Appropriateness

The two previous sections have focused on a quantitative analysis of the linguistic accuracy, interaction features, and amount of language that learners and native speakers produced during discussions centered on problem-solving tasks. This last section describes a qualitative analysis of the data to answer the following question: "Is the language produced by learners in these discussions appropriate for use in settings outside the language classroom?" To answer this question, the learners' language was compared with the native speakers'. The underlying issue is whether the learners can learn various features of sociolinguistic competence from each other. The findings suggest that they cannot.

Three speech acts were selected as central to the discourse of the discussions: expressing opinions, agreeing, and disagreeing. The native speaker data were used as a baseline measure of appropriateness, with the language of both groups being analyzed in terms of some positive and negative politeness strategies described by Brown and Levinson (1978). Findings on the language used for the three speech acts are discussed in the following sections.

Expressing opinions The finding was that learners used most of the strategies that native speakers used, but with far less frequency. The strategies and examples of each are presented in Table 4. Learners seems to be more like native speakers in their use of the first four strategies (all positive politeness strategies) than they were in their use of the last four strategies (all negative strategies). For example, native speakers used past forms most of the time for expressing their rankings and ideas ("I thought"), whereas learners rarely used them, and when they did, they frequently used a present form even within the same sentence or turn ("My fourth was a teacher. What is your fifth?"). Learners never used impersonal verbs ("seem") and rarely hedged, using only five forms.

Expressing agreement Both natives and learners used the strategy of focusing on agreement when it was immediate, although here too the native speakers were able to hedge ("We're kind of agreed on some of them") and the

TABLE 4   Strategies and Examples of Language Used for Expressing Opinions

Expressing opinions	
Native speakers	*Learners*
Use informal language	
I mean	I mean
y'know	y'know
freaked out	Oh my God
dig this	wow
the damn senator	hombre
just kina like wow	
Use "we"	
Now what do we have	We can discuss
We could start a fire	We are agree
How about if we	We disagree here
What we have to consider is	What do you think we have to do?
Show attention to the other's ideas	
That's a very good point	Yeah, I know what you mean
Good question	As you said,
You have a point there	Yeah, you have reason
Like you said,	Yeah, that's true, that's a good arguing
That's a very logical way of thinking	
Solicit the other's opinion	
What do you think	Who do you prefer better-best
Do you feel	What do you think
How did yours compare	O.K. Go ahead. What about you?
Why did you have the child first?	What is the number four for you?
How would you put	
Use past forms for rankings and ideas	
I thought	I thought
It seemed to me	The problem here was survivors
I would argue that	I chose
I figured	My fourth was a teacher. What is your fifth?
	At the time I thought how the famous doctor can arrive
Use impersonal verbs	
It seemed to me	
It doesn't seem that	
That seems very logical	
Hedge	
Well, it's just a guess.	Is too old to me
I thought maybe	I think is better
It's possible that	Perhaps one person can use it
I would choose	I think maybe
I would put X just on the basis	For me, the spiritual is important
Use tags	
right? don't you?	y'know? no? right?
reckon? d'ya think?	

TABLE 5 Strategies and Examples of Language Used for Expressing Agreement and Disagreement

Expressing agreement	
Native speakers	Learners
Immediate: Focus on agreement	Well, in the first, third we have the same
That's the same as mine	It's agree, no? We're agree.
Well, that's close	We are agree.
We're kind of agreed on some of them	
Well, I thought she was pretty bad too, but . . .	
After some discussion: Hedge	Don't hedge.
I could go along with switching a little bit.	All right.
Well, I'm somewhat convinced by what you say.	I changed my mind.
That is a somewhat good idea, I guess, in the extreme case.	I am agree. I can change it.
I think basically you have a somewhat legitimate argument.	It's OK. I think is OK.
	Yeah, I change to seven.

Expressing disagreement	
Native speakers	Learners
Don't directly disagree.	Express disagreement directly
Acknowledge other's view and state your own.	No!
A: I ranked them—those two the worst.	Well, I disagree with you.
B: Really. I ranked Abigail and Slug the worst.	I'm no agree with that.
	But that is not important.
	Is wrong.
	No, no, forget it!
Focus on own ignorance or task difficulty	
At this point, I was very arbitrary	I'm not sure about
But I don't know how it works	Is very difficult
I thought . . . but who would know for sure	I didn't really pay attention of that part
Oh! It didn't even enter my head.	
Hedge disagreements if expressed at all	
I wouldn't necessarily agree with that even though	
So I had him kind of towards the end of my list	

learners were direct ("We are agree"). A bigger difference is that when after some discussion an agreement was reached and a participant "came around" to his partner's way of thinking, the native speakers expressed such agreement with hedges ("I'm somewhat convinced"), whereas the learners expressed such agreement directly ("I am agree. I can change it."). Examples are presented in Table 5.

    Expressing disagreement The greatest difference between native speakers and learners was in expressing disagreement. Although both natives and learners occasionally used the face-saving strategy of focusing on their own ignorance or the task difficulty, the main difference was that learners expressed disagreement directly and natives did not. The latter group avoided mentioning the disagreement or hedged their statements of disagreement. See Table 5 for examples of disagreement strategies.

From this analysis of politeness strategies in the speech of learners and native speakers, it seems clear that while the learners were familiar with some of the strategies, overall they were not using them to the same extent as the native speakers. And, as sociolinguists such as Labov have pointed out, it is not the presence or absence of a feature that marks a particular speech style, but the relative frequency of its occurrence (1966). The learners' low frequency of the negative strategies marks their speech as more direct than that of the native speakers in their expression of opinions, agreement, and disagreement.

One possible explanation for this directness is interference from Spanish discourse patterns. However, a small-scale study done by Porter and Richardson (1982) suggests that this is not the case. When a comparable group of learners did the same tasks in Spanish, the strategies turned out to be identical to those used by native speakers of English. Thus, while the learners in this study could have transferred the strategies directly from Spanish, they did not apparently do so. The likelihood is that at their particular levels of proficiency, the majority of their energy was taken up by comprehending and speaking, by their focus on the referential content of the language they heard and used. They probably had insufficient attention left to be concerned about the effect or force of what they were saying, even if they had been consciously aware of such strategies. The findings here support Fraser's idea that it is not necessary to teach strategies for conveying politeness and for mitigating the force of an utterance, but it is necessary to teach *when* the strategies ought to be used (1978).

These findings regarding the learners' lack of appropriate language use patterns suggest that only native speakers (or perhaps very advanced nonnative speakers) can provide truly "appropriate" input that will build sociolinguistic competence. The important implication for language teaching is that teachers will have to make explicit presentation of such appropriate language in the classroom through the use of natural texts by native speakers or materials based on natural texts. Such an implication is clearly in line with a suggestion of Crymes that teachers move away from "contrived materials towards natural texts as the primary in-class vehicles for the language data on which we base our instruction" (1978: 3). In sum, communicative activities in the classroom will provide valuable production practice for learners, but they will not generate the type of sociocultural input that learners need.

SUMMARY AND CONCLUSIONS

The major focus of this study was how learners talk to each other in task-centered discussions of the sort often used in the ESL classroom. The findings and implications are best summarized according to the three questions posed by the study. The first asked about differences in *input* to learners provided by native speakers and by other learners at two levels of proficiency. The findings suggest that if learners can get accurate native speaker models outside the classroom, then communicating with other learners in the classroom has certain advantages. Even though the learners provided ungrammatical input to each other, their input contained at least two interaction features (repairs, prompts) that may be vital to second language acquisition.

The similarity of repair and prompting undertaken by native speakers, advanced learners, and intermediate learners is of theoretical interest in regard to Long's ideas (1981) about the importance of interaction features for second language acquisition. Long has demonstrated how native speakers help their nonnative conversational partners both to participate and to comprehend in a variety of ways and has hypothesized that the interactional devices native speakers use are the crucial features of comprehensible input. The findings of this study, although not contradicting Long's hypothesis in any way, show that learners at the intermediate and advanced levels are also able to help their conversational partners in similar ways. This in turn implies that in considering the value of comprehensible input for second language acquisition, we need to broaden our focus to include the possibility of acquisition through communicative interaction with other learners.

Also in relation to comprehensibility, the study indicates that because there were no phonological problems in learner-learner discussions and because there were comparable amounts of repair in native-learner and learner-learner discussions, input from learners was just as comprehensible as that from native speakers, showing no clear advantage for a native speaker as an input provider.

Pedagogically, the findings on input provide evidence that teachers need not be concerned about learners picking up each others' errors or miscorrecting each other: such miscorrections and error incorporations were extremely rare in the data. In regard to level differences, the finding was that learners got more input and better-quality input from advanced learners than from intermediates, suggesting an advantage for practice with a higher-level partner from the perspective of quality and quantity of input. Thus, teachers might wish to pair students of differing proficiency levels in the language classroom.

Such a mixing of proficiency levels for language practice would be consistent with Krashen's belief that the best input language contains structure a bit beyond the current level of competence of the learner. In Krashen's view (1982), learners need to be exposed to target language forms that are just a little ahead of their current level of knowledge, and they need to hear these forms embedded in language that they understand; furthermore, they need to be focused on understanding the meaning of that language rather than focused on form. The intermediate learners in this study were in fact in such an ideal input situation, as learners would be in a classroom if paired with higher-level learners and engaged in communicative tasks.

The second question asked about differences in *production* by learners when they spoke to the three levels of interlocutors. The findings suggest that if quantity and quality of production is a goal, learners will derive greater benefit from talking to other learners than to native speakers: the learners in this study talked more and got more practice in one interactive feature, prompting, in discussions with other learners; furthermore, their level of accuracy and amount of repair work and monitoring were virtually the same whether talking to natives or to learners.

Educators such as Rivers and researchers such as Canale and Swain have emphasized the importance of production in language acquisition. Swain (1983) has proposed the "comprehensible output hypothesis," and argues that learners must have opportunities to produce the new forms they are exposed to in the input. In this study, learners were able to take the new forms that appeared in the tasks and turn them into comprehensible output in their discussions with native speakers and each other. While all learners got more practice and more input in discussions with advanced-level learners, they got more practice in repair work with intermediate-level learners. Thus, here is a way in which a higher-level learner may benefit from being paired with a lower-level learner: the learner will have ample opportunities to produce comprehensible output and more opportunities to practice the negotiation of meaning than with a matched partner.

The third question of study asked about the *appropriateness* of the language that learners used with each other. The finding was that learners did not provide socioculturally accurate models for expressing opinions, agreements, and especially disagreements. This finding does not mean, however, that learners should stop interacting with each other; it suggests the need for contact with native speakers or the need for explicit classroom presentation of the forms and strategies necessary to develop sociolinguistic competence.

In sum, then, though learners cannot provide each other with the accurate grammatical and sociolinguistic input that native speakers can provide them, learners can offer each other genuine communicative practice, including the negotiations for meaning that may aid second language acquisition.

This study is clearly limited by the homogeneous language background of the learner participants, the quasi-laboratory context of the data collection, and the single task type. In addition, the cross-sectional design of the study limits predictions about what the long-term effects of learner-learner practice may be. If we are truly committed to communicative language teaching, we need to determine the optimum balance of learner input and teacher-controlled input so that our students can get sufficient practice in genuine communication in addition to sufficient exposure to accurate language models.

REFERENCES

Arthur, B., R. Weiner, M. Culver, Y. J. Lee, and D. Thomas. 1980. The register of impersonal discourse to foreigners: verbal adjustments to foreign accent. In D. Larsen-Freeman (ed.). *Discourse Analysis in Second Language Research*. Rowley, Mass.: Newbury House.

Breen, M. P., and C. N. Candlin. 1980. The essentials of a communicative curriculum in language teaching. *Applied Linguistics*, 1(2): 89–112.

Brown, P., and S. Levinson. 1978. Universals in language usage: politeness phenomena. In E. N. Goody (ed.). *Questions and Politeness: Strategies in Social Interaction*. Cambridge: Cambridge University Press.

Bruton, A., and V. Samuda. 1980. Learner and teacher roles in the treatment of error in group work. *RELC Journal*, 11(2): 49–63.

Canale, M., and M. Swain. 1980. Theoretical bases of communicative approaches to second language teaching and resting. *Applied Linguistics*, 1(1): 1–47.

Chun, A. E., R. R. Day, N. A. Chenoweth, and S. Luppescu. 1982. Errors, interaction, and correction: A study of native-nonnative conversations. *TESOL Quarterly*, 16(4): 537–547.

Crymes, R. 1978. The developing art of TESOL: Theory and practice. In C. H. Blatchford and J. Schachter (eds.). *On TESOL '78: EFL Policies, Programs, Practices*. Washington, D.C.: TESOL.

Day, R. R., N. A. Chenoweth, A. E. Chun, and S. Luppescu. 1984. Corrective feedback in native-nonnative discourse. *Language Learning*, 34(2): 19–45.

Fathman, A. K. 1980. Repetition and correction as an indication of speech planning and execution processes among second language learners. In H. W. Dechert and M. Raupach (ed.). *Towards a Cross-linguistic Assessment of Speech Production, Kasseler Arbeiten zur Sprache und Literatur*, No. 7. Frankfurt am Main: Lang.

Fraser, B. 1978. Acquiring social competence in a second language. *RELC Journal*, 9(2): 1–21.

Freed, B. F. 1978. Foreigner talk: A study of speech adjustments made by native speakers of English in conversation with non-native speakers. Unpublished Ph.D. dissertation, University of Pennsylvania.

Gaies, S. J. 1977. The nature of linguistic input in formal second language learning: Linguistic and communicative strategies in ESL teachers' classroom language. In H. D. Brown, C. A. Yorio, and R. H. Crymes (eds.). *On TESOL '77: Teaching and Learning English as a Second Language: Trends in Research and Practice*. Washington, D.C.: TESOL.

Gaies, S. J. 1983. Learner feedback: an exploratory study of its role in the second language classroom. In H. W. Seliger and M. H. Long (eds.). *Classroom-Oriented Research in Second Language Acquisition*. Rowley, Mass.: Newbury House.

Hatch, E. M. 1978. Discourse analysis and second language acquisition. In E. Hatch (ed.). *Second Language Acquisition: A Book of Readings*. Rowley, Mass.: Newbury House.

Hatch, E. M. 1983. *Psycholinguistics: A Second Language Perspective*. Rowley, Mass.: Newbury House.

Henzl, V. M. 1979. Foreigner talk in the classroom. *International Review of Applied Linguistics*, 17(2): 159–167.

Krashen, S. 1978. The monitor model for second language acquisition. In R. C. Gingras (ed.). *Second Language Acquisition and Foreign Language Teaching*. Arlington, Va.: Center for Applied Linguistics.

Krashen, S. 1982. *Principles and Practice in Second Language Acquisition*. Oxford: Pergamon Press.

Labov, W. 1966. *The Social Stratification of English in New York City*. Washington, D.C.: Center for Applied Linguistics.

Long, M. H. 1981. Input, interaction, and second language acquisition. In H. Winitz (ed.). *Native Languages and Foreign Language Acquisition, Annals of the New York Academy of Sciences*, 379: 259–278.

Long, M. H., L. Adams, M. McLean, and F. Castaños. 1976. Doing things with words—verbal interaction in lockstep and small group classroom situations. In J. Fanselow and R. Crymes (eds.). *On TESOL '76.* Washington, D.C.: TESOL.

Maclay, H. and C. E. Osgood. 1959. Hesitation phenomena in spontaneous English speech. *Word,* 15: 19–44.

McCurdy, P. L. 1980. Talking to foreigners: The role of rapport. Unpublished Ph.D. dissertation, University of California, Berkeley.

Pica, T., and C. Doughty. 1983. Input and interaction in the communicative language classroom: a comparison of teacher-fronted and group activities. Paper presented at the 10th University of Michigan Conference on Applied Linguistics, Ann Arbor, Michigan.

Pica, T., and C. Doughty. 1984. The role of group work in classroom second language acquisition. Paper presented at the 18th annual TESOL Conference, Houston, Tex.

Porter, P. A. 1983. Variations in the conversations of adult learners of English as a function of the proficiency level of the participants. Unpublished Ph.D. dissertation, Stanford University.

Porter, P. A., and C. Richardson. 1982. Language use in problem-solving tasks: English and Spanish. Paper presented at the 16th annual TESOL Conference, Honolulu, Hawaii.

Rivers, W. 1981. *Teaching Foreign Language Skills.* Chicago: University of Chicago Press.

Scarcella, R. C., and C. A. Higa. 1982. Input and age differences in second language acquisition. In S. D. Krashen, R. C. Scarcella, and M. H. Long (eds.). *Child-Adult Differences in Second Language Acquisition.* Rowley, Mass.: Newbury House.

Schegloff, E., G. Jefferson, and H. Sacks. 1977. The preference for self-correction in the organization of repair in conversation. *Language,* 53(2): 361–382.

Swain, M. 1983. Understanding input through output. Paper presented at the 10th University of Michigan Conference on Applied Linguistics, Ann Arbor, Mich.

Tarone, E. 1981. Some thoughts on the notion of communication strategy. *TESOL Quarterly,* 15(3): 285–295.

Varonis, E. M., and S. Gass. 1983. Target language input from non-native speakers. Paper presented at the 17th annual TESOL Conference, Toronto, Canada.

Section Four

OUTSIDE THE CLASSROOM

INTRODUCTION

Richard R. Day

Section Four deals with conversations of second language learners outside the classroom. The three chapters in this final section examine various aspects of learning a second or a foreign language in informal contexts, and treat such topics as the role of corrective feedback (Chapter 11), informal versus formal learning (Chapter 12), and sex differences in the speech of ESL students (Chapter 13).

Brock, Crookes, Day, and Long, in Chapter 11, explore the crucial question of the effect of corrective feedback supplied by NSs in response to errors made by their NNS friends who are learning ESL. It has been an unexamined assumption that correction plays an important role in second language learning by providing learners information about the correctness of their speech, and that, in so doing, it helps them to modify their current interlanguage rules. In an earlier study, Chun, Day, Chenoweth, and Luppescu (1982) demonstrated that native speakers of English provided corrective feedback to their NNS friends on only about 8 percent of their errors (excluding phonological mistakes). Day, Chenoweth, Chun, and Luppescu (1984), using the same data, claimed that the corrective feedback that the NSs provided was more often "on-record" (direct, unambiguous) than "off-record" (indirect, ambiguous). What was not treated in that research, however, was the result, or effect, of the NS corrective feedback.

Brock et al., using the data from Day and his colleagues, explore this issue, and address two questions:

1. What types of NNS error lead to what types of NS response constituting negative input available to the NNS?
2. What relationship exists betwen type of NS response and subsequent NNS speech in a given conversation?

They find that NS corrective feedback has little observable effect on subsequent NNS speech. This suggests to them that corrective feedback plays a minor role as an aid in acquisition. Brock et al., however, note several limitations to their study, including the fact that they were looking only for observable short-term effects, and that the absence of short-term effects does not necessarily imply that there are no long-term effects of corrective feedback.

In Chapter 12, Schmidt and Frota provide a descriptive, analytical study of the development of conversational ability in Portuguese by Schmidt during a 5-month stay in Brazil in an attempt to address two issues:

1. The kind and amount of Portuguese he learned in his attempts to communicate with native speakers of Portuguese
2. The ways in which formal instruction and informal conversations outside the classroom aided in learning Portuguese

The data examined by Schmidt and Frota come primarily from Schmidt's diary of his experiences. In an attempt to overcome the limitations of research based solely on a diary study, they provide data from a more objective source—a series of four tape-recorded conversations in Portuguese between themselves. Frota, incidentally, is a native speaker of Brazilian Portuguese.

Schmidt and Frota find, not unexpectedly, that there were some grammatical constructions that were relatively easy for Schmidt to learn, and that there were others that were relatively difficult. For example, Schmidt found number agreement between noun and adjective easier to learn than gender agreement. He barely made any headway in learning how to express mood in Brazilian Portuguese; learning the correct conjugation was easier than number and person marking. They are unable to find one single explanation for the differences, and attempt to account for them by such notions as "markedness, morphological confusion, psycholinguistic and discourse-based processing difficulties, transfer from the L1 and in some cases from an L3 (Arabic), innate developmental patterns, and overgeneralizations of target language norms."

The development of Schmidt's conversational abilities followed a pattern that Schmidt and Frota believe is normal—a beginning state in which the NS controls topics by the use of questions leading to a later stage in which NS-NNS conversations are done through the use of an exchange of statements, similar to NS-NS conversations.

They next examine the roles of instruction, interaction, and correction. They conclude that instruction helps in many cases by providing comprehensible input not available outside the classroom. Formal instruction is also helpful as a source for new forms in Portuguese which Schmidt discovered he was able to use immediately in conversations outside the classroom with NSs. In addition, Schmidt and Frota claim that instruction is beneficial because it gave Schmidt interpretations of linguistic phenomena that he could have obtained outside the classroom only with difficulty.

Schmidt and Frota, however, believe that formal instruction was neither a necessary nor a sufficient factor in Schmidt's learning of Portuguese. They report that he did not always learn what was taught in the classroom; for a taught form to be learned by Schmidt, it must have been present in input outside the classroom—a necessary condition.

The role that conversational interaction with NSs played in Schmidt's acquisition of Brazilian Portuguese was a mixed one. For example, only some of the routine or formulaic expressions that he learned in informal conversations led to the extraction of material for productive use. Further, he learned some forms used by NSs which were not explicitly taught to him, but other forms were not similarly learned.

In looking at the role of correction, Schmidt and Frota, unlike Brock et al., find evidence that some NSs's corrections did seem to help Schmidt in learning the target language. They also report, however, that there were times when NS corrections seem to have made no impact on him. Perhaps the difference between the finding in this chapter and the one by Brock et al. is due to the longer observation period available to Schmidt and Frota; corrections might have importance only in long-term learning.

They conclude by challenging some widely held assumptions and "hypotheses" in second language learning and teaching by discussing three issues: the creative and noncreative aspects of language and learning, the process by which a learner progresses from one stage to another, and the role of production in second language learning. This section of the chapter is exciting and stimulating, and will most likely provoke discussion and research.

Section Four concludes with a chapter by Gass and Varonis on the differences between male and female speech in second language learning. Gender-based differences in first languages are well known and have received the attention of researchers for a long time. However, such differences have been neglected in second language acquisition research. Gass and Varonis examined sex differences in NNS-NNS conversation in an initial attempt to fill the gap.

They examine 30 taped conversations of 10 NNS-NNS dyads of native speakers of Japanese learning ESL. Four of the ten dyads were male/female, three were male/male, and three were female/female. The recordings come from three tasks: a conversation task and two picture-description tasks. The data are analyzed in four categories: negotiation of meaning, topics, dominance, and interpersonal phenomena.

Their results are interesting. Gass and Varonis demonstrate that in certain ways the male subjects appear to dominate the male-female conversations. However, females initiate more meaning negotiations than men. The conversations in the male-male dyads display more involvement in the topic.

Gass and Varonis argue that the different interactional styles exhibited by their subjects may have important effects on the acquisition of langue. For example, the male subjects in their study might have produced more comprehensible output because of the ways in which they dominated the conversations. But the female subjects might have received more comprehensible input since they initiated more meaning negotiations in the mixed-sex dyads.

REFERENCES

Chun, A. E., R. R. Day, N. A. Chenoweth, and S. Luppescu. 1982. Errors, interaction, and correction: A study of native-nonnative conversations. *TESOL Quarterly,* 16(4): 537–547.

Day, R. R., N. A. Chenoweth, A. E. Chun, and S. Luppescu. 1984. Corrective feedback in native-nonnative discourse. *Language Learning,* 34(2): 19–45.

11

DIFFERENTIAL EFFECTS OF CORRECTIVE FEEDBACK IN NATIVE SPEAKER–NONNATIVE SPEAKER CONVERSATION

Cynthia Brock, Graham Crookes, Richard Day, and Michael Long
University of Hawaii at Manoa

This study analyzes informal native speaker (NS)–nonnative speaker (NNS) conversation to see what types of NNS error lead to what types of NS response constituting negative input available to the NNS. This study further examines the differential effect of the NS response on subsequent NNS speech in a given conversation.

In their consideration of rule fossilization, Vigil and Oller (1976) claimed that a certain minimum, although unspecified, amount of "corrective feedback" from a NNS's interlocutors' indication of comprehension problems or needed changes in the form of the NNS's utterance is necessary for the continued development of a NNS's interlanguage (IL). Selinker and Lamendella (1979) pointed out, however, that it is necessary to distinguish potentially available feedback and corrective feedback that is actually part of a NNS's intake.

Schachter (1984) suggested that it is necessary to consider not only corrective feedback on the form of a particular NNS utterance but also the broad range of what she calls "negative input," any information provided to the NNS that "something has gone wrong in the transmission of a message," On one end of the continuum this information may occur as explicit corrective feedback, an indication that there is something unacceptable to the native speaker about the form of a comprehended message. At the other end, it may occur as an indication that the NNS's utterance was not comprehended. In between lie implicit corrective feedback, confirmation checks, and clarification requests.

In research on French immersion classrooms, Chaudron (1977) found differential short-term effects in learner response for variations in one type of error correction—repetition—by teachers. It may be the case, then, that different types of negative input may have different effects on NNS speech as well.

The availability to and the effect on the NNS of negative input is relevant to any theory of second language acquisition (SLA) that includes the concept of hypothesis formation and testing on the part of the NNS. Schachter (1984) draws attention to a phenomenon observed and labeled blank trials laws by Levine (1975). In Levine's research, in constructing and revising conscious hypotheses related to problem solving, learners treated no response from the experimenter in the same way they treated responses of "right." Responses of "wrong," on the other hand, caused learners to change their hypotheses. As Schachter points out, negative input may have a similar effect on the NNS's unconscious hypotheses about the rules for generating the target language (TL), and lack of negative input may serve as affirmation of a NNS's incorrect hypotheses. However, available negative input can potentially have a modifying effect on the NNS IL only if it is, in fact, part of the NNS's intake. In other words, only input that is both comprehensible and being attended to can possibly produce alterations in IL forms.

RESEARCH QUESTIONS AND HYPOTHESES

The present study was undertaken to investigate possible relationships between certain types of errors—errors in lexis, phonology, and morphosyntax—made by NNSs in informal conversation and the ways in which their NS interlocutors respond. In addition, possible relationships were sought between the different types of NS response to errors and subsequent alterations in NNS speech in a given conversation. It was hypothesized that corrective feedback occurring in side sequences would influence subsequent NNS output to a greater degree than corrective feedback occurring in NS responses that did not disrupt the main line of conversational discourse. This was motivated by the assumption that participants' attention to form should be greater in side sequences, when the flow of communication is threatened.

The research questions addressed, then, were as follows:

1. What types of NNS error lead to what types of NS response constituting negative input available to the NNS?
2. What relationship exists between type of NS response and subsequent NNS speech in a given conversation?

METHOD

Data

Twenty-three NS-NNS conversations were analyzed in this study. Seventeen were recorded by students enrolled in beginning and intermediate classes at Hawaii Pacific College (HPC) and six were recorded by advanced learners enrolled in the English Language Institute (ELI) at the University of Hawaii at Manoa, both institutions located in Honolulu, Hawaii. The native speakers were asked to record informal conversations of approximately 20 minutes on topics of their choice with NS friends outside the classroom. These conversations formed the corpus for an earlier study of repair techniques (Chun, Day, Chenoweth, and Luppescu 1982).

Analysis

After the conversations were transcribed, errors were agreed on by the raters acting in consensus. "Error" was defined for the purpose of this study, following Richards, Platt, and Weber (1985), as "the use of a linguistic item in a way, which, according to fluent users of the language indicates faulty or incomplete learning of the TL."

Every NNS turn containing an error or errors was identified. The ensuing NS turn was then classified according to the categories of NS response illustrated in the constructed example in Figure 1.

Numbers 1a and 1b are categories of moves that continue the main sequence of the discourse in terms of topic. In both instances the NNS's message has been clearly comprehended. However, category 1a contains implicit corrective feedback in that the error in the NNS's statement has been

		NNS: I goed to New York yesterday.
Continue main sequence	1a	NS: I went there yesterday too. (+ corrective feedback)
	1b	NS: It's a nice town, isn't it?
First move in a side sequence	2	explicit correction (+ corrective feedback) NS: You went. (declaratory intonation)
	3	message checks
	3a	NS: You went yesterday? (+ corrective feedback)
	3b	NS: Yesterday?

FIGURE 1

231

transformed to its TL form because it happens to be used by the NS in his or her response to the NNS. Category 1b, on the other hand, does not contain this implicit corrective feedback.

Categories 2, 3a, and 3b, on the other hand, are the first moves in side sequences. We use the term side sequence, following Jefferson (1972), to indicate a break in the main topic of conversation that is directly related to it. Category 2 constitutes explicit corrective feedback. It is a response to the form of the NNS's message. The NS's declaratory intonation indicates that the NS has clearly understood the message (or believes so). This NS response contains and emphasizes the TL version of the errorful item, and the provision of the TL form is the major thrust of the NS's turn.

Categories 3a and 3b are also the first moves in side sequences, but they are message checks, indicating that the NNS's utterance has not been clearly understood or clearly heard. Category 3a includes confirmation checks or clarification requests that happen to contain the TL form of the errorful item and thus contains implicit corrective feedback. Category 3b does not contain the TL form and therefore does not contain implicit corrective feedback on the form on the NNS's errorful item. It does, however, indicate to the NNS that "something has gone wrong in the transmission." This category also includes clarification requests without the TL form, as in, for example, "Where?"

After extensive practice sessions, and careful agreement of errors, an interrater reliability coefficient of .95 was obtained for coding the NS responses according to the above categories using Cohen's formula for kappa to correct for chance agreement (Cohen 1960, Frick and Semmel 1978).

The NNS turn immediately following an NS response falling into any category except 1b was then analyzed for NNS reaction. The NNS turn immediately following a response falling into categories 1a, 2, and 3a was examined to see if the NNS correctly or incorrectly repeated the supplied TL form and/or used it productively. If this occurred, the supplied form could then be said to be reliably part of the NNS intake and to have had an observable effect. The NNS turn immediately following a response falling into category 3b was examined to see if the NNS recoded an errorful item into a TL form. The NNS's subsequent speech within the remainder of the same conversation was checked for observable effect, that is, for TL or non-TL use of the supplied form. Errors were separated into errors of lexis, phonology, and morphosyntax. Differential effects for error type on NS response were sought, as were differential observable effects on NS speech of different NS response types.

RESULTS

Comparing errors in morphosyntax with NS turns that continue the main line of discourse, morphosyntactic errors were found less likely to result in a side sequence than other errors ($\chi^2 = 9.08$, df = 1, p < 0.005). On the other hand, lexis errors were more likely to result in side sequences than other errors ($\chi^2 = 9.87$, df = 1, p < 0.005). Phonological errors did not appear to be related to a particular type of NS turn ($\chi^2 = 2.96$, df = 1, p < 0.25, ns).

TABLE 1 Relationship between Error Type and Type of NS Turn Following a NNS Error

NS turn type	1a	2	3a	3b	Total
Lexis	5	12	14	12	43
Phonology	12	10	15	11	48
Morphosyntax	29	7	8	17	61
Total errors	46	29	37	40	152

TABLE 2 Error Type vs. Sequence Comparisons

	χ^2	df	
Morphosyntactic errors vs. sequence type	9.08	1	p<0.005
Lexis errors vs. sequence type	9.87	1	p<0.005
Phonological errors vs. NS turn type	2.96	1	ns

Differences in observable effects were tested (χ^2 , df = 1) but were found to be not significant (see Tables 2 and 3) in the following four areas:

1. Main sequences as opposed to side sequences (1a + 1b vs. 2 + 3a + 3b)
2. Explicit correction as opposed to implicit correction (2 vs. 1a + 3a)
3. Explicit correction as opposed to meaning checks (2 vs. 3a + 3b)
4. Implicit correction, main sequence as opposed to side sequence (1a vs. 2 + 3a)

TABLE 3 Relationship between Number of Occurrences of Incorporation and NS Turn Type

NS turn	1a	2	3a	3b
Observable effects:				
raw	6/46	7/29	12/37	2/40
%	13	24	32	5

TABLE 4 Observable Effects Comparisons

	χ^2	df	
Main sequence vs. side sequence	0.596	1	ns
Explicit correction vs. implicit correction	0.0002	1	ns
Explicit correction vs. meaning checks	0.464	1	ns
Implicit correction, main vs. side sequence	3.02	1	ns

DISCUSSION

The significant relations between type of error and ensuing NS turn shown in our data apply to lexis and morphosyntax. They may reflect the different potential each has for communicative distress. Lexical errors are more likely than others to trigger a side sequence in which an attempt is made to clarify the message. Morphosyntactic errors, perhaps because of their lesser communicative significance, are more likely to permit the main line of discourse to be continued.

Whether repetitions or cases of productive use, few effects of the NS response were observed on subsequent NNS conversation. No pattern regarding type of NS turn most likely to produce an effect of any kind on the IL emerged, even though, at the very least, the extra attention focused on the error by a side sequence might have been expected to lead to a significant relation.

Even when the definition of corrective feedback is expanded beyond that used in the Chun et al. (1982) study to include other sources of "negative input" besides explicit correction, an extremely small proportion of errors receive any kind of response that is potentially destabilizing. Of the 152 that did, in only 26 cases was an observable effect exhibited, even when this category includes mere repetition. This suggests, prima facie, the weakness of corrective feedback as an aid to acquisition. Consequently, the failure to observe significant relations between observable effect and NS turn type is not surprising.

CONCLUSION

Obviously, the n size in this study is small, and the ILs were followed for only, at a maximum, 20 minutes after any potentially destabilizing event. However, the general implications run contrary to those of a theory of SLA based on concepts of hypothesis testing, or the need for NS feedback as an important source for IL destabilization, unless the processes involved are conceived as gradual in nature.

It may also be the case that attention needs to be given to the effect of task. We have observed (though not quantified) examples of incorporations following NS provision of corrective feedback following error when conversation takes place in the context of communication games. The significant difference here is probably that the situation prevents the topic's being switched, dropped, or avoided, with the result that far more attention is directed, over a longer period, to a particular area in which the IL is deficient. This impressionistic observation would suggest that ILs *can* be quickly destabilized, if sufficient attention is given to the area in question.

By focusing on corrective feedback to linguistic errors contained in an NNS turn, the analysis used in this study does not capture every instance of corrective feedback. Discourse errors and errors of fact were not included. Also excluded were instances of what might be termed comprehension errors, as illustrated in the following examples from the corpus:

NS: How long will you be going to this school?
NNS: Uh from this year. Last — last September.
NS: No. How long *will* you be going to this school
NNS: oh yeah
        I don't know. I don't know. Maybe four or five years at least.

Furthermore, in limiting our analysis of potentially available corrective feedback to that contained in NS turns immediately following the NNS turns containing errors, corrective feedback provided at the end of a side sequence was not included, as in the following example:

1   NS: What ki- what size bed do you have?
2   NNS: I don't know. I don't know the inches, you know.
3   NS: No no. Is it just- Is it for one person or two people?
4   NNS: One person.
5   NS: Single.
6   NNS: Single yeah single.
7   NS: Mm. I should look around.
8   NNS: I have two single beds.

Since the NNS utterance in line 5 did not contain a linguistic error, neither the NS suppliance in line 6 of the correct lexical item nor the NNS's TL productive use of it in line 8 was coded.

Finally, by looking only for TL or non-TL use of the supplied form, our analysis did not capture alterations in the IL form subsequent to corrective feedback, as in the following sequence of corrective feedback occurring in one conversation:

NNS: Uh how- how do you feel Taiwan?
NS: How did I like it?
NNS: Yeah how do you like it?

                    .
                    .
                    .

NNS: And how- how do you feel the Taiwan uh New Year?
NS: You didn't let me finish my question- your question. You asked me how do I like Taiwan what do I think about it.

                    .
                    .

NNS: . . . LaiLai (a department store in Taiwan). Do you know that?
NS: Yes I went to LaiLai.
NNS: How- how about you feel?
NS: My feeling?
NNS: Uhhuh

The results of this examination of the immediately observable effect of corrective feedback contained in various types of NS response must be considered in the light of the phenomenon, which Schachter (1984) draws attention to, called processing time. A learner may require a certain amount of time to make use of negative input, and in the interim will continue to operate with old, as-yet-unmodified hypotheses.

A related phenomenon was observed by Nelson (1980) in a study of intervention input and first language acquisition of tag questions by children. During an observation session, one of the children, a 3-year-old, used a tag question for the first time "20 hours and 37 minutes after the child had last heard an experimenter's use of a tag question." Since the child's parents were reported virtually never to use tag questions with the child, Nelson assumed the original tag question formation occurred, after a considerable amount of elapsed time, as a result of the intervention input.

It is reasonable to assume that if a NNS repeats a supplied form correctly or incorrectly, or uses it in subsequent speech in a TL or non-TL manner, then that supplied form is part of a NNS's intake. On the other hand, it is not reasonable to say that if he or she does not use the supplied form in any way, then the corrective feedback is not part of the NNS intake. Thus, while we have been looking for observable effects of corrective feedback on NNS' ILs, and have not yet found much evidence of such effects, their absence in the short term does not necessarily mean that they do not exist over time.

REFERENCES

Chaudron, C. 1977. A descriptive model of discourse in the corrective treatment of learners' errors. *Language Learning*, 27(1): 29–49.

Chun, A. E., R. R. Day, N. A. Chenoweth, and S. Luppescu. 1982. Errors, interaction and correction: a study of native-nonnative conversations. *TESOL Quarterly,* 16(4): 537–547.

Cohen, J. A. 1960. A coefficient of agreement for nominal scales. *Educational and Psychological Measurement*, 20: 37–46.

Frick, T., and M. I. Semmel. 1978. Observer agreements and reliabilities of classroom observational measures. *Review of Educational Research*, 48(1): 157–184.

Jefferson, G. 1972. Side sequences. In D. Sudnow (ed.). *Studies in Social Interaction.* New York: The Free Press.

Levine, M. 1975. *A Cognitive Theory of Learning: Research in Hypothesis Testing.* Hillsdale, N.J.: Lawrence Erlbaum Associates.

Nelson, K. E. 1980. Theories of the child's acquisition of syntax: a look at rare events and at necessary, catalytic, and irrelevant components of mother-child conversation. *Annals of the New York Academy of Sciences*, 345: 45–67.

Richards, J. C., J. Platt, and H. Weber. 1985. *Longman Dictionary of Applied Linguistics.* London: Longman.

Schachter, J. 1982. Nutritional needs of language learners. In M. Clarke and J. Handscombe (eds.). *On TESOL '82.* Washington, D.C.: TESOL.

Schachter, J. 1984. A universal input condition. In W. Rutherford (ed.). *Universals and Second Language Acquisition.* Amsterdam: John Benjamins.

Selinker, L., and J. Lamendella. 1979. The role of extrinsic feedback in interlanguage fossilization. *Language Learning*, 29(2): 363–375.

Vigil, N., and J. Oller. 1976. Rule fossilization: a tentative model. *Language Learning,* 26(2): 281–295.

12

DEVELOPING BASIC CONVERSATIONAL ABILITY IN A SECOND LANGUAGE: A CASE STUDY OF AN ADULT LEARNER OF PORTUGUESE[1]

Richard W. Schmidt
The University of Hawaii at Manoa

Sylvia Nagem Frota
Pontifícia Universidade Católica do Rio de Janeiro
Universidade Federal do Maranhão

This chapter is a descriptive, analytical study of the development of conversational ability in Portuguese by one subject during a 5-month stay in Rio de Janeiro, Brazil. The chapter attempts to deal with two basic issues: (1) the kind and amount of language that was learned in order to communicate with native speakers, and (2) the ways in which both instruction and conversational interaction contributed to learning the language.[2] The chapter is based on two data sources. The learner, the first coauthor of this paper, hereafter referred to as R, kept a journal throughout his 5 months of exposure to Portuguese, recording whatever seemed on a day-to-day basis the most salient aspects of his learning experience. As in numerous other diary studies, R recorded his experiences and observations only semisystematically, in greater or lesser detail at various times, and with varying time intervals between events and the journal entries reporting them. Some conversational exchanges were written down within seconds, while other events were recorded at the end of a day or even several days after the fact. Many of the entries deal with communication and learning strategies, hypotheses being formulated concerning the target language, and the degree to which these seemed confirmed or disconfirmed in interaction, issues especially relevant to SLA theory.

Baltra has pointed out that only language learners themselves can be in a position to observe their experiences, but the fact that we cannot observe what goes on in another person's mind should not automatically lead us to assume that we necessarily do know what goes on in our own (Armando Baltra, personal communication). The weaknesses of diary studies are in general well recognized (Bailey and Ochsner 1983). In addition to being idiosyncratic and of dubious generalizability, what they report is subjective, already filtered through the perceptions and possibly the biases of the learner (especially important when the learner is a linguist professionally interested in SLA theory), and exceedingly difficult to verify. With respect to the processes of learning, these are important limitations, since those who believe that language acquisition goes on almost entirely below the level of conscious awareness might argue that one simply cannot observe oneself learning a language (Seliger 1983; Derek Bickerton, personal communication). McLaughlin, Rossman, and McLeod (1983) have argued that introspection and subjective reports are notoriously unreliable and easily mistaken, and as we shall see, R was not able to identify accurately some of the hypotheses and rules that define his Portuguese interlanguage. Even with regard to the products of language learning, there are important limitations to self-report data. Learners cannot say with assurance when their rules and outputs match those of native speakers, cannot be relied upon to identify their errors and areas of difficulty, and may not even be able to report accurately what they have said (still less, what was said by native speakers) on particular occasions.

In order to compensate partially for such weaknesses in the self-report data, the paper also draws upon the evidence from a second, more objective data source, a series of four tape-recorded conversations in Portuguese between the two coauthors, varying from 30 to 60 minutes per conversation, recorded at approximately 1-month intervals. These conversations were unstructured, and covered a range of topics dealing with biography, current activities, and future plans. The tapes were transcribed, errors were identified, and various aspects of the Portuguese noun phrase and verb phrase were analyzed by the second coauthor, a linguist who is a native speaker of Brazilian Portuguese. This analysis is complementary to that which emerges from R's journal, and in the development of the paper there has been an interplay between the data sources, a method recommended by Cohen (1984). Subjective reports in the journal have suggested things to look for in the recorded data, and phenomena initially identified from the conversational transcripts have often been illumintated by comments in the journal. When hypotheses and explanations are offered here, these represent the combined perspectives of the learner and the native speaker observer.

R's Language Learning History

R's previous personal language learning history, with self-assessments of his proficiency in each language, is summarized below. Languages are listed in descending order of proficiency.

Arabic   Arabic is the only language other than English that I have ever been able to speak well. I first studied Arabic in a 6-month intensive audio-lingual course in the United States. This was followed by 8 years' residence (spread over a total of 12 years) in Egypt and Lebanon, during which I also studied intermittently with private tutors. I was evaluated and assigned official FSI ratings twice: after finishing the initial course, I was rated an FSI S-1+; after 2 years of exposure, I was rated an FSI S-3+. I'm not sure of my final level of attained proficiency, since while I was very comfortable in the language there were still things I had trouble expressing, especially in higher registers, and still gaps in my comprehension. I have always thought that the reason I learned Arabic quite well (which most English speakers I knew in the Arab world did not do) was that I made a point from the beginning of making friends who were monolinguals: whatever was to be said had to be said in Arabic. For the past 8 years, I have neither spoken nor heard Arabic except for a few brief encounters with native speakers.

French   I studied French for 3 years in high school and a year in college, but my competence in French is almost entirely passive. I attribute this mainly to patterns of interaction developed in Lebanon. Many Lebanese are bilingual in Arabic and French and prefer to speak French with foreigners. I therefore heard a lot of French during the period in which I was committed to improving my Arabic, and it was not uncommon for me to have long and detailed conversations in which I spoke only Arabic and my interlocutor spoke only French, both of us unable or unwilling to switch. To this day, I am extremely inhibited about speaking French, and I'm not sure what kind of French I would produce if I had no way to avoid trying.

Japanese   I have never studied Japanese, but I have lived with several native speakers and made four trips to Japan, varying between a week and a month. I know about 100 vocabulary items in Japanese and perhaps a dozen formulaic expressions, only one of which (subject-wa NP desu) is at all productive. My comprehension is poor, and I can only rarely get the gist of overheard conversations.

German   I studied German for one semester in graduate school, with intensive cramming before taking a foreign language proficiency exam and almost zero retention thereafter.

Dutch, Italian, Greek, Hebrew, Farsi   These are all languages I have been exposed to only as a tourist, in each case picking up a handful of expressions and vocabulary items for survival and temporary use.

Portuguese (predeparture exposure) I did not study Portuguese before going to Brazil, because my trip was not planned far in advance and final confirmation came less than 2 weeks before I boarded a plane. However, during the 6 weeks immediately preceding my departure, I was teaching a course in comparative grammar in which students worked in groups several times a week, each group eliciting facts about a particular language from a native speaker. One of the languages investigated was Portuguese, and my intention was to spend as much time as possible with the Portuguese group. For practical reasons, it did not work out that way, but I did spend approximately 3 hours listening to students elicit sentences for grammatical analysis from the Portuguese informant. What I got from that was an idea of the basic sentence structure of Portuguese, a handful of vocabulary items (which tended to be repeated over and over in various manipulations of sentences), and a general familiarity with the sounds of the language. Portuguese sounded familiar when I arrived in Brazil.

Instruction and Interaction in Portuguese

R arrived in Brazil with virtually no ability in Portuguese and was unofficially tested 20 weeks later at the S-2 level on the FSI scale.[3] In describing the development of R's command of Portuguese during his stay in Brazil, we have for convenience divided the period of exposure into three unequal stages, defined according to distinct patterns of interaction and instruction: stage 1, 3 weeks (–instruction) and (–interaction); stage 2, 5 weeks, (+instruction) and (+interaction); and stage 3, 14 weeks, (–instruction) and (+interaction). These three stages, which will be discussed first in terms of R's subjective reports in the journal, are indicated graphically in Figure 1, which indicates the period of instruction and the dates of the unofficial FSI exam and the conversational recordings. The amount of interaction at each stage is represented impressionistically, although the points at which increases in interaction are shown are keyed to specific changes mentioned in R's journal.

Stage 1 During the first 3 weeks in Brazil, R had no instruction and almost no interaction in Portuguese. R began his journal in the middle of the second week. The first entry summarizes his experiences up to that point:[4]

Journal entry, Week 2
P and I [R was accompanied by his teenaged son for the first 6 weeks in Brazil] arrived in Rio 10 days ago after an overnight flight from New York. We didn't see anyone to meet us, but had no difficulty getting through customs, into a cab, and across the city to the hotel . . . where we had reservations. After we checked in, D called . . . [and shortly after] arrived to take us to lunch with her family . . . It's a polyglot family . . but the only languages spoken that afternoon were English among the adults and Portuguese with the kids. Of course I didn't understand a word [of the Portuguese]. I noticed that when D talked to her son, she frequently asked *já?*, and he always replied *já*, but I don't know what that means. My dictionary [Berlitz 1982] says "adv., at once, immediately, already."

Week

1 2 3 4 5 6 7 8 9 10 11 12 13 14 15 16 17 18 19 20 21 22

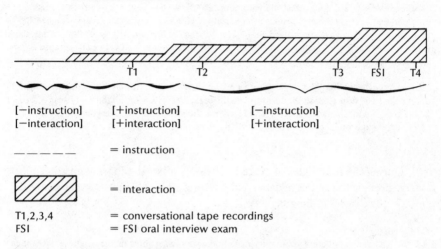

T1		T2	T3	FSI	T4

[−instruction]   [+instruction]   [−instruction]
[−interaction]   [+interaction]   [+interaction]

_ _ _ _ _   = instruction

[hatched box]   = interaction

T1,2,3,4   = conversational tape recordings
FSI   = FSI oral interview exam

FIGURE 1   Patterns of Instruction and Interaction Over a 22-week Period

Sunday we all got together again . . . and went to a soccer game at the Maracaña. Besides enjoying the game I tried to decipher the banners hung around the stadium. French gave me some clues, and I could figure out that they were advertising banks, insurance programs and government health clinics.

Monday . . . I went to the Consulate and met the folks who administer the Fulbright program. Got some information on Portuguese classes available and went immediately . . . to sign up . . . Unfortunately, we will have to wait [3 weeks] until classes begin. In the afternoon, I went to the university and met a few of the English staff I'll be working with . . . . I met a member of the French section, and she spoke to me in French and I spoke back in English, which gave me a vivid flashback to days in Beirut. I was really surprised a moment later when she was talking to D in Portuguese and mentioned *Senhor Fulano*, which must mean "Mr. so-and-so," a loan from Arabic. I also met J . . . [who is] in charge of an exchange program which brought about a dozen American undergraduates to the university a month or so ago. J suggested that I sit in on their classes. However, it turns out that they have all studied Portuguese for two or more semesters before coming to Brazil . . . The course I could sit in on is the tail-end of a rapid grammar review. I know that's not for me, although J said, "why not? You're a linguist."

Other than that, P and I have been alone almost all the time we're been here . . . We've been spending a lot of time at the beach, which requires no language, and exploring the neighborhood, which requires very little more. When we want to go somewhere, I ask at the hotel desk first, repeat whatever I was told to the cab driver, and read the meter to see how much it cost. Buying necessities and eating require a bit more. The night before we left Honolulu, X and Y gave me a dictionary and a phrase book [Figueiredo and Norman 1979], both pocket-sized, and I carry them everywhere. So when I went to a pharmacy the second day I could ask for *pasta de dente* instead of just pointing at the toothpaste. When a clerk says how much something costs, I try to understand the price (so far I cannot) before handing over a bill I've already calculated to be more than enough. . . Unfortunately, the phrase book is meant for Portugal, not Brazil . . . and I think that might turn out to be a major problem. My solution in restaurants: order something I don't know, and I'll know what it is the next time. I've been frustrated at breakfast, though, because the waitress always brings my coffee with milk, which I detest. She always asks first: *café com leite?* and I've tried saying *leite não*, meaning that I want it black, but it still comes with milk or not at all.

So far I have noticed very little about the language. One of the first things P and I learned was our room number (202). One desk clerk pronounces "2" as [dois] and the other says [doish] . . . I wonder if that's geographical or social or free variation. I immediately noticed that Portuguese "r" is frequently [h], as in *rua* ("street"), *correio ("mail"), and the first one Arpoador,* the neighborhood where we are staying. It's satisfying being able to say those words, and very easy because Arabic also has post- and inter-vocalic [h], but I suspect that I'm probably not matching the phonetic value for Portuguese very closely.

I have the textbook for Portuguese 1 [Abrue and Rameh 1972] and I've been studying it in the evenings and at breakfast, reading through the dialogues and doing all the exercises . . . except for the greetings in Chapter 1, which P and I have practiced and use with everyone we encounter, so far I cannot make any connection between what I'm reading in the text and the noise I hear around me.

During the remainder of stage 1, virtually all of R's journal entries report noncomprehension of Portuguese and a strong sense of frustration at not being able to break into the language system:

Journal entry, Week 2
Even though I can't start class yet, I'm trying to find a way to get going on the language. Not much luck! There's a TV in the lobby. While that might be culturally interesting, I've been giving my students the line for years that you can't begin to learn a language from television, and I'm not going to waste my time sitting in front of it . . . P came up with something that might turn out a bit better. There is an FM station that plays two English songs every night . . . with translations into Portuguese after every phrase. The translator has a magnificent, resonanat voice . . . Portuguese is certainly a beautiful language. I'm going to stick with this show for a while, even though so far it hasn't taught me anything. The first problem is that I find it difficult to understand the English lyrics to songs. When I can understand the English, I can't hold even a phrase in memory if I'm trying to listen to the Portuguese at the same time.

Journal entry, Week 2
I *hate* the feeling of being unable to talk to people around me. I'm used to chatting with people all day long, and I don't like this silence. Language is the only barrier, since it is certainly easy to meet Brazilians. I've noticed that it is acceptable to ask anyone on the street for a cigarette. It . . . appears to have no relationship to age, sex or class. Last night an attractive and obviously respectable young woman, accompanied by her boyfriend, stopped me and bummed a cigarette. If I take a pack to the beach, it disappears within an hour, so that's 20 people I could have met. . . . Today P and I were at the beach, a guy came up for a cigarette, sat down and wanted to talk. He asked if I were an American and I said *sim*. He said something I didn't comprehend at all, so I didn't respond. He said, "well, obviously communication with you would be very difficult" (I *did* understand that, though I can't remember any of the words now), and left.

Journal entry, Week 3
The first department meeting was today . . . It started off well, and I actually got the gist of the first topic . . . about university personnel policies and changes in the requirements for appointment and promotion to various ranks (*níveis,* my word for the day). No doubt I understood that much because it's all too familiar in my own work, and the chairperson had a clear diagram on the blackboard. However, after that topic was closed, I did not understand another word for the remainder of the meeting, which dragged on to 9 p.m. I am totally exhausted. The only observation I can report is that

turn-taking rules for meetings in Brazil are different from those in the U.S. There was a great deal of overlap among participants, and the general atmosphere was a lot rowdier than what I'm used to.

Journal entry, Week 3
Just came back from [a sidewalk café], where I finally had something close to a conversation with someone . . . another nonnative speaker . . . a linguist, half Chinese, half Spanish, who works on comparative Romance phonology somewhere in France. . . . I was amazed that I could understand a fair bit of what he said. He spoke slowly and with difficulty and it didn't sound like Portuguese, but French. . . .I said very little, and I guess it was about a third English, a third French and a third Portuguese, but words only. No Portuguese sentences I am sure . . . . Now I must break out of the trap I'm in. I want to be fluent in Portuguese by the time I leave here, and I want to get started. Krashen is absolutely right that native speakers are generally unable or unwilling to provide comprehensible input to beginning nonnative speakers. I wouldn't waste my time talking to someone who knew as little English as I know Portuguese. I know some people prefer to wait and get settled before tackling a language, but in my case this silent period has been maddening and against my will. I can't wait for class to start on Monday.

Stage 2, which we have characterized as (+instruction, +interaction), begins with R's starting formal lessons in Portuguese and, almost simultaneously, beginning to meet and interact with native speakers. R's first day in class was perceived by him as successful:

Journal entry, Week 4
P and I started class yesterday. There are 11 in the class (of various nationalities). The teacher is young and very good. She introduced herself to us (in Portuguese): I am X, my name is X, I am your teacher, I am a teacher, I am a teacher of Portuguese, I'm also a teacher of English, I'm from [place], I'm single, I'm not married, I don't have children, I have a degree in applied linguistics, etc. She went around the class, asking the same kinds of questions: what's your name?, where are you from?, what kind of work do you do?, do you have children?, etc. Most of the students could answer some of the questions, e.g., I know what my title is at the university. Everyone was rapidly picking up new things from the others' answers. For the rest of the class, we circulated, introducing ourselves to each other and talking until we exhausted the possibilities. At the end of the class, X put the paradigm for SER on the board, plus a few vocabulary items. Great! This is better than *bom dia* and then silence. . . . I'm sure I'll be asked all those questions thousands of times before I leave here. So I went out last night and talked to four people. It worked, and I'm invited to a party tomorrow night. Of course I quickly ran out of things to say and quickly stopped understanding what people said to me, but that just makes me eager to get back to class.

R's second class day was much less satisfying:

Journal entry, Week 4
A half hour into the class, X showed up and pulled me out. There's a new section of the intensive course that's just opened and if I want I can move. I said yes . . . and went to the new class, which was already in session . . . . When I sat down, a drill was in progress. SER again, which must be every teacher's lesson one. Teacher asks, student responds: *Você é americana?* ["Are you an American?"]; *Sou, sim* ["I am, yes"]. When it was my turn the question was *Você é casado?* ["Are you married?"], so I said *não*. L corrected me:*sou, sim*. I objected: *eu não sou casado*. L said [in English], "We are practicing affirmative answers." I objected again, I'm not married, and L said, "These questions have nothing to do with real life." My blood was boiling, but I shut up. The remainder of the class was choral repetition of the first conjugation verb FALAR: *falo, fala, falamos, falam,* over and over. I didn't like that much either, and when it was my turn to perform

individually I tried to put the forms in sentences: *eu falo português* ["I speak Portuguese:], *você fala inglês* ["you speak English"]. L did not appreciate that at all. What a sour start! But I think I will stick with it. There are only three students in the class, and the other two are as eager as I am... This class will give me almost twice as many hours a week as the other one, and L says we will cover about twice the material I would get in that course. So I guess I can remember that I am not the teacher here, try not to provoke L too much, and make the best use of the resources that I get.

Although R was never happy with the methodology and techniques used in the class, he found that it improved with time:

Journal entry, Week 6
L and I are still giving each other a hard time. Today in class, K's sentence in a substitution drill had a negative before the verb, followed by *nada*. I wanted to find out whether other double negatives are possible, so when it was my turn I said *eu não conhecia ninguém* ["I didn't know anyone"]. This wasn't the sentence I was supposed to produce. I don't remember whether L corrected me to *alguém* or not. I only remember her annoyance that I was not performing the drill as I was supposed to, so I didn't find out what I was after. But in general, the class is OK now, even though much too structured. We start out every day with "what did you do yesterday?" and always end with "what are you going to do today after class?" In between, we have the structures of the day, each beginning with explanations and a few examples and far too many drills. I don't mind the drills as much as at first, but I will not say sentences which I don't understand, so I ask a lot of questions. This has not endeared me to L, but I think we are now getting to the point of grudging mutual respect. I have to admit that whenever we are doing anything except drills she does have a superb ability to monitor our conversations and adjust up or down as appropriate... Maybe that's possible if you are teaching a beginning class. Most of the native speakers I'm meeting outside of class don't come very close. I also like L's stories, most of which are quite clever. And she doesn't overburden us with rules... We have a text [Magro and DePaula 1981], but it's basically an exercise book, with very few explanations. We don't use the text much, and when we do, L skips around.

During stage 2, R started making Brazilian friends with whom he conversed only in Portuguese. At the beginning of this stage, he could converse for only a few minutes, but by the end of stage 2 he could carry on a conversation for several hours, although he depended on patient and helpful conversational partners to do so. There was also an important limitation in whom he would attempt Portuguese conversation with, which never completely disappeared. During this stage, he was comfortable only speaking Portuguese with monolingual native speakers:

Journal entry, Week 6
I also understand [P's] reluctance to speak to me in Portuguese, since I find it strange to speak Portuguese to English speakers also.... Night before last, J had a party for the American exchange group, my first chance to meet most of them. I was very impressed by the fact that they all spoke mostly Portuguese all evening, even though there was no one present who couldn't speak English. I tried to go along with it as far as I could, but I'm so limited in what I can say that I couldn't maintain it.

Journal entry, Week 7
S and I made the first recording today for our project. I felt very strange at first, because this was absolutely the first time we have ever talked to each other in Portuguese .... This is somewhat

different from my difficulty in using Portuguese with native speakers of English. In that case, it's just so much easier to say it in English that it's hard to avoid switching. But with native speakers of Portuguese who are English teachers . . . I am ashamed to show my ignorance of their language when they speak mine so well. With monolinguals, it's different: we are equally ignorant of each other's language and I feel no embarrassment at all. So S and I talked in English right up to the moment she turned the tape-recorder on. Then it was fine. It was good to find that I wasn't as embarrassed as I expected to be, in fact quite comfortable.

In addition to going to class, R used several strategies to try to enhance his learning:

Journal entry, Week 7
Since we don't have a real grammar book . . . I've been organizing my own, mostly verb tables, vocabulary lists, and whatever comes up in class that's interesting. I review these every day on the bus. I've started reading the *Journal do Brasil*, but it's beyond me, so about half the time I buy the English paper instead. . . . A few times I've bought *Última Hora*, a tabloid, which I find I can read with better comprehension. . . . I still carry my dictionary, but it seldom answers my questions. Too many of the entries are just cognates with English, with no indication of how the meanings vary. This a.m., A came by and kept talking about the *cohenteza* at the beach. I knew from context that he must mean "undertow" or "riptide," but I didn't know which, so I tried to look it up. It took me a while to realize that the spelling must be *correnteza*. I have no trouble pronouncing a word with "rr" as [h], but I usually get fooled going from the pronunciation to the spelling. When I figured that out, I found that the dictionary only has *corrente*, "current," which was less informative than what I had already figured out.

Journal entry, Week 7
Last night we [the members of the Portuguese class] and L's other class went to a Japanese restaurant in Copacabana . . . an official exercise in communication outside of the class . . . . The event went well . . . . I was proud of myself because I managed to produce a couple of instances of *tão* + adj. and *mais do que* constructions [comparatives], which is what we practiced in class yesterday morning. K noticed it, and said she was impressed because she never remembers to use in conversation what we learn in class. I think it's easier for me because I've been making it a habit, and . . . simply because I have fewer resources [than K] to draw on. Whatever I can get, I need.

By the end of the course (50 hours of instruction in all), R was satisfied that he had gotten the foundation he was looking for:

Journal entry, Week 8
Today was the last day of class. X sat in, and she and L agreed that after the between-term break [of one month] I should register for Portuguese 3, not 2. I put less stock in X's evaluation, because I think she was influenced a lot by the joke I told in class . . . X didn't realize that I had written out the joke at home using my dictionary, memorized it and practiced my delivery. However, L knows my ability, and seems satisfied. I am also satisfied . . . . When I started the class I could hardly say anything to anyone. Now I am at least at the point where I can get conversations going and stay in the conversation if my interlocuter is patient enough. I've certainly met a lot of people in a short time, and although the communication breaks down with frustrating regularity the friends that I've been making have been helpful in getting things started up again. Some, like A, are quite sensitive to the problems I have in expressing myself, while some like H are pretty hopeless . . . . I'm confident that I can get along without class for a while.

Stage 3   R planned to reenroll in a Portuguese language class when the next term began, but after the first day of class decided to drop out and try to learn the language through interaction alone:

Journal entry, Week 12
Portuguese 3 met for the first time this morning. From my point of view, it's a disaster. The first sign that things were not going to be perfect was when I arrived and found 17–18 people outside a classroom that only holds 10. K was there and told me . . . Portuguese 4 had been cancelled and everyone is being put into one class. When we were re-located to another room, things started off with the obligatory introductions. The first student to speak was housewife, native speaker of Spanish, who has lived in Brazil for 8 years and wants to polish her grammar. I saw C . . . [who has] acted in Brazilian theater. For the group as a whole, the average length of residence in Brazil seemed to be about 4 years . . . I do not belong in this group. The class started off with a discussion of the imperfeito vs. perfeito . . . Then Y said we would do a communicative exercise. She got us into groups of three and passed out pictures. The exercise was for each of us to make up three sentences about our picture, using the present subjunctive. I have no idea how you make the present subjunctive or any other subjunctive . . . What really bothered me most was that Y speaks so rapidly that I didn't understand much of what she said at all. She apologized for it, said that everyone tells her she speaks much faster than most native speakers, but she can't control it. I don't know what to do about this situation. I have the option of going back to Portuguese 2, but I might be bored there . . . . I'm tempted to drop completely . . . I'm doing pretty well outside of class, meeting people constantly, speaking Portuguese 2–3 hours every day and I think learning something from almost every interaction . . . Even if I stick with this class, I'm going to miss at least a third of the meetings because of workshops I've got scheduled. That sounds like a rationalization to me. Am I going to feel guilty if I drop out? What are my goals? . . . . Would I rather get up early to go to class, or . . . stay out very late at night partying, with Brazilians, in Portuguese? An obvious choice. I have until Monday to change my mind, because that's when I have to pay my tuition.

During stage 3, R continually increased the circle of friends with whom he spoke only Portuguese. Throughout this stage, he continued to feel that he required interlocuters who were not only patient but also talented at communicating with native speakers, although on occasion he also felt that he needed less help than friends had become used to providing:

Journal entry, Week 11
H and I ate dinner at Caneco 70. He complained non-stop about his job. I tried to say "you don't seem comfortable" with the job: *sinto que você não está comfortável,* and his face showed complete non-comprehension. I grabbed my dictionary. "Comfortable" is *comfortável,* but it flashed through my mind that perhaps you can only say chairs are comfortable, not people. A few minutes later H said something with *não deve.* I was taught DEVER as "have to" or "must," and I've been thinking that *não deve* + Verb would mean "don't have to" and *deve não* + Verb would mean "must not," but H's remark obviously meant "should not." So I learned something, but in general H is a terrible conversationalist for me. He doesn't understand things I say that everyone else understands. When I don't understand him, all he can ever do is repeat.

Journal entry, Week 12
V and I were waiting for the bus when A spotted us and came over and talked for a few minutes. After he left, V complained that A speaks very simplified Portuguese to me and speaks much too slowly. I . . . protested that I have really needed slower than normal speech. However, it's true that I now understand almost everything A says to me . . . I need more challenge than this, new blood. Perhaps I should propose the vampire principle for SLA.

Journal entry, Week 18
Last night I was really up, self-confident, feeling fluent. . . . At one point, M said to F that she should speak more slowly for me, but I said no, please don't, I don't need it anymore.

Although R was conscious that most Brazilians modified their speech for his benefit, he was also impressed by the fact that they did expect him to learn Portuguese. He was constantly encouraged by friends, but also frequently corrected and criticized for errors:

Journal entry, Week 10
X and Y, both Americans married to Brazilians, talked only in Portuguese. I remarked to X that this seemed quite unusual to me, but he commented that almost all foreigners living in Brazil learn Portuguese quickly and well. I find this a different attitude from what I've encountered in other countries. Perhaps it's because Brazil attracts many immigrants, not just expatriates who work a few years and move on.

Journal entry, Week 16
I had a conversation with Y, the manager, who said my Portuguese seems to be coming along. She then said that she learned Portuguese perfectly in three weeks after she arrived here from Italy 20 years ago.

Journal entry, Week 20
Last night I met X, who's just come back from Argentina. Before we were introduced, I overheard M and U talking to X about me at the other end of the table. X: *ele fala português?* ["Does he speak Portuguese?"]; U: *fala mal* ["He speaks poorly"]. M said I make lots of mistakes, and mentioned *marida* and *pais*. X saw me looking at them and said: *mas você entende tudo?* ["But you understand everything?"] I was annoyed and wanted to let them know I had been listening, so I replied: *entendo mal também* ["I also understand poorly"].

During the last few months of his stay in Brazil, R increased his use of Portuguese in spurts. In the fourth month, he made several trips to other cities with friends and spoke only Portuguese for 3 to 4 days at a time. During the last month, he shared an apartment with a monolingual native speaker. R felt that the most significant expansion of his interaction and ability in Portuguese came when he began spending most of his free time with an informal social group of Brazilians:

Journal entry, Week 17
Two weeks ago, M took me to a sidewalk restaurant in Copacabana to meet some friends. I've been back almost every night since . . . . Between 11 and 1 about 20 regulars show up for dinner. Everyone knows everyone, and there's lots of moving about and putting tables together. Later, smaller groups split off, either to party in someone's apartment nearby or to go dancing. I've seen a lot of sunrises, and I think I've found a place where I can really fit in. They have welcomed me, and there's a critical mass of very intelligent people whom I find very stimulating. The people I've met so far have been mostly writers (journalists, novelists) or theater people (actors, producers, directors). It's a big challenge. Part of the problem is cultural. . . . The language problem is severe. I frequently get so exhausted trying to keep up at least with the main topic of each conversation that I just drift off for a while. In spite of that, I've felt positively euphoric since I started to hang out there.

At the end of his stay in Brazil, R summed up what progress he thought he had made, and attributed a large part of his improvement in Portuguese to interaction with this group:

Journal entry, Week 22
The area where I think I've made the steadiest progress is comprehension. There are still plenty of things I cannot follow and even television is still difficult . . . but I am not so discouraged anymore. Even when my Arabic was at its best, I still couldn't follow NS-NS conversations a lot of the time. I think the biggest help has been interacting with lots of people regularly at Trattoria. There I don't restrict myself to highly negotiated one-on-one conversations, but really strain to understand what everyone is saying. When I do get lost, usually someone will notice and will negotiate me back in. . . . Last night was my last there, and also M's birthday. Z had champagne sent to our table and N and E made short speeches. . . . U, who has been the harshest critic of my Portuguese, said I've improved a lot and my Portuguese is now almost as good as her English.

As time progressed, R was more able to carry on conversations in Portuguese even when English was available as a much easier means of communication:

Journal entry, Week 16
O and Q came by about 9 for the trip to a samba club out of town. V decided to come along, and while we were waiting for our ride she insisted that we speak only Portuguese all evening. I agreed. It was a strange feeling, because of the dozen in our group more than half were English teachers from [a language institute], but . . . with this group, maybe I can manage it so that it's English at work, Portuguese after dark.

Journal entry, Week 19
Z showed up with N and Y. His head was freshly shaved, because yesterday was the last shoot of the prison film he's acting in. I found out that he lived in New York for five years and has acted off Broadway. I'm glad I didn't know that before, or I probably would have spoken English with him. As it was, we did not switch to English even after I discovered his English is probably nearly perfect.

However, R's use of Portuguese throughout his stay in Brazil was exclusively for social, not professional purposes. He lectured on applied linguistics at a university in Rio de Janeiro and gave workshops at various institutions for language teachers, but always in English. He felt that he could not have carried out these functions in Portuguese, even at the end of his stay:

Journal entry, Week 11
Being simultaneously translated today was a new experience, but I'm glad I didn't attempt the paper in Portuguese . . . . I saw T before the conference and he was in a panic . . . told them he could do it in Portuguese and wished he hadn't. Shortly after my presentation, X gave her paper on Amerindian Linguistics. It was excellent, and I really admire her bravery and ability. I was surprised to find that I could understand her talk completely . . . the first clear example I've had of the superior comprehensibility of Portuguese spoken by another English-speaker. Almost made me feel I could have done it myself, though I know I could not have. I was even nervous fielding questions in Portuguese after my presentation (I replied in English), and I know I misinterpreted at least one of them.

The last few meetings of the English section have been mostly in Portuguese . . . . D told me that before I arrived the meetings were always in Portuguese but some members of the staff thought they should not be, and my presence was a good excuse to switch. Now they think I know enough at least to follow. I do not . . . . I don't have the vocabulary for talking about academic subjects, and I still cannot follow conversations at full speed when Brazilians are talking to each other . . . in a group melee, I have to focus my full attention on the overall topic . . . if I once lose track of what's being talked about I'm lost.

WHAT WAS LEARNED? LINGUISTIC ANALYSIS

In describing the development of R's Portuguese from a linguistic point of view, we are hampered by the fact that there has been very little research describing other second or foreign language learners of Portuguese. We will identify some areas of ease and difficulty for R, but we do not know the extent to which he will have ultimately been seen to be typical of adult learners of Portuguese. Some of the grammatical features that were learned by R with difficulty may turn out to be problems for all learners; others may later be seen to have been idiosyncratic problems of just this one learner.

Table 1 presents accuracy data (percentages of correctly supplied forms in obligatory contexts) for 17 grammatical features of the Portuguese simple clause at two times. Conversation tape 1 was recorded during R's seventh week in Brazil (fourth week of instruction); conversation tape 4 was recorded during R's last week in Brazil (week 22), the end of a 14-week period of interaction only. While we are aware of the various objections raised against morpheme counting in second language acquisition research (Hatch 1983: 44–57) and agree that these numbers do not tell the whole story, an array such as that in Table 1 has several advantages. It allows us to succinctly characterize some of the most noticeable features of R's interlanguage. While Table 1 shows some improvement in grammatical correctness over time, R's interlanguage at both the earlier and later stages recorded was characterized by a strong tendency to make errors in the use of articles, the copula, and (to a lesser extent) prepositions. The accuracy figures presented in Table 1 also allow us to make some comparisons with a study by van Naerssen (1980) on the acquisition of grammatical constructions in Spanish (the constructions are similar, though not identical, in Spanish and Portuguese). Van Naerssen collected data on 15 first-year college students of Spanish as a foreign language whose native language was English and scored the following grammatical constructions: present indicative tense, perfect past tense, imperfect past tense, adjective/noun number agreement, and the copulas SER and ESTAR. We started with the same list of constructions but have broken down several of them into subcategories and have added categories for prepositions and articles, in order to give a slightly more comprehensive picture of the grammar of the Portuguese simple sentence.[5]

249

TABLE 1 Accuracy Ratings (Percentages of Correct Forms in Obligatory Contexts) for 19
Grammatical Features of the Portuguese Simple Sentence

	Tape 1	Tape 4
Noun-phrase features:		
Noun gender (phonological shape)	98% (182/186)	99% (132/134)
Gender agreement, articles	95% (105/111)	96% (184/191)
Gender agreement, premodifiers	79% (23/29)	92% (95/103)
Gender agreement, adjectives	78% (59/76)	94% (45/48)
Noun-adjective order	92% (36/39)	97% (38/39)
Adjectives, number agreement	95% (75/79)	92% (55/60)
Prepositions	70% (139/199)	77% (201/260)
Definite article	66% (91/137)	67% (122/181)
Indefinite article	40% (10/25)	56% (52/93)
Verb-phrase features:		
Regular verbs, correct conjugation	99% (89/90)	98% (162/165)
Irregular verbs, correct form (not regularized)	99% (74/75)	100% (294/294)
Number agreement, regular verbs	99% (89/90)	94% (155/165)
Number agreement, irregular verbs	99% (74/75)	99% (292/294)
Person, regular verbs	92% (83/90)	95% (156/165)
Person, irregular verbs	99% (74/75)	99% (290/294)
Choice of tense: present	99% (119/120)	97% (204/210)
Choice of tense: perfect past	80% (28/35)	92% (85/92)
Choice of tense: imperfect past	85% (11/13)	74% (34/46)
Copula	44% (39/88)	54% (60/111)

Noun Phrase Features

Gender In Portuguese and Spanish, articles, other premodifiers, and
adjectives (which generally follow the noun) agree with nouns in both number
and gender. For Spanish as a foreign language, van Naerssen reports that
(1) students had little difficulty with initially choosing the gender of the noun to
be modified, (2) gender agreement was more difficult than number agreement,
and (3) students perceived the masculine form to be the basic form for
adjectives. These three conclusions apply also to R's learning of Portuguese. R
appears to have perceived the masculine form of adjectives to be basic, possibly
because there are more O-nouns than A-nouns in Portuguese (Raymond
Moody, personal communication): 19 of R's 20 adjective gender errors (on the
two tapes combined) consisted of using a masculine adjective when a feminine
one was required. R also showed better accuracy in inflecting adjectives for
number than for gender (95 vs. 78 percent on tape 1).

R also showed little difficulty in initially choosing the gender of the noun to
be modified, although a consideration of this issue has led us to examine some
additional aspects of Portuguese gender and ultimately to view gender as a
multidimensional rather than a unitary phenomenon. The gender of the noun in a
Portuguese phrase such as *a comida brasileira* ("Brazilian food") is indicated
in three ways, all realized by *-a* in this example: the choice of the feminine article

a, the phonological shape of the noun (the vast majority of nouns ending in-*a* are feminine), and the feminine singular adjective *brasileira* (the masculine form is *brasileiro*). In determining R's initial choice of noun gender, we found that the criteria of phonological shape and accompanying article both had to be considered. Both have been shown to be important in the first language acquisition of languages with grammatical gender (Slobin in press: 9, 41), but neither alone tells us unambiguously whether R acquired the gender of a noun. Reliance on articles alone as a criterion may underestimate the learner's knowledge, because R frequently omitted them but sometimes indicated elsewhere in the data (for example, by providing a correctly inflected adjective) that he indeed knew the gender of a particular noun. Phonological shape as a criterion may overestimate the learner's knowledge, because some nominal endings do not betray gender or may be misleading (for example, there are exceptions to the generalization that nouns ending in -*a* are feminine).

Table 1 suggests that phonological shape is the more important factor in R's acquisition of gender, consistent with the data from Romance language L1 studies. R almost always got the phonological shape correct, even at the beginning, and also identifies almost all the errors he did make as nouns that he had never heard in Portuguese but was simply guessing, attempting to transfer an English cognate, e.g.: *gramático comparativo* as an on-the-spot translation of English "comparative grammar" (Portuguese is *gramática comparativa*); *diária*, based on English "diary" (Portuguese has *diário*, though in context the correct word was *memórias*). The single error not of this type is identified by R as a performance slip, a momentary confusion between two nouns with different genders: *tango* (the dance) and *tanga* (Brazilian-style bikini).

Selection of an appropriate masculine or feminine article was only slightly more difficult for R than remembering the phonological shape of nouns. Both were much easier than adjective agreement. We do notice a difference over time in those article errors which R did make. On conversation tape 1, R showed some variation in article gender even when the phonological shape of the noun was fixed: tape 1 contains both *da guerra* (correct) and *o guerra* (incorrect), *a PUC* (correct) and *no PUC* (incorrect). By the time of tape 4, R was consistent in the articles he used with particular nouns and, possibly because the phonological rhyming pattern had gotten stronger, he was more likely to make errors when the phonological shape of the noun was misleading. Three of the seven errors on tape 4 were nouns ending in-*ema* or-*ama*, which are of Greek origin and always masculine in Portuguese. R misinterpreted them as feminine nouns, based on the final -*a* alone.

In addition to articles, other determiners and premodifiers in Portuguese must also agree with the noun in number and gender. We computed accuracy figures for gender in premodifiers other than articles separately, partly to see if there might be evidence suggesting whether the discrepancy between gender agreement of articles (relatively easy) and adjectives (relatively difficult) derives from the contrast between pre- and postmodification or possibly, as suggested by Slobin (in press: 9), from the storage of nouns with co-occurring articles once these are learned. The latter suggestion seems more plausible in light of the accuracy figures presented in Table 1. Gender agreement with determiners such as *todo/a* ("every"), *muito/a* ("many"), etc., as well as with the possessive pronouns *meu/minha, seu/sua,* etc., was much more difficult than article agreement, and the numbers for gender agreement of premodifiers and adjectives are almost identical on both tapes.

Noun-adjective order   Van Naerssen reports that learners of Spanish as a foreign language had virtually no problem learning the order of nouns and adjectives. R also had little difficulty producing Portuguese constructions in which adjectives follow the noun rather than precede as in English. R may have found this aspect of Portuguese syntax easy because in Arabic, his strongest L2, adjectives also follow the noun. However, if it turns out that second or foreign language learners of Portuguese in general have little difficulty with noun-adjective pairings, as we suspect is the case, this may be contrasted with the fact that Portuguese-speaking learners of English do have problems with the English order, producing constructions such as *sons and daughters adopteds*, on the Portuguese pattern. A handy explanation for this one-way transfer may be found in the suggestion of numerous SLA scholars that L1 patterns that are marked are unlikely to be transferred (Krashen 1983, Zobl 1980, Kellerman 1978). With regard to noun-adjective order, Portuguese is unmarked and English marked, since a consistent SVO language places nominal modifiers such as adjective, genitive, and relative clause after the noun, while OV languages do the opposite (Greenberg 1963, Lehmann 1978).

Examination of the errors that R did make in this category indicates one possible conditioning factor. Half of the errors were translations of proper nouns (adjective-noun compounds) in English, e.g., *média este* for "Middle East" (Portuguese is *Oriente Médio*); *festa de novo ano* for "New Year celebration" (Portuguese is *ano novo*).[6]

Prepositions   Prepositions, which typically involve numerous lexical and syntactic complexities, are difficult in any language; so it is no surprise that prepositions were more difficult for R than any other feature of the noun phrase discussed so far, with accuracy figures of 70 percent for tape 1 and 77 percent for tape 4.

The error rates of 30 percent on tape 1 and 23 percent on tape 4 conflate two types of errors, omission and incorrect choice of preposition. (There are also a few "extra" prepositions on both tapes, which are not included in the figures in Table 1.) On tape 1, R omitted 18 percent (35/199) of all obligatory prepositions. There are a few cases in which transfer from English is the suspected culprit, since there are some verbs that are simple transitives in English but require prepositions before the object in Portuguese. One such verb is GOSTAR ("like"), which R used six times on tape 1, always without its required preposition *de*. Most omissions of prepositions are not susceptible to a transfer explanation, however, since in the majority of cases English and

Portuguese both require a preposition. When R did provide prepositions, another 15 percent (25/164) were incorrect. Again, some of these errors are susceptible to a transfer explanation, e.g., *ao fim de mês ("at the end of [the] month"),* where Portuguese requires *no* ("in"), but other errors occur when English would have been a reliable guide, e.g., *Hawaii é do Pacífico,* "Hawaii is of the Pacific," where both English and Portuguese require "in." Other errors arose when R simply had not mastered a distinction between two Portuguese prepositions (especially *a* vs. *para*) for which English has no parallel distinction.

By the time of tape 4, R showed greater control over Portuguese prepositions when he used them: 93 percent (201/206) of the prepositions he used were correct. But his tendency to omit prepositions altogether continued unabated. Although the verb GOSTAR was used another six times on tape 4, with the preposition *de* correctly supplied five of those six, R's overall rate of preposition omission of 17 percent (44/206) showed virtually no improvement from tape 1.

Articles Articles posed major problems for R in his acquisition of Portuguese. As indicated in Table 1, R's accuracy rates for definite and indefinite articles on tape 1 were only 66 and 40 percent, respectively, and showed only slight improvement on tape 4. In fact, if the figures for definite and indefinite articles are summed, R's overall accuracy rate increased only from 62 percent on tape 1 to 63 percent on tape 4.

Errors of omission and incorrect choice are again conflated in Table 1, but in the case of articles, omission was overwhelmingly the problem. Of the total of 161 article errors on the two tapes analyzed, 155 (96 percent) were errors of omission, while only six were incorrectly chosen articles (definite where indefinite was required in all cases).[7]

R deleted the definite article in all environments, including those in which an article is required in both English and Portuguese, e.g., *diretor de centro cultural americano* ("director of [the] American cultural center"), but as Table 2 indicates there are two respects in which the Portuguese definite article posed particular learning problems for R.

TABLE 2   Percentage of Definite Articles Supplied in Obligatory Contexts with All Nouns, Following Contracting Prepositions and Preceding Place Names

	Tape 1	*Tape 4*
Definite article, all nouns	66% (91/137)	67% (122/181)
After contracting prepositions	45% (21/47)	68% (63/93)
Before place names	28% (9/32)	66% (41/62)

Geographical names (neighborhoods, cities, states, countries) and some other proper nouns (such as names of institutions) cause difficulties because these usually do not require articles in English but usually do in Portuguese. The information required is lexical in most cases; e.g., if one lives in the city of Rio de Janeiro (which takes a definite article, *o Rio*, though most cities do not), one must learn individually whether one lives *em Copacabana* ("in Copacabana," no article), *no Leblon* (masculine article), *na Barra da Tijuca* (two feminine articles), etc. In other cases, the rule is more general; e.g., all names of countries except for a half dozen exceptions do take an article.

On tape 1, R did not distribute the articles he used randomly but produced specific nouns consistently either with or without an article. Of all place names that appear more than once on tape 1, there are only two (*Egito, Japão*) that appear both with and without an article. There are four nouns (*o Brasil, o Rio, os Estados Unidos, a PUC*), all taught in class, which R invariably produced with their obligatory definite articles. All other place names (including *Hawaii*, which appears 12 times on tape 1) were consistently produced without any article.

The problem with articles that follow prepositions, on the other hand, is less a problem of lexical knowledge than one of automatizing a complex psycholinguistic procedure. In order to produce a simple Portuguese sentence such as *eu gosto do Brasil* ("I like [of the] Brazil"), a speaker/learner must: (1) realize that the verb GOSTAR requires the preposition *de*; (2) identify *Brasil* as a noun that must be preceded by the masculine definite article *o*; and (3) contract the preposition with the article (or re-retrieve the contracted form from memory). There are five common prepositions that contract with the article (*de, em, a, por, para*), and on tape 1 R seldom managed the contraction with any of them.

By the time of tape 4, R's particular difficulty with articles before place names seemed to have disappeared. Most nouns that R produced on tape 1 without an article showed some variation on tape 4 (e.g., *Hawaii* appeared again 16 times, 6 times with the required article and 10 times without), while most new place names and other proper nouns and other proper nouns had been learned with their accompanying articles, which were used consistently. There are a handful of new geographical nouns that R had learned without any article, e.g., [o] *Flamengo*, a neighborhood name about which R commented:

Journal entry, Week 22
S and I did our last taping today. I think it went very well, and it was fun to do. We were both relaxed and joking, but I was still aware of monitoring a lot (as she could tell), especially my articles. I know one I missed: Flamengo. I just asked M if it takes an article and he said yes, *você mora agora no bairro do Flamengo* [you live now in the Flamengo district].

R's specific difficulty with articles following contracting prepositions also seemed to have been resolved with time, except for the contraction *para* + *o* = *pro*, which he never produced correctly. The result of improvement in these two troublesome environments was not, however, a general improvement over time in supplying required definite articles. R continued to omit a third of all obligatory definite articles, but we are unable to identify any further conditioning factors that might explain this.

The case of the indefinite article, which R omitted even more frequently than the definite article on both tape 1 and tape 4, is even more puzzling. Although the Portuguese indefinite article is less regular in its use than the definite article (Thomas 1969: 35), a contrastive analysis between English and Portuguese would not predict wholescale omission of the indefinite article. Most of the striking differences between Portuguese and English involve cases where English requires the article and Portuguese omits it, e.g., before nouns denoting profession, religion, and nationality; before unmodified nouns in the predicate; and after negatives. Yet R never made L1 transfer errors such as *você tem um carro?* ("Do you have a car"), incorrectly supplying an indefinite article where Portuguese disallows it.[8] We find no apparent conditioning factors for R's omission of the indefinite article,[9] nor do we know if he is typical of second language learners of Portuguese in this regard. We do have two hypotheses to suggest, which might be resolved by comparisons with other learners with different backgrounds:

1. R was well aware that Portuguese speakers of English make errors in English constructions such as *she is doctor, he has car.* Observing that Portuguese sometimes omits articles that English requires, R may have unconsciously decided not to bother much with providing them. (This was not a conscious strategy.)

2. R's strongest L2, Arabic, has no indefinite article. R subjectively felt that his Portuguese was greatly affected by transfer from Arabic, and this would explain why R deleted the indefinite article more frequently than the definite. While we hesitate to claim syntactic transfer from a third language, R recorded several of his own errors that seem to have no reasonable explanation other than transfer from Arabic:[10]

Journal entry, Week 5
Today in class I talked about hanging out at Caneco 70, and L corrected my pronunciation to *setenta* ["70"]. I realized that I have been saying [sittenta]. That's from Arabic, a clang association. Portuguese *setenta* sounds closer to me to Arabic *sitta* ["six"] than it does to Portuguese [Rio] *sete* ["seven"], which is pronounced [seči].

Journal entry, Week 5
I'm beginning to wonder if I have English stored in one part of my brain and Arabic in another. If so, I'm putting Portuguese where the Arabic is. Or maybe I've got a translate-to-foreign-language program. Arabic words slip out of my mouth at the darndest times, not when I realize that I don't know a Portuguese word and am groping, but just automatically, fluently, unreflectingly. This morning in class I said *yimkin* [Arabic, "perhaps"] without realizing it wasn't Portuguese until L looked at me and signalled noncomprehension. Now I know the word: *talvez*. It even sounds Arabic, rhymes with *ma'leesh* [Arabic, "never mind"]. Weirder still, a few moments later we did a drill with nouns and adjectives and I said *as moças as bonitas* ["the women the [sic] beautifuls"]. L corrected me immediately, but I knew at that instant that it was from Arabic. I can see the logic in it. In Arabic and Portuguese adjectives follow the noun and agree in number and gender, so if Arabic reduplicates the article before the adjective then Portuguese must too. But I didn't think any of that *before* I said it. Maybe schema theory fits it best: top-down processing, filling in the Arabic schema once it's been activated by what I know so far about Portuguese.

Verb-phrase Features

Conjugation class, person, number　Van Naerssen has discussed areas of difficulty in verb forms for college learners of Spanish and concluded that the choice of the appropriate tense was most difficult, followed by the use of correct person, while choice of the correct conjugation class caused relatively few problems (van Naerssen 1980:150). While van Naerssen presents no figures for precise comparison, these general conclusions also hold for R's learning of Portuguese.

As indicated in Table 1, R made few errors of conjugation class, and also seemed little tempted to regularize irregular verbs by assigning them to a regular conjugation. On tape 1, R made one error of each type, both of them in the same phrase: *no pensia* [PENSAR, first conjugation, should have been *pensava*] *que via* [irregular VIR, should have been *vinha*] *à América Latina* ("I didn't think that I would come to Latin America"). The single error of conjugation class that occurred on this tape was the same one that R had recorded having made one week earlier in class:

Journal entry, Week 6
The paradigm [the imperfect] is also straightforward, more regular and less confusing than the pretérito, although maybe not as easy as I first thought. In class I produced *pensia*, which is incorrect . . . . I treated a first conjugation verb as a 2nd/3rd.

On tape 4, R made a few more conjugation errors, but no errors of treating an irregular verb as a regular one. There is no apparent pattern to the substitutions of one conjugation for another; for the three errors recorded, the substitutions were first for third, third for first and third for second.

Correctly inflecting verbs for person (first vs. second/third[11]) was more difficult for R than either choosing the correct conjugation class or inflecting for number, at least for regular verbs. On tape 1, R made seven person errors on regular verbs (92 percent accuracy), as opposed to one each for number and conjugation class. We have two suggestions for why person inflections are more difficult than number inflections. First, in the singular, there is no stable correspondence among vowels of the personal inflections across tenses. For example, for first conjugation verbs, the singular inflections for the present and the perfect past are:

	Present	Perfect
First person	-o	-ei
Second/third person	-a	-ou

Second, there is a discourse-based difficulty in the learning of person markers on verbs. As we will discuss more fully in the following section, one normally responds to a yes/no question in Portuguese by repeating the main verb or auxiliary of the question. When the question refers to the hearer (or speaker), the personal endings must be changed in the response:

1.386–387
S: Você gosta de clube?   You like [second/third singular] clubs?
R: Gosto, gosto.   Like [first singular], like.

One of R's typical strategies for answering questions was simply to repeat some part of the question with declarative intonation, without any other change. When first and second person subjects were involved, this led to error and, we suspect, to further confusion between verb forms.[12]

Choice of tense   Choice of tense (only three are considered here: the present, the perfect past, and the imperfect past) caused more problems for R than person, number, or conjugation class. In her study of learners of Spanish as a foreign language, van Naerssen was able to conclude that the imperfect is easier than the perfect for foreign language learners (van Naerssen 1980:151–152). This conclusion does not seem warranted in the case of R's acquisition of Portuguese. On the first conversational tape, R had 85 percent accuracy for the choice of imperfect vs. 80 percent for the perfect, but on tape 4 this was reversed, with 92 percent on the perfect but only 74 percent for the imperfect.

There are several reasons that may account for the fact that our results are not the same as van Naerssen's. First, our scoring systems may have been different. Van Naerssen implies that errors of person and number as well as tense choice were counted in the scoring of the three tenses. We have not counted person and number errors (reported in the previous section) in this category. If we had done so, our figures would be shifted generally in the direction of van Naerssen's findings, since there are no person errors in the imperfect (the singular person endings for the imperfect are identical in the spoken Portuguese of Rio). Second, there appear to be discourse factors that affected R's use of the imperfect on tape 4 which might not have affected van Naerssen's subjects, who were responding to specific oral exam questions. Many of R's errors in the imperfect (cases where he should have used the imperfect but did not) were substitutions of the present tense in stories and descriptions, contexts that might elicit the historical present in English. Third, if we focus solely on the issue of choice of one of the two past tenses, perfect vs. imperfect (the distinction here is really aspect, not tense), we do not find as van Naerssen did that only the perfect replaces the imperfect. In R's Portuguese, either of the two past tenses may substitute for the other.

Looking more closely at the contrast between the imperfect and perfect past tenses, we have found that one of the assumptions of most morpheme acquisition studies (as well as displays such as that in Table 1), that grammatical morphemes are learned sequentially and apply generally to all relevant members of a category, does not hold. We assumed, on the basis of comments in R's journal, that he would probably vary his use of perfect and imperfect forms of particular verbs, with the choice on specific occasions determined by some simplification of the complex semantics involved:

Journal entry, Week 6
This week we were introduced to and drilled on the imperfect. Very useful! The basic distinction [between perfect and imperfect] seems straightforward enough: *ontem eu fui ao clube* ["yesterday I went to the club"] vs. *antigamente eu ia ao clube* ["formerly I used to go to the club"].

Journal entry, Week 12
The class started off with a discussion of the imperfect vs. perfect, with C eliciting rules from the class. She ended up with more than a dozen rules on the board . . . which I am never going to remember when I need them. I'm just going to think of it as background and foreground and hope that I can get a feel for the rest of it.

Britto (1984) has called the Portuguese aspectual system wildly complicated and inconsistent. However, the basic distinction between perfective and imperfective is reasonably clear-cut. The imperfect indicates a nonpunctual structure (durative, iterative, or habitual), while the perfect is either punctual or indicates that none of the aspectual information given by any element in a structure is being taken into account. R's initial strategy for breaking into this system (in fact a very reasonable first approximation, although he had no conscious awareness of what he was doing) was, first of all, lexical. Verbs that appeared frequently in R's speech did not vary between the two past tenses. Instead, R settled on one of the two past tenses (i.e., one aspect in the past) for each individual verb, and used that form consistently. The figures are presented in Table 3.

TABLE 3 Distribution of Perfect and Imperfect Past Tenses among Lexical Verbs That Appear More Than Once per Conversation Tape

	Tape 1	Tape 2	Tape 3	Tape 4
Verbs in perfect only	5	6	8	17
Verbs in imperfect only	2	3	1	4
Verbs in both perfect and imperfect	1	2	1	1

As Table 3 shows, on tape 1, of eight verbs that R used more than once in one of the past tenses (frequencies range from 2 to 13 per conversational tape), seven (88 percent) appeared in only one of them, and only one showed variation. The figures are similar for the other three tapes, and also remarkably consistent over time. There were 29 verbs that R used more than once on the four tapes combined, with frequencies ranging from 2 to 38. Of these, 24 verbs (83 percent) occurred consistently in just one of the past tenses, and only five showed any alternation at all, either within a single tape or across the series.

There is the further question, of course, of why particular verbs were assigned to an aspectual category. We have considered two hypotheses, either of which might explain how a lexical strategy resulted in much better than random contextual accuracy: the semantics of individual verbs, and the frequency of those verbs in input from native speakers. The distinction among semantic classes of lexical verbs fits the data better. The five verbs that appear exclusively in the imperfect (ESTAR, "Be"; PENSAR, "Think"; QUERER, "Want"; TER, "Have"; and SABER, "Know") are all statives, while of the 19 that appear exclusively in the perfect almost all are dynamic verbs (e.g., COMPRAR, "Buy"; CONVIDAR, "Invite"; FALAR, "Speak"; IR, "Go"). There are two verbs in the [+ perfective] category, VER ("See") and OUVIR ("Hear") which are statives, but these can be considered in past tense usage as punctual (nondurative), activity verbs.[13]

Copulas SER and ESTAR The copulas SER and ESTAR were difficult for R (44 percent accuracy on tape 1 and 54 percent accuracy on tape 4), as would be predicted by several models of second language acquisition. Since Portuguese obligatorily distinguishes between two verbs on semantic grounds while English has only one, a contrastive analysis such as that proposed by Stockwell, Bowen, and Martin (1965) identifies the choice as occupying the highest level of difficulty for the second language learner. On the other hand, children learning many different languages frequently omit linking verbs; so an SLA model that generally identifies L1 and L2 acquisition would predict errors of omission.

Van Naerssen found that students of Spanish as a foreign language had a moderately good command of the copulas SER and ESTAR (73.3 percent accuracy) and that there were only two omissions of the copula (total obligatory contexts not given). Once again, our figures are not directly comparable with van Naerssen's, who included tense, person, number, and the semantic distinctions between the two verbs in determining correct use of the copulas. As van Naerssen suggests, perhaps researchers should not try to determine when a copula is acquired as a whole in this way (van Naerssen 1980:150), and we have not. Our figures therefore include only errors of omission of the copula and incorrect choice of the two verbs. In Table 1, these two factors were combined, but they are broken down in Table 4.

TABLE 4 Errors of Omission and Commission in the Use of SER and ESTAR

	Tape 1	*Tape 4*
Correct copula:		
SER	46% (37/81)	55% (51/92)
ESTAR	29% (2/7)	47% (9/19)
SER + ESTAR	44% (39/88)	54% (60/111)
Omissions:		
SER	47% (38/81)	45% (41/92)
ESTAR	29% (2/7)	42% (8/19)
SER + ESTAR	45% (40/88)	44% (49/111)
Incorrect choice:		
SER required	7% (6/81)	0% (0/92)
ESTAR required	43% (3/7)	11% (2/19)
Combined	10% (9/88)	2% (2/111)

Table 4 indicates that R did choose the wrong copula 10 percent of the time on tape 1, but only 2 percent of the time on tape 4. The pattern was for SER to substitute for ESTAR in the present and for ESTAR to substitute for SER in the past. With regard to the basic distinction between the two verbs, R commented:

Journal entry, Week 4
We've started off with the contrast between SER and ESTAR, which I suppose I should expect to cause difficulties. It does not seem that hard, although there are some arbitrary aspects of the distinction. If it's raining outside, that's ESTAR because it's temporary. But if it's 12:15, which seems pretty temporary to me, it has to be SER. My status as a student in this class is certainly temporary, but it has to be SER. L explained that this moment in time will be forever frozen with the label 12:15 and the relationship between student and teacher is enduring. Nice rationalization, but I'm sure I'll do better just paying attention to what people say in specific situations.

While the temporary/permanent distinction does account for virtually all the examples of SER incorrect replacing ESTAR in the present in our data, the problem with SER vs. ESTAR in the past is quite different. As mentioned above in our discussion of perfect vs. imperfect, ESTAR was one of the verbs that R used frequently, always in the imperfect. SER, on the other hand, appeared very infrequently in R's speech in the past and seems to have assigned to neither aspectual category. R was aware of the problem:

Journal entry, Week 6
The last thing he corrected was *estava* [ESTAR + imperfect] *meu aluno* to *era* [SER + imperfect] *meu aluno*. I know I have problems with that. How does a permanent state of affairs become past tense?

Journal entry, Week 19
G told a joke about a former minister who had been fired after only a few days in office. He told the press *não era* [SER + imperfect] *ministro, estava* [ESTAR + imperfect] *ministro*. The joke is clear, he was emphasizing the extreme temporariness of his tenure. What I don't understand is why *era* would be the preferred form in the first place. If it's got to be a form of SER, why not *fui* [SER + perfect]? Would that imply that he was speaking from the dead?[14]

Journal entry, Week 22
In our session S told me she was robbed last week at knife-point. I just told M about that and said *ela tava assaltada*. But I think that should have been made with SER. *Ela foi assaltada? Era assaltada?* Probably not *foi*. I think the only time I've ever heard *foi* as the past of SER is in *foi um barato*.

The above excerpt from R's journal is factually incorrect on two points. *Foi* (perfect of SER, R's third guess), not *estava* or *era*, was the required form. And it is not true that he never heard native speakers say the past tense forms of SER. There are 40 instances of SER in the past (perfect and imperfect combined) in S's speech on the conversational tapes.

Recognizing that some of R's errors in using the Portuguese copula are attributable to confusion between the two verbs, gaps in the paradigms, or nonuse of some forms, omission was nevertheless a much greater problem, one that did not diminish over the time of this study. R omitted the copula 45 percent of the time on tape 1 and 44 percent of the time on tape 4. We are not sure why R omitted the copula so frequently, while van Naerssen's learners of Spanish hardly did so at all, but suggest four possibilities:

Context of learning Future research might show copula deletion to be a problem affecting second language learners of Portuguese but not of Spanish (unlikely, we think) or possibly second as opposed to foreign language learning. Pica (1983) found that Spanish-speaking learners of English under different conditions of exposure (instruction only, naturalistic and mixed) used different language learning strategies, although treatment of the copula was not one of the areas in which differences were found among the groups.

Avoidance Since R made some errors of copula choice, copula omission could be a strategy to avoid error. We think this a rather implausible hypothesis, however, since (1) R had no conscious awareness of such an avoidance strategy (did not know he deleted copulas, in fact), (2) R improved his choices between the two copulas over time but did not stop omitting them, and (3) the environments in which he had difficulty in choosing the correct copula were not those in which he was especially likely to omit the copula. For example, there were contexts for ESTAR (as the auxiliary of the progressive, not counted in our copula statistics) where R never made an error between SER and ESTAR but still omitted ESTAR several times.

L3 influence Arabic does not have a present tense copula. When R was told that he tended to delete the copula in Portuguese, he was surprised and immediately suspected Arabic as the source of the error.

Journal entry, Week 9
I had no idea that I have been leaving out my copulas! Why haven't I been aware of it? Why hasn't anyone corrected me? Why am I forgetting them anyway? I suppose it's the influence of Arabic again. Damn it, why can't I keep these two languages apart?

We should note, as a counterargument to this hypothesis, that R's copula omissions in Portuguese did not follow the constraints of Arabic: R deleted SER and ESTAR in the perfect, imperfect, and future as well as in the present, the only environment in which Arabic has the zero copula.

Learning style Possibly the most promising hypothesis is that some learners, including R, begin language learning with a preference for a telegraphic style, concentrating on the big things (content words) and letting the details wait. R also omitted verbs other than the copula on occasion (12 times on tape 1; 11 times on tape 4). In some of these cases this may have been because R did not know the appropriate verb to use in a particular utterance, e.g., tape 1, *toda dia [contam] piadas, piadas, piadas* ("every day [they tell] jokes, jokes, jokes"), for which R did not know the appropriate verb CONTAR. In other cases, R did know the appropriate verb but omitted it anyway, e.g., tape 1, não, *[vou] a Nova Iorque primeiro* ("no, [I'll go] to New York first"); tape 4, *depois eu não sei, [vai ter uma] festa da Trattoria, acho* ("later I don't know, [there will be a] party at Trattoria, I think"). In these cases, the verbs that were omitted resulted in little loss of meaning.

At the beginning of this section, we characterized R's Portuguese interlanguage in terms of difficulties in the use of the copula, articles, and prepositions. We have now seen that in each of these grammatical areas, R overwhelmingly tended to simply omit the required grammatical morphemes. We have also seen, in each of these categories, that while R improved his grammatical accuracy over time whenever he produced those morphemes (choices among alternatives), his rate of deletion remained virtually unchanged over the period of this study.

CONVERSATIONAL ABILITY

Without any target language vocabulary and without some rudiments of grammar, a nonnative speaker cannot begin to communicate with native speakers of the target language. At the same time, the ability to carry on conversations is not just a reflection of grammatical competence. The second language learner must also come to control the rules for turn taking and adjacency pairings in the new language, must nominate topics for conversation and recognize topics nominated by native speakers, respond relevantly, and so on. As Hatch (1978b, 1983) has frequently pointed out, topics in adult discourse cover an incredibly wide range when compared with those involved in child first and second language learning, and the conversational ambitions of adult learners are complex and abstract. In the case of adult second language learners, there is also pressure to respond in conversation intelligently, to say something coherent and reasonably interesting, both to protect one's own good image of oneself (face) and to minimize as much as possible the conversational burden that must be carried by native speakers.

When we compare R's conversational behavior in the early stages with that toward the end of his stay in Brazil, we find several ways in which R's communicative ability developed. On the first conversational tape, R spoke hesitantly and had a great deal of difficulty in expressing his intended messages, even when these were not very complex:

1.1–5

S: Como é que você se sentiu quando você sabia, soube, que vinha pró Brasil? Qual era sua idéia do Brasil?

How did you feel when you knew, knew that you were coming to Brazil? What was your idea of Brazil?

R: Um ... no pensia, no pensia nada, no pensia que via a América Latina mas uh ... porque eu sei e conheço Média Este e conheço também Asia ... uh, Japon.

Um ... I didn't think, I didn't think anything, didn't think I would go to Latin America but uh ... because I know the Middle East and I know also Asia ... uh, Japan.

Even ignoring the errors of pronunciation, lexis, and grammar in R's response, what he said did not adequately communicate what he intended to say: I had never really thought of going to Latin America before, since all my previous experience had been in the Middle East and a bit in Asia.

By the end of his stay in Brazil, R was able to express notions of similar complexity in a smoother and communicatively more effective manner.[15]

4.381–386

S:	É muito comum você ver um rapaz de 30 anos morando com pai e mãe.	It's very common for you to see a 30 year old guy living with father and mother.
R:	Ah, eu sei. Aos Estados Unidos se tem um rapaz de 25 anos ainda mora com os pais, ah . . . toda gente pensam que coisa estranha mas aqui, não, aqui talvez um cara de 25 anos mora sozinho a gente falam: uma coisa estranha.	Ah, I know. In the U.S. if there's a 25 year old guy [who] still lives with the parents, ah . . . everybody thinks that strange thing, but here no, here maybe a 25 year old guy lives alone and people say: a strange thing.
S:	É o opos . . .	It's the oppo-
R:	O oposto!	The opposite!

Nevertheless, there are still instances on the last tape in which R's style of delivery deteriorates and becomes very choppy, as well as less grammatical, especially when he is excited:

4.114–122

R:	Fomos lá . . . mas foi, foi um barato! Sorte, sorte e . . . fomos a Cabo Frio em rua muito longe da cidade. Fomos lá prá ver as praias bonitas, tem ilha também, esqueci nome rua, não tem pessoa nada. Ninguém, ninguém. Nós dirigimos, tudo bem, e vem polícia. Tudo fora, tudo fora.	We went there. But something fantastic happened! Luck, luck . . . we were in Cabo Frio on a road far from town. We went there to see the beautiful beaches there's an island too. I forgot the name [of the] road. We drove, OK, and police comes. Everything out, Everything out.
S:	Meu Deus do Céu!	My God in Heaven!
R:	Temos em carro fitas, abriu: tem alguma coisa dentro lá? Todos corpo: tem alguma coisa. Bolsas, tudo . . .	We have in car tapes, he opened: is there something inside there? All body: do you have something? Bags, everything . . .

Misunderstandings

On the first conversational tape, there are numerous examples of minor or serious communicative breakdowns and misunderstandings:

1.188–193

S:	E a Havaí também é muito bonito o campus.	And at [the University of] Hawaii also the campus is beautiful.
R:	Mmm . . .	Mmm . . .
S:	Aqui é mais bonito, né?	Here is more beautiful, isn't it?
R:	Ah, sim, sim. A Hawaii?	Ah, yes, yes. In Hawaii?
S:	É.	Yes.
R:	Não. Campus?	No. The campus?

1.297–309

S:	A tua mulher, a tua ex-mulher tem descendência oriental?	Is your wife, your ex-wife of oriental descent?
R:	Hum?	Huh?
S:	Qual é a descendência dela? É oriental ou inglesa ou noroeguesa ou é . . .	What is her descent? Is it oriental or English or Norwegian or is it . . .
R:	Não entendo.	I don't understand.
S:	Não entendeu?	You didn't understand?
R:	Não entendo.	I don't understand.
S:	A família dela é oriental? Como a minha, por exemplo, meu avô, minha avó . . .	Is her family oriental? Like mine, for example, my grandfather, my grandmother . . .
R:	Non, non. Minha ex-marida?	No, no. My ex-wife?
S:	É, isso.	That's it.
R:	Hum, americana de Boston, também.	Uh, American also from Boston.
S:	De Boston, mas digo os descendentes.	From Boston, but I'm talking about descendents.

In the last example above, the problem from the perspective of the native speaker, S, was that R did not understand the question ("is she of oriental descent?") even when rephrased into an or-choice type of question ("oriental or English or Norwegian or . . ."), and when he finally did seem to answer the question he still did not answer appropriately. From R's perspective the problem was quite different. He did not recognize S's question about *tua ex-mulher* as referring to his ex-wife. After the question had been paraphrased twice, he guessed whom it might be about, and asked for confirmation, using *ex-marida*, which is a nonoccurring word in Portuguese although formed according to a regular pattern ("husband" is *marido*). By the time the topic of the question had been clarified, he had forgotten exactly what the question had been.

There are still some (though fewer) examples of similar communicative difficulties on conversation tape 4:

4.196–202

S:	. . . mas o americano não faz isso. Ele tá te icentivando.	. . . but the American doesn't do that. He encourages you.
R:	Porque os Americanos são famosos . . .	Because Americans are famous . . .
S:	Como assim?	What's that?
R:	Ah, os americanos não corrigem?	Ah, Americans don't correct?
S:	Não. Eles icentivam, falam que você fala bem inglês quando você não fala.	No. They encourage, say that you speak English well when you don't speak.

In this example, R wanted to say "Americans are famous for not correcting people," but the beginning of that utterance sounded strange to S, who thought R was off the topic. While the majority of the communicative breakdowns and misunderstandings on four tapes involve R's failure to comprehend S, there are a few additional cases on tape 4 where the opposite occurs:

4.485–492

| R: | Mas depois 30, começa a diminuir. | But after 30, it [your age] starts to decrease. |
| S: | Exatamente, não faço mais aniversário. | Exactly, I'm not going to have any more birthdays. |

R:	Tenho agora só 18.	I'm only 18 now.
S:	18?	18?
R:	42, ahm?	[I'm] 42, right?
S:	43.	43.
R:	42.	42.
S:	Quando é teu aniversário?	When is your birthday?

In this case, S either did not get or was distracted from R's attempted joke: 30 + 12 = 42, but 30 − 12 = 18.

Analysis of Discourse

Because most of the differences over time in R's conversational ability and in the quality of interaction between R and S appear to be quantitative rather than qualitative in nature, we have carried out an analysis of the discourse contained in the first and last conversational tapes. For tapes 1 and 4, we analyzed the first 400 turns (200 turns by each speaker), categorizing utterances into the following discourse categories:

Statements. Following Hunt (1970), Loban (1976), and Beebe (1983), we have counted each independent grammatical predication as a statement. An utterance consisting of an independent clause and a dependent clause constitutes one such unit, while an utterance consisting of two independent clauses constitutes two units.[16]

Questions, further categorized into Wh-questions, yes/no questions (univerted in Portuguese), tag-questions, and or-choice questions (e.g., "did you go out last night or stay home?").

Imperatives, including both second singular and first plural forms.

Self-repetitions, in which a speaker repeats his or her own words, without significant additional information, either exactly or in an attempt (successful or unsuccessful) at self-correction.

Other-repetitions, in which a speaker repeats part of his or her interlocuter's speech, with declarative intonation, with or without correction.

Confirmation checks, in which a speaker repeats part of his or her interlocuter's speech with question intonation, with or without correction.

Comprehension checks, attempts by a speaker to establish that the interlocuter is following what he or she is saying, e.g., "right?" "do you understand?"

Clarification requests, in which the speaker attempts to clarify what the previous speaker meant to say or ask, but without repeating the exact words of the interlocuter, e.g., "huh?" "who, me?"

Requests for help. A speaker requests language assistance, by pronouncing a word or part of a word with question intonation, or by asking directly, "how do you say . . .?"

Minimal responses. Answers to questions consisting of "yes," "no," *sim, não,* etc.

Backchannel responses. Responses to statements, minimal comments such as "yeah," "uh-huh," *ah é? ah não?* and *pois é.*

Table 5 gives the number of occurrences of each coded feature and the extent to which the differences between the frequencies in the early and late recordings are significant, based on chi-squared scores.

Looking at R's conversational behavior as represented in Table 5, we find that virtually all the changes between tape 1 and tape 4 are in the direction that we would expect given increased conversational proficiency. On tape 4, R used fewer comprehension checks, confirmation checks, requests for help, etc. However, taking .025 as the level of significance, only 4 of the 15 categories coded for R and 5 of those codes for S show statistically significant change. For R, the significant decrease in the number of clarification requests used seems a reflection of generally improved comprehension, while the significant increase in the number of statements produced appears to be reflection of improved productive fluency. R had more that he was able to say. A general increase in productive fluency on R's part also seems reflected in two additional measures not included in Table 5: the number of words per turn produced by R increased from 6.9 on tape 1 to 12.13 on tape 4, and the rate of speech in words per minute of R and S combined increased from 72.55 on tape 1 to 80.33 on tape 4.[17] However, both of those measures are statistically nonsignificant.

Repetitions One of the more striking aspects of R's speech, as represented in Table 5, is the amount of self- and other-repetition that R did in comparison with S, the native speaker. Repetition was one of the more obvious characteristics of R's early conversational behavior in Portuguese:

1.483–490

R:	Nada, nada, nunca, nunca e . . . ele, ele gosta a comida italiano, italiano.	Nothing, nothing, never, never and . . . he likes, he likes Italian food, Italian.
S:	Massa?	Pasta?
R:	Massa, massa. Por isso agora, agora comendo, estamos, estamos comendo, estamos comendo ao restaurante italiano, toda noite.	Pasta, pasta. So now, now eating, we are, we are eating, we are eating at the Italian restaurant, every night.
S:	Toda noite?	Every night?
R:	Toda noite, toda noite.	Every night, every night.

We do not know the extent to which R may be typical of beginning adult language learners in this respect, on which the SLA literature has generally been silent. Such repetitions have been well documented in the literature on child L1 and L2 acquisition. Keenan (1977) cites extensive examples of repetition in L1 child-child discourse, to which she attributes various discourse functions. Peck (1978) and Itoh and Hatch (1978) have documented cases of "repeaters" in child L2 acquisition, using repetition for similar functions.

R's repetitions run the gamut of discourse functions identified for child L1 and L2 acquirers. Other-repetitions were used to answer questions:

TABLE 5 Comparison of 15 Discoursal Features in R's and S's Speech at Different Times

Discoursal feature	R's speech				S's speech			
	Tape 1	Tape 4	$\chi^2 (df=1)$	p	Tape 1	Tape 4	$\chi^2 (df=1)$	p
Wh-questions	2	5	1.29	NS	42	40	0.05	NS
Yes/no questions	7	4	0.82	NS	68	44	5.14	.025
Tag questions	5	12	2.88	NS	27	23	0.32	NS
Or-choice questions	0	0	0.00	NS	7	0	7.00	.01
Total all questions	14	21	1.40	NS	144	107	5.45	.025
Statements	160	307	46.27	.01	79	165	30.31	.01
Imperatives	0	2	2.00	NS	5	4	0.11	NS
Self-repetitions	92	64	5.02	.025	10	10	0.00	NS
Other-repetitions	53	35	3.68	NS	11	13	0.17	NS
Confirmation checks	11	5	2.25	NS	24	9	6.82	.01
Comprehension checks	4	0	4.00	NS	4	0	4.00	NS
Clarification requests	16	4	7.20	.01	3	10	3.77	NS
Requests for help	5	2	1.28	NS	1	0	1.00	NS
Minimal responses	57	31	7.68	.01	16	22	0.95	NS
Backchannel responses	2	8	3.60	NS	14	12	0.15	NS

1.281–282

S: Os dois registros?	The two registers?
R: Dois, mas dois, três, quatro, continum.	Two, but two, three, four, [a] continuum.

to delay answering questions briefly:

1.44–45

S: Por que?	Why?
R: Porque, ah . . . Beirute é	Why, ah . . . Beirut is

to agree with statements:

1.206–208

R: 4%	4%
S: É?, mais ou menos.	Yes? more or less.
R: Mais ou menos, mais ou menos.	More or less, more or less.

to accept topics:

1.99–100

S: E o Japão? Como é que é o Japão? Eu tenho muita curiosidade.	And Japan? How is Japan? I'm very curious.
R: O Japon, Japon, se você . . .	Japan, Japan, if you . . .

to acknowledge corrections and feedback:

1.229–231

R: Disse não.	I said no.
S: Não vou.	I won't go.
R: Não vou, não, não vou.	I won't go, no, I won't go.

and to acknowledge requested assistance:

1.329–331

R: . . . muito feliz, "even though?"	. . . very happy, "even though?"
S: apesar	even though
R: apesar, apesar crises financial mas . . .	even though, even though financial crises, but . . .

Confirmation checks (other-repetitions with question intonation) were used by R in cases where he really was unsure of what was said or asked:

1.325–326

S: Como é que é esse jeito brasileiro?	What is this Brazilian way?
R: Jeito brasileiro?	Brazilian way? (R did not know the expression)

But just as frequently when there was no real comprehension problem:

1.439–440

S: Já surfou alguma vez no Havaí:	Have you ever surfed in Hawaii?
R: Surfou? Não, body surf só.	Surfed? No, only body surf.

Self-repetitions were used sometimes to self-correct:

1.178
R: ... todos os alunos adaltos, são adultos.   ... all the students adults, are adults.

or for emphasis:

1.402
R: ... na praia mas é bem longe, bem longe.   ... at the beach, but it's very far, very far.

The role of repetition, especially other-repetition (imitation), as a learning and production device has been hotly debated in the L1 acquisition literature, with attitudes toward imitation strongly colored by theoretical disputes about the nature of language (Clark 1977). As Snow (1981) points out, the imitation of adult utterances by children has been viewed as an epiphenomenon of language acquisition that makes no contribution to development; a process that primarily supports vocabulary development; a process that makes a limited contribution to morphological and syntactic development for some children (those who do imitate); and a process of central importance in language acquisition. While much of the debate about the relevance of imitation has focused on the use of chunked or formulaic speech for comparison and factoring (a topic we will address below), Bloom et al. (1974) have suggested that selective imitation is a strategy that allows a child to encode a state of affairs with the perceptual support of a relevant message. Peters (1983) has suggested that both other-repetition and self-repetition (which she calls imitation and repetition, respectively) are important strategies for the formation and automatization of production routines.

Many of R's repetitions are of the type that Peters identifies in child language acquisition as "repetition and build-up":

1.123
R: ... nào morei   ... I didn't live
     não morei lá   I didn't live there

1.486
R: agora   now
     agora comendo   now eating
     estamos   we are
     estamos comendo   we are eating
     estamos comendo ao restaurante italiano,   we are eating at the Italian restaurant,
     toda noite   every night

In fact, many of the examples in the discourse categories listed above also seem to serve an important encoding and production function. R used repetitions (both self- and other-) to hold the floor and gain planning time and, often, to say a second time more completely or more smoothly what he said first incompletely or hesitantly.

Repetitions did not disappear from R's discourse behavior by the time of tape 4, but the three categories of self- and other-repetitions and confirmation checks do show a combined 34 percent decrease from 156 instances to 104 ($\chi^2 = 10.40$, df = 1, p. < .01). Considered separately, only the category of self-repetitions shows a statistically significant decrease (see Table 5), and here we note as well a shift in the functions for which this conversational device was used. In the discourse on tape 1, the majority of instances of self-repetition fell into the rehearsal or stalling-for-time categories, or could be viewed as having those functions in addition to their other discourse functions. These types of self-repetition decreased on tape 4, while the number of self-repetitions for the purpose of self-correction increased:

4.350
R: E aqui no Rio também é uma cidade de, da liberdade também.

And here in Rio, it's a city of, of (de + art.) liberty also.

4.288–289
R: Não, estava fazendo mas quando, quando mudou, quando mudei prá Flamengo . . .

No, I was doing, but when, when you moved, when I moved to Flamengo . . .

4.88–90
S: E as praias de Búzios? Que que cê achou?

And the beaches of Buzios? What did you think?

R: Muito bonito! Muito bonitas, praias.

Very beautiful (m.sg.)! Very beautiful (f.pl.), beaches (f.pl.).

S: "Monitoring" hein?

Monitoring, huh?

On tape 1, 17 self-repetitions (18 percent) contained corrections, while 75 did not; on tape 4, there were 24 self-repetitions containing corrections (38 percent) as opposed to 40 without correction ($\chi^2 = 7.05$, df = 1, p. < .01).

Questions and answers Discourse is more than simply individual utterances, fragments, repetitions, and the like, strung together like beads on a string. Conversation is organized at various levels, for example, in talk about topics. At the lowest level of organization, which we analyze here, discourse moves may be seen as linked together in terms of adjacency pairs such as greeting-greeting, compliment-acceptance, complaint-apology, and request-grant (Schegloff and Sacks 1973, Coulthard 1977, Richards and Schmidt 1983b). We deal here with only one adjacency pair type, question-answer, one of the most common types in our conversational data.

We turn our attention first to the distribution of statements and questions in the speech of S, the native speaker. In doing so, we are making two assumptions that we hope are justified by the results of the analysis. First, we assume that some aspects of foreigner talk discourse (the speech of native speakers addressed to nonnative speakers) identified in research on English interlanguage communication are not language-specific but will be found in Brazilian foreigner talk discourse as well.[18] Second, we assume that some of the interactional aspects of foreigner talk discourse are sensitive to the level of competence of the nonnative partner in the conversation.[19] In other words, we present here a partial analysis of S's conversational behavior as a reflection of R's developing conversational proficiency.

Long (1981) has reported that one of the most striking and significant aspects of foreigner talk discourse when compared with native-native discourse is the preponderance of questions in the former and statements in the latter. Analyzing 36 5-minute conversations between speakers of American English and Japanese young adults with elementary English proficiency, Long found that 66 percent of all t-units in the native speaker speech directed at those learners were questions, while in a comparable corpus of native-native discourse 83 percent of all t-units were statements. Moreover, the distribution of question types was different in the two corpora. While Wh-questions were the most favored type in the native-native discourse, closed questions (those in which the propositional content of the answer is encoded in the question, i.e., yes/no, tag, and or-choice questions) predominated in the foreigner talk discourse.

As can be seen from Table 5, S's conversational behavior when talking to R on tape 1 was remarkably similar to the way Long found native speakers of English behaving when talking to low-level Japanese speakers of English. On tape 1, S used 144 questions (63 percent), 79 statements (35 percent), and only 5 imperatives (2 percent). The figures are almost identical to those presented by Long (1981:Table 5). Yes/no questions (uninverted in Portuguese) were S's most favored type of question, followed by Wh-questions, tag questions, and or-choice questions.

Hatch (1978b) has noted that native speakers frequently repeat questions, shifting down what is required of the learner by rephrasing Wh-questions (open) as yes/no or or-choice questions. We find this phenomenon in S's speech to R on tape 1:

1.299
S: Qual é a descendência dela? É oriental ou inglesa ou é norueguesa ou é . . .

What is her descent? Is it oriental or English, or is Norwegian or is it . . .

1.133
S: Me diz uma coisa. E no Rio, Que que você tá achando da cidade. Tá achando ela bonita, tá achando interessante?

Tell me something. And Rio, what do you think of the city? Do you find it beautiful, do you find it interesting?

In fact, on tape 1, S frequently repeated her questions within the same turn without waiting to see if R had comprehended the question. Twenty-three percent of all questions on the first tape were immediately repeated. Not all these repeats involved shifting to a different question type, however; the majority of the questions that were repeated (57 percent) were repeated as the same type of question.

By the time of tape 4, S had significantly reduced her questions and increased her statements (X^2 values in Table 5). Assuming that the proportions of questions and statements in English and Brazilian Portuguese native-native discourse are roughly equal, an assumption that may not be justified and for which we have no baseline data,[20] S was presumably still not talking to R the way she would talk to a native speaker. Long found that native-native discourse contained 83 percent statements vs. 16 percent questions; S used 165 statements (60 percent) vs. 107 questions (39 percent) on tape 4. However, in general the picture is clear: on tape 1, S was talking to an elementary-level speaker; on tape 4, she was talking to someone she believed to be a more competent interlocutor, not limited to simply answering conveniently phrased questions.

We now turn our attention back to R's speech. R increased his statements significantly between tape 1 and tape 4 but did not increase his questions to S as she decreased hers to him. Most of the questions asked on the later tapes continue to be asked by S, and R therefore does a lot of answering. As mentioned briefly above, herein lies a tricky learning problem in Portuguese. Whereas in English and many other languages, one may answer yes/no questions simply with "yes" or "no," that is, lexically, in Portuguese questions may be answered negatively with *não* but are rarely answered affirmatively with *sim*. The use of *sim* alone as a response is restricted to emphatic agreement or disagreement (Thomas 1969):

1.411–412
R: Mas onda aqui não é muito grande.　　　But wave here is not big.
S: É sim R. Você acha que não?　　　Oh yes, R. You think not?

Sim, with ironic tone and "long" pronunciation, may also mean "no." The way in which yes/no questions are normally answered affirmatively in Portuguese is by repeating the verb of the question, or the auxiliary if there was one, changing the personal inflections on the verb or auxiliary as appropriate, or repeating one of a closed set of high-frequency adverbs (Tarallo and Kato 1984). If *sim* is used, it follows the repeated element.

4.214–243
R: . . . sabe "98"? FM "good times," "good　　　[Do you] know [second/third singular] 98?
    times 98"?　　　FM good times, good times 98?
S: Sei　　　[I] know [first singular]

4.560–561
R: 12 quilos, mas acho que tem problema,　　　12 kilos, but I think there's a problem, huh?
    huh?
S: É, tem sim. Nossa Senhora!　　　Is, there is. Our Lady!

The use of inappropriate affirmative responses is a characteristic of nonnative Brazilian Portuguese, previously identified for native speakers of

Spanish (Baltra 1981). R clearly had major problems in this regard. On tape 1, he answered questions inappropriately, with *sim* alone, 36 times, e.g.:

1.9–10
S: Você morou no Egito? É?   You lived in Egypt? Yeah?
R: Sim, 5 anos.   Yes, 5 years.
1.110–111
S: Deve ser fascinante.   It must be fascinating.
R: Sim.   Yes.

In the above two examples, appropriate responses would have been *morei* ("I lived") and *é* ("it is"), respectively. Besides responding with *sim*, R's next most common strategy was to simply repeat part of the question, but usually not the correct part (31 examples), e.g.:

1.446–447
S: Tá gostando?   Are you enjoying [it]?
R: Gostando.   Enjoying.

1.521–523
S: Carne nos Estados Unidos é muito caro,   Meat in the United States is very expensive,
    né? A carne nos Estados Unidos?   isn't it? Meat in the United States?
R: Muito caro, muito caro . . .   Very expensive, very expensive.

In only seven cases on tape 1 did R attempt to respond by repeating the verb. In three cases the interchange referred to third persons; so no change in the verb was required and R got it correct. But of the four cases in which R attempted to answer questions about himself, requiring a verb change, he failed to make the required changes in three of them, e.g.:

1.439–440
S: Já surfou alguma vez no Havaí?   Have you ever surfed in Hawaii?
R: Surfou? Não, body surf só.   You surfed? No, only body surf.

1.513–515
S: . . . você já comeu a comida brasileira   . . . have you eaten real Brazilian food yet,
    mesmo, já comeu?   have you eaten?
R: Comeu, comeu canja e . . .   You ate, you ate chicken soup and . . .

In these examples, the appropriate responses would have been *surfei* ("I surfed") and *comi* ("I ate"), or simply *já* ("already") in both cases. In only one case on tape 1 did R answer a question in the Brazilian way, repeating the verb and reinflecting it:

1.386–387
S: Você gosta de clube?   Do you like clubs?
R: Gosto, gosto.   I like, I like.

It seems to us that there are several possible reasons why this aspect of Portuguese discourse was difficult for R (and also is difficult for children learning Portuguese as their first language, Robert Blust, personal communication), in spite of the fact that as noted earlier in the diary notes he was drilled on affirmative answers on the second day of class and frequently thereafter. First, it is different from English. Second, answering questions in Portuguese involves an actual manipulation of the form of the verb. We view this as a transformation, not in the well-known sense of Chomsky (1965 and thereafter), a rule intervening between meaning and surface structure, but in the original sense of Harris (1952, 1957), who viewed transformations as relations among sentences in connected discourse. In order to answer Portuguese questions affirmatively, a speaker must (1) store the verb form of the question in memory; (2) analyze that form, identifying both the lexical verb and the person and number markers on the question form; and (3) reassemble the verb with the appropriate personal inflection for a reply. An alternative explanation (Richard Day, personal communication) would be simply to assume that question-and-answer forms of verbs are memorized as pairs. This seems plausible also, and we have no evidence on which to prefer one analysis to another, but the basic principle is the same: hear one form, produce another.

A final reason why affirmative answers involving changes in verbal inflections were difficult for R may be that such responses appear infrequent in input, at least in foreigner talk discourse. S produced only three examples of transformed verbs as affirmative answers on tape 4, and none at all on tape 1. This was not only because R asked relatively few questions for S to answer, but also because S generally used other strategies of affirmation and confirmation. On occasion, S repeated some part of the question other than the verb (one of R's most common strategies), e.g.:

1.380–381

R:	Há muitos libaneses lá?		Are there many Lebanese there?
S:	Muitos, muitos.		Many, many.

In the majority of cases, whether answering a question or agreeing with a statement, S simply responded with é:

1.126–128

S:	Já?		Have [you]?
R:	Eu?		Me?
S:	É. Você fala francês?		Yes [é]. Do you speak French?

1.367–368

R:	Interessante mas todas as pessoas lá são muito pobres.		Interesting, but all the people there are very poor.
S:	É, lá você vai ver o Brasil.		Yes [é], there you will see Brazil.

In both examples above, S's response form é can be analyzed as an appropriately inflected form if it is seen as an elliptical version of "[that] is [what

I'm talking about]," although that interpretation is less plausible for the second example, which has a third plural verb form (*são*) in the question but gets a third singular form (*é*) in the response. Here, *é* seems to be just a lexicalized confirmation form. É is also the standard way of responding to questions whenever the question is an implied one or otherwise does not contain a verb (Thomas 1969:243).

By the end of his stay in Brazil, R had mastered some but by no means all aspects of answering in Portuguese. On tape 4, R answered affirmatively with *sim* alone (inappropriate) only twice, and there were five instances in which he responded by repeating the verb. In all five cases, the verb was properly inflected, e.g.:

4.318–319
S: E você ligou?   And you called?
R: Liguei, mas eu sabia antes também.   I called, but I knew before also.

What R did not do was answer with *é* when appropriate, nor did he use other available Portuguese response forms such as *claro, pois é* and *tá*. Instead, on six occasions, he used a typical English response form:

4.164–165
S: É a Elba Ramalho, né?   That's Elba Ramalho, isn't it?
R: Uh-huh.   Uh-huh.

Why R failed to learn the simple Brazilian Portuguese response *é* to questions is unclear to us. It was not taught in class, though it was presumably heard there and was certainly present in other output to R from the beginning. He recorded nothing about it in his diary and does not remember ever having noticed it, though he did notice the related form *é, isso*, meaning "that's it" or "correct":

Journal entry, Week 5
... and I notice that when we are doing our drills, L keeps saying something that sounds like ee-yes-u, sort of like a Japanese saying "yes" .... it obviously means "right."

It seems to R now, as an afterthought, that one possibility for his failure to learn and use *é* might be the fact that a similar or identical vocalic sound occurs in the languages he knows, with several different meanings: [e] means "yes" in Lebanese Arabic, "what?" in Egyptian Arabic, and is a question tag in Canadian English. Such thoughts are not represented in the journal, although R was aware that he used the form "uh-huh":

Journal entry, Week 16
I wish I could stop saying "uh-huh" everytime M asks me a question. I know this is totally un-Portuguese, but it just comes out. If I stop myself and try to think about it, I don't know what to say instead. Oh well, he and everyone else seem to understand me when I say it.[21]

Did Instruction Make a Difference?

As indicated by several of the journal entries already presented, instruction was perceived by R to make a great deal of difference. Before class started, R could not talk to speakers of Portuguese; as soon as class began, he could. The classroom provided resources that could immediately be put to use. In addition to comments from the journal already presented, the following are typical:

Journal entry, Week 5
The class is getting better, since L has started telling us some brief stories. The first one was about her elderly father. Once he was too tired to walk home from the park, so he told the police he was lost and got a ride. I got at least one useful expression from that: *você vai andando todo dia prá lá e prá cá*, "you walk there and back every day." Since I walk to and from the university, I've been able to use this several times already.

Journal entry, Week 6
I went back to the gym today and signed up. Amazing . . . three weeks ago I could not manage any interaction there at all in Portuguese, but today I not only registered but chatted with the instructor, who said, "what happened? You didn't speak and now you do."

Classroom instruction was also useful in providing quick answers to problems that R could not figure out from context:

Journal entry, Week 4
B called up last night. Talking on the phone is next to impossible! The long silences are stressful, and I have no idea at all how to get off the phone. I'm sure I cannot say *tchau* out of the blue and hang up, so I had to wait (and wait) for her to say it. I didn't understand the simplest things. I said *hoje praia* ["today beach"] and B said *foi?*, several times. I had no idea at all what that meant. Today in class I asked and learned that *foi* is the past of IR (also SER). B meant "did you go?" and I should have answered *fui*, "I went."

On the whole, the influence of instruction was clearly positive. At the same time, in our discussion of R's developing grammatical competence we identified numerous aspects of Portuguese that R was taught but did not learn to produce accurately. Other such phenomena have been identified in R's conversational behavior, such as R's failure to learn the pattern that was taught (and mentioned above in the entry about *foi?: fui*) for answering questions. In this section, we attempt to deal more directly with the effects of instruction on learning, by examining the relationship between what was taught and what was learned. The discussion is limited to Portuguese verbs, for convenience and because many of the more difficult points of Portuguese grammar are found in the forms and distribution of verbal inflections. Verbs are also the focus of most teaching.

Table 6 lists those aspects of the Portuguese verb presented in R's Portuguese class, in the order in which they were presented. The teacher's

TABLE 6 Portuguese Verb Forms. Order of Instruction, Presence in Input, Presence in Output

Verbal feature taught	Present in input?				Present in output?			
	T1	T2	T3	T4	T1	T2	T3	T4
Present of SER, ESTAR	+	+	+	+	+	+	+	+
Present, regular verbs ending in -ar, -er, -ir	+	+	+	+	+	+	+	+
Progressive (ESTAR + V-ndo)	+	I	+	+	I	−	R	R
Irregular verbs: VIR, IR, TER, VER, FAZER, SABER, DIZER, QUERER	+	+	+	+	+	+	+	+
Future with IR	I	I	+	+	I	I	I	I
Perfect past tense	+	+	+	+	+	+	+	+
Imperfect past tense	I	+	I	I	+	+	+	+
Imperfect of ESTAR + V-ndo	−	I	I	I	−	I	I	+
Compound present	−	I	−	I	−	−	−	−
Compound past perfect	−	−	I	−	−	−	−	−
Inflected future	I	I	−	−	−	−	−	I
Irregular verbs: FICAR, PODER, LER, SAIR, OUVIR, PEDIR, POR, DAR	+	I	+	+	I	−	I	+
Conditional	+	+	−	I	R	I	−	I
Reflexive	I	I	−	I	I	I	I	I

+ = present   I = (< five instances per conversational tape)
− = absent   R = present only as a repetition

lesson plans and order of presentation appear to be based on the order of presentation in Abreu and Rameh (1972, 1973), although this text was not used by the class. In contrast to our previous discussion of R's grammatical competence, we are concerned here primarily with whether and how frequently R produced forms in conversation, and only secondarily with the accuracy with which he produced the forms when these were attempted. We also include in Table 6 some information about the frequency of such forms in input. This is of course limited, based only on S's speech to R on the conversational tapes. We are assuming that S's speech to R was not bizaarely atypical, that if S used a form with very high frequency then probably others did also when interacting with R and that if S consistently avoided certain forms then probably other native speakers did also, regardless of how common such forms might be in native-native interaction.

As Table 6 indicates, it is clearly not the case that whatever was taught was learned and used by R, even leaving aside here the question of whether it was used correctly. It does not even seem to be true that the order of presentation in class determined whether or not R would use a form. This accounts for part of the data, for example, the fact that of two groupings of irregular verbs, R produced first and most frequently those which were introduced early, one by one, and individually drilled, while seldom producing any of the group 2 irregular verbs that were introduced late and only superficially drilled. The periphrastic future with IR, which shows up with low frequency in R's speech although it was taught early, is probably not a substantial exception to a principle of first-taught-most-used, since it is clearly influenced by topic. The early conversational tapes deal primarily with biographic and current topics. Only the last conversational tape contains much talk about future plans, and for R this was mostly about travel (the verb IR, "to go," is used in the present to talk about the future)f. The low frequency in R's speech of the progressive (ESTAR + V-ndo) is more difficiult to explain. It was taught early, drilled often, is highly regular, and was topically relevant on all tapes. One possible reason for R's nonuse of this "easy" form may be the fact that the progressive is commonly used in Portuguese in utterances in which it is unlikely, or in a few cases (with statives) not permissible in English. While S's speech to R contains numerous examples of the progressive, many of them fall into this category, such as S's frequent formulaic utterance, *que que você tá achando de NP?* ("what do you think of NP?") where English would not permit a progressive form.[22]

The clearest example of the lack of good fit between what was taught and what was learned and used is R's nonuse of the compound present tense (very roughly equivalent to the English present perfect progressive) and the compound past perfect. Both of these tenses were drilled extensively. R produced no instances of either (there were obligatory contexts for both), although he did produce verb forms that were introduced later in the course and drilled less frequently.

A second generalization fits the data better: R learned and used what he was taught if he subsequently heard it; i.e., what was more frequent in input was more likely to be used. Although R's nonuse of the progressive remains an exception to this generalization also, R's nonuse of the compound present and the past perfect can now be related to the fact that these were seldom present in input. Again, there are some exceptions to the generalization. R overused the imperfect in comparison to S's speech. There is also a discrepancy in the frequency of input and output in the use of the reflexive that is not revealed by Table 6. While both S and R produced the reflexive infrequently, S used the reflexive productively with various different verbs, whereas all of R's examples of the reflexive are with a single verb, SE CHAMAR ("be called"). R recorded the following in his journal about this verb:[23]

Journal entry, Week 6

Today L told us a story in class about *o homem que decidiu suicidar-se,* the man who tried to commit suicide, but failed because he hadn't paid his gas bill . . . After the story, K asked about reflexive verbs. I already know one, *se chama.* That's because when X visited about 10 years ago, he was taking high school Spanish. We went to the zoo and he kept saying to all the animals *como se chama, llama?* He thought it was very clever. I thought it was extremely annoying, but the phrase has stuck to this day. L says that reflexive verbs are common in Portuguese, and there is often no difference in meaning between reflexive and nonreflexive verbs. She gave a few examples [not recorded].

The situation is similar with regard to the inflected future, which was present in input with several verbs but was used by R only with one verb, SER.[24]

A third generalization fits the data best: R learned and used what he was taught if he subsequently heard it and if he *noticed* it. R's journal entries contain references to all the verb forms listed in Table 6, with the exception of the conditional. As an afterthought, R now believes that he did indeed notice native speakers using the conditional , which he himself used only occasionally (but correctly), but recorded no observations about it in his journal. Each of the other forms listed in Table 6 is represented in the journal, minimally by being contained in native speaker utterances that R wrote down and in most cases with some additional discussion.

R noticed some verbs in input before they were taught (see previously quoted journal entry concerning *foi* as the past of IR/SER), but more commonly he noticed verb forms in input immediately after they were taught. Several journal entries deal with the imperfect, e.g.:

Journal entry, Week 6
This week we were introduced to and drilled on the imperfect. Very useful! The basic contrast seems straightforward enough: *ontem eu fui ao clube* ["yesterday I went to the club"] vs. *antigamente eu ia ao clube* ["formerly I used to go to the club"]. L gave us a third model: *ontem eu ia ao clube,* "yesterday I was going to the club... but I didn't", which L says is a common way of making excuses. The paradigm is also straightforward... though maybe not as easy as I first thought. ... Wednesday night A came over to play cards, and the first thing he said was: *eu ia telefonar para você* ["I was going to call you"], exactly the kind of excuse L had said we could expect. I noticed that his speech was full of the imperfect, which I never heard (or understood) before, and during the evening I managed to produce quite a few myself, without hesitating much. Very satisfying!

Other verb forms were frequently noticed, but with a perception of difficulty:

Journal entry, Week 7
We went over IR, VER, and VIR again today. What a mess those verbs are. . . . On the bright side, A stopped by at 5 p.m. and in our conversation he said *quis*, which I guessed from context [correctly] to be the past of QUERER.

Journal entry, Week 20
Just now talking to N I wanted to contrast what I thought about Brazil before I came here and what I think now. I said: *eu sabia* . . . He responded: *e o que veio? Veio?* I'm sure I use *veio* to mean "did you come?", but have I mixed it up again with VER ["see"]? Did he mean "what do you see?" or "what came?", something like "how did it turn out?"? While I was thinking about this, N got fed up and said *esquece* ["forget it"]. I need about a year more to figure this language out.

However, not everything that was taught in class was noticed by R in the input. In some cases, this was because some standard Portuguese forms taught in class are seldom used in the Portuguese of Rio de Janeiro:

Journal entry, Week 6
There are some things in class that I know immediately are going to be difficult. Today we went over indirect object pronouns, changing sentences like *você comprou um livro prá ele* to *eu lhe comprei um livro*. Forget it! It's clear that I can always use the alternative form, with preposition and pronoun after the verb.

Today in my SLA class I mentioned that some things I was taught I immediately heard all around me, like the imperfect, which I heard frequently from the day it was taught. The class agreed that this is common in L1 as well, that when you learn a new vocabulary item you often start hearing it, although it was being said around you all along. There are other things which I've been taught which I never hear anyone say, however, for example *lhe*, the indirect object pronoun. I suggested that perhaps I couldn't hear it because it's a marked structure, but the class said no, the reason I haven't heard it is that no one says it in Rio. . . . They suggested I should listen next week in Salvador, because it's used in that dialect.

But there are other cases in which a particular verb form did occur in the input, but R simply did not "hear," i.e., notice, it. As indicated in Table 6, two forms did occur in input (albeit infrequently) but were never produced by R, the compound present and compound past perfect. We have also indicated that the reflexive and the inflected future occurred with various verbs in input but were never produced by R except with one verb each. For all four of these verbal forms, R claimed in his journal that he did not hear native speakers producing them. The two perfect tenses were never noticed at all:

Journal entry, Week 15
Tonight M called and we decided to go to Trattoria. Just got back. On the bus going there, I wanted to ask him if he had been going there for a long time. I had time to think about it, and carefully composed my sentence: *há muito tempo você inha vido á Trattoria?* I immediately realized that I probably got the participle wrong, mixing IR, VER and VIR again. M answered: *eu vou lá há muito tempo* ["I go there it's a long time"]. So I didn't accomplish what I wanted: I wanted to try out a perfective verb, which I have never used and never heard anyone else use. Was what he gave me back foreigner talk?[25]

The remaining two verb forms, the inflected future and the reflexive, were noticed by R, but only very late in his stay in Brazil:

Journal entry, Week 16
I complained to N that the São Paulo trip is just talk and never comes off, and he said *faremos*. The first time I've heard that form. I figured it to be a form of FAZER, which one? Conditional, subjunctive, future? My books are at the office, but I really wanted to figure this one out. Is the trip on or off or what? N said he couldn't help, he doesn't know grammatical terminology. I asked him if it's equivalent to *vamos fazer*, and he said yes. Great. The inflected future, which L said was uncommon but very emphatic. N then said it's not uncommon and it's not emphatic, there's no difference in meaning. I conclude that the trip is on, but I'm not sure how emphatically.

Journal entry, Week 21
I've reached a new take-off point and I wish I weren't leaving in 10 days. The main thing that's happened is that I'm suddenly hearing things I never heard before, including things mentioned in class. Way back in the beginning, when we learned question words, we were told that there are alternate short and long forms like *o que* and *o que é que, quem* or *quem é que*. I have never heard the long forms, ever, and concluded that they were just another classroom fiction. But today, just before we left Cabo Frio, M said something to me that I didn't catch right away. It sounded like French *que'est-ce que c'est*, only much abbreviated, approximately [kekse], which must be *(o) que (é) que (vo)cê*. The other thing I just started hearing is reflexives. Maybe I just didn't pay attention to them before, but I really never noticed any. In print, I've seen signs like *aluga-se* ["for rent"] and

vende-se ["for sale"] which look like they have reflexive pronouns but also seem similar to passives. Suddenly I'm hearing those forms. E was just here and while she was talking to M she said *me lembra não*. Or possibly she said *me lembro não*. I'm not sure of the verb, but I'm sure the negative was after the verb, and I'm sure she used *me*, which I think is a reflexive. I've heard other examples too in the past few days. Last night on an FM 98 tape I heard: *você perdeu aquele adorado sentimeto, e agora se foi, foi, foi*. "You've lost that lovin' feeling, now it's gone (reflexive), gone, gone."

Journal entry, Week 22
I just said to N *o que é que você quer*, but quickly: [kekseker]. Previously I would have said just *o que*. N didn't blink, so I guess I got it right, except now I wonder if it should have been *quiser*. I can't believe that what I notice isn't crucial for what I can do.

It seems, then, that if R was to learn and use a particular type of verbal form, it was not enough for it to have been taught and drilled in class. It was also not enough for the form to occur in input, but R had to notice the form in the input. As indicated by the last journal entry above, R subjectively felt as he was going through the learning process that conscious awareness of what was present in the input was causal. One of the most important questions for current SLA theory is whether noticing features of the language consciously in this way is a necessary step in the process of acquisition or whether, as is commonly assumed on very weak evidence, this all goes on below the level of conscious awareness. We are not suggesting, however, that R was free to notice whatever features he chose in the input. Looking at specific instances of things that R did not notice, frequency in input was probably a factor in some cases, while in other cases the forms were frequent but phonologically reduced and perceptually nonsalient. *E que* variants of question words were used by S 43 percent of the time on the conversational tapes, but in virtually all instances these were pronounced in a phonologically reduced form. One reason R may have been slow to notice and identify the reflexive form *se* is that it is homophonous with *ĉe*, the shortened form of the second singular subject pronoun *você*, which may have been what R misperceived in utterances such as *mas pode se transferir?* ("But (you) can transfer (reflex.)?")

Did Interaction Help?

Instruction was helpful but did not guarantee grammaticality. Likewise, as we show in this section, interaction with native speakers provided input that sometimes led to language learning, but interaction guaranteed neither grammaticality nor idiomaticity. We have already reported that while R clearly became a more competent conversationalist as time progressed, there were some basic aspects of conversational behavior (e.g., how to say "yes" in Portuguese) that he never caught on to.

In trying to answer the question of whether and how interaction helped in the acquisiton of *grammar*, we have looked at the conversational tapes to see if there might be general grammatical rules or constructions that R was not taught in class but induced from input. Again, we have focused on Portuguese verbs, taking as our guide the syllabus of the course that R dropped out of. Had R continued with that course, he would have been taught: six tenses of the subjunctive (present, imperfect, future, compound present, compound imperfect, compound future), the personal infinitive, passive voice, and the future progressive. We have again followed the procedure of going through the conversational tapes to ascertain the frequency of each form in S's input and R's output. None of the forms just listed appear frequently (i.e., more than five times per tape) in the input. Four of them, the three compound tenses of the subjunctive and the personal infinitive, do not appear at all in the input available to us. None of these were ever produced by R. The passive also appears infrequently in the input, only on tape 4 and only three times in the context of one story, when discussing a mugging. S then asked R if he had ever been robbed, and he answered using a passive modeled on what S had just said:

4.33–34

S:	Cê foi alguma vez assaltado enquanto cê tava aqui?	Have you ever been mugged while you've been here?
R:	Não, aqui não, no Hawaii fui.	No, here no, in Hawaii I have.

There is also some indication from the journal notes that R had begun to notice the passive at the end of his stay:

Journal entry, Week 20
M said that his bookcase *é feito pelo Y.* Ah- hah, a passive.

Journal entry, Week 22
In our session S told me she was robbed last week at knife-point. I just told M about that and said *ela tava assaltada.* But I think that should have been made with SER.

The remaining verb forms, the present, imperfect, and future subjunctives, do occur in S's input to R, a dozen times on the four tapes. R did not attempt to produce any subjunctive forms until tape 2, and did not produce any correctly until tape 4. As noted earlier, the present subjunctive was tested in an exercise on the one day that R went to his second Portuguese course. He could not do the exercise but either picked up there or already had some information about when the subjunctive is required. This is reflected in the following exchange a few days later on conversation tape 2:

2.139–147

R:	... se eu, se eu vir... subjuntivo, huh? Subjuntivo eu não sei. Se eu vi aqui aqui no Brasil antes de vinte anos...	... if I, if I come (infinitive)... subjunctive, huh? Subjunctive I don't know. If I saw (intended as *vim*, "came") here in Brazil before twenty years...

S:	Se eu viesse, se eu viesse. Se eu viesse antes de vinte anos o que aconteceria?	If I came, if I came. If I came before twenty years what would have happened?
R:	Se eu viesse?	If I came?
S:	É. Que que acontecia antes de vinte anos, cè não ia mais embora? Que que você ia dizer? Se eu viesse pró Brasil antes de 20 anos . . .	Yes. What would have happened before twenty years, you wouldn't have left? What were you going to say? If I came to Brazil before 20 years . . .

S's part in the above exchange is a good example of foreigner talk, in four respects: (1) she was talking the way R talked, using one of R's more frequent self-created formulaic expressions, *antes de vinte anos,* instead of the correct form *há vinte anos atrás;* (2) she simplified the subjunctive, giving the imperfect form *viesse* instead of the correct and more natural compound form *tivesse vindo;* (3) she was speaking for R, using the first pronoun pronoun *eu* consistently, trying to get R only to repeat; and (4) the second time she used the verb ACONTECER (which R did not know the lexical meaning of) she used the imperfect instead of the conditional form. Nevertheless, she supplied the subjunctive form, labeled as such, which R repeated. A few turns later, R attempted to produce his own subjunctive:

2.224
R:	. . . se você vesse, visse, homem ou moça andando talvez você sabe de onde.	. . . if you see, see, a man or woman walking maybe you know where (they are) from.

In this case, *visse* happens to be the correct imperfect subjunctive form of VER, "see." However, R's reaction on seeing the transcript was that he got the form right purely by accident. He was frequently confused between the forms VIR and VER and was simply trying to remember the form *viesse* (which would have been incorrect) which S had modeled for him a few minutes previously.

The first subjunctive form that R began to use with any consistency at all (though it does not appear on the conversational tapes) was the future subjunctive of QUERER:

Journal entry, Week 14
V and I went to the clube de samba last night. When we were talking about whether to go by bus or cab, I said como você quer, "as you like," and she corrected me emphatically, *como você quiser.* It should be subjunctive.

Journal entry, Week 14
A was here and said *como você quer?* I asked him why he didn't say *quiser* and he said he knows I don't know the subjunctive and *quer* is OK. No matter, I have been saying *como você quiser* at every opportunity for the past three days.

R's knowledge of this subjunctive form was of course thoroughly formulaic. Even a slight modification of the frame made him unsure whether the subjunctive or the indicative was to be used:

M needed a bus token, so I offered him mine, *eu tenho um se você quer, não, dois.* ("I have one if you want, no, two") He said *duas?* He may only have meant to confirm what I said, but I took it as a correction, so I replied *duas*, to let him know that I got it, that the number should agree with the understood *fichas* ("tokens") . . . But now I wonder if that *quer* should have been *quiser*.

The only occurence of any subjunctive form on tape is also formulaic, and R's use of the form was deliberate:

4.355

R: Acho que se eu tivesse nessa mesma exper-iência a Minas Gerais. . . .	I think that if I had this same experience in Minas Gerais . . . .

Journal entry, Week 22

S and I did our last taping today. . . . I also used *se eu tivesse*, but I'm not sure I managed a reasonable place to do it. It was semi-premeditated. It flashed through my mind that I could use it, even though I didn't have the rest of the sentence in mind.

R's subjunctive in this case was well formed, although not for the reason he thought it might be. S interpreted R's *tivesse* as a short form of *estivesse* (imperfect subjunctive of ESTAR) and his utterance as "if I were in this same experience." While R did use shortened, colloquial forms of ESTAR such as *tô, tá, tava,* he had no idea that *tivesse* could be a form of ESTAR but was producing what he thought of only a form of TER. Under R's interpretation, the utterance contains a preposition error, while under S's interpretation R's utterance was completely grammatical.

It seems, then, that none of the forms of the Portuguese verb that R would have been taught had he stayed in class were learned by him through interaction to the extent of permitting productive use, though he had begun to use a few of them in the formulaic frames in which he noticed the forms in input. We have looked for other aspects of Portuguese grammar that R was not taught but learned from interaction. We find only one clear case, the use of the verb TER to make existential sentences.

On conversation tape 1, R used existential TER once correctly, in a formula:

1.568

R: No, no há problema, não tem problema.	No, there's no problem, there's no problem.

In this utterance, R first used *há* to form the existential sentence, which is correct. *Há* is a form of HAVER ("have") but is the only really common form of that verb in colloquial Brazilian speech and has been called a "quasi-preposition" by Britto (1984). Then R self-corrected to the somewhat more idiomatic formula *não tem problema.* Elsewhere on tape 1, R correctly used *há* several times, but in five cases where an existential with TER would have been appropriate, R tried to figure out what to do, using both SER and ESTAR unsuccessfully.[26]

1.259

R: 73 queria voltar para os países árabes e não estava, não fui, não estava, não estava trabalho de linguística teoretical . . .

(In 19)73 I wanted to return to Arab countries and there wasn't (ESTAR), wasn't (SER), wasn't (ESTAR), wasn't (ESTAR) work in theoretical linguistics . .

Five weeks laters, on conversation tape 2, R produced existential sentences frequently and more or less correctly using TER:

2.245

R: Não, ruim por que? Tudo igual, ainda tem, tem cultura diferência

No, bad why? Everything('s) the same, still there's, there's cultural difference.

2.285

R: Mas você sabe, feriado, férias aqui, tem férias lá também.

But you know, holiday, vacation here, there's vacation there too.

In between tapes 1 and 2, R had made the following observations:

Journal entry, Week 10
Não tem problema is A's favorite expression, and I think he uses *tem* in lots of other sentences too. Tonight he said *tem aqui cartas de jogar?*, which might mean "do you have any playing cards here?", but I think it might also mean "are there any playing cards here?"

Journal entry, Week 10
I've been listening closely . . . and I'm pretty sure now that *tem* is "there is/are," in addition to "have." Reminds me of Hawaii creole English *no mo*, which means both "there aren't" and "don't have." So if it's *tem* in the present, should I say *tinha* in the past?

Having found a way to make existential sentences, R produced many of them on the later tapes. In a few cases, he clearly overused the construction:

4.622

R: . . . mas proibido, cheque não tem negócio no Brasil.

. . . but [it's] prohibited, check there isn't business [intended: cannot be negotiated] in Brazil.

There are some other cases in which formulaic expressions learned by R through interaction were made at least partially productive. The expression ESTAR + *morrendo* + NP is common in S's speech on the conversational tapes and was heard by R:

Journal entry, Week 18
M frequently says *vou morrer de fome* ["I'm going to die of hunger"] or *tô morrendo de fome* ["I'm dying of hunger"]. When he came back tonight he said *tô morrendo de calor* ["I'm dying of the heat"]. So a few minutes later I tried one, saying *tô morrendo de cansa,* meaning "I'm dying of exhaustion." It passed without notice. [Note: R's principle was correct, but he should have said *morrendo de cansado* or *de cansaço.]*

In other cases, R failed to extract relevant parts from formulaic utterance for productive use in other contexts.

Journal entry, Week 7
Last night I went to K's house for dinner and had my most successful conversation so far, talking to a helpful but also critical listener. It was a full 20 minutes before I said everything I can now say in Portuguese. I got a nice slang expression, *foi um barato*, which means "it was terrific." I know *barato* as "cheap," but X said this expression was originally drug culture jargon and now everyone uses it.

Although R used *foi um barato* frequently, he never derived from the expression any other use for *foi*, the perfective of SER.

In still other cases, R did extract material from formulas for productive use, but then proceeded to use the material in entirely inappropriate ways:

Journal entry, Week 5
D told me the expression *o que a gente vai fazer*, "what shall we do?", although *a gente* usually means "people."

Journal entry, Week 16
I noticed that N always orders from X using *a gente*, for example *café prá gente*, "coffee for the person," but meaning "coffee for *me*." Seems odd, but I've used it a few times.

Having discovered the form *a gente*, which seemed very colloquial to R, he began to use it frequently, but always incorrectly. In Brazilian Portuguese, *gente*, with no article, means "people." *A gente*, with the definite article, means "we/us." Thus, *gente como a gente* (the translation of the film title, "Ordinary People") means "people like us." Both *gente* and *a gente* are very frequent in informal speech. There are in addition some uses of *a gente* in which the identity of referents other than the speaker may be obscure or indefinite, some of which are parallel to similar uses of "we" in English (e.g., the editorial/imperial/ poetic/pastoral or group representative "we"). Other cases in which *a gente* is used might be more likely to trigger the use of impersonal "one" or "you" in English, e.g., *quando a gente está apaixonada, a gente fica com vontade de morrer,* "when you're in love, you want to die," in which the speaker is talking about his or her current situation but is expressing feelings as though they were universally felt. A further complication is introduced by the fact that both *gente* and *a gente* are semantically plural (or collective) but syntactically both are third singular.

This is a case where direct explanation might have been very useful, as R was unable to infer the meanings of the two forms from context. First, he did not realize that there were two forms, missing the significance of the article entirely (note that in his prototype utterance *café prá gente* the article has been absorbed by the preposition). Second, misinterpreting some utterances (*café prá gente* means "coffee for us," not "coffee for me"), R concluded that *(a) gente* was a pro-form that could be used to refer vaguely to almost any person. He made two types of systematic errors. When using *gente* to mean "people" (semantically

286

correct), he used third plural verbs (grammatically incorrect). When he did use third singular verbs, it was because he intended a third singular referent (semantically incorrect). e.g.:

4.204
R: ... eu falei uma hora ou mais com gente que estava sentando ao lado de mim ...

I spoke for an hour or more with people [*gente*, but intended meaning was "someone," *uma pessoa*] sitting beside me ...

R's ability to generalize accurately from formulaics to more productive use was therefore limited. However, we do not view the relevance of formulaic speech simply as a way "into the system" but also as a way *out* of the system. Pawley and Syder (1983) have argued that even when constructions are fully derivable by productive rules of the grammar, speakers do not utilize the creative power of syntactic rules to anything like their full extent, and "indeed, if they did so they would not be accepted as exhibiting nativelike control of the language" (Pawley and Syder 1983:193). The gist of Pawley and Syder's argument is that the ability of native speakers to routinely convey meanings fluently, in the face of limited human capacities for encoding novel speech, and in a way that is not only grammatical but also idiomatic and nativelike, rests to a great extent on prepackaged material: memorized sentences and phrases, lexicalized sentence stems (with open slots), familiar collocations, and the like. Such prepackaged items include true idioms with arbitrary construction and usage, but also regular form-meaning pairings, which Pawley and Syder claim must be known both holistically (as lexicalized units) and analytically (as products of syntactic rules). Pawley and Syder argue that the stock of lexicalized sentence stems alone must be in the hundreds of thousands for an ordinary mature speaker of a language.

In the speech of S on the conversational tapes, there are many examples of idiomatic "chunks," readily identifiable by the fact that they occur repeatedly, with minimal change, e.g.:

que que você tá achando de NP?	what do you think of NP?
	7 examples on tape 1, no variation
me diz uma coisa	tell me something
	6 examples on tape 1, no variation
quer dizer que	I mean, that is to say
	5 examples on tape 1, no variation

Other examples that occur less frequently on tape are still recognizable as things frequently said, e.g.:

quem sabe seja isso mesmo	who knows if it's really that
te leva a pensar	it makes you think
aí é que é bom	then it's good
ia te falar	I was going to tell you
se você quiser	if you like/want

cada um na sua	everyone minds their own business
tem mania de NP	is crazy/compulsive about NP
pois é	indeed
é uma festa	it's a party (i.e., something terrific)
que sorte/bom/interessante	how lucky/good/interesting
seria bom/interessante	it would be good/interesting

An increase in idiomaticity, and particularly the use of idiomatic, prepackaged strings, might be one of the expected benefits of learning a language through interaction with native speakers. When we look at R's language on the conversational tapes, the evidence is mixed. We do find some examples of slang, for example, in R's speech, beginning with conversation tape 2 and increasing on the last two tapes, such as the formulaic *foi um barato*, lexical items such as *cara* ("guy"), *loucura* ("lunacy"), *baseado* ("joint"), and abbreviated (more colloquial) forms of the verb ESTAR such as *tô (estou), tá (está),* and *tava (estava).* In a few cases, slang was explained by native speakers:

Journal entry, Week 20
Q gave me some more slang: *tô na minha, tá na dele,* etc., meaning "I do it my way," "he does it his way," etc.

Other times, R figured out the meaning of slang expressions from context:

Journal entry, Week 12
During our first conversation, I noticed that N has a favorite expression, which sounded to me like [dehepentsh]. It seemed from context that it must mean "maybe," "perhaps," a hedge of some kind. So I started using it back.... Now I'm really embarrassed. I tried to look it up in my dictionary, but couldn't find it at first. Today I realized that it must be "r," not "h," and I found *repente, de,* "suddenly." If I misinterpreted what N said to me, that's pretty normal, but what stupidities have I produced by saying "suddenly" when I thought I was saying "perhaps"? Also, I just checked my class notes. We were given *de repente* in class.

Journal entry, Week 13
I mentioned the *de repente* example in class today, to illustrate the difficulties of figuring out the language through conversation with a monolingual native speaker. Everyone had a good laugh on me, until O piped up and said, "wait a minute, *de repente* also does mean "maybe"; it's very current slang and I use it constantly with that meaning. The rest of the class was skeptical, but O insisted. I just stopped by N's place and asked him. He said *de repente* is just a sign of reflection, automatic, doesn't mean anything. And he used it three or four times while we were talking. even as a filler in the midst of his explanation.

There are other cases in which R noticed idiomatic usage, including a few cases in which what he observed was accurate although it contradicted what he had been taught in class:

Journal entry, Week 11
We were taught that Brazilian Portuguese does not use the T-forms, but I hear them used. A always leaves saying *eu te ligo,* "I'll call you," and I also hear the possessives *teu* and *tua,* though never a subject T-form.

288

Of the forms that R noticed, *não* + V is standard Portuguese, *não* + V + *não* is
typical of Rio de Janeiro, and V + *não* is generally considered to be typical of
speakers from the northeast of Brazil. R was aware that some of his friends were
originally nordestinos but does not know if the particular friends who produced
those constructions were.

Looking through the conversational transcripts for idiomatic, prepackaged chunks, the evidence is more discouraging, although we do not know
how much idiomaticity should be expected after 4 months of interaction with
native speakers. It is clear that R did rely whenever possible on familiar material
for communication, including language he had picked up verbatim from native
speakers. There are several cases where R can identify his language on tape as
things he heard people say to him in the context of the event reported. On tape 3,
R reported having swum a long distance, from one beach to another, *duma até a
outra* ["from one to the other"]. The phrase, which contains R's only correctly
contracted preposition with an indefinite article on any tape, was exactly what
one friend had said to another when describing R's swimming a few days
previously. R also used, and often overused, common expressions like *tudo
bem/bom/legal* ("everything's OK, fine"), *mais ou menos* ("more or less"),
são X horas ("it's X o'clock"), chunks that virtually all nonnative learners of
Portuguese quickly pick up and use. In other cases, R relied heavily on chunks
that he himself had constructed. Some of these are reasonable Portuguese. On
tape 4, R said what he always said when people asked him if he had studied
Portuguese before arriving in Brazil:

4.246
R: ... e quando eu vi [intended: vim] aqui no   ... and when I say [intended: came] here to
Rio ... eu non sabia nenhuma palavra em   Rio ... I didn't know a single word of
português.   Portuguese.

The majority of R's familiar ways of saying things, however, are simply not
idiomatic Portuguese. They are either Portuguese chunks used in noticeably

nonnativelike ways or, more commonly, nonnativelike chunks, R's own frozen interlanguage forms. Some of the more striking examples are:

antes de X anos	"Before X years" Occurs many times on tape. The correct form is *há X anos atrás*. Source of R's form unknown.
falamos X juntos	"We speak X together," presumably from English. Occurs on all four tapes. In Portuguese, the *juntos* is not used and is felt to be redundant.
a coisa de NP	This also appears as *a causa de NP* on a note which R wrote to a friend. Intended as "because of NP," which in Portuguese is *por causa de*.
companheiro da casa	"Housemate" Normally in Portuguese, one would say *moro com um amigo* ("I live with a friend"), although there is an expression *companheiro de quarto*, "roommate." R learned that expression from a native speaker and used it correctly on tape 3. Between tapes 3 and 4, he apparently reconstructed the form, and for a time did not remember ever having heard or used it with *quarto*.
V + com + pronoun	A possible construction, but overused and incorrectly used by R. R first learned the phrase *vou levar comigo* ("I'll take [it] with me"), used that phrase when CARREGAR ("carry") was required, and generalize the pattern incorrectly, e.g., *falou comigo que* ("talked to me that") instead of *me contou* ("told me").
preciso + V	"I must/need to/have to" On tape 1, R expressed this notion with DEVER + V, then used PRECISAR + V from tape 2 to the end of his stay in Brazil, although he constantly heard and understood the more common form *TER que + V*. R's forms were correct. The problem is partly one of register and partly semantic. PRECISAR has a connotation of personal responsibility, as opposed to the connotation of external forces in the case of *TER que* (comparable with the contrast between "must" (internal) and "have to" (external) in English).
alguma coisa *algumas vezes*	"something," "sometimes" The forms are correct, but R used these formulaics in semantic contexts in which they don't occur in native speech: *alguma coisa* was used when a native speaker would say *uma coisa* (cf. S's formulaic *me diz uma coisa*, "tell me a thing"); *algumas vezes* was used when a native speaker would say *várias vezes* ("several times").

Did Correction Help?

When nonnative speakers make errors, they are sometimes able to identify and self-correct their errors, and native speakers sometimes react to errors with corrective feedback. Both kinds of correction, self- and other-, are part of the phenomenon of repair, in which the parties to a conversation attempt to rectify conversational trouble (Day, Chenoweth, Chun, and Luppescu, 1984). But does repair help? Is an error that is repaired therefore less likely to recur? While the extensive literature on the subject of error treatment still provides no conclusive evidence, current opinion on the meaning of errors and the desirability of correction ranges between two extremes. Hammerly (1982:274–280) views errors as failures that must be counteracted, urging that "we should not allow early free speaking, which results in linguistic monstrosities." Vigil and Oller (1976) argue that errors that do not receive negative cognitive feedback are likely to fossilize, and Schachter (1984) has suggested that "negative input," including but not limited to correction, may be a universal input condition for successful second language acquisition. Others have argued that errors are inevitable and that error correction is a mistake, since correction raised the "affective filter" and is of no direct benefit to language acquisition (Krashen 1982:74–76). Error correction in free conversation has been much less discussed. In the only study we know of to date that attempts to find out if such correction produces any results, Brock, Crookes, Day, and Long (this volume) found few if any observable effects of corrective feedback but do not argue that corrective feedback produces no results; they suggest that longitudinal research would help resolve the issue.

The issue of self-correction has been less discussed in the language learning literature, but there are various possibilities that have been proposed. Krashen (1982:104–112) has discussed self-correction in connection with the concept of monitor use, the application of learned rules as an editing device that may improve performance, but only slightly and under certain conditions. Krashen has also suggested frequently that learners may monitor by "feel" in addition but has not yet in his published writings suggested any place for self-correction in the acquisition process itself. Morrison and Low (1983) have raised this possibility. They suggest that it might be possible to show that the act of detecting and repairing certain mistakes has longitudinal repercussions. We might find that learners who monitor and self-correct their own speech make faster progress or progress further in language learning than those who do not monitor, or that those who monitor primarily at the level of phonology would show improvement in phonology while those who monitor their syntax would show improvement in syntax, etc.

When dealing with a single learner, we are limited in the ways in which we may look for possible effects of self- and other-correction. This is also an area in which we feel especially keenly the limitations of our data. Out of all the interactions in Portuguese in which R took part we have only a small sample on tape, which may or may not be typical in various ways. Other native speakers may have corrected R more or less than S; R may have monitored and self-corrected more in the taped conversations than in other interactions, and possibly less than in some other situations. R also took note of corrections of his Portuguese by various interlocuters, but these clearly represent only a small sample of the corrections that native speakers must have made in a 5-month period. Nevertheless, a few patterns emerge and there are a few cases in which errors and the attempts made to correct them are sufficiently documented in our data that we can give a sketchy natural history of their evolution.

First, it is clear that native speakers do indeed correct errors that their nonnative speaking friends make, even though they correct only a small percentage of the errors that are made (Chun, Day, Chenoweth, and Luppescu 1982). R reported in his journal being corrected by friends quite often. There is almost certainly some variation by personality: R reported that one friend "never" corrected him, while others did so frequently. It is also clear that correction does have potentially adverse effects on the quality of interaction. While R felt in principle that he would rather be corrected than not, there are several journal entries that show clearly his discomfort and ill feelings when native speakers overdid it:

Journal entry, Week 7
I'm glad I was wearing my sense of humor, because Y corrected me constantly. The ones I can remember now were *muitas problemas* (I know *problema* is masculine but made the error anyway), *nominal* to *substantivo, silência* to *silêncio* and *corpo diplomática* to *corpo diplomático*. I didn't want to take that one lying down, and objected that it was just a guess. I knew "foreign service" would not translate, but I figured CD would. Y said: guess better . . . He works for the Tax Ministry, so maybe that explains his authoritarian personality.

Journal entry, Week 20
X corrected me frequently throughout the exam. She corrected the stress on *níveis* (not the first time I've made that mistake), and corrected *confusando* to *confuso* (I think), pointing out that it's irregular. I don't know if she was giving me the word for "confused" or "confusing". . . . X also corrected *prefero* to *prefiro*, but I think I didn't make that mistake. . . . I think she just heard the error because she was expecting it. I didn't appreciate the correction.

Journal entry, Week 20
I'm feeling very discouraged by how little I've managed to learn. I had a great time last night until I said something about my trip today and I must have said *de mánha* again (stress error) . . . Y corrected me sharply. I wish I could learn with only one correction too, but I would also appreciate a softer touch in correction. I was so angry I didn't talk at all for a couple of hours.

Table 7 gives the frequency of self- and other-corrections, taken from the conversational transcripts and R's journal notes, and their distribution according to type of error repaired. Except for errors of pronunciation (which we will not deal with) and lexis (which we will deal with for only a few examples), the categories into which repairs have been sorted are roughly the same as those discussed on pages 249–261; so some comparisons between what was repaired and what improved are possible.

Self-correction If self-correction facilitates second language learning, we might expect to find various manifestations of this in the data. Looking across the series of tapes, we might find that those grammatical categories in which errors were most often self-corrected were those which showed the greatest improvement over time. Looking at the tapes one by one, we might find a pattern in which at one stage R did not self-correct an error type, a second stage at which errors continued to occur but were self-corrected, and a third stage in which the error did not occur. We do not find any of these patterns in our data, and we are

TABLE 7 Repair. Self-Correction and Other-Correction on Conversational Tapes, Other-Correction Noted in Journal

	Self-correct	Other-correct	Noted in journal	Total
Lexicon	5	7	7	19
Articles	8	4	2	14
Gender	9	1	5	15
Pronunciation	5	4	6	15
Copula	7		2	9
Perfect past	5	3		8
Prepositions	1	4	1	6
Person	4	1		5
Conjugation		1	2	3
Discourse		4		4
Subjunctive	1	1	2	4
Miscellaneous	16	10	6	32
Total	63	40	33	136

unable to discern any clear effect from self-correction to improved performance over time. Three areas in which R concentrated his self-corrections but which received relatively little other-correction illustrate the variety of patterns that we do find:

Gender   As indicated in Table 7, gender errors were the most frequently self-corrected of any of our categories but do not show up with equivalent high rank in our tabulations of other-corrections. Gender seems to be a good candidate for something that R was working on by himself. However, if we refer back to Table 1, we see that the various aspects of gender in Portuguese were things that R was already good at in the beginning. Instead of self-correction being a precursor of improved performance, it seems here to be the reflection of already established good performance, an ability to detect and remedy those occasional (performance) errors that do occur. This interpretation is strengthened if we look at the distribution of self-corrections within the various aspects of gender. Twice as many of R's self-corrections repaired problems with article gender and phonological shape (those aspects of gender on which he performed best at the beginning) as repaired problems with pre- and postmodifiers, the categories in which he originally made the most errors but showed the most improvement over time.

Copula   Copula errors were corrected relatively frequently by R (rank 3 in Table 7) but seldom by native speakers. Self-monitoring and correction seem to have had no effect here at all. Five of R's seven corrections of copula errors on tape consisted in restoring omitted copulas, but as discussed on pages 259–262 this was an area in which R did not improve at all during his stay in Brazil.

Person   As noted above, R made errors confusing first and second/third person verb forms, especially in the perfect and on tape 1 especially when answering questions when the answer required changing the personal inflection.

Person errors are another area in which self-corrections were focused, and again there is little evidence that self-correction contributed to improved performance subsequently. The area in which improvement occurred over time was in answering questions, yet none of R's self-corrections were in answers to questions. All his self-corrections of verb person errors were in self-initiated utterances. In this case, R's self-corrections appear to be an attempt to control a part of the grammar that actually was showing a slight deterioration over time.

Gender, copula, and verb person are thus three areas on which self-corrections were focused, with no apparent effect on subsequent production. While our data are limited, they seem to us to support the Krashen position that the ability to monitor and self-correct in the midst of a communicatively meaningful interaction is a rather minor output control mechanism, not a significant part of the acquisition process. Two other categories listed in Table 7, articles and the perfect past tense, present a somewhat different picture. However, both of those areas of the grammar also received significant other-correction and joint work by the native and nonnative speaker, so we deal with them below under the category of apparent successes of other-correction.

In discussing the issue of whether instruction helped, we proposed that it was important that R noticed certain features of Portuguese, a type of metalinguistic awareness. Self-correction is another aspect of metalinguistic awareness, which seems this time to have had no effect. A study by Schlue (1977) suggests a possible reason why. Schlue recorded three university ESL students once a week for 10 weeks, and immediately after each recording had her subjects listen to the tapes of their conversations and try to identify and correct their own errors. Schlue found no clear indication that overall error sensitivity either increased or decreased for these subjects during the 10-week period, and she does not report any relationship between the ability to self-correct during the course of a conversation and progress in grammatical development. Schlue does report, however, that with one subject ("Dr. F"), there was a dramatic shift in the development of noun plurals, from an initial stage in which errors went unrecognized to a second stage of *belated* awareness of error (when listening to the tape being replayed) to a third stage of improved performance. We have no comparable data for R, who did not listen to the tapes of his own conversations and did not look at any of the transcripts until just before his departure from Brazil.

Other-correction While R recorded instances of corrective feedback in his journal, the 33 specific corrections recorded must represent only a small fraction of the error corrections that he must have received over a 5-month period. No doubt R failed to remember many corrections long enough to write them down, and negative feedback was frequently not the most salient aspect of the language learning experience on most occasions when R wrote in his journal. We believe there is also another reason for the small number of examples recorded: R frequently did not know that he was being corrected. In the transcripts of the conversational tapes there are numerous examples in which it is clear that while the native speaker provided corrective feedback, and intended to do so, R did not recognize it as such. Some examples from tape 1, corroborated by discussion between S and R concerning what each one thought was going on, are the following:

1.124–128

S:	Você já estudou francês?	Have you studied French?
R:	Sim.	Yes.
S:	Já?	Have you? (lit: already?)
R:	Eu?	Me?
S:	É. Você fala francês?	Yes. Do you speak French?

1.251–254

S:	Foi com você pro Líbano?	Did she go with you to Lebanon?
R:	Sim.	Yes.
S:	Foi, né?	She went, huh?
R:	Sim, e . . .	Yes, and . . .

1.84–88

S:	Que que você tá achando do carioca em relação ao Egito?, aos egípcios?	What do you think of Cariocas (residents of Rio) compared with Egypt, with Egyptians?
R:	Ah . . . muito perto.	Ah . . . very close.
S:	Muito perto, né? Muito parecidos?	Very close, huh? Very similar?
R:	Sim, muito, muito.	Yes, very, very.

The first two examples above deal with R's inappropriate answers to questions in Portuguese, and in both cases S supplied what would have been a more appropriate response. However, these were heard by R not as error corrections but simply as confirmation checks. In the classification of Day et al. (1984), these are examples of off-record corrective feedback, corrections embedded in utterances with more than one function. The third examples treats a lexical error. *Perto* means "proximate in space," as does English "close," but cannot be extended to mean "proximate in relation." R's error was an overgeneralization of a Portuguese item along lines suggested by English. When R produced the error, S responded first by repeating the incorrect form, then providing the correction. The correction was not "heard" by R, who once again took the potentially corrective feedback as a confirmation check, and provided the confirmation that he thought had been requested. From R's point of view, *perto* was confirmed, not disconfirmed by this interaction, which might be part of the reason why he continued to produce the form with this meaning throughout his stay in Brazil. On tape 4 we find the following exchange. This time *perto* is not corrected by S:

4.370–372

R:	Mas não é confuson, é diferente.	But it's not "confusion". It's different.
S:	É, é diferente.	Yes, it's different.
R:	É perto, mas tem diferença.	It's close, but there's a difference.
S:	É.	Yes.

Cases like these, in which intended corrections were not noticed by R, are common on each tape. It is also possible that at least on some occasions, the opposite happened: something said by a native speaker and not intended as correction might be taken as correction. We doubt that this happened often, but there is one example on tape:

1.71–73, 84–85

R:	Uh, mas os egipitios?	Uh, but the "Egyptians"?	
S:	Egípitos?	Egyptians?	
R:	Os egípitos é, não son fanáticos . . .	The Egyptians is, are not fanatic.	
. . . .		. . . .	
S:	Que que voce tá achando do carioca em relação ao Egito?, aos egípcios?	What do you think of Cariocas compared to Egypt, to Egyptians?	

R did not know how to say "Egyptians" in Portuguese, so asked for help. S responded, but was not sure about the word the moment she said it. What she said was a native speaker performance error. She found an opportunity to say it again correctly, but in the meantime R had taken her initial response as a correction of his original pronunciation and had repeated it.

It may well be that in order for corrective feedback to have any effect, the nonnative speaker must, as a minimum, realize that he or she had been corrected. At least, we have not been able to find in our data any examples of cases where R made an error, was corrected, did not realize that he was being corrected, but nevertheless soon after improved his performance. On the other hand, being corrected is certainly no guarantee that one will not make the same error again, as every classroom teacher is fully aware.

In the remainder of this section we discuss some cases where correction apparently worked, and some others where it apparently did not work. We consider a correction to have worked if R did not make the same error again, a failure if he continued to make the same error. We must restrict our claims to *apparent* successes, since additional errors may have occurred of which we have no record, and improved performance may have other origins than error correction. Failures must also be identified tentatively, since the ultimate effects of some corrections might yet remain to be seen. We also restrict our discussion to examples of corrections for which we have enough documentation to look for positive effects. Many items that were corrected once on tape never occur again in our corpus and are never mentioned in the journal.

Apparent failures Several examples of correction that had no effect on R's subsequent performance have already been mentioned: the subjunctive, which was corrected several times (see pages 282–284 and Table 7), but except for the case of the formulaic *como você quiser* (which is mentioned in the journal but does not appear on tape) was not learned by R; the imperfect form of PENSAR, which R produced incorrectly in class and again a week later on tape 1 (page 256); *a causa de* NP, which R wrote on a note that a friend corrected and later produced in conversation on tape 4 (page 290); *perto* in the sense of "similar," corrected although the correction was not perceived by R. Several journal entries report errors that persisted in spite of multiple corrections by friends, including three stress errors: *de mánha* instead of *de manhá* ("in the morning"); *errós* instead of *érros* ("mistakes"); and *país* instead of *páis*, which resulted in a confusion between "parents" and "country."

There are other cases in which correction of an error that reflects a general grammatical problem seemed to have had a temporary effect but did not result in any general improvement in R's performance in the long run, e.g.:

3.209–211

R: Fui a Hula's?	Did I go to Hula's?
S: Foi? Não, não fui não, fui só ao cinema.	Did you go? No, I didn't go, I only went to the theater.
R: Mas vi, viu Hula's?	But I saw, you saw Hula's?

R's error was with the personal inflection on the verb; his questions should have been *foi?* not *fui?* S's initial response, *foi*, can be seen as what-R-should-have-said, or as a confirmation check on what he did say (reversing person as appropriate when questioning). Her subsequent *não fui não* makes R's error clear. In his next turn, R made the same mistake again and, possibly under the influence of S's correction, he self-corrected the error. But there was no subsequent general improvement in R's performance on verb person by the time of the next tape.

4.90–99

R: E sabe também, eu lembro agora, em árabe também eu tenho problema, uma, um problema: em árabe também tem concordância adjetivo substantivo mas eu lembro agora que o problema prá mim é como falar adjetivo mas eu não tenho subjuntivo.	And you know also, I remember now, in Arabic also I have a problem, a [feminine singular], a [masculine singular] problem: in Arabic also there is adjective-noun agreement but I remember now that the problem for me is how to speak adjective but I don't have subjunctive.
S: Substantivo.	Noun.
R: Substantivo, quando não tem substantivo, par exemplo, nós falamos sobre as ruas bonitas e depois eu falo . . .	Noun, when there is no noun, for example, we speak about the beautiful streets [feminine plural] and later I speak . . .
S: Bonitos.	Beautiful [masculine plural]
R: Bonitos. Sem, sem o subjuntivo, substantivo e também em português é problema, huh?	Beautiful. Without, without the subjunctive, noun, and also in Portuguese it's [a] problem, huh?

In the above example, R made an error confusing *substantivo* ("noun") and *subjuntivo* ("subjunctive"), S corrected the error, R repeated it but then just a few seconds later made the same error again and self-corrected himself. We have no data that indicate the *final* outcome of this and many similar corrections.

Apparent successes Two examples have been mentioned in passing of corrections that seemed to work immediately. *As moças as bonitas,* an article-noun-article-adjective construction that we have attributed to transfer from Arabic, was produced in class, corrected, and never produced again (page 255). *Corpo diplomática,* a guess by R on the basis on his knowledge of French *corps diplomatique,* was corrected in conversation to *diplomático* and appears in the corrected form on tape 1. It may (or may not) be significant that these errors were corrected the first time that R made them.

Articles Articles are an aspect of Portuguese grammar in which R made numerous errors (see pages 253–255), and as indicated in Table 7, article errors were among those most often other-corrected and self-corrected in conversation. There may be some relationship between the fact that 10 of the 14 self- and other-corrections on the conversational tapes were focused on R's specific problem of omitting the definite article between a contracting preposition and a place name or other proper noun and the fact that these were precisely the environments in which R's performance improved over time. There seems to be an especially significant repair sequence on the third conversational tape:

3.91–105

S: Cê foi com quem? — Who did you go with?

R: Com O, você conhece, huh? Que trabalha Cultura Inglesa e algumas pessoas, professores . . . — With O, you know [her], huh? Who works [at the] Cultura Inglesa and some people, teachers . . .

S: *Da* Cultura. — *From the* Cultura.

R: *Da* Cultura, agora "*da* Cultura," tudo com artigo. — *From the* Cultura, now "from the Cultura," everything with article.

S: A tua palesta *na* Cultura eu achei que foi mais . . . foi mais bem concluida do que *no* IBEU. — Your lecture *at the* Cultura I think was more, finished better than [the one] *at the* IBEU.

R: *Na* Cultura. — *At the* Cultura.

S: É, *na* Cultura. — Yes, *at the* Cultura.

R: Acho que sim. O grupo muito bom. — I think so. The group very good.

S: A O me convidou prá dar aula *na* Cultura. — The O invited me to give classes *at the* Cultura.

R: Eu ouvi. — I heard.

S: Se você quiser vir morar *no* Brasil, cê já vai dar aula *na* Cultura, *no* IBEU. — If you want to live *in the* Brazil, you already are going to give classes *at the* Cultura, *at the* IBEU.

R: *Na* Cultura, *no* IBEU. — *At the* Cultura, *at the* IBEU.

S: *Na* PUC. E aqui *na* PUC. — *At the* PUC. And here *at the* PUC.

In this exchange, there are 15 occurrences of articles contracted with prepositions preceding proper nouns, and both S and R were aware and amused by the fact that they were producing so many of them while continuing to focus on the topic of conversation. Such repair sequences may have had something to do with the fact that on the next (final) conversational tape R no longer had a particular problem in supplying articles in those particular environments. While he continued to omit articles in general, his omissions after prepositions and before proper nouns were no more frequent than any others. However, we must point out two other possibilities: (1) the improvement might have happened without either self- or other-correction, and (2) exchanges such as that cited above from tape 3 might have only accelerated, or perhaps been a reflection of, a change already in progress. Between tapes 1 and 2, R's performance on definite articles contracted with prepositions had already increased from 45 to 51 percent; his accuracy on definite articles before place names and other proper nouns had already increased from 28 to 44 percent.

Perfect vs. imperfect past tense   On pages 257–259, we reported that the distribution of the two past tenses, perfect and imperfect, in R's speech was lexical: the great majority of verbs that R used repeatedly appeared either in the perfect or in the imperfect consistently, not both. We also reported that the underlying basis for R's assignment of specific verbs to the classes of [+ perfect] and [+ imperfect] was a semantic distinction between inherently stative and nonstative lexical verbs, rather than the frequency with which the verbs appeared in one of the two past tenses in input. Nevertheless, interesting questions remain concerning the roles of input and interaction, including correction, in the assignment of specific verbs to one of the past tenses.

Input frequency as a factor was suggested by the fact that although R used a lexical strategy for the distribution of the tenses he was still able to achieve a reasonable level of contextual accuracy. When either the perfect or the imperfect was required, R had a combined accuracy rate of 81 percent (39/48) on tape 1 and 86 percent (119/138) on tape 4. This suggested to us that while all Portuguese verbs have both perfect and imperfect past tense forms, native speakers of Portuguese might also strongly prefer one of the past tenses for particular verbs, or common conversational contexts might force particular choices, possibly to the extent that R might have heard only one past tense form for many verbs.

Table 8 lists all verbs used more than once by R in some past tense on the conversational tapes, and indicates the distribution by tense in both R's speech and the input provided by S.

In general, the frequency of the perfect in the input from S was much higher than the frequency of the imperfect. One result of this, as indicated in Table 8, is that there were indeed some verbs (COMPRAR, CONVIDAR, LER, NADAR, OUVIR, PAGAR, and VER) that R produced exclusively in the perfect and that were also present exclusively in the perfect in the sample of input available to us. On the other hand, the five verbs that R used exclusively in the imperfect past tense were not present in input either exclusively or overwhelmingly in the imperfect.

The pattern presented in Table 8, including discrepancies between the categories of [+ stative] and [+ imperfect] and the few cases of verbs that show variation can be accounted for if we adopt two sets of assumptions:

1. R operated under a (subconscious) hypothesis that stative (or durative) verbs would be [+ imperfect] in the past, while nonstative (or punctual) verbs would be [+ perfect] in the past.

TABLE 8 Lexical Verbs Used More Than Once by R; Distribution of Perfect and Imperfect Forms in Input and Output

Lexical verb	Stative?	Output		Input	
		Perfect	Imperfect	Perfect	Imperfect
ESTAR (Be)	+	−	23	2	5
PENSAR (Think)	+	−	2	4	−
QUERER (Want)	+	−	7	1	2
SABER (Know)	+	−	10	3	2
TER (Have)	+	−	11	3	3
COMPRAR (Buy)	−	7	−	8	−
CONVIDAR* (Invite)	−	2	−	1	−
DIZER (Say)	−	12	−	5	1
FALAR (Speak)	−	7	−	3	1
FAZER (do)	−	8	−	8	1
FICAR (Become)	−	2	−	−	−
IR (Go)	−	38	−	34	6
LER (Read)	−	2	−	2	−
MANDAR (Order)	−	2	−	−	−
MUDAR (Change)	−	2	−	−	−
NADAR (Swim)	−	5	−	5	−
OUVIR (Hear)	+	9	−	1	−
PAGAR (Pay)	−	2	−	1	−
PLANEJAR (Plan)	−	2	−	−	−
RECEBER (Receive)	−	6	−	−	−
VER (See)	+	11	−	12	−
VIR (Come)	−	3	−	−	1
VISITAR (Visit)	−	2	−	−	−
GOSTAR (Like)	+	11	1	23	−
JOGAR (Play)	−	1	1	2	−
MORAR (Live)	?	3	5	3	−
SER (Be)	+	4	2	30	10
TRABALHAR (Work)	?	2	4	1	−

*CONVIDAR also includes *envidar*, an incorrect form sometimes used by R.

2. Language learning is subject to the "easy confirmation principle." Learners look for verification of their hypotheses, not disconfirmation (Schachter 1983, 1984). Hypotheses can be disconfirmed, but if the learner has hypothesized that a particular form X is appropriate in some environment Y, then disconfirmation requires either that some other form Z occurs in environment Y either exclusively or with overwhelming frequency, or that the learner produces form X and is explicitly corrected to form Z.

An initial assumption that statives would be imperfect, combined with the easy confirmation principle, explains why R produced five stative verbs exclusively in the imperfect, even though he only heard them *sometimes* in the imperfect.[27] The principle that disconfirmation is difficult, but possible, will explain why two stative verbs, VER and GOSTAR, appeared exclusively in the perfect in R's speech: those two verbs were among the most frequent in the input to R, and in the data available to us appear exclusively in the perfect in the input. The other stative verb that R used in the perfect, OUVIR, is not explained by this principle, since in our data it occurred only once in input, and we are not sure why R produced OUVIR in the perfect. It might be because OUVIR in the past is (relatively) punctual, or it might be that it occurred more frequently and always in the perfect in other input not available to us, or it might be that OUVIR was assigned to the perfect category under the influence of VER (the perfect of VER is *vi/viu;* that of OUVIR, *ouvi/ouviu*).

Four verbs on which R's performance was variable remain to be explained: JOGAR, SER, MORAR, and TRABALHAR. R produced the verb JOGAR twice in the past on tape, once in the perfect (as predicted, since "play" is nonstative) and once in the imperfect. R's use of JOGAR in the imperfect appears to have been triggered by the verb form of the question he was answering:

2.205–206

S; Mas o que que ele fazia? Só cantava?	But what was he doing [imperfect]? Just singing [imperfect]?
R: Só cantava, só cantava mas as moças também jogavam, jogavam com ele e brincavam, brincavam com ele . . .	Just singing [imperfect] just singing but the girls were playing [imperfect], playing with him and playing [imperfect] playing with him . . .

R's response to a question phrased in the imperfect contained not only the imperfect of JOGAR but also the imperfect of two other nonstatives, CANTAR (modeled by the question) and BRINCAR. In Table 8 we listed only those verbs that R used more than once in the past on tape. If we consider *all* verbs that R used in the past (including those which appear only once), then the occurrences of BRINCAR and CANTAR in this example constitute the only additional exceptions to the principle that nonstatives are in the perfect.

The verb SER appears in R's speech in the past four times on the tapes, twice in the imperfect (as predicted) and four times in the perfect (not predicted), which violates both the hypothesis that statives should be imperfect and the easy confirmation hypothesis, since there are 10 occurrences of SER in the perfect in the input on tape. However, it seems to us that R did not really have this verb assigned to either aspect. R seldom used SER in the past, preferring to use the imperfect of ESTAR. In addition, the four occurrences of SER in the perfect are each odd in some way: one was a bungled attempt at an existential sentence (see page 285); two were in the formula *foi um barato* (see page 286), the last was as the auxiliary of a passive, modeled on what S had said in the previous turn (see page 282).

The final two verbs that show variation between the two aspects of the past, MORAR and TRABALHAR, are interesting in a number of respects. First, it is unclear to us whether they should be classified as statives or nonstatives (grammarians we have consulted have not all agreed), though it is clear that they are both nonpunctual verbs. Second, these verbs indicate one of the inadequacies of R's lexical solution to the problem of aspect. While the imperfect in Portuguese is used for nonpunctual structures, as Britto (1984) points out, there is no contradiction in Portuguese between a marker of perfectiveness and other markers of durativeness in the same sentence:

a.	João morava [imperfect] na Europa quando o conheci.	John lived in Europe when I met him.
b.	*João marou [perfect] no Europa quando o conheci.	
c.	João morou [perfect] na Europa muitos anos.	John lived in Europe for many years.
d.	*João morava [imperfect] na Europa muitos anos.	

Sentences a and b show that the imperfect must be used in Portuguese whenever reference is made to a point in time contained within the period indicated by MORAR. There is also in Portuguese, as in English, the alternative of using a past progessive construction in such sentences, a construction with which R had no problems. Sentences c and d, on the other hand, indicate that while both the adverbial and the lexical meaning of the verb itself make it clear that MORAR takes time, sometimes the perfect is required, whenever the segment of time is "seen from the outside."

Finally, this is a case where we think that explicit correction (in the case of MORAR) and modeling (in the case of TRABALHAR) may have played a significant role in destabilizing one of R's characteristic errors. The error here was R's producing sentences of type d, e.g.:

1.7–8
R:	... e vous sabe que eu é, eu morava no Egito e Lebanon, Líbano.	... and you know that, uh, I lived [imperfect] in Egypt and Lebanon, Lebanon.
S:	Você morou no Egito? É?	You lived [perfect] in Egypt? Yeah?

1.45
R:	Beirute é, é eu morava em Beirute de 75 até 79 e ...	Beirut, uh, I lived [imperfect] in Beirut from 75 to 79 and ...

.343
R:	Trabalhava, trabalhava cinco anos em Salvador ...	He worked [imperfect], worked five years in Salvador ...

On tape 1, R first produced the form *morava* [imperfect] and was corrected by S to the imperfect form *morei/morou*, in the first example above. R's reaction later when looking at the transcript of this conversation was that he had noticed the correction but had not understood it: since he had intended to convey the idea "used to live" ("used to" is a marker of nonpunctualness for English) and since he had been told to use the imperfect as an equivalent of "used to" (see journal entry, page 258, what was wrong with this utterance? A minute or so later, R again produced the form *morava*, again incorrectly (second example above), and then, with a little help from S, produced the correct form *morei*:

1.119–122

S: E me diz uma coisa R, você morou na França também?	Tell me something R, have you lived [perfect] in France too?
R: Não.	No.
S: Nunca?	Never?
R: Nunca, nunca, visitei França 3 vezes ou 4 vezes mas não morei, não morei lá.	Never, never, I visited [perfect] France 3 times or 4 times, but I didn't live [perfect], didn't live there.

Looking for a longer-range outcome of a possible shift in R's interlanguage in the use of MORAR, we find no occurrences of that verb on tape 2 in either R's or S's speech, and only one on tape 3, where R used the imperfect in an utterance in which the perfect would have been more acceptable though not obligatory. On the last tape, R used the verb three more times: first correctly in the perfect, then correctly in the imperfect (*ano passado morava comigo no Havái*, "last year he lived with me in Hawaii," an utterance in which native speakers also prefer the imperfect), and one final time, correctly in the perfect.

The verb TRABALHAR occurs less frequently in both R's and S's speech on the tapes and was not corrected by S when R first used it incorrectly in the imperfect on the first tape. On the second tape, S modeled the form *trabalhou* [perfect] for R in a question. A few minutes later, R once again incorrectly used the imperfect form of the verb. Several turns later in the conversation, R again used the imperfect but immediately self-corrected to the perfect:

2.99

R: Trabalhava, trabalhei lá, huh? e . . não, eles não pagaram . . .	I worked [imperfect], worked [perfect], huh? and . . . no, they didn't pay . . .

Something had clearly made R aware that the imperfect was not the form to use, but we don't know if the crucial factor was S's use of the form earlier in the conversation or perhaps the correction he had received for MORAR, since MORAR and TRABALHAR were the only two verbs for which he thought he was using the imperfect to mean "used to." TRABALHAR does not appear on the last two tapes.

Marida The final example we discuss illustrates both the easy confirmation/difficult disconfirmation principle and the principle that correction can work, if you keep at it.

In Portuguese, *marido* is "husband," but there is no corresponding word *marida* for "wife." R made up the form, overgeneralizing the principle that there are masculine/feminine pairs ending in *o/a*. We do not know when R first produced the form, but it appears on the first conversational tape. Although S was amused and was tempted to correct the error, she did not:

1.245–246

R: . . . e minha ex-marida também professora de inglês.	. . . and my ex-wife also English teacher.
S: Ah é?	Oh yeah?

A few turns later in the same conversation, S asked R a question about his ex-wife, using the normal form *mulher* (literally, "woman"), which R did not understand. In attempting to clarify the question S had asked him, R finally asked if she was talking about his *ex-marida*, and S replied "yes" (see page 264 for the entire exchange).

Two weeks later, when beginning to transcribe tape 1, S mentioned to R that she had immediately noticed some exciting things. Specifically, she mentioned that R was deleting many of his copulas, and that there was a classic overgeneralization in his creation of a word *marida* for "wife." R's reaction was the following:

Journal entry, Week 9
I saw S this afternoon. She has started to transcribe the tape and is excited about the project. She told me that I am omitting my copulas and I've created a word *marida* for wife, when it should be *esposa*. I responded as non-comittally as possible, but I was amazed. I had no idea that I have been leaving out my copulas. . . . The word I've apparently made up for "wife" astounds me even more. Now that the error is pointed out, I see that it is an overgeneralization . . . . I'm shocked because I did that tidy bit of analysis entirely without awareness. There are plenty of times when I don't know a word and consciously guess, but this is not one of them. I have the strongest feeling, in fact I'm ready to insist, that I have never heard the word *esposa*, but I have heard *marida* many times. I've been thinking about this all afternoon. S-san used to talk about his wife in class. Didn't he always refer to his wife as *minha marida*? I guess not, or L would have corrected him. I have a very weird feeling about all this.

Three weeks later on tape 2, R used the word to which he had been corrected, *esposa*:

2.265

R: E a esposa de meu amigo lá trabalhava turística . . .	And the wife of my friend there used to work in tourism . . .

This was not the end of the matter, however. While R did not use *marida* again on tape, he did so in conversation, frequently enough that friends not only corrected him frequently but also used the word to characterize his faulty interlanguage:

Journal entry, Week 19
Talking about X, I referred to Y as *a marida dele* ["his *marida*" Note: this refers to the same person R called *a esposa de meu amigo* on tape 2.] E gave me a big frown, and said that was at least the third

time I've said that to her. She's started to react as though I'm a real dummy. I can't blame her, but I also cannot shake the feeling that I didn't make it up, in spite of what everyone says. . . . Now I have a strong feeling that if it's not Portuguese it must be Arabic. But it isn't, I don't think. After suffering from such strong interference from Arabic in the beginning, now I find I've repressed that language so well that I can't think of Arabic words when I try.[28]

Journal entry, Week 20
M said I make lots of mistakes, and mentioned *marida* and *pais* [stress error].

Gradually, the balance seems to have shifted from *marida* to *esposa*:

Journal entry, Week 21
At the beach today I said *esposa*. I realized it after, not before I said it.

4.405–406 (Week 22)

R:	. . . eu vou lá, a Boston, e vou discutir com minha ex-esposa.	. . . I'm going there, to Boston, and I'll discuss it with my ex-wife.
S:	Tá acertando tudo hoje, hein?	You're getting everything right today, huh?
R:	Estava procurando oportunidade.	I was looking for a chance.

And then, three days before leaving Brazil, R finally noticed in input the word that Brazilians usually use for "wife":

Journal entry, Week 22
I'm watching TV and just saw a preview of a coming show entitled *Sozinho, marido e mulher,* which clearly means "alone, husband and wife." *Mulher!* No wonder it's been difficult to remember to say *esposa* instead of *marida*. People have not been saying *esposa* unless they were correcting me. But I can't remember having ever heard people say *mulher* before either, and I'm sure it's not the form people have said I should use. Five months to figure out such a simple thing!

But Brazilians had certainly been saying *mulher* to R. We have two occurrences in S's speech to R on tape. Although, as we have mentioned, R did not understand the word the first time S said it to him, the second time, on tape 3, R's response indicated that he did comprehend:

3.383–385

S;	Cê gosta da mulher dele? A mulher do Pepeu Gomes que também é cantora?	Do you like his wife? The wife of Pepeu Gomes who is also [a] singer?
R:	Mas . . . nunca junto.	But . . . never together.
S:	Não, cantam separados, é.	No, [they] sing separately, yes.

Note that R did not have to interpret the word *mulher* in order to understand who was the "X" of Pepeu Gomes, also a singer. He had already heard the story of the husband and wife who are both singers but never perform or record together. This looks like a good example of something just beyond R's current level of competence which was present in comprehensible input with the use of extralinguistic information but was not thereby learned. Instead, R continued to fluctuate between a self-created form and a form he was told to use.

CONCLUSIONS

Some of the findings that we have discussed in this report on the development of R's grammatical and conversational ability in Portuguese have been quite specific, in some cases possibly idiosyncratic to this single learner and in some cases probably generalizable only to other adult learners of Portuguese, with the distinction between the two categories to be settled by further research with other learners (Frota, in progress). In the realm of grammar, we have reported that some constructions were relatively easy for R to learn and others were relatively difficult. We found, for example, that gender is best viewed as a multifaceted phenomenon, with the phonological shape of nouns and article-agreement easier to master than agreement of determiners and adjectives. Between noun and adjective, we found number agreement easier than gender agreement. In the verb phrase, we found choice of the correct conjugation to be easier than number and person marking, which in turn were easier than tense/aspect choice. The most difficult dimension of verbs was mood (indicative vs. subjunctive), which R barely began to make progress on. We found that R had a very strong tendency to omit free (usually unstressed) grammatical morphemes, i.e., the articles, the copulas and prepositions, a tendency that did not diminish during the time of this study. We have not found a single grand explanatory principle for all these observations but have offered various explanations for various aspects of R's learning of Portuguese: markedness, morphological confusion, psycholinguistic and discourse-based processing difficulties, transfer from the L1 and in some cases from an L3 (Arabic), innate developmental patterns, and overgeneralizations of target language norms. In the realm of conversational abilities per se, we have observed what is likely to be a normal progression from an early stage in which native-nonnative conversation is characterized by native speaker topic control through the use of questions to a later stage in which the native and nonnative speakers carry on conversations through an exchange of statements, more nearly approximating native-native discourse. We have characterized R's personal conversational style in terms of a great deal of repetition, of himself and of what his interlocuters said, and we have traced R's incomplete learning of one specific speech act: answering questions affirmatively.

We have also examined the self-report and tape-recorded data in an effort to shed light on three questions of current interest and importance in SLA theory. In all three cases, the evidence was mixed. In asking whether and how instruction helped R's learning of Portuguese, we concluded that in many cases it was of great help, in providing comprehensible input that was not available in the wider environment, in providing resources and grammatical forms that could be immediately put to use in conversation outside the classroom, and in efficiently providing interpretations that could be derived only with difficulty through interaction alone. However, we have not argued that instruction played a necessary role in R's learning of Portuguese, and it clearly did not play a sufficient one. It was not true that whatever was taught was learned. It was also not true that whatever was taught was learned if it also appeared in input to the learner, though presence in input seems to have been a necessary condition (for all the cases we have examined here) for the ultimate learning of taught forms. In examining the question of whether and how interaction with native speakers fostered R's learning of Portuguese, we found that some forms that were not taught but that were used by native speakers in interaction with R were learned by him, but others were not. Some formulaic expressions led to the extraction of material for productive use; some did not. We also found that just as instruction does not guarantee grammaticality, so interaction does not guarantee idiomaticity. Our third question was whether correction helped R's learning of Portuguese. We found that he was indeed corrected by native speaking friends, and also corrected himself. Self-corrections were found to have no detectable effect. Corrections by native speakers fell into two categories: those that seemed to have worked and those that seemed not to have worked.

One of the questions that originally motivated this study was whether an approach that combined the perspectives of both the "insider" (the learner) and the outside observer would produce interesting results. We believe that it has done so. There have been many cases in which only the learner himself could have been in a position to say what he meant to convey on a particular occasion, what he heard others saying to him, and what he thought was going on in particular interactions. At the same time, there have been clear instances in which what R thought was true (about what people said, about how he spoke Portuguese, etc.) was not correct and does not correspond to the harder evidence from the tape-recorded conversations. We believe that the approach used here has justified itself and could fruitfully be used by other researchers.

We remain aware of the problems inherent in the self-report data that form the basis for some of the arguments that follow, as well as the general limitations of case studies for both proposing and evaluating general theories and models. Each learner's biography is not only unique but also complex, so that the relative importance of variables hypothesized to be important in language learning cannot be completely unraveled. Nevertheless, in this concluding section we would like to suggest some hypotheses about the processes and products of adult language learning in general that are consistent with both the subjective and objective data available to us. We deal with three aspects of the puzzle of language learning: the creative and noncreative aspects of language and learning, the process by which a learner progresses from one stage or form to another in the course of learning, and the role of production in the learning of second languages. In all three cases, we challenge some widely held assumptions and hypotheses.

Creativity and Routine

For more than 20 years, the most basic assumption in linguistics has been that language is creative, not a set of learned responses to environmental stimuli but a set of powerful, internalized rules that generate an infinite number of grammatical sentences of a language and that make it possible for speakers to regularly produce and understand sentences never heard before. In this sense, the ultimate state of the learner's linguistic knowledge exceeds the specific data (always finite) to which the learner has been exposed during the process of learning. Creativity in language learning also refers to learner independence from external factors such as the forms of utterances in input. Brown (1973) observed that the occurrence of systematic errors is "the best evidence we have that the child produces construction rules." The position is also almost universally accepted in SLA that learners' systematic use of novel construction rules is very strong evidence for the role of an internal cognitive organizer in learning (Dulay and Burt 1978:73).

We have provided abundant evidence, we think, of creativity, especially creative errors, in R's learning of Portuguese, but we do not intend to pursue the issue of creativity much further, for several reasons. First, one consequence of attributing a central or even all-subsuming role to the creative aspects of language learning is that the problem of language acquisition theory is often seen as the purely *logical* problem of how a child is able to internalize the complete system of productive rules, "from fairly restricted primary data, in a sufficiently quick time, with limited use of memory" (Wexler and Cullicover 1980:18). Much current work on "learnability" in linguistics is, in our opinion, less useful for language acquisition research than it might be, partly because of some obviously false assumptions that are adopted "so that serious inquiry may proceed" (Wexler and Cullicover 1980:11). The most serious of these, which may put the grammarian and the student of acquisition in separate fields (Matthews 1983), is the assumption that language learning is instantaneous (Chomsky 1965), that all the data are available to the language learner at one time and the learner selects a grammar at one fell swoop. This model, proposed with full knowledge that it contains false assumptions, may ultimately prove to have been useful, but at the present time the result has been to transform the problem of langauge learning into the question of what constitutes a possible language, and within linguistics has encouraged a continued preoccupation with extremely rare and complex sentences, not the kind of sentences that beginning second language learners (or children) are concerned with.[29]

Second, we will not focus further on creativity because we think it useful to look at the other side of the coin, which is that neither linguistic knowledge nor language use nor language learning is exclusively or even mostly creative. Creativity exists; we do not doubt it. But routine aspects of language also exist, and we think that considering the role of routine in language and learning may also lead to progress in explaining the puzzles we face in SLA theory.

The primary evidence for limitations on creativity in linguistic knowledge (competence) comes from recent work in linguistics on the degree to which grammatical constructions are lexically constrained. While it is common to view language as dichotomized between a dictionary (containing words and frozen expressions) and productive rules, many linguists have suggested that some aspects of the grammar are best accounted for not by transformations but by rules relating lexical entries. First suggested by Chomsky with regard to derivational processes in English, which are "typically sporadic and only quasi-productive" (Chomsky 1965:184), lexical approaches have been extended to such phenomena as passive and dative, and there are a number of linguistic models that reject the use of any transformations whatsoever (e.g., Brame 1978, Bresnan 1978, Starosta 1984). While many other linguists still prefer to look for categorical rather than lexical explanations to identify the heart or "core" of grammar, Lakoff has argued that a continued focus on core grammar, that portion of the grammar that happens to work by fully productive general principles of compositionality, is unfortunate, since by his estimate the continuum between fully productive constructions and completely frozen expressions includes 95 to 98 percent of the constructions in English (Lakoff 1982: 157).

A lexicalist approach has been fruitfully applied to the study of first language acquisition by Bloom and her colleagues, who have found that the acquisition of verbal inflections (Bloom, Lifter, and Hafitz 1980), Wh-questions (Bloom, Merkin, and Wooton 1982), and complement constructions (Bloom, Tackeff, and Lahey 1984) are all highly constrained by the particular lexical verbs that children know and use, indicating that the development of the verb lexicon and of grammar are mutually dependent. Lexical approaches have been advanced recently in the field of SLA to account for patterns of acquisition and use of the dative (Mazurkewich 1984, LeCompagnon 1984) and the third person singular-*s* (Abraham 1984). Abraham analyzed correctly and incorrectly formed third person singular verbs produced by ESL learners, and found that subjects tended to cluster the *s*'s on a few verbs rather than randomly distributing them over all verbs. Factors that Abraham suggests may have influenced which verbs were acquired with the morpheme include the frequency with which they were heard and used by the learners, the perceptual saliency of the morpheme when attached to particular verbs, and the difficulty of pronouncing specific verbs with the morpheme. In this study we have identified two points at which R's learning of Portuguese grammatical constructions showed a strong lexical influence: the acquisition of the definite article (for which the adult native speaker grammar must also contain lexical information) and the distribution of perfect and imperfect past tenses to different verbs (for which an adult native speaker grammar could be defined lexically but need not be as a result of the linguistic facts alone).

Studies of language use, including both sociolinguistic work dealing with conversational routines and stereotypical expressions (e.g., Coulmas 1981) and psycholinguistic research on the role of productive syntactic rules in comprehension and production (e.g., Foss and Hakes 1978), also indicate that we seldom as native speakers utilize the full creative power of the grammar. Most sentences that one produces and hears during the course of a day are really not creative or novel in any interesting sense. Moreover, there is very little evidence that when we utter familiar and ordinary sentences we are being creative "because the speaker generated such sentences from an internalized rule system" (Dulay and Burt 1978:67). Chomsky himself has repeatedly pointed out that his use of "generate" and "generative" in linguistics refers only to a formal algorithm for language, linguistic competence, and that "it would be tempting but quite absurd to regard it as a model of performance as well" (Chomsky 1967:435). When we actually produce language in ordinary conversation (and also in more "creative" activities such as scholarly writing), it seems much more reasonable to assume as the psychological basis of fluency that we alternate between two modes of production, one creative and hesitant, the other rehearsed, formulaic to varying degrees, and fluent (Goldman-Eisler 1968, Miller 1951, Pawley and Syder 1983).

For second language learning and production we propose the same alternation between creativity and consolidation.[30] We have found that R repeated himself almost constantly when beginning to learn Portuguese, not only within clauses and phrases but also by retelling stories in almost the same words and by relying repeatedly on the same constructions, some nativelike and some not. We suggest that only the first occurrence of each such construction represents the actual operation of the creative language faculty. When a language learner faces a novel communication problem, a creative solution is required. But the next time the learner faces essentially the "same" communication problem, we believe that in most cases the learner does not work through the problem again but simply remembers the solution. Especially when errors are idiosyncratic, it seems unlikely that the cognitive organizer has somehow repeatedly worked through a problem and repeatedly arrived at the same solution. When R said *antes de X anos* for the fifth time, we doubt that he had just created it for the fifth time. He simply remembered it.

Notice the Gap

Krashen has long argued that the only way in which a learner acquires a language is through understanding input (Krashen 1980, 1981, 1982, 1983). When a learner is at a particular stage of competence i with regard to a particular structure or set of structures, he or she will progress to the next stage $(i + 1)$ if and only if he or she is exposed to and understands (with the help of extralinguistic cues) language that contains structures $i + 1$. While Krashen's basic position has been extremely influential, it has not met with universal acceptance among scholars, and until recently one of the major criticisms directed against the input hypothesis has been that Krashen fails to provide any explanation of how the step from understanding to acquisition is made (Gregg 1984:89). However, in a recent paper, Krashen has provided at least a sketch of the internal processes involved in moving from one form to another (Krashen

1983:138–140 and Figure 1, the "Krashen-Andersen schema"). Briefly, Krashen proposes that (1) New forms may be presented to the language learner in two ways, via input that is understood or through the creative construction process. Either of these two processes can present the acquirer with an $i + 1$, a potential new rule. (2) For acquisition to occur, acquirers need to notice a difference between their current form or competence i and the new form or structure $i + 1$. (3) If the comparison of i and $i + 1$ shows a gap, the $i + 1$ form becomes a candidate for acquisition. If it turns up in input with some minimum frequency, it can be confirmed and acquired. If it does not turn up, it is a transitional form and will eventually be discarded.

Although Chaudron (1984) has pointed out that this model is rather simplistic and relies on the very difficult task of identifying what constitutes $i + 1$, it seems to us that the process of comparative operations and the principle that learners must "notice the gap" are extremely important and potentially useful additions to the theory of second language acquisition that Krashen has been developing for more than 10 years. However, we propose to make a significant modification of the principle, with which Krashen would surely not agree. While Krashen proposes that both the product and the process of acquisition are subconscious, and specifically that differences between competing forms i and $i + 1$ are noticed at a subconsious level (Krashen 1983:140), we propose instead that in the particular case of a nontargetlike form i and a targetlike form $i + 1$ a second language learner will begin to acquire the targetlike form if and only if it is present in comprehended input and "noticed" in the normal sense of the word, that is, consciously.

We should make it clear that we are not claiming at all that the products and processes of language learning are readily accessible to consciousness. Indeed, one of the major findings of this study has been that although R was sometimes able to recognize accurately what was difficult about Portuguese grammar (e.g., the verbs IR, VIR, and VER, which he confused and knew he confused; the subjunctive, which he did not learn) and the cognitive strategies that affected his learning (e.g., the influence of Arabic, which would have been difficult for anyone else to identify), in many cases his subjective beliefs concerning how and what he was learning about Portuguese were incorrect. R was totally unaware that he had devised a lexical strategy to distribute Portuguese verbs between the two past tenses. He did not know that he deleted copulas and articles until he was told. When told that he had made up a lexical item *marida*, he was completely surprised and amazed. These are specific examples of what appears to be a general phenomenon: the operations of the cognitive organizer, the language-creating faculty, are not accessible to conscious awareness except (sometimes) in retrospect.

What we are hypothesizing is that Krashen may have identified a crucial point, perhaps the crucial point, at which awareness may play an important role in language learning: the comparison of nontarget forms produced by the learner with target forms that appear in input. We are not suggesting that any particularly abstract generalization be made, only that the learner must notice the difference. Our hypothesis is similar to the position of Munsell and Carr, that:

acquisition takes place when the acquirer reaches a stage of *awareness* of a particular crucial feature of the tacit rule, but we agree that this most often does not require either explicit understanding of the whole rule, nor is it often the case that the acquirer can systematically state, after the fact, what had reached awareness, nor what its significance was. In other words, we hypothesize that if we looked at the right time and asked the right questions, we would get from the acquirer . . . responses that would in fact be quite specific and would in some general sense show a passing yet crucial "consciousness" of what was being acquired. (Munsell and Carr 1981:497–498)

The evidence we have presented in support of this hypothesis is the following:

1. Looking at 14 verbal constructions that R was taught in class, we found four (the compound present, the past perfect, the reflexive, and the inflected future) that were present in input at least occasionally but were never produced by R. What strikes us as being most significant about these cases is that, in contrast to 10 verbal construction types that he did use, R never noticed them in input. They were present, but R did not notice their presence.

2. Looking at additional aspects of the Portuguese verb phrase that R was not taught but that were present in the input to him from native speakers, we found only one clear example of something that was not taught but was learned. Existential sentences made with TER were not, however, an example of "acquisition" in the Krashen sense, i.e., subconscious learning, but were consciously noticed by R in the input.

3. Corrective feedback that was not noticed by R (embedded in ambiguous utterances such as confirmation checks) seems to have had no effect. In order for R to profit from correction by native speakers, it seems to have been a necessary (but not a sufficient) condition that he realize that he was being corrected.

One of the advantages of a conscious notice-the-gap principle is that it provides a way to include a role for correction, and instruction in general, in an integrated theory of second language learning.[31] We do not claim that correction is the only way in which learners come to notice the gap. Repeated exposure to input may also do the trick. While we have not found many examples of this in our data, we have one that seems clear:

Journal entry, Week 17
I often say *dois anos antes,* for "two years ago." I think it should be *anos atrás.* I have been hearing it that way in conversation, I *think* . . . [Later the same day] I asked M which is correct and he says both are OK, but I'm suspicious. Check with S tomorrow.[32]

However, there are some obvious difficulties with the ability of nonnative speakers to notice the gap between two forms or constructions simply by being exposed to more input. In many cases, the learner may not recognize that what he or she says and what is heard are both "the same thing" (represent the same semantic intention) and also "not the same thing" (different form). Thus, R was unable for many months to realize that a verb that he often heard and didn't understand, ACONTECER, was "the same" as a verb he wanted, "to happen." Corrective feedback provides a potential solution to this problem, since it juxtaposes the learner's form i with a target language form $i + 1$ and the learner is put in an ideal position to notice the gap.

We recognize that the data on which we have based our arguments for a conscious notice-the-gap principle, as well as the principle itself, are open to question from a number of points of view. We anticipate at least the following objections, with which we include our responses:

1. This study does not count, because R has been trained as a linguist, and linguists have an edge in language learning and approach language learning differently from ordinary people. This is the most common objection we have encountered when discussing the general outlines of this study with various people, but we think it has very little validity. Granted that linguists may have more metalinguistic awareness of a particular type than most people, but all adults have some degree of such awareness. We know of no evidence showing that linguists are superior language learners (which, were it true, would support rather than detract from a position that conscious awareness counts), and R does not appear to be an exceptional learner of Portuguese. In addition, the observations that we think counted are not of a type that linguists alone make. We do not think it important at all that R identified sentences with the verb TER as "existentials," only that he noticed that this was a way in which Portuguese speakers expressed the concept of "there is/are," the sort of observation that anyone might make. We do think, even so, that not all learners are alike. Some notice more facts about a new language than do others. Our hypothesis is that those who notice most, learn most.

2. Experimenter bias. This derives not only from the fact that R was both subject and experimenter, a dual role with both advantages and disadvantages (Linton 1975), but also the fact that R had posed questions relating to the role of conscious awareness and induction in language learning in relation to another study (Schmidt 1983, 1984), and began keeping a language learner's journal in Brazil partly in order to shed light on this particular issue. Having set out to find evidence bearing on the question, he trained himself to notice his noticings and write them down, which might in itself have had some effect on the outcome. Ultimately, these questions as well as those raised under objection 1 can only be resolved through further research, preferably with linguistically naive subjects.

3. For some of our examples, it might be the case that what R did not learn was not a candidate because it was not presented in comprehensible input. While we agree that language that is not comprehensible will not lead to any significant learning, it is not the case that the particular examples we have used in our argument fit this situation. Looking at the conversations in which verb constructions used by native speakers were taught but not learned by R

(compound present, present perfect, etc.), we find only one example for which the discourse indicates that R did not understand what was said. This was an occurrence of a reflexive, in a question that R failed to understand not because he did not recognize the reflexive nature of the verb but because he did not know the lexical verb itself. All other cases of the four verb structures that were taught, heard (but not noticed), and not learned were embedded in utterances that R's responses indicate were not only comprehensible but comprehended.

4. It could also be argued that R failed to learn certain features of Portuguese grammar not because he did not notice them but because he was not ready to notice them or learn them; they were not yet $i + 1$, candidates for learning. This argument is a rather circular one. Given our present state of ignorance regarding a natural order for all second language learners of Portuguese, what was $i + 1$ for R at a particular time can only be determined by what he did learn next; so the argument is impossible to prove or falsify. Nevertheless, this line of argument contains the seeds of one that could be much more serious. We readily grant that R was not free to notice whatever he wished in the input. Noticing was contingent on perceptibility, itself apparently due to several factors. In general, it seems that learners have no alternative to noticing the "big" things first, gradually progressing to details. The point is that we may someday know enough about the linguistic structures that enter into the processes of learning, the innate perceptual filters that constrain which parts of the input are available to the language learning faculty at particular points, and the types of hypotheses that are and are not possible to ultimately view language learning as a maze through which there is only one path (Helmut Zobl, personal communication). This would of course be a very strong nativist position, but one that shared a point of view with its archrival, radical behaviorism, that what the creature is thinking while learning its way through the maze is really irrelevant to the process. R's subjective feeling that his active noticing was important might in the end turn out to have been a language learner's delusion.

We do not ourselves believe that the course of language learning is so completely determined. Miller and Johnson-Laird (1976) have proposed an information-processing model of language and perception that is relevant to this problem. Miller and Johnson-Laird point out that in order to talk about any information-processing system, it is necessary to identify basic predicates that correspond to inputs, outputs, and memory. For language, the basic predicates identified by Miller and Johnson-Laird are PERCEIVE, INTEND, and REMEMBER. What is interesting about these is that they are not instructions that are under voluntary control. We cannot ask someone to PERCEIVE something, because he or she will perceive whatever he can. We cannot ask someone to REMEMBER a specific item (we remember what we can), though we can ask someone to *search* in memory for any relevant stored information. Similarly, we can ask someone to try to *achieve* a goal, and a cooperative person may try, but we cannot instruct someone to INTEND to achieve that goal. In addition to the basic predicates of the system, Miller and Johnson-Laird also identify a set of "control instructions" (e.g., *find, test, store, generate, achieve, infer, utter*) as another category, which the conceptual system uses to call on the perceptual system for information. With regard to instructions such as *notice* and *attend* (both special cases of the general instruction *find*), Miller and Johnson-Laird argue that there is a basic human ability to pay attention to different aspects of perceptual experiences. A person's ability to attend to some properties and ignore others is not unlimited, but we do have some control over the features we attend to, and can control to some extent which features are most salient.

In light of the above objections (and possibly others we have not anticipated), we do not claim to have produced conclusive evidence in support of a conscious notice-the-gap principle, but we believe that the principle is a viable hypothesis, at least as viable as the hypothesis that the process of language learning is in all respects subconscious. In particular, we know of no evidence supporting the opposing claim that language learning (or "acquisition") is almost exclusively incidental learning, best accomplished when we think we are doing something else, with our focus consistently on the message rather than on the form (Krashen 1983:136). Such a paradoxical claim, that we learn what we systematically ignore, requires evidence and explanation more than assertion, and in light of the tremendous consequences for language teaching methodology we urge that the supremacy of incidental learning not be taken as an established finding of research to date and that applications to language pedagogy be made with caution.

A final advantage of a conscious and voluntary notice-the-gap principle is that it permits a more common sense and intuitively satisfying conception of the "affective filter," which Krashen has proposed (following Dulay and Burt 1978) to incorporate motivational and affective variables into an overall theory of second language acquisition. The affective filter is hypothesized to be a device that prevents input from reaching "that part of the brain responsible for language acquisition, or the language acquisition device" (Krashen 1982:31). Various criticisms have been leveled against the affective filter hypothesis, including the observation that the function and operation of such a filter is not explained (Gregg 1984:95), that the filter is a purely metaphorical image (Schmidt 1984), and that it is strange to posit conscious factors such as desire to learn a language or affect toward native speakers as having an effect on unconscious processes (Michael Long, personal communication). However, if the notice-the-gap principle is taken to pertain (either exclusively or partly) to conscious and voluntary noticings, then affective factors may reasonably be assumed to play a role through the general mechanism of selective attention.

Autoinput in SLA

The principle of notice-the-gap provides a partial answer to the question of fossilization, one of the most significant characteristics of adult second language learning, which any SLA theory must attempt to explain. We have proposed that the process of noticing the gap may be the crucial point at which affective variables, individual differences, conscious awareness, and "paying attention" enter into the language learning process.[33] We have proposed that negative input, in the form of overt correction by native speakers in conversation, also exists and can potentially have salutory effects on the learner's ability to notice the gap.

A major problem remains to be addressed. One reason why many learnability theorists have rejected a role for negative information in language learning is that while negative information is powerful and would (if it existed) greatly reduce the problem of learnability and require a much less powerful innate component, the evidence from child L1 research is that negative information is not systematically provided, and when it is provided it does not seem to have much effect (Wexler and Cullicover 1980). With the principles we have been proposing here, the major question is: why, if individual learners arrive at a point (either by themselves or with the assistance of native speakers) at which they notice a gap between their own and native speaker language, do they often continue to make the same errors and not profit from the comparisons made through the notice-the-gap process? Two easy answers are readily available. One could claim that while the learner has consciously adopted a new hypothesis, he or she has not done so subconsciously (this is not a possible resolution of the problem if one assumes that all hypotheses and all operations of the notice-the-gap principle are subconscious), or one could claim that old forms, structures, and rules do not disappear because they are habits, and habits take time to be extinguished. While both of these formulations have what we believe to be a grain of truth in them, we prefer a third formulation, the autoinput hypothesis. The autoinput hypothesis is a hypothesis that the learner's own input is a very significant part of his or her input, which affects the course of language learning.

The autoinput hypothesis is not original with us. Something like it has been proposed for second language learning by Sharwood-Smith (1981) and Gregg (1984). We have been most influenced, however, by the autoinstruction hypothesis as proposed for child L1 acquisition by Platt and MacWhinney (1983). Platt and MacWhinney have argued, as we have, that language learner errors are not *just* examples of creativity in language learning. While childlike forms like *foots* cannot have been produced initially by rote memorization (because such forms do not appear in the input to the child from adults), one possibility not usually considered is that having produced *foots* once by combination (i.e., creatively), the child may then have listened to his or her own error and then learned it as a whole by rote. Children may learn their own solutions to language structure problems, to such an extent that these errors dominate for a while over the correct forms to which the child is more frequently exposed via reception.

Platt and MacWhinney tested some predictions from this hypothesis, including the claim that the primary source of incorrect forms were the children who produced them rather than other children, by eliciting grammaticality judgments from 4-year-old children to four types of sentences: sentences containing subject-generated errors; sentences with similar errors, exactly parallel syntactic structures with different lexical items; "baby errors," typical of much younger children; and correct sentences. They found significant differences in responses to the four sentence types, including a significant difference in the percentage corrected between the self-generated errors and the similar errors.

Applied to adult second language learning, the autoinput hypothesis can help explain why it is difficult to notice the gap and why errors persist even once the gap has been noticed. Specifically applied to this study, autoinput can explain the following about R's learning of Portuguese:

1. The lexical distribution of perfect and imperfect past tenses. According to the autoinput hypothesis, each time a new verb was used in a past tense, a creative decision had to be made. Every successive time that R wanted to use the same verb in a past tense, he simply retrieved the solution from memory.

2. The fact that structures containing errors as well as more nativelike structures attained the psycholinguistic status of formulaic speech, things often said, with varying degrees of lexicalization and openness in those structures.

3. The persistence of errors in the face of abundant evidence in input that what R said was not what native speakers said, even when errors were corrected by native speakers and R recognized and understood the corrections.

4. The fact that when R had to supply definite articles between contracting prepositions and place names, he did so invariably when he had produced an article with that noun from the beginning (as with o Rio, o Brasil, etc., except in cases when a "new" solution was required for the preposition prá/pró), but in those cases where he began producing the noun without an article (e.g., Hawaii) he improved but always performed variably.

5. R's subjective reaction when faced with his own errors, especially in the case of marida, that these could not be errors because he had certainly heard them before.

The subjective feeling of a learner that errors are not errors but correct productions (as opposed to simply a feeling of uncertainty about one's own speech) is also reflected in Schlue's finding that 65 percent of the errors committed by her subjects went unrecognized, with subjects putting utterances containing these errors into a category labeled "There is no error here; all parts of this sentence are easy for me now." In general, however, there is not a great deal of research reported in the literature that bears directly on the hypothesis. While there are quite a number of studies in the general area of error detection (see Chaudron 1983 for a review), most do not deal with errors that were produced by the same subjects who were later asked to judge them. For example, Schachter, Tyson, and Diffley (1976) presented ESL students with transfer errors identified as characteristic of particular groups, but not necessarily produced by the students in the study, while a study by Ioup and Kruse (1977) looked at transfer errors that might be predicted on the basis of contrastive analysis, not errors that the subjects actually made. One study that did elicit students' reactions to their own errors was that by Gass (1983), which used errors gathered from individual students' own written compositions as well as from other students. The results were much less clear-cut than in the Platt and MacWhinney study of 4-year-olds. Gass's intermediate subjects had a better idea of when they were right than of when they were wrong, while the advanced subjects had about equal abilities in determining their own correctness and incorrectness; both groups were less willing to accept others' grammatical sentences than their own grammatical sentences; the intermediate group was more willing to accept others' ungrammatical sentences than their own, while the opposite was the case for the advanced group.

More research needs to be done in this area, but we would not in any case predict that learners would be unable to recognize their own errors when these are selected randomly from either speech or writing. Since the feeling of correctness probably derives from the strength of a particular form or structure in memory, and since all memories represent earlier processes (Neisser 1967), both those of comprehension and those of production, we would need in addition some information concerning both input and output frequencies before any predictions could be made. We also expect changes with time: at one point R had no idea at all that *marida* was an incorrect form; at a later time he realized fully that it was an error, although he continued to produce it.

In our discussion of the evidence for the autoinput hypothesis and its implications so far, we have dwelt primarily on the negative aspects, especially the persistence of errors and the constraints that the autoinput hypothesis puts on the principle of noticing the gap. We would like to conclude by considering some possible positive aspects of the autoinput hypothesis, and a positive role for production in language learning.

Sharwood Smith (1981) and Gregg (1984) have both suggested the same potentially positive role of output in language acquisition. Assuming that monitoring (in some sense, not necessarily that of applying learned, fully explicit rules to conversation) can increase the incidence of correct utterances of a given structure, then the results would presumably be available to the speaker as feedback (autoinput) into acquired knowledge. Krashen has considered this idea also (Krashen 1981:118) but rejected productions under the conscious control of the monitor as only a trivial source of help. Krashen argues that if a language learner consistently applied a learned rule to his own output, when the day came that such a learner was "ready" to acquire the already learned rule, his or her own performance of it would qualify as comprehensible input at $i + 1$ and he would acquire it. However, this is a trivial sense of a conscious rule helping acquisition, because such a learner would have acquired the rule at that time without it, on the basis of input from native speakers. We tend to agree with Krashen, but for different reasons. Under the principles we have proposed here, speaker productions, including, for example, self-corrections (whatever the knowledge source underlying such productions), will count not only as input but as very significant input. Theoretically then, self-correction should lead to improved performance. However, we found no effect for self-correction in R's learning of Portuguese, and we think in general that the role of self-correction is limited, because it is simply too difficult to self-correct in any systematic fashion when engaged in real and meaningful conversation. Even in the case of definite articles between prepositions and place names, the focus of many of R's self-corrections, he never managed to self-correct more than 10 percent of his errors. And if one were able to self-correct a higher percentage of one's errors, say 50 percent, the frequency of correct forms in output (and subsequently in input) would be only 25 percent higher than if one had not produced the utterance at all. Considering in addition the fact that overmonitoring and excessive self-correction greatly interfere with meaningful communication, we believe that the primary source of correct forms must be input from native speaker models.

Yet we do see many positive aspects of the autoinput hypothesis and for the role of production in language learning. One obvious benefit of production is that it is through production, i.e., practice, that second language structures become more automatic and easily produced (McLaughlin, Rossman, and McLeod 1983). As second language learners produce (speak) more, we expect to find and do find a general increase in conversational fluency: faster speech, fewer pauses and hesitations, etc. On the level of conversational content, it is through rehearsal and production that we hone our ideas and our ways of expressing them in order to hold the attention and appeal to the sympathies of our conversational partners. Consider, for example, the ways in which we all tell and retell significant stories about our lives, adding, deleting, and modifying details until we have a formulation that will work with most audiences. On the level of grammatical expression, it is not only our errors and incorrect productions that we learn, but also our correct productions, which must (except for those cases in which we are being truly creative) be learned holistically if we are to speak natively and fluently. Errors themselves may not be all bad (it is possible that you cannot learn without making mistakes), especially in the case of transitional forms that may be necessary steppingstones to a more targetlike level of competence. Platt and MacWhinney point out for L1 acquisition that their findings suggest that children do receive and use negative data, by generating and learning their own negative instances, which they eventually come to know as incorrect.[34] Finally, from the point of view of SLA theory, there are two notable virtues to the autoinput hypothesis: (a) it is parsimonious, since something like it needs to be posited not only for second language learning but also for native language performance; and (2) it preserves the integrity of a view that holds (correctly, we think) that there is only one basic cause of language acquisition, understanding what is presented through input. The only difference here is that what is presented through input and learned is not produced by native speaker models but by the language learners themselves.

NOTES

1. We have benefited greatly from comments on an earlier draft of this paper by Armando Baltra, Mary Brown, Richard Day, Fred Genesee, Michael Long, Raymond Moody, Ann Peters, Charlene Sato, and Helmut Zobl, none of whom are responsible for flaws that may remain.

2. We use the terms *learning* and *acquisition* roughly synonymously throughout, using *acquisition* when we mean specifically unconscious or subconscious acquisition.

3. FSL S-2 means: "Can handle with confidence, but not with facility, most situations, including introductions and casual conversations about current events, as well as work, family, and autobiographical information. Can handle limited work requirements, needs help in handling any complications or difficulties; can get the gist of most conversations on non-technical subjects (for example, topics which require no specialized knowledge) and has a speaking vocabulary sufficient to be understood simply with some circumlocutions; accent, though often quite faulty, is intelligible; can usually handle elementary constructions quite accurately but does not have thorough or confident control of the grammar." Memo, Post Language Officer, American Consulate General, Rio de Janeiro.

4. R rewrote his journal entries shortly after his departure from Brazil, eliminating highly personal material, revising the orthography (e.g., putting all citation forms of verbs in uppercase), and in some cases expanding elliptical or cryptic entries. Material added later to journal entries cited is enclosed in square brackets ([ ]). Names have been replaced by initials, which in most cases do not correspond to the real initials of the persons referred to. R and S do consistently refer to the coauthors of this paper. X and Y are variables, used to refer to a number of people, each of whom is mentioned only once in the journal materials included here.

5. In Table 1, the numbers for adjectives scored for word order, number agreement, and gender agreement are not equal because noun-adjective order is not relevant for predicative adjectives, and because more adjectives inflect for number than for gender. The figures for definite and indefinite articles supplied in obligatory contexts do not equal the figures for articles with correct gender agreement because both incorrectly selected and extra articles may be correctly inflected for gender (and were in most cases).

6. Not all adjectives follow the noun in Portuguese, and there are some semantic contrasts between N + Adj. and Adj. + N constructions, e.g., *boa mulher*, a (morally) good woman vs. *mulher boa*, a woman with an excellent figure. There is no evidence that R was aware of such contrasts.

7. Errors of gender, already discussed, were not counted when scoring the categories of definite and indefinite articles.

8. R did use some articles that are not allowed in Portuguese. All of these were definite articles, and none are explained by contrastive analysis. On tape 4, all his extra articles were either before place names or after prepositions (in most cases, both), an apparent case of hypercorrection.

9. Indefinite articles, like definite articles, seem especially difficult when they follow contracting prepositions, but we have too few obligatory cases to make a strong argument.

10. R's feeling that he had pronounced the Portuguese word for "seventy" under the influence of the Arabic stem for "six" is supported by the fact that on tape 1 he told S in Portuguese that he had lived in Beirut from 1975 to 1979. In fact, he lived there from 1965 to 1969.

11. In an earlier stage of the language, still preserved in formal usage and in some dialects in the north and south of Brazil, the second singular pronoun *tu* had its own distinctive set of verb inflections. In the dialect of Rio de Janeiro (and many other areas), *tu* was replaced by *você* (derived from the historical polite form *Vossa Mercê*), which takes a third singular verb. When *tu* is heard in Rio, it is also now used with third singular verb forms.

12. By the time of tape 4, there was no longer any difference between R's performance on verbal inflections for number and person, but it seems to us that person is still the problematic category. Seven of his ten errors of number agreement on the last tape involved the single lexical item *gente*, while person errors remained more general. Errors of person are also more likely to cause misunderstandings than are errors of number.

13. R's lexical approach to solving the problem of perfect vs. imperfect is similar to the strategies identified for children learning verbal inflections in various languages. Simões and Stoel-Gammon (1979) have reported that in Portuguese L1 acquisition perfect inflections occurred early, but only on some verbs, those expressing a completed action in the immediate past. Antinucci and Miller (1976) observed that past tense inflections appeared only with certain lexical verbs in the acquisition of Italian and English. Bloom, Lifter, and Hafitz (1980) report that in English the occurrence of different verbal inflections coincides with other differences in children's verbs that are lexical, and that the selective use of different morphemes is largely determined by the inherent aspectual meanings of the individual verbs, with the stative/nonstative opposition as the superordinate prime. Bickerton (1981) has argued that both the state-process distinction and the punctual-nonpunctual distinction are part of the innate bioprogram for language.

14. The anecdote reported by R is well known and much admired in Brazil. R's version of the story was incorrect on several points (e.g., the minister in question had been in office for 2 years, not a few days), but R's understanding of the point was essentially correct. The remark was intended both as a threat to resign and as a criticism of those who think power is forever.

15. These two examples are compared because in both cases these were concepts that R had expressed before in English (the content was rehearsed) but had never attempted to say in Portuguese before the conversational tapes in which they appear.

16. The analysis of statements into t-units or communication units also follows Beebe (1983) in allowing various kinds of ellipsis. While Loban (1976) counts as statements only those answers to questions that lack only the repetition of question elements to satisfy the criterion of independent predication, Beebe points out that nonnative speakers often omit much more than just the question elements, but such answers may still be usefully considered as communication units.

17. We did not attempt to measure the rate of speech of R and S separately, in order to avoid the problem of assigning time between turns to last or next speaker, but simply timed the tapes through the 400th turn, and divided by the total number of words.

18. Although we are aware of studies showing cultural differences in baby talk (e.g. Heath 1982), comparative studies of speech addressed to foreigners are rare. With respect to the specific issue examined here, the distribution of questions and statements, Long, Gambhiar, Gambhiar, and Nishimura (1983) have reported that Hindi-Urdu and Japanese, like English, exhibit a preponderance of questions over statements in foreigner talk, while Chan and Choy (1980) report the same for Mandarin. There is no discussion of the phenomenon in Portuguese that we know of, and no studies at all of foreigner talk in Brazilian Portuguese. In addition, we lack baseline data on the distribution of questions and statements in Portuguese native-native conversations.

19. There are a few studies that report that in some ways native speaker speech is sensitive to the general proficiency level of nonnative interlocuters (Henzl 1975, Henzl 1979, Gaies 1979). Ellis (1983), in the only longitudinal study we are aware of, reports that several (but not all) interactional features in teacher speech were sensitive to the developing competence of two Punjabi-speaking boys learning English. None of these studies deal with the distribution of questions and statements.

20. We suspect that tag questions may be more frequent in native-native speech in Portuguese than in English.

21. The irony here is that while not the most typical Brazilian response form, "uh-huh" really was not inappropriate, since the form has been borrowed from English and is used frequently by many Brazilians.

22. It is clear that R often failed to use the progessive when he should, but this was not included in our tallies of forms correctly supplied in obligatory contexts because of the high percentage of cases in which the present or progessive would have been more natural though not obligatory.

23. R's memory concerning *como se chama, llama* is incorrect. CHAMAR is only Portuguese, not Spanish; so what he heard must have been *como se llama, llama?*

24. R attributes his use of *será*, the future of SER, to the song *"Que será, será."*

25. The participles of IR, VER, and VIR are *ido, visto,* and *vindo,* respectively. *Vido was R's invention. The native speaker's response was not foreigner talk at all, but a correction. R

attempted a past perfect, apparently thinking it was a compound present, in an environment in which the present perfect is required in English but its closest equivalent is prohibited in Portuguese.

26. Literary Portuguese uses HAVER, not TER, SER, or ESTAR, for existential sentences. R's attempts at using SER and ESTAR may have been prompted by a story he was told in class which begain *era uma vez um casal idoso sem filhos* . . . [remainder of line not recorded in class notes], which means "once upon a time an elderly couple without children . . . ," but which R interpreted as "once upon a time there was an elderly couple without children." *Era uma vez*, "once upon a time," is a frozen form.

27. As indicated by Table 8, PENSAR did not occur in the input on tape in the imperfect. However, we know that the form PENSAR + imperfect was confirmed for R because in class he produced an incorrectly derived imperfect form *pensia* and was corrected to the imperfect *pensava* (see page 256, Journal entry, Week 6).

28. There is an Arabic word [mariDa], with an emphatic (pharyngealized) voiced stop, which is the feminine singular adjective "sick." To what extent this may have contributed to R's feeling that he had heard *marida* before is unclear.

29. The collection of papers edited by Hornstein and Lightfoot (1981) illustrates this aspect of current learnability theory. It is difficult to find there specific examples of what it is that children acquire from limited primary data, but when examples are found they turn out to be things such as the manifestations of the parameters of subjacency in various languages. Most of the sentences used for illustration are not sentences that any child could make sense of. As Matthews (1983) has pointed out, one of the most interesting papers in the collection is that by White on the responsibility of grammatical theory to acquisition data, which concludes in essence that there is no responsibility at all.

30. One difference between the newly created/rehearsed status of utterances in beginning second language learning as opposed to adult native speaker speech may be that for the beginning second language learner rate of speech may be a reflection of this, while experiments with native speakers show that speakers do not talk any faster after practice in particular description tasks but that the length of fluent, pause-free units increases significantly (Pawley and Syder 1983:222).

31. In Krashen's model, there is no advantage to being able to incorporate a role for correction in the language acquisition process, since correction is hypothesized to play a role in "learning," not "acquisition."

32. The form that appears on the conversational tapes is *antes de X anos*. We do not know if R's observation that he often said *X anos antes* is correct or, if so, at what point he may have made a transition between those two forms on the way to eventual recognition that *X anos atrás* was the form he wanted. Both *X anos atrás* ("X years ago") and *X anos antes* ("X years before") are correct, though they do not mean the same thing.

33. Peters (1984) argues, similarly, that children learning their first language are able to make selective use of the processes of discrimination and classification and that our observations of such selectivity allow us to account for individual differences in L1 acquisition. Wong-Fillmore (1976) reports that one of her 5-year-old learners, Nora, was not only especially adept at the social skills that encourage exposure and interaction but also attentive to the structural possibilities of language.

34. The psychological status of incorrect forms once they have been recognized as such is unclear to us, but it is clear that abandonment of a hypothesis does not mean that the relevant forms are purged from memory. For example, native speakers of English whose dialects do not contain such structures as "me and my boss are having an argument" can easily and fluently produce such structures (L1 transitional forms) if they want. In this sense, transitional forms that are not a part of current competence may be similar to dialectal variants.

REFERENCES

Abraham, R. 1984. Patterns in the use of the present tense third person singular -s by university-level ESL speakers. *TESOL Quarterly,* 18 (1): 55–69.

Abreu, M. I., and C. Rameh. 1972. *Português contemporâneo* 1. Washington, D.C.: Georgetown Univesity Press.

Abreu, M. I., and C. Rameh. 1973. *Português contemporâneo* 2. Washington, D.C.: Georgetown University Press.

Antinucci, F., and R. Miller. 1976. How children talk about what happened. *Journal of Child Language,* 3: 169–189.

Bailey, K. M., and R. Ochsner. 1983. A methodological review of the diary studies: windmill tilting or social science? In K. M. Bailey, M. H. Long, and S. Peck (eds.). *Second Language Acquisition Studies.* Rowley, Mass.: Newbury House.

Baltra, A. 1981. My acquisition of Portuguese. *Cadernos PUC: Lingüística* No. 9, 109–120. São Paulo: PUC/SP.

Beebe, L. M. 1983. Risk-taking and the language learner. In H. W. Seliger and M. H. Long (ed.). *Classroom-Oriented Research in Second Language Acquisition.* Rowley, Mass.: Newbury House.

Berlitz. 1982. *Portuguese-English English-Portuguese Dictionary.* Lausanne: Editions Berlitz.

Bickerton, D. 1981. *Roots of Language.* Ann Arbor, Mich.: Karoma.

Bloom, L., L. Hood, and P. Lightbown. 1974. Imitation in language development: if, when and why. *Cognitive Psychology,* 6: 380–420.

Bloom, L, K. Lifter, and J. Hafitz. 1980. Semantics of verbs and the development of verb inflections in child language. *Language,* 56 (2): 386–412.

Bloom, L., W. Merkin, and J. Wootten. 1982. WH-questions: linguistic factors that contribute to the sequence of acquisition. *Child Development,* 53: 1084–1092.

Bloom, L., J. Tackeff, and M. Lahey. 1984. Learning "to" in complement constructions. *Journal of Child Language,* 11: 391–406.

Brame, M. 1978. *Base Generated Syntax.* Seattle: Noit Amrofer.

Bresnan, J. 1978. A realistic transformational grammar. In M. Halle, J. Bresnan, and G. A. Miller (eds.). *Linguistic Theory and Psychological Reality.* Cambridge, Mass.: MIT Press.

Britto, P. H. 1984. Unpublished lecture notes for contrastive analysis of English and Portuguese. Rio de Janeiro: Pontifícia Universidade Católica do Rio de Janeiro.

Brown, R. 1973. *A First Language: The Early Stages.* Cambridge, Mass.: Harvard University Press.

Chan, B. L., and C. Choy. 1980. Foreigner talk in Chinese. Term paper, Department of English as a Second Language, the University of Hawaii at Manoa.

Chaudron, C. 1983. Research on metalinguistic judgments: a review of theory, methods and results. *Language Learning,* 33 (3): 343–377.

Chaudron, C. 1984. Intake: on models and methods for discovering learners' processing of input. Paper presented at the 18th Annual TESOL Convention, Houston.

Chomsky, N. 1965. *Aspects of the Theory of Syntax.* Cambridge, Mass.: MIT Press.

Chomsky, N. 1967. The formal nature of language. In E. Lenneberg, *Biological Foundations of Language.* New York: Wiley.

Chun, A. E., R. R. Day, N. A. Chenoweth, and S. Luppescu. 1982. Errors, interaction, and correction: a study of native-nonnative conversations. *TESOL Quarterly,* 16 (4): 537–547.

Clark, R. 1977. What's the use of imitation? *Journal of Child Language,* 4: 354–358.

Cohen, A. 1984. Studying second language learning strategies: how do we get the information? *Applied Linguistics,* 5 (2): 101–112.

Coulmas, F. (ed.). 1981. *Conversational Routine.* The Hague: Mouton.

Coulthard, M. 1977. *An Introduction to Discourse Analysis.* London: Longman.

Day, R. R., N. A. Chenoweth, A. E. Chum, and S. Luppescu. 1984. Corrective feedback in native-nonnative discourse. *Language Learning,* 34 (2): 19–45.

Dulay, H., and M. Burt. 1978. Some remarks on creativity in language acquisition. In W. C. Ritchie (ed.). *Second Language Acquisition Research.* New York: Academic Press.

Ellis, R. 1983. Teacher-pupil interaction in second language development. Paper read at the Input in Second Language Acquisition Conference, University of Michigan.

Ferguson, C. A. 1971. Absence of copula and the notion of simplicity: a study of normal speech, baby talk, foreigner talk and pidgins. In D. H. Hymes (ed.). *Pidginization and creolization of languages.* Cambridge: Cambridge University Press.

Figueiredo, A., and J. Norman. 1979. *Portuguese Phrase Book.* 2d ed. Harmondsworth: Penguin Books.

Foss, D. J., and D. T. Hakes. 1978. *Psycholinguistics: An Introduction to the Psychology of Language.* Englewood Cliffs, N.J.: Prentice-Hall.

Frota, S. N. In progress. Learning Portuguese as a second/foreign language under different conditions of exposure. Ph.D. dissertation, Pontificia Universidade Católica do Rio de Janeiro.

Gaies, S. 1979. Linguistic input in first and second language learning. In F. Eckman and A. Hastings (ed.). *Studies in First and Second Language Acquisition.* Rowley, Mass.: Newbury House.

Gass, S. 1983. The development of L2 intuitions. *TESOL Quarterly,* 17 (2): 273–291.

Gleitman, H., and L. Gleitman. 1979. Language use and language judgement. In C. J. Fillmore, D. Kempler, and W. S-Y. Wang (eds.). *Individual Differences in Language Ability and Language Behavior.* New York: Academic Press.

Goldman-Eisler, F. 1968. *Psycholinguistics: Experiments in Spontaneous Speech.* New York: Academic Press.

Greenberg, J. H. (ed.). 1963. *Universals of Language.* 2d ed. Cambridge, Mass.: MIT Press.

Gregg, K. R. 1984. Krashen's monitor and Occam's razor. *Applied Linguistics,* 5 (2): 79–100.

Hammerly, H. 1982. *Synthesis in Second Language Teaching.* Blaine, Wash.: Second Language Publications.

Harris, Z. S. 1952. Discourse analysis. *Language,* 28 (1): 8–23.

Harris, Z. S. 1957. Co-occurrence and transformation in linguistic structure. *Language,* 33 (3): 283–340.

Hatch, E. M. (ed.), 1978a. *Second Language Acquisition: A Book of Readings.* Rowley, Mass.: Newbury House.

Hatch E. M. 1978b. Discourse analysis and second language acquisition. In E. M. Hatch (ed.). *Second Language Acquisition: A Book of Readings.* Rowley, Mass.: Newbury House.

Hatch, E. M. 1983. *Psycholinguistics: A Second Language Perspective.* Rowley, Mass.: Newbury House.

Heath, S. B. 1982. Questioning at home and at school: a comparative study. In G. Spindler (ed.). *Doing the Ethnography of Schooling: Educational Anthropology in Action.* New York: Holt, Rinehart and Winston.

Henzl, V. 1975. Speech of foreign language teachers: a sociolinguistic register study. Paper read at AILA, Stuttgart, Germany.

Henzl, V. 1979. Foreigner talk in the classroom. *IRAL,* 17 (2): 159–165.

Hornstein, N., and D. Lightfoot (eds.). 1981. *Explanation in Linguistics: The Logical Problem of Language Acquisition.* London: Longman Linguistic Library. 25.

Hunt, K. W. 1970. Syntactic maturity in school children and adults. *Monographs of the Society for Research in Child Development,* 53:1.

Ioup, G., and A. Kruse. 1977. Interference versus structural complexity in second language acquisition: language universals as a basis for natural sequencing. In H. D. Brown, C. A. Yorio, and R. H. Crymes (eds.). *On TESOL '77, Teaching and Learning English as a Second Language: Trends in Research and Practice.* Washington, D.C.: TESOL.

Itoh, H., and E. M. Hatch. 1978. Second language acquisition: a case study. In E. M. Hatch (eds.). *Second Language Acquisition: A Book of Readings.* Rowley, Mass.: Newbury House.

Keenan, Elinor Ochs. 1977. Making it last: repetition in children's discourse. In S. Ervin-Tripp and C. Mitchell-Kernan (eds.). *Child Discourse.* New York: Academic Press.

Kellerman, E. 1978. Giving learners a break: native language intuitions as a source of predictions about transferability. *Working Papers on Bilingualism,* 15: 59–92.

Krashen, S. D. 1980. The input hypothesis. In J. Alatis (ed.). *Current Issues in Bilingual Education. Georgetown University Roundtable on Languages and Linguistics.* Washington, D.C.: Georgetown University Press.

Krashen, S.D. 1981. *Second Language Acquisition and Second Language Learning.* Oxford: Pergamon Press.

Krashen, S. D. 1982. *Principles and Practice in Second Language Acquisition.* Oxford and New York: Pergamon Institute of English.

Krashen, S. D. 1983. Newmark's "ignorance hypothesis" and current second language acquisition theory. In S. Gass and L. Selinker (eds.). *Language Transfer in Language Learning.* Rowley, Mass.: Newbury House.

Lakoff, G. 1982. Categories: an essay in cognitive linguistics. In The Linguistic Society of Korea, *Linguistics in the Morning Calm: Selected Papers from SICOL-1981.* Seoul: Hanshin Publishing Company.

LeCompagnon, B. 1984. Interference and overgeneralization in second language learning: the acquisition of English dative verbs by native speakers of French. *Language Learning,* 34 (3): 39–67.

Lehmann, W. P. (ed.). 1978. *Syntactic Typology: Studies in the Phenomenology of Language.* Austin, Tex.: University of Texas Press.

Linton, M. 1975. Memory for real-word events. In D. A. Norman and D. E. Rumelhart (eds.). *Explorations in Cognition.* San Francisco: W. H. Freeman and Company.

Loban, W. 1976. *Language Development: Kindergarten through Grade Twelve.* NCTE Research Report 18. Urbana, Ill.: National Council of Teachers of English.

Long, M. H. 1981. Questions in foreigner talk discourse. *Language Learning,* 31 (1): 135–157.

Long, M. H., and S. K. Gambhiar, V. Gambhiar, and M. Nishimura. 1983. Regularization in foreigner talk and interlanguage. Paper delivered at the 17th Annual TESOL Convention, Toronto.

McLaughlin, B., T. Rossman, and B. McLeod. 1983. Second language learning: an information-processing perspective. *Language Learning,* 33(2): 135–158.

Matthews, P. H. 1983. Review of N. Hornstein and D. Lightfoot (eds.): Explanation in linguistics. *Journal of Child Language,* 10 (2): 491–493.

Mazurkewich, I. 1984. The acquisition of the dative alternation by second language learners and linguistic theory. *Language Learning,* 34 (1): 91–109.

Miller, G. A. 1951. *Language and Communication.* New York: McGraw-Hill.

Miller, G. A., and P. N. Johnson-Laird. 1976. *Language and Perception.* Cambridge, Mass.: The Belknap Press of Harvard University Press.

Morrison, D. M., and G. Low. 1983. Monitoring and the second language learner. In J. C. Richards and R. W. Schmidt (eds.). *Language and Communication.* London: Longman.

Munsell, P., and T. H. Carr. 1981. Monitoring the monitor: a review of S. D. Krashen, Second language acquisition and second language learning. *Language Learning,* 31 (2): 493–502.

Naerssen, M. van. 1980. How similar are Spanish as a first language and Spanish as a foreign language? In R. C. Scarcella and S. D. Krashen (eds.). *Research in Second Language Acquisition.* Rowley, Mass.: Newbury House.

Neisser, U. 1967. *Cognitive Psychology.* New York: Prentice-Hall.

Pawley, A., and F. Syder. 1983. Two puzzles for linguistic theory: nativelike selection and nativelike fluency. In J. C. Richards and R. W. Schmidt (eds.). *Language and Communication.* London: Longman.

Peck, S. 1978. Child-child discourse in second language acquisition. In E. M. Hatch (ed.). *Second Language Acquisition: A Book of Readings.* Rowley, Mass.: Newbury House.

Peters, A. M. 1983. Finding a place for imitation in theories of language acquisition. Paper given at the Western Regional Meeting of the American Speech and Hearing Association, Honolulu.

Peters, A. M. 1984. Early syntax. In P. Fletcher and M. Garman(eds.). *Language Acquisition*. 2d ed. Cambridge: Cambridge University Press.

Pica, T. 1983. Adult acquisition of English as a second language under different conditions of exposure. *Language Learning*, 33 (4): 465–497.

Platt, C. B., and B. MacWhinney. 1983. Error assimilation as a mechanism in language learning. *Journal of Child Language*, 10 (2): 401–414.

Richards, J. C., and R. W. Schmidt (eds.). 1983a. *Language and Communication*. London: Longman.

Richards, J. C., and R. W. Schmidt. 1983b. Conversational analysis. In J. C. Richards and R. W. Schmidt (eds.). *Language and Communication*. London: Longman.

Schachter, J. 1983. A new account of language transfer. In S. Gass and L. Selinker (eds.). *Language Transfer in Language Learning*. Rowley, Mass.: Newbury House.

Schachter, J. 1984. On negative input. In W. Rutherford (ed.). *Language Universals and Second Language Acquisition*. Philadelphia: John Benjamins.

Schachter, J., A. Tyson, and F. Diffley. 1976. Learner intuitions of grammaticality. *Language Learning*, 26 (1): 67–76.

Schegloff, E., and H. Sacks. 1973. Opening up closings. *Semiotica*, 8: 289–237.

Schlue, K. 1977. An inside view of interlanguage. In C. Henning (ed.). *Proceedings of the Los Angeles Second Language Research Forum*. Los Angeles: UCLA TESL Department.

Schmidt, R. W. 1983. Interaction, acculturation and the acquisition of communicative competence. In N. Wolfson and E. Judd (ed.): *Sociolinguistics and Language Acquisition*. Rowley, Mass.: Newbury House.

Schmidt, R. W. 1984. The strengths and limitations of acquisition: a case study of an untutored language learner. *Language Learning and Communication*, 3 (1): 1–16.

Seliger, H. W. 1983. The language learner as linguist: of metaphors and realities. *Applied Linguistics*, 4 (3): 179–191.

Sharwood Smith, M. 1981. Consciousness-raising and the second language learner. *Applied Linguistics*, 2 (2): 159–168.

Simões, M. C., and C. Stoel-Gammon. 1979. The acquisition of inflections in Portuguese: a study of the development of person markers on verbs. *Journal of Child Language*, 6: 53–67.

Slobin, D. I. In press. Crosslinguistic evidence for the language-making capacity. In D. I. Slobin (ed.). *The crosslinguistic study of language acquisition*. Hillsdale, N.J.: Lawrence Erlbaum Associates.

Snow, C. E. 1981. The uses of imitation. *Journal of Child Language*, 8: 205–212.

Starosta, S. 1984. *Lexicase and Japanese language processing*. Ms., University of Hawaii at Manoa.

Stockwell, R., J. D. Bowen, and J. Martin. 1965. *The Grammatical Structures of English and Spanish*. Chicago: University of Chicago Press.

Tarallo, F., and M. Kato. 1984. Sim: respondendo afirmativamente em Português. Paper presented at the IX Encontro Nacional de Lingüística, PUC/RJ, Rio de Janeiro.

Thomas, E. W. 1969. *The Syntax of Spoken Brazilian Portuguese*. Nashville, Tenn.: Vanderbilt University Press.

Vigil, N. A., and J. W. Oller. 1976. Rule fossilization: a tentative model. *Language Learning*, 26 (2): 281–296.

Wexler, K., and P. W. Cullicover. 1980. *Formal Principles of Language Acquisition*. Cambridge, Mass.: The MIT Press.

Wong-Fillmore, L. 1976. The second time around: cognitive and social strategies in language acquisition. Ph.D. dissertation, Stanford University.

Zobl, H. 1980. The formal and developmental selectivity of L1 influence on L2 acquisition. *Language Learning*, 30: 43–57.

Zobl, H. 1983. Markedness and the projection problem. *Language Learning*, 33 (3): 293–313.

13

SEX DIFFERENCES IN NNS/NNS INTERACTIONS[1]

Susan M. Gass
Evangeline Marlos Varonis
The University of Michigan

The study of nonnative speaker (NNS) interactions has been approached from a number of perspectives. For example, researchers have considered ethnic differences as a variable contributing to conversational analysis involving NNSs (Sato 1982, Scarcella 1983, Varonis and Gass 1985a). Others (e.g., Zuengler 1985) have attempted to weight the effect of status differences on talk directed to NNSs. Still others (e.g., Long and Pica, this volume; Gass and Varonis 1984) have noted differences in speech based on proficiency level and degree of familiarity of the interlocutors or teachers with NNS discourse. Similarly, Beebe (1985) has noted differences in the input to which learners are sensitive, based largely on sociocultural factors. These studies have contributed to our understanding of some of the variables that influence the nature of what is called "foreigner talk" and foreigner talk discourse. However, one potentially crucial variable has not received attention in the NNS literature: that of male-female differences.

Differences between male and female speech have long been noted. Gauchat (1905) observes that women in Switzerland are instrumental in furthering linguistic change, an observation supported by the work of Labov in New York City (e.g., 1966), Wolfram in Detroit (1969), Trudgill in England (1972), Cedergren (1973) in Panama, and others. More recently, Labov (1984) has argued that sex differences in interaction with other variables is a crucial area for understanding the mechanism of linguistic change, pointing out that in

Philadelphia, men and women participate equally in the early stages of sound change but that their role becomes differentiated as sound change progresses. However, not all studies cast women in such an important linguistic role. Jespersen (1922) argues that women use fewer hesitations in speech, not because of "intellectual power" but because of lack of deep thought. Lakoff (1973) suggests the existence of a "woman's language" that avoids strong or forceful statements and encourages uncertainty by the use of linguistic devices such as tags. While Hirschman (1974, cited in Thorne and Henley 1975) was unable to quantify such differences with data from four same-sex and mixed-sex dyads, Argyle et al. (1968, cited in Thorne and Henley 1975) and Zimmerman and West (1975) claim that males interrupt more than females, perhaps in an attempt to dominate the conversation. Conversely, Keenan (1976) points out that Malagasy women are "norm breakers" in that they are associated with more straightforward and even impolite manner of speech.

Where there is a growing, albeit controversial, literature on male-female differences among native language speakers, this is an area that has heretofore been neglected among L2 acquisition researchers. Gass and Varonis (1985) note that in conversational pairs, males signal a lack of understanding (i.e., initiate nonunderstanding routines or negotiate meaning) more often than females in two picture-describing tasks. On the other hand, females tended to increase in their use of these signals on the second task, while men did not. This suggests that women, at least initially, feel less confident in signaling a lack of understanding in interactions with men (assuming that men and women understood equally well). However, that study was designed to control for ethnic as opposed to sex differences as a variable in NNS interactions, and thus any conclusions are best regarded as tentative. The present study, then, was conceived specifically to test for sex differences in NNS/NNS interactions between ESL learners of a single language background.

METHODOLOGY

The data base for the present study consists of 30 taped conversations of 10 NNS/NNS dyads. In order to control for ethnic differences, all subjects were native Japanese speakers. The subjects were adults studying in an intensive language program at the English Language Institute of the University of Michigan. Of the 10 dyads, four were male/female pairs, three were male/male pairs, and three were female/female pairs. Each dyad participated in three tasks: a conversation task and two picture-description tasks. The presentation of these tasks was varied to control for any effect of order: subjects participated in free conversation before the picture tasks or vice versa. In the conversation task, subjects were instructed to converse upon topics of interest to them with no other constraints placed on them. In the picture-description tasks, one interlocutor described a picture while the other attempted to draw it; then they switched roles and proceeded with a different picture. The pictures, with cartoonlike characters, are the same as those used in Gass and Varonis (1985). Each of the tasks was tape-recorded using lavaliere microphones. The first 10 minutes of each task was then transcribed. These transcripts serve as the data base for this study.

RESULTS AND DISCUSSION

The analysis of the results is divided into four main sections: (1) negotiation of meaning, (2) topics, (3) dominance, and (4) interpersonal phenomena.

Negotiation of Meaning

The Model In a previous study (Varonis and Gass 1985a), we presented a model to account for the form of the negotiation of meaning that takes place in nonnative discourse. The crucial part of this model was one interlocutor's indication of nonunderstanding, signaled by what we termed as "indicator" (I). Indicators could be of two types: direct, employing such terms as "what?" or "hunh?" and indirect, typically consisting of a repetition of all or part of the interlocutor's previous utterance with rising intonation. The other parts of the model included the utterance (T) that triggered the indicator, the response (R) to the indicator, and an optional reaction to the response (RR). Examples from the present study appear in 1.

1. Indicators of nonunderstanding
   a. Direct
         Hiro: What type of chair?   (T)
         Nobue: Hmm?   (I)
         Hiro: What type of chair?   (R)
         Nobue: Like this one.
         Hiro: Oh.
   b. Indirect   (T)
         Nobue: uh . . . uh, there's uh two people.
         Hiro: Two people?   (I)
         Nobue: umm   (R)
         Hiro: Uh-hmn   (RR)

In 1a, Nobue directly signals a lack of understanding by saying "Hmm?" Hiro responds by repeating his previous utterance completely, Nobue then appropriately responds to the question, and the conversation continues. In 1b, Hiro indirectly signals incomplete understanding by repeating part of Nobue's previous utterance: "Two people?" Nobue responds by acknowledging that Hiro's interpretation is correct: "umm," and Hiro reacts to the response with "uh-hmn," thus completing the negotiation routine.

In the 1985a study we found that conversational dyads involving NNSs included significantly more negotiation routines than did dyads including only native speakers of English, with dyads involving two NNSs showing the highest negotiation. In addition, within the NNS dyads, the lowest incidence of negotiation occurred in those dyads where interlocutors shared a native language and were at the same proficiency in English; thus, the interlocutors who had the most in common had the least negotiation.

Sex Differences in Negotiation of Meaning   We first analyze the effect of type of dyad on negotiation of meaning. Results are presented in Table 1. Female/female dyads exhibited the least amount of negotiation ($X = 2.67$ per 10-minute task, across tasks), with male/male dyads evidencing just slightly more ($X = 2.78$). In contrast, dyads involving both males and females evidenced a much greater proportion of negotiation. In these dyads, males initiated an average of 4.42 negotiations with females (male-to-female), while females initiated an average of 8.25 negotiations with males (female-to-male). The results are graphed in Figure 1 as a function of speaker and hearer; clearly, both the person speaking and the person to whom speech is addressed are important variables. Males initiate more negotiation to females than they do to males, while females initiate more negotiation to males than they do to females.

TABLE 1   Mean Negotiations per Task as a Function of Sex Interlocutors

	Female/Female	*Male/Male*	*Male-to-Female*	*Female-to-Male*
X negotiations	2.67	2.78	4.42	8.25

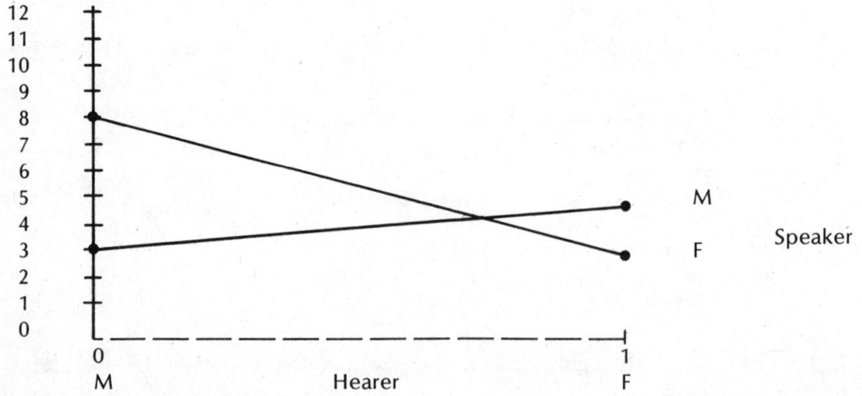

FIGURE 1   Mean Negotiations

Sex Differences in Use of Direct vs. Indirect Indicators   In Gass and Varonis (1985), we noted that all speakers evidenced a much greater proportion of direct as opposed to indirect indications of nonunderstanding. The results for

330

the present study are presented in Table 2. As with mean number of negotiations as a whole, female/female and male/male pairs evidenced the smallest number of both direct and indirect indicators, while mixed dyads evidenced the largest. Males initiated the same number of direct negotiations to females (male-to-female) as females did to males (female-to-male) ($X = .5$), but female-to-male negotiations ($X = 7.75$) were much greater than male-to-female ones ($X = 3.92$). Results are graphed in Figure 2, along with the results for total (direct and indirect) negotiations. The lack of curvilinear pattern indicates that directness does not interact with sex. However, the very low incidence of direct indicators even in the mixed-sex dyads suggests that such overt demonstration of nonunderstanding is not favored.

TABLE 2   Direct vs. Indirect Indicators of Nonunderstanding as a Function of Sex of Interlocutors

	Female/Female	Male/Male	Male-to-Female	Female-to-Male
X direct indicators	.11	.33	.5	.5
X indirect indicators	1.67	2.44	3.92	7.75

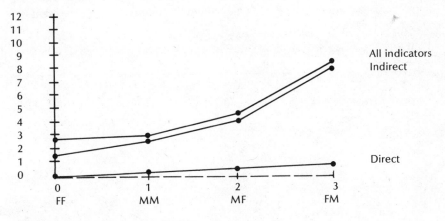

FIGURE 2   Direct vs. Indirect Indicators

Sex Differences in Negotiation as a Function of Task   The issue of conconversational task has been examined by a number of researchers. Long (1983) notes that interlocutors tend to modify input more in two-way tasks, that is, tasks in which each interlocutor has information that the other needs, than in one-way tasks in which one interlocutor must obtain information from the other. Gass and Varonis (1985), on the other hand, note more negotiation in one-way picture-drawing tasks (identical to those in the present study) than in a two-way task. However, the one-way task in that study was qualitatively different from that of Long, perhaps explaining the seemingly contradictory results. Doughty and Pica (1984) report more modified interaction when the information exchange is required as opposed to optional. The present study contrasts amount of negotiation in free conversation vs. two one-way picture-drawing tasks. We point out that the order of presentation of these tasks was varied to control for the effect of familiarity.

Results are presented in Table 3. Overall, the picture tasks evidenced a much greater degree of negotiation than did free conversation. This may be explained by considering that interlocutors had a given task to accomplish in a set period of time, necessitating them to question each other if understanding was incomplete. In free conversation, a nonunderstanding is not as important unless interlocutors are desperate to understand something in particular about each other. Conversation may proceed even if a nonunderstanding is rampant (see Varonis and Gass 1985b for an example). Furthermore, in free conversation topic grows as a result of a shared exchange of information. In contrast, the development of the exchanges in the picture-drawing tasks is controlled to a larger extent by external factors, e.g., the task itself.

Just as with the results for negotiations as a whole, same-sex pairs exhibited much less negotiation than did mixed-sex pairs for both free conversation and the picture tasks. Results are graphed in Figure 3. Consistent with the results overall, for both tasks female/female dyads show the least amount of negotiation while the female-to-female condition shows the greatest.

TABLE 3   Mean Negotiation on Free Conversation vs. Picture Tasks as a Function of Sex of Interlocutors

	Female/Female	Male/Male	Male-to-Female	Female-to-Male
X free conversation	.5	1.5	2.75	6.5
X picture tasks	2.41	3.42	5.25	9.13

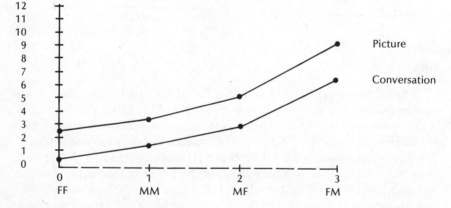

FIGURE 3   Pictures vs. Conversation

Sex Differences in Negotiation as a Function of Role in Picture Task   Gass and Varonis (1985) showed that, in a picture-drawing task, the drawer initiates far more negotiation than does the describer. Since it is the drawer who has ultimate responsibility for producing the end result of the task, namely, a representation of the drawing the describer holds, the drawer has the need to indicate nonunderstanding when it occurs. In addition, the describer may generate more speech to be questioned simply by virtue of the fact that she is describing the picture to be drawn.

Results for the present study are presented in Table 4. As with the previous study, all groups show a much higher number of negotiations for the drawers than for the describers. Consistent with the results above, same-sex dyads show the least negotiation for both conditions, while mixed-sex dyads show the most. Additionally, in both roles, female/female dyads show the least negotiation of all while the female-to-male condition shows the most. Thus, the role of the interlocutor in the picture task does not interact with sex.

Sex Differences in Picture-Task Negotiation as a Function of Task Order   Gass and Varonis (1984) show that the ability of native speakers to comprehend NNS speech is influenced by the familiarity of the native speakers with NNS speech in general and with that of certain NNS speakers in particular. In doing this analysis we proposed to discover whether familiarity could also be a factor when NNSs converse with each other. Specifically, would subjects who interacted with each other before the picture tasks, e.g., with free conversation, evidence less negotiation in the picture tasks than interlocutors who did not have this opportunity? Results are presented in Table 5. Three out of four of the sex conditions evidenced less negotiation in the picture tasks when free conversation preceded the tasks than when free conversation followed. The only group that did not evidence this result was the male/male group, as is obvious in Figure 4; not only did this group evidence less negotiation on the picture task when it

TABLE 4   Mean Negotiation in Picture Task Descrciber vs. Drawer Roles as a Function of Sex of Interlocutors

	Female/Female	Male/Male	Male-to-Female	Female-to-Male
X describer-initiated	4.66	6.5	10.0	16.5
X drawer-initiated	.17	.33	.5	1.75

TABLE 5   Mean Negotiation in Picture Tasks as a Function of Order of Presentation (Pre- vs. Postconversation) and Sex of Interlocutors

	Female/Female	Male/Male	Male-to-Female	Female-to-Male
X preconversation	4.5	2.25	6.0	12.0
X postconversation	1.38	4.0	4.5	6.25

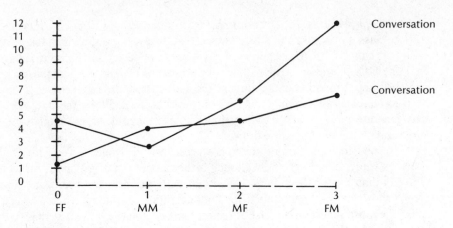

FIGURE 4 Negotiations as a Function of Task Order

preceded conversation, but also it evidenced less negotiation than did the female/female group under this condition. Unfortunately, the data do not easily lend themselves to an interpretation of this phenomenon.

Sex Differences in Negotiation vs. Echoes A Description of Echoes Up to this point, the discussion has revolved around the negotiation of meaning as specified on page 329. However, close examination of the data revealed a related but qualitatively different phenomenon in the form of one interlocutor's echo of all or part of the other's speech. An important difference between an echo and an indirect indication of nonunderstasnding lies in the intonation of the utterance: indirect indicators that repeat part of the previous utterance evidence rising intonation, while echoes evidence falling intonation. An example contrasting indicators and echoes is given in 2.

2. Indicators vs. echoes

Keiko:	And left-left-left side woman are standing and he's— he's s having a string to the dog.	
Shigeru:	Pardon me? Point out?	Direct indicator
Keiko:	He has a dog.	
Shigeru:	He has a dog?	Indirect indicator
Keiko:	No, she has a dog.	
Shigeru:	She has a dog.	Echo

In this example, Shigeru signals initial incomplete understanding directly by "Pardon me?" Keiko simplifies her response, and Shigeru responds with an indirect indicator, repeating the utterance in full with rising intonation: "He has a dog?" Finally, Keiko corrects her pronoun mistake and Shigeru responds with an echo: "She has a dog." Further examples of echoes are given in 3.

3.   Echoes
    a. Shin: Oh there is uh two persons.
       Tadahiro: Two person.
       Shin: Yeah.
       Tadahiro: OK.
    b. Tadahiro: mmm I'm not sure but I guess she's a middle-aged.
       Shin: Middle-aged.
       Tadahiro: Yes.
       Shin: Uh-huh.

In each of these examples, and in general, the echoer picks out exactly that portion of the previous utterance that seems to constitute new information, whether it be existential ("Two person") or descriptive ("middle-aged").

   Sex Differences in Use of Echoes   Analyzed as a function of sex of interlocutors, the results for echoes differ sharply from the results for negotiation (see Table 6). While female/female pairs again evidence the lowest incidence, female-to-male responses, highest in negotiation, are uncharacteristically low. Results are graphed in Figure 5. Variation in use of echoes is clearly more conditioned by sex of the speaker than by sex of the hearer: males use more echoes than females, regardless of whether the hearer is male or female. Thus, echoing seems to be characteristic of male Japanese speakers in English conversation.

TABLE 6   Mean Echoes as a Function of Sex of Interlocutors

	Female/Female	Male/Male	Male-to-Female	Female-to-Male
X echoes	4.06	6.06	6.83	4.25

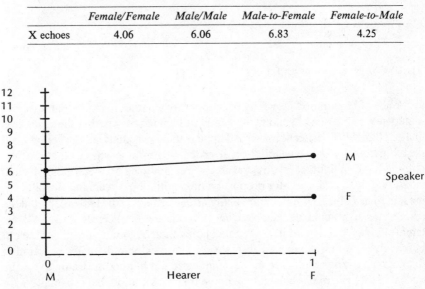

FIGURE 5 Use of Echoes

335

Sex Differences in Use of Echoes vs. Negotiations of Meaning For ease of comparison, data on the negotiation of meaning across tasks are displayed again next to data on echoes across tasks. Results are displayed in Table 7. For three of the four conditions, there is greater echoing than there is negotiation; only females addressing males have greater negotiation, with an average of 8.25 vs. 4.25. Results are graphed in Figure 6. It is clear from the graph that while

TABLE 7   Mean Echoes vs. Mean Negotiations as a Function of Sex of Interlocutors

	Female/Female	Male/Male	Male-to-Female	Female-to-Male
X negotiations	2.67	2.78	4.42	8.25
X echoes	4.06	6.06	6.83	4.25

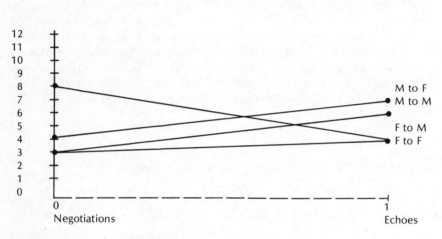

FIGURE 6   Negotiations vs. Echoes

incidence of negotiation is greatly influenced by whether a dyad is same-sex or mixed-sex, incidence of echoing is greatly influenced by whether the speaker is male or female. Thus, echoing would appear to be pragmatically different from the indicators that signal negotiation. In order to determine whether these results obtained for individual dyads, results were analyzed to determine if each individual dyad had a greater proportion of negotiation or echoing. Results are presented in Table 8. A chi-square analysis performed on the table indicated the results are significant at the .05 level (chi square = 6.47; df = 3). All the female/female pairs exhibited greater echoing than negotiation, while three out of four dyads under the female-to-male condition exhibited greater negotiation than echoing. The results are in the same direction but not as dramatic for the males: in general, males use more echoing than negotiation, but especially so in same-sex dyads. Thus, it seems the greater the solidarity with one's interlocutor, the greater the likelihood of echoing rather than negotiating meaning. This is especially true in female/female dyads.

TABLE 8 Relative Preponderance of Negotiations vs. Echoes as a Function of Sex of Interlocutors

	Female/Female	Male/Male	Male-to-Female	Female-to-Male
Number of dyads with more negotiations than echoes	0	1	1	3
Number of dyads with more than or equal echoes to negotiations	6	5	3	1

chi square=6.47; df=3; p<.05

Topics

We now turn to an analysis of (1) topics that the NNSs discussed and (2) topic shifts that occurred in the discourse. It has been noted in the literature on NS/NNS interactions that cultural background is a determining factor in the selection of conversational topics (Richards 1980). This has been directly observed by Scarcella (1983), who found that native Spanish speakers selected topics of a more personal nature than did English speakers. In fact, personal topics were all but absent in the English conversations. Cultural differences are also indirectly noted by Tannen (1980), who found that a narrative report by different cultural groups will witness different foci in the narrative.

Differences in topic selection are noted in the present data, falling along male/female lines. In Table 9 is a list of topics discussed in the 10 dyads of this study.

What was interesting and unexpected was that only in male/male conversations is the majority of the conversation devoted to personal topics. In both the female/female and the male/female groups, the conversation tends to be more objective, dealing with such topics as past and future university studies, job status and job description, planned return to Japan, and intended length of stay at the ELI. In one of the male/female conversations, there is a brief discussion of opposite sex preferences. However, this discussion occurs toward the end of the conversation and was of short duration. Similarly, there was an attempt in one of the female/female groups to turn the conversation to a discussion of an upcoming party. As can be seen in 4, the attempt failed and the conversation continued with a discussion of the intended return to Japan of one member of the pair.

4. Female/female
    Miyuki   Are you going to attend today's party?
    Akiko   I don't know yet, but probably I'll attend. (long pause, with intermittent 'hm's). So, when will you go back Japan?

On the other hand, conversations between two men often began with personal topics. For example, one of the male/male pairs talked only about women, in

TABLE 9 List of Topics Discussed

Male/Male	Male/Female	Female/Female
1. a. Women b. Experiences with American women	1. a. Where they live b. What and where studied c. Why in U.S.	1. a. Past education b. Proposed return to Japan c. Major d. Future studies e. Literature f. Party g. Return to Japan
2. a. Buying car b. Living experiences c. Spouses	2. a. Reasons for studying b. Jobs c. Difficulties with English d. Story about misunderstanding e. Shared lack of English ability	2. a. Purpose of interview
3. a. Hobbies b. Working hours c. Wife of one d. "Girls" in Ann Arbor	3. a. Where they live b. Roommates c. Restaurants in Ann Arbor d. American friends e. Shopping/recent purchases	3. a. Jobs
	4. a. University studies b. Japanese history c. Extracurricular activities d. Jobs e. Past living experiences f. School experiences g. U.S. and Japanese heroes h. Japanese history i. Japanese dialects	

particular their experiences with American women. Within this conversation there was a long narrative about a party to which one had gone. Thus, there appears to be a greater amount of personal involvement in the male/male pairs than in any of the other pairs.

Another indication of more personal involvement in terms of topic selection in conversations with men is the reference they make to spouses. In three conversations, two involving a male/male pair and the other a female/female pair, a speaker mentioned his or her spouse. In the male/male conversation, one part of the discussion centered around the fact that one interlocutor's wife was pregnant and was about to have an ultrasound. They further discussed her upcoming arrival in the United States. The other interlocutor also talked about his wife, making additional reference to his family and their living conditions. In the other male/male pair the discussion centered around where one of them had met his wife and whether she plays tennis. The conversation then turned to the "girls" the other one likes. In contrast, in the female/female conversation, discussion of the spouse was brief, being limited only to where he was from and his college. The extent of the female/female conversation is given in 5.

5. Female/female
    Junko   nnnnnnn no, no . . m I moved to Totori just for my . . . marrimarriage
    Megumi — ah, I see
              I see . . . . So he is from Totori?
    Junko   No, ... He is also . . from . . . Kobe
    Megumi —No, hh -uh hunh
              Kobe, I see. So, his co—his college . . . is located . . on Totori
    Junko   Yes, that's right.
    Megumi —yes   —hhh, I see. I was born in Tokyo . . . . . .

What this suggests is a greater involvement of self in the conversation on the part of the men in the male/male pair.

Topic Shifts   Within the general area of conversational topic, we now turn to a discussion of the topic shifts made in these conversations. As a preliminary observation, we note that in quantity alone, there was a greater number of topics discussed in the male/female conversations than in either of the other groups. In fact, in one of the male/male and one of the female/female conversations only one topic was discussed throughout the duration of the conversation: in the case of the male/male pair, it was American women; in the case of the female/female pair, it was a discussion of the purpose of the task including a lengthy analysis of communication and the speech of Japanese speakers. There was another female conversation that dealt with a single topic, that of jobs, although the participants took turns discussing their own occupations.

Long (1983) and Scarcella (1983) have pointed out that NS/NNS conversations evidence a greater number of abrupt topic shifts than do NS/NS conversations. Furthermore, NSs in conversations with NNSs are willing to accept a topic shift despite its abruptness. This relates to the general issue of uneasiness that occurs in conversations when one or the other participant is slow to take a conversational turn (cf. Coulthard 1977), resulting in silence. Changing topics is a way out of the uncomfortable situation.

Relating these findings to the present study, we find that within the same sex dyads there are only two examples of abrupt topic shifts. One occurs in one of the male/male conversations and the other in a female/female conversation. In the first instance the two men are discussing buying a car and driving in the United States. In particular, they were discussing the fact that Ichiro doesn't have a driver's license but that his wife does. Akira responds by saying that he hasn't driven for 10 years. This is followed by the exchange in 6.

6. Male/male

Ichiro   How about your uh fiancee not wife?

Akira   My wife my wife? She's going to have a baby this end of this September but she said on
the . . .

What we cannot tell is whether or not the question by M1 was intended as a topic shift or not. In other words, Ichiro may have been asking only whether Akira's wife drives. Regardless of the intent, it was interpreted and accepted by Akira as a topic shift and the ensuing conversation dealt with his wife's pregnancy and arrival in the United States.

The single abrupt topic shift in a female/female dyad was illustrated in 4. Prior to that exchange the topic had been the French language and French literature. In fact, the utterance that immediately preceded the question regarding the party was a translation of a French word.

In the male/female dyads the abrupt topic shifts were more frequent (although it is important to remember that this could be an artifact of there being a greater number of topic shifts in general in these dyads). In the five examples of abrupt topic shifts in the male/female conversations, four were initiated by men. Twice before the new topic was nominated there appeared to be overt awkwardness or a feeling of discomfort on the part of the male (7b and 7e). In 7 are the five instances of abrupt topic shifts in the male/female dyads.

7. Male/female

a. Talking about a book

M: Did you read it?

F: Yes, of cou . . .

M: Yes, I read it too.

F: Oh really? I decided . .

M: well, you don't come from Kochi prefecture do you? . . . . . .

b. Talking about Japanese students at the ELI

M: I think uh there are so many Japanese at ELI so sometimes we would uh have roommates
Japanese roommates. mmmmm Are you oh used to American food now?

c. Talking about Sushi restaurants in Ann Arbor

M: . . . but I doubt if we can get wonderful Sushi

F: laughs

M: uh Do you think we have too many assignments?

d. Talking about their lack of knowledge of English

M: yeah, yeah, but it takes time. mm mm

F: Did you enjoy weekend?

e. Talking about his company

M: and Japanese invoice.

F: Yeah.

M: Everything. But uh uh uh I think uh uh uh I have a lot of trouble in English.

There were other examples of men deliberately taking responsibility for the continuation of the discourse. In a number of instances (all within male/female pairs and all by men), the man paused and uttered "What else?" before continuing. While all these instances showed hesitation, they did not result in topic shifts. Thus, it appears that the men in these conversations assumed a greater burden for keeping the conversation going and attempted to resolve a problem or potential problem of breakdown by taking the floor and, when necessary, nominating a new topic.

Dominance

The next area we deal with is dominance, questioning in particular who dominates the conversation. We use four measures in our investigation: (1) amount of talk, (2) number of turns, (3) leading, and (4) overlaps.

Amount of Talk   In this measure we considered only the results of the free conversation task and not the results of the picture-description task, since the conversation provided a less restricted environment and was thus more appropriate for a consideration of dominance, both parties having equal opportunity to participate. Our independent variable is number of words. The results are given in Table 10.

TABLE 10   Number of Words in Free Conversation:
Percentages in parentheses

Male/Male	Male/Female	Female/Female
1. 617----453	1. 904----271	1. 364----260
(57.7) (42.3)	(76.9) (23.1)	(58.3) (41.7)
2. 456----414	2. 572----377	2. 311----311
(52.4) (47.6)	(60.3) (39.7)	(50.0) (50.0)
3. 417----312	3. 459----204	3. 403----303
(57.2) (42.8)	(69.2) (30.8)	(57.1) (42.9)
	4. 454----618	
	(42.4) (57.7)	

As can be seen, in three of the four male/female conversations, the men dominated the conversation in terms of the amount of talk. On the other hand, within the same sex dyads the amount of talk was more or less evenly distributed between both members of the dyad. This presumably reflects the amount of time each held the floor. In the one instance in which the woman dominated in the male/female pairs, the male had in fact dominated throughout most of the conversation. It was only at the end that the female took the floor and reported on how her interest in Japanese history had been sparked. These results corroborate those of Argyle et al. (1968) and Bernard (1972), who also found that men produced a greater amount of talk than women, but are dissimilar to those of Hirschman (1974), who found no sex-related differences in amount of speech.

Related to the issue of who has the greater amount of talking time is the issue of who begins the conversation. In all four of the male/female dyads it was the male who began, either with a question of what they should talk about or with the nomination of a topic. This can be seen in 8.

8. Male/female
   a. M1: uh . . . I will talk about uh my object uh uh . . in ELI uh
   b. M2: You told me you graduated from university in Japan
   c. M3: Can you understand what this questionnaires or so means? or intends?
   d. M4: So now imagine just-uh- we are now we are foreigners and-uh just we arrived here and I happen to meet you . . . .

As is evident in the above examples, it was the male who initially attempted to determine the direction of the conversation.

Number of turns   While the word count given above provides us with an indication of who dominated the conversation in terms of who held the floor longer, it does not tell us whether the interlocutors had equal opportunity to gain access to the floor as opposed to just keeping it. To determine the issue of access, we counted the number of turns each had in the free conversation task. These results are given in Table 11. As can be seen, men and women do not differ much in the number of turns each takes. A comparison of these results with the word count results suggests that men, when they have a turn, hold it for a longer period of time. That is, while the opportunities provided for "practice in talking" appear more or less equal, there are differences between men and women in the advantage they take of these opportunities.

TABLE 11   Number of Turns in Male/Female Dyads—Free Conversation

Dyad No.	Male	Female
1	65	61
2	37	32
3	42	38
4	56	57

Leading   In trying to understand who assumes a major role in guiding the conversation, we focus on the results of the picture-description task since it is in this task that there is a definite expectation of who will and who will not provide direction to the conversation. It is particularly striking when those expectations are violated. Within the setting of the picture-description task, recall that one person describes a picture to the other in such a way that the second person is able to draw the picture despite the fact that he or she does not have visual access to it. The normal expectation (and one that is corroborated through data from Gass and Varonis 1985) is that it will be the describer who leads the conversation, selected which aspects of the picture to describe and in what order. It is to be further expected that the drawer will intervene only to ask for clarification or perhaps for more time to draw. This was the case for only some of the conversations—in particular, in the same sex dyads.

In the male/female dyads men tended to lead the conversation even when that responsibility belonged to the women by virtue of the task itself. Examples of this type of dominance can be seen in 9.

9. Woman describing picture to man
   a. (She has not yet mentioned what the woman has on her feet)
      M: She's wearing boots? lo —long boots?
      F: no only shoes
   b.
      M: Dog. So man- which-um- which side man sit?
         they-he-di-does he-does he sit on the floor?
      F: No, no. I'll explain it.
      M: Okay, so which one does man sit- I mean the left side or right side?
      F: There is a man standing to the right side.
   c.
      F: She has she wears a hat.
      M: hat
      F: hat, yeah.
      M: A hat
      F: A hat
      M: mmm um What is he doing?

In 9 the man raises a new area of description, one that the woman had not at that time dealt with. In 9b he attempts to guide the description the way he wants to. She resists. He ignores her resistance and clarifies the question. Her response, however, while providing him with the information he needs, contradicts his question because the man was standing, not sitting. Finally, in 9c there is a period of silence that he breaks with his question.

To investigate quantitatively this indication of dominance, we determined the number of questions (other than clarification requests) that the drawer asked. There was one additional example that we included in this count. It was a statement in the form of "Tell me about . . ." which, despite the fact that it was not in the form of a question, served the function of leading the content of the description. The results from this analysis are given in Table 12. As can be seen, in three of the four dyads it was the male who dominated the description, asking leading questions, as opposed to the female who was actually describing. The reverse is not true. That is, the female does not take the same leading role when she is drawing: she waits for descriptions from her partner. In the same sex dyads the roles were dictated to a greater extent by the task itself. Even when one drawer did ask questions, as in No. 3 female/female, the interlocutor also asked

TABLE 12   Leading Questions asked by Drawer in Picture-Description Task

Dyad No.	Male/Male		Female/Female		Male/Female	
1	1	1	0	1	14	3
2	1	4	4	4	1	1
3	2	2	7	7	11	1
4					13	4

questions when roles were reversed. That is, both women in the dyad asking leading questions to the other.

Questions within a free conversation structure are difficult to interpret with regard to dominance. On the one hand, they serve the function of shaping the direction of the discourse. On the other hand, they serve the function of shifting the turn to the partner and away from the speaker. The former can be interpreted as dominance, while the latter can only in part. In fact the results (see Table 13) of a count to determine who asked questions in this task show a great deal of variation, with no clear pattern emerging. It may be that questions are used for a different purpose by different people.

TABLE 13   Leading Questions in Free Conversation

Dyad No.	Male/Male		Female/Female		Male/Female	
1	6	1	11	6	15	7
2	7	7	1	0	1	7
3	6	0	6	0	9	7
4					10	14

Overlaps   The final area of dominance we consider is that of overlaps. For this analysis we limit ourselves to the male/female free conversation data.

A basic tenet of conversation is that the participants alternate turns. This, in fact, is inherent in the definition of conversation itself. When this does not occur, the situation is given another name such as lecture or monologue. Sacks (ms.) (cited in Coulthard 1977) claims that in American English conversation "at least and not more than one party talks at a time." As Coulthard points out, when this "rule" is violated, it is noticeable and there is an immediate attempt to resolve the situation by the selection of one and only one participant to continue the conversation. With regard to overlaps, Coulthard states that "overlapping is dealt with by one speaker ending his turn quickly..." (1977:53). We further this notion by considering who it is who ends his or her turn.

What we are interested in is who "wins" in situations where both members of the conversational pair begin an utterance simultaneously. In general, men were the ones to take the conversational turn following these overlaps. Examples are given below:

10. Male/female
    a. Talking about a book
       M: Did you read it?
       F: Yes, of cou ...
       M: Yes, I read it too.
       F: Oh really? I decided ..
                        well, you don't come from
          Kochi prefecture do you? ....

b.
>
> M: Where — where do you live?
> F: In-
> M: Where do you live?
> F: In United States?

In the first example interlocutors had been talking about a particular book. The female's response was an appropriate one given the topic. Yet, she ends her turn and the man continues after the overlap despite the fact that continuation on his part entails a change of topic. In 10b the man continues by repeating his original question. This was unnecessary, since she had already begun to answer the question in the overlap.

Within the male/female dyads there were nine instances of overlaps; they occurred in two of the four pairs. In eight of nine times it was the male who took the floor as a result. As mentioned above, this was the case even in those instances in which, because of the preceding turn, the floor actually belonged to the woman. This corresponds to the asymmetry found by Zimmerman and West (1975) in male/female dyads. In their data men dominated in overlaps 100 percent of the time.

In considering the general area of turn taking two further aspects of the male/female dyads are of relevance, as they further demonstrate the dominant role of one party over the other. In two cases there is an attempt by the male to relinquish the floor by asking the female a question.

11. Male/female
>
> a. M: How about you?
>   F: laughs
>   M: uh uh Are you now in William's house?
>   F: Yes.
> b. M: ... and after that uh I must come back to Japan
>   F: Oh. and
>   M: and you?
>   F: Oh your company send to send you?
>   M: Yes.
>   F: And for the purpose of uh um uh do will you have a position in USA of your com-company?
>   M: uh uh My accounting office is is uh uh foreign uh foreign company. Therefore uh a few Americans ... (continues about his company).

In both cases the female does not accept the turn (the first example may be a lack of understanding). In 11b she quickly attempts to throw the turn back to him. He accepts it only after her second attempt. It is only toward the end of the conversation that she accepts the floor and talks about her perceived abilities in English. This exemplifies a reluctance to talk and assume conversational responsibility, not dissimilar to what was discussed above with regard to the amount of talk by each person.

The second example relevant to the issue of dominance is given in 12. As can be seen, not only does the female not take a turn, but the man takes what should be her turn for her, responding appropriately to his own remark.

12. Male/female (picture-description task)
   F: oh her pants the design her pants is check
   M: check uh hunh check striped or check? check.

Interpersonal Phenomena

The final topic we deal with in this chapter is the area of interpersonal aspects of the conversation. There are three subareas of this topic that provide insight into this area: (1) encouragement, (2) apologies, and (3) hedges.

Encouragement By indications of encouragement we intend those utterances that reinforce the positive behavior of one's interlocutor, whether it concerns his or her drawing (in the case of the picture-description task) or what he or she has just said (in the case of the free conversation task). Examples are given in 13.

13. Male/female
   a. Picture description
      M: ah it's very difficult one OK.
      F: see it is hard to draw.
   b. Female/female (free conversation)
      Majumi: it's easy to find out our mistakes
      Haruko: yeah that's right
      Mayumi: and what kind of mistakes grammatical . . . .

With the exception of one female/female dyad, all the indications of encouragement came in the picture-description task; that is, they were indications of approval of the drawing. Within the one female/female pair where this restriction did not hold, there were five indications (three by one and two by the other) of encouragement or approval with regard to the content of her partner's utterance. In general there is a greater frequency of encouragement signals in the same sex dyads, as can be seen in Table 14.

This suggests a greater sense of cooperation and perhaps involvement in the discourse when both members are of the same sex. On the other hand, opposite-sex dyads display a greater sense of distance between the participants. We return to this issue below.

Apologies Apologetic phrases within discourse serve the function of mitigating against the effect of dominance. In the present corpus they were found most frequently in the form of "I'm sorry" or "Excuse me." The quantitative results of apologies are given in Table 15.

There is only one dyad in which there is a large discrepancy between the number of apologies each person utters. This occurs in male/female dyad 4, with

TABLE 14 Signals of Encouragement

Dyad No.	Male/Male		Female/Female		Male/Female	
1	5	3	1	0	0	1
2	1	3	5	11	0	0
3	3	2	2	0	4	1
4					0	0

TABLE 15 Apologies

Dyad No.	Male/Male		Female/Female		Male/Female	
1	4	2	0	1	3	2
2	0	0	2	2	0	0
3	2	3	5	8	2	0
4					3	10

the woman apologizing more frequently. For the most part in all the other conversations, the number of apologies are more or less distributed evenly. What is more interesting is the content of the apology. With one exception, all the male apologies relate to either an English language deficit or a drawing deficit; i.e., they openly admit their inability to either speak English or draw. On the other hand, while women also apologize for the two above-mentioned deficits, there are additional areas for which they apologize: giving incorrect information, giving insufficient information, self-correction, not understanding, taking a turn, or changing the topic. In our corpus men did not apologize in these areas.

Hedges The final category we discuss is that of hedges. Hedges are those phrases that soften the power of an utterance, particularly when one is unsure of what one is saying. Thus, they provide a way out in case the content (or form) of the utterance turns out to be incorrect. In other words, they are face-saving devices. In this sense, they are less powerful than apologies, forming one end of a continuum with apologies on the other. When one apologizes, there is an admission of error. When one hedges, there is an indication that there may be an error but that the speaker believes there is enough information to suggest otherwise.

The hedges in these conversations were primarily "I think," "maybe," "perhaps," and "I guess." In 14 is an example.

14. Male/female
   (a bottle of gin was clearly evident in the picture)
   M: And-Uh- man and woman are drinking maybe alcohol.

The quantitative results are given in Table 16. On the average there were more of these hedges in the male/male as opposed to the female/female dyads. The largest number appeared in the opposite-sex dyads. In three of the four

TABLE 16   Hedges

Dyad No.	Male/Male		Female/Female		Male/Female	
1	16	6	4	2	16	5
2	2	4	10	8	5	3
3	8	7	5	2	15	1
4					9	11

male/female pairs men used more hedging devices than the women, and in two of those three the discrepancy was great. In fact, the four men in the male/female pairs used a total of 45 hedging devices when in conversations with women, for an average of 11.25 per male. (Women in mixed-sex dyads averaged 5.00.) Yet, in male/male dyads there was a total of 43 hedges used by the six men, for an average of 7.17 per male. Female/female dyads averaged 5.17 hedges per person.

DISCUSSION

An early view of L2 acquisition held that people learn grammatical structures and then apply these structures in a conversational setting. That is, conversation is a vehicle for practice. In 1975, Wagner-Gough and Hatch argued that syntax developed out of conversation. Conversation thus provided the input that learners used for building syntactic structures. Ellis (1985) in a discussion of the L2 acquisition of English by two Punjabi children showed how the children used conversational interactions to move from one-word utterances to two-word utterances and then to three-word utterances. While these studies provide us with a different perspective on the interrelationship between conversation and the development of IL grammars, there is yet an important question that these studies do not address. Do NNSs have equal opportunities to utilize conversation in a way that can promote acquisition?

In this study we noted differences between men and women in the amount each participated in the conversation and in the control each had over the direction of the conversation.

Krashen (1980) argued that learners must receive comprehensible input in order for acquisition to proceed. Input that is not comprehensible is of no value for acquisition (cf. also Long 1983, 1985). Comprehensible input can be obtained in a number of ways, e.g., through speech modification on the part of one's interlocutor or through negotiation of meaning (cf. Varonis and Gass 1985a).

Another dimension to consider is the notion of comprehensible output developed by Swain (1985). She argues that a refinement of the notion of comprehensible input is necessary. Comprehensible output, or the productive use of language, plays a central role in acquisition, since it provides learners with a forum for testing out hypotheses about the target language.

In an earlier paper (Varonis and Gass 1985a) we argued that successful communication depends on attentiveness and involvement by the participants in the conversation itself. In that paper we referred to the work of Stevick (1976, 1980, 1981), who argues that acquisition is facilitated precisely by active involvement in the discourse since the input becomes charged, allowing it to penetrate. We extend the concept of input to output as well (cf. Swain 1985), suggesting that the active personal involvement in the conversation makes the entire conversation more meaningful—in Stevick's terms, a precondition for acquisition. This is further supported by work by Scarcella and Higa (1981), who argued that the optimal input for acquisition is that input that comes as a result of negotiation work as opposed to simplification by one's interlocutor.

Taking into account the notions of comprehensible input and comprehensible output, it is clear that an important forum in which to obtain both is conversation itself. What we have seen in this study is a situation of unequal partnerships (cf. Scollon and Scollon 1983 for a discussion of unequal encounters). Men took greater advantage of the opportunities to use the conversation in a way that allowed them to produce a greater amount of "comprehensible output," whereas women utilized the conversation to obtain a greater amount of comprehensible input.

The overall dominance of men in the conversation may be influenced by cultural norms. Nonetheless, there are clear implications for the advantages that learners have in different kinds of paired situations. In an earlier paper we suggested that learners could benefit from conversational interaction with one another, since it provided them with a nonthreatening environment in which to obtain comprehensible input (Varonis and Gass 1985a). While that is generally the case, further considerations may be necessary. If it is the case that in same-sex dyads there is less negotiation, then this might provide an opportunity to share information to a greater extent. In contrast, in mixed-sex dyads there is a greater amount of negotiation that provides an opportunity for a greater amount of language focus. Thus, the advantages provided by different dyadic arrangements depend on the purpose of the interaction itself. We point out the limitations of this study and we utter a caution in terms of interpreting the results, since the domain of inquiry was limited to one ethnic group. Only investigations of many different kinds of dyadic arrangements can begin to provide answers to the question of the optimal relationship between conversation and second language development.

CONCLUSION

We have shown that the role of participants in a conversational setting is by no means equal. In this study we have seen differences in the ways men and women interact in conversation in same-sex and opposite-sex dyads. While the men appeared to dominate in conversations with women in ways that provided opportunities for producing comprehensible output, women initiated more meaning negotiations than men in mixed-sex dyads. This suggests that each is able to use the conversation in a different way. We have also shown that male/male pairs exhibit more involvement in the conversation itself and argued that this plays an important role in obtaining comprehensible input. This study raises a number of issues with regard to male/female interactions. The central issue relating to language development is: what is the effect of the varying roles in conversation? We suggest that if further studies on male/female role differences support our findings, in particular relating to differences found in the negotiation of meaning and obtaining comprehensible input (females) versus production of comprehensible output (males), then this would provide a fertile testing ground for tearing apart the relative influence of comprehensible input and comprehensible output on L2 acquisition in a conversation of neutral content.

NOTE

1. We would like to acknowledge the support of Orestes Varonis as well as the assistance in transcribing and data analysis of Betsy Carpenter, Charmie Hamilton, and Sharon Lasky. All errors are of course our own.

REFERENCES

Argyle, M., M. Lalljee, and M. Cook. 1968. The effects of visibility on interaction in a dyad. *Human Relations,* 21: 3–17.

Beebe, L. 1985. Input: choosing the right stuff. In S. Gass and C. Madden (eds.). *Input in Second Language Acquisition.* Rowley, Mass.: Newbury House.

Bernard, J. 1972. *The Sex Game.* New York: Atenum.

Cedergren, H. 1973. The interplay of social and linguistic factors in Panama. Ph.D. dissertation, Cornell University.

Coulthard, M. 1977. *An Introduction to Discourse Analysis.* London: Longman.

Doughty, C., and T. Pica. 1984. Small group work in the ESL classroom: does it facilitate language acquisition? Paper presented at TESOL 1984. Houston.

Ellis, R. 1985. Teacher pupil interaction in second language development. In S. Gass and C. Madden (eds.). *Input in Second Language Acquisition.* Rowley, Mass.: Newbury House.

Gass, S., and E. Marlos Varonis. 1984. The effect of familiarity on the comprehensibility of non-native speech. *Language Learning,* 34 (2): 115–132.

Gass, S., and E. Marlos Varonis. 1985. Task variation and NNS/NNS negotiation of meaning. In S. Gass and C. Madden (eds.). *Input in Second Language Acquisition.* Rowley, Mass.: Newbury House.

Gauchat, L. 1905. L'unite phonetique dans le patois d'une commune. In *Aus Romanischen Sprachen und Literaturen: Festschrift Heinrich Mort.* Halle: Max Niemeyer.

Hirschman, L. 1974. Analysis of supportive behavior in conversations. Paper presented at LSA summer meeting.

Jespersen, O. 1922. *Language: Its Nature, Development and Origin.* London: Allen and Unwin.

Keenan, E. Ochs. 1976. On the universality of conversational implicatures. *Language in Society,* 5 (1): 67–80.

Krashen, S. 1980. The input hypothesis. In J. E. Alatis (ed.). *Current Issues in Bilingual Education.* Washington, D.C.: Georgetown University Press.

Labov, W. 1966. *The Social Stratification of English in New York City.* Washington, D.C.: Center for Applied Linguistics.

Labov, W. 1984. The intersection of sex and class in the social origins of sound change. Paper presented at N-Wave 13. Philadelphia.

Lakoff, R. 1973. Language and Woman's Place. *Language in Society,* 2: 45–79.

Long, M. 1983. Native speaker/non-native speaker conversation in the second languge classroom. In M. Clarke and J. Handscombe (eds.). *On TESOL '82.* Washington, D.C.: TESOL.

Long, M. 1985. Input and second language acquisition theory. In S. Gass and C. Madden (eds.). *Input in Second Language Acquisition.* Rowley, Mass.: Newbury House.

Richards, J. 1980. Conversation. *TESOL Quarterly,* 14: 413–432.

Sacks, H. ms. Aspects of the sequential organisation of conversation.

Sato, C. 1982. Ethnic styles in classroom discourse. In M. Hines and W. Rutherford (eds.). *On TESOL '81.* Washington, D.C.: TESOL.

Scarcella, R. 1983. Discourse accent in second language performance. In S. Gass and L. Selinker (eds.). *Language Transfer in Language Learning.* Rowley, Mass.: Newbury House.

Scarcella, R., and C. Higa. 1981. Input, negotiation and age differences in second language acquisition. *Language Learning,* 31 (2): 409–437.

Scollon, R. and S. B. K. Scollon. 1983. Face in interethnic communication. In J. C. Richards and R. W. Schmidt (eds.) *Language and Communication.* London: Longman. 156–188.

Stevick, E. 1976. *Memory, Meaning and Method.* Rowley, Mass.: Newbury House.

Stevick, E. 1980. *Teaching Languages: A Way and Ways.* Rowley, Mass.: Newbury House.

Stevick, E. 1981. The Levertov machine. In R. Scarcella and S. Krashen (eds.). *Research in Second Language Acquisition.* Rowley, Mass.: Newbury House.

Swain, M. 1985. Communicative competence: some roles of comprehensible input and comprehensible output in its development. In S. Gass and C. Madden (eds.). *Input in Second Language Acquisition.* Rowley, Mass.: Newbury House.

Tannen, D. 1980. A comparative analysis of narrative strategies. In W. Chafe (ed.). *The Pear Stories.* Norwood, N.J.: ABLEX.

Thomas, J. Cross-cultural discourse as "unequal encounter": towards a pragmatic analysis. *Applied Linguistics,* 5 (3): 226–235.

Thorne, B., and N. Henley (eds.). 1975. *Language and Sex: Difference and Dominance.* Rowley, Mass.: Newbury House.

Trudgill, P. 1972. Sex, covert prestige, and linguistic change in the urban British English of Norwich. *Language in Society,* 1: 179–195.

Varonis, E. Marlos, and S. Gass. 1985a. Non-native/non-native conversations: a model for negotiation of meaning. Applied Linguistics, 6 (1): 71–90.

Varonis, E. Marlos, and S. Gass. 1985b. Miscommunication in native/non-native conversation. *Language in Society,* 14:2.

Wagner-Gough, J., and E. Hatch. 1975. The importance of input data in second language studies. *Language Learning,* 25 (2): 297–307.

Wolfram, W. 1969. *A Sociolinguistic Description of Detroit Negro Speech.* Washington, D.C.: Center for Applied Linguistics.

Zimmerman, D., and C. West. 1975. Sex roles, interruptions and silences in conversation. In B. Thorne and N. Henley (eds.). *Language and Sex: Difference and Dominance.* Rowley, Mass.: Newbury House.

Zuengler, J. 1985. Phonological aspects of input in NS-NNS interactions. In S. Gass and C. Madden (eds.). *Input in Second Language Acquisition.* Rowley, Mass.: Newbury House.